D0170120

Owen,
Merry Christmas.
Good people do good
things.
Good Luck
Love,
Colette

why freedom matters

why freedom matters

The Spirit of
the Declaration of Independence
in Prose, Poetry, and Song
from 1776 to the Present

Edited by DANIEL R. KATZ

Workman Publishing • New York

Cataloging-in-Publication data is available from the Library of Congress

ISBN 0-7611-3268-6 (hc)—ISBN 0-7611-3165-5 (pbk)

Workman books are available at special discounts when purchased in bulk for premiums and sales promotions, as well as for fund-raising or educational use. Special editions or book excerpts can also be created to specification. For details, contact the Special Sales Director at the address below.

Workman Publishing Company, Inc.
708 Broadway
New York, NY 10003-9555
www.workman.com

Printed in the United States of America

Printed on 80% recycled paper with 50% post-consumer waste content, processed chlorine free

First printing August 2003

10 9 8 7 6 5 4 3 2 1

This book is dedicated to our future defenders of democracy—
Ben, Madeline, Brianna, Daniel, Noah, Stephanie, Melanie,
Dante, Bo, and most of all, to Griffin.

TABLE OF CONTENTS

3: LIBERTY

4: THE PURSUIT OF HAPPINESS

5: OUR LIVES, OUR FORTUNES, OUR SACRED HONOR

APPENDIX

ACKNOWLEDGEMENTS

Above all, I'd like to thank the Declaration of Independence Road Trip, the inspiration for this book. The Declaration of Independence Road Trip is a three-and-a-half-year tour, launched in July of 2001 to commemorate the 225th anniversary of this seminal document. The mission of the nonprofit, nonpartisan project is to take an original copy of the Declaration of Independence, along with a multimedia exhibit, directly to the American people, particularly young Americans, to inspire them to become more civic-minded, to exercise their rights, and, above all, to vote.

The project is made possible by the support of Home Depot, the presenting sponsor; the United States Postal Service, the official carrier; and AXA Financial, Inc. The project includes a filmed reading of the Declaration of Independence by distinguished actors, a national curriculum program distributed to millions of middle and high school students, and an interactive Web site. More can be learned about this project by going to *www.independenceroadtrip.org*.

Many people assisted in creating this anthology. I am grateful to those who reviewed, commented on, made suggestions, and helped secure permissions for the collection, including Caty Borum, David Bollier, David Bloom, Craig Harshaw, Dan Jordan, Steve Jordan, and Richard Sarnoff. Many thanks to the researchers, writers, and friends who helped shape this book, including Labeeb Abboud, Tom Craughwell, Charles Salzberg, Fawn Stehlin, Rebecca Schiff, and Dawn Ward. And many thanks to Diana Ayton-Shenkar for her meaningful contribution. Kris Dahl at ICM continues to be the world's best agent. Thank you to Suzie Bolotin at Workman for seeing the value of this project, and to Peter Workman for supporting it. Richard Rosen was much more than the book's editor at Workman—he was a true team leader in the project and his talent, creativity, and wit made the book so much stronger and the process so much more enjoyable.

I'm grateful to Cherie Simon at the Declaration of Independence Road Trip for supporting the project from beginning to end; and to Norman Lear, the visionary behind the Road Trip, whose help was invaluable. To me, Norman is the model for leadership in a democratic society. I am always proud to work with him.

A special thanks to former Presidents Jimmy Carter and Gerald Ford for lending their time and assistance; and also to the many wonderfully gifted writers, poets, and others who gave us permission to reprint their works.

My partner on this project was Iara Peng. Iara provided the much-needed research, inspiration, organizational ability, and moral support for this compilation from day one and never relented on her commitment to seeing it through to completion. This book would not have been possible without her dedication to perfection.

Most important, thanks to Maggie and Griffin, the joys of my life.

Lastly, we wanted to preserve some of the flavor of the different times during which these pieces were originally published, so the grammar and usage may vary from entry to entry. While all efforts have been made to cite original sources and find original texts, all errors and omissions are fully the responsibility of the editor.

Daniel R. Katz

EDITOR'S NOTE

DANIEL R. KATZ

As you will read in the pages to come, democracy is messy, difficult to articulate, and almost impossible to perfect. Yet for over two hundred years, the people of United States have struggled to do just that: create a more perfect union. Along the way, the original words and sentiments of the Declaration of Independence have been echoed many times.

This book is a collection of those echoes. We have sifted through thousands and thousands of documents, speeches, letters, essays, poems, and songs to find an accessible collection of writings that best express the values first articulated in the Declaration of Independence. Researching this book has been the most uplifting experience imaginable, as time and time again we were reminded of the great sacrifices individuals have made in order for democracy first to take hold and then stick. What a remarkably rich history we have experienced in such a short period.

The selections in this book come from people with different outlooks, writing in different centuries and different countries—but, at their heart, these writings all embrace the same issues, the same human struggles. A contemporary hip-hop poem written by Beau Sia, an Asian American, echoes the plea of black abolitionist Frederick Douglass exactly 150 years earlier. A poem by Maya Angelou mirrors the struggles described in an essay by Albert Camus. A song by Bob Dylan resonates hauntingly with Emma Lazarus's sonnet inscribed at the Statue of Liberty.

The book is divided into five sections, each built around a central pillar of the Declaration of Independence. But within each section, you will find a great deal of diversity, one of the very virtues of a working democracy. The first section, "In the Course of Human Events," celebrates the Founding Fathers and looks back to help explain the context of quite possibly the most important document ever written. It also captures the essence of the Fourth of July—Independence Day—as less about waving flags and more about getting involved in our participatory democracy, and as a time to reflect on the fact that, as Chief Seattle reminds us, this was not always "our" nation, and our growth as a country often came at a great cost to others.

The second section, "Life," looks at both our fragility and remarkable durability. The writers contemplate the meaning of being alive from many angles, including from miles above the Earth. The pieces in the third section of the book, "Liberty," concern our nation's great struggles to overcome racism, sexism, poverty, and oppression in all its forms. We are reminded that, for all its faults, this country has been a beacon of freedom for the entire world. And the truest mark of that freedom is our right—and responsibility—to protest, argue, and struggle for a more perfect democracy. That, in fact, is the purest form of patriotism.

"The Pursuit of Happiness," the fourth section, addresses the individual. The Declaration of Independence guarantees no one happiness—just the right to pursue it without interference. It's a concept unique to our founding document. Section Five, "Our Lives, Our Fortunes, Our Sacred Honor," looks forward to a future in which we can all be, to quote Eleanor Roosevelt, "keepers of democracy." Although this section contains the sentiments of many contemporary writers, journalists, and politicians, it also looks to the past, as far back as the 17th century, to find words to inspire us in the years to come.

The history of the United States is peopled with countless heroes and their stories of struggle, longing, and hope. This book captures many of their voices, reminding us of all that is possible, celebrating what wonderful progress has already been made, and outlining the unique and important challenges that lie ahead.

FOREWORDS

This is a time for us to pause and to think about our history: the history of our country, our people, their diversity, and the progress we've made. The wisdom of our Founding Fathers gave us not only a vision that excites the human spirit, but also a form of government that has permitted this nation to be flexible enough to progress—so we the citizens can analyze our own progress, our own achievements, our own greatness, and at the same time, with the same thoughts, analyze our mistakes, our failures, our shortcomings, and our opportunities for improvement.

We've come through some difficult times. A war that divided our nation resulted in the end of slavery, followed by another hundred years of official and condoned racial discrimination—and then continued progress, slow but steady, to correct additional problems we have faced. We've seen women given the right to vote—something that was unheard of 220 years ago, along with other changes that have made us all proud. The inspiration of the Declaration of Independence has shaped our lives to a major degree.

America's birth opened a new chance in mankind's history. Ours was the first nation to dedicate itself clearly to basic moral and philosophical principles that all people are created equal and endowed with unalienable rights to liberty and the pursuit of happiness—and that the power of government is derived from the consent of the governed. This national commitment was a singular act of wisdom and courage, and it has brought the best and the bravest from other nations to our shores. It was a revolutionary development that captured the imagination of mankind. It created a basis for a unique role for America: that of a pioneer in shaping more decent and just relations among people and societies. We hope all of us, in our minds and thoughts and words will never let freedom, democracy, human rights, and other principles of the Declaration of Independence be separated.

Jimmy Carter

President Jimmy Carter

———•◆•———

On July 4, 1776, delegates to the Continental Congress adopted a Declaration of Independence, and proclaimed to the world the birth of the United States of America. Their quest was nothing less than a courageous attempt to build a new order in which free people govern themselves and fulfill their individual destinies. In 1976, I had the great honor and high privilege of serving as President of the United States during our nation's 200th birthday. Even now, more than a quarter century later, my words and thoughts from the Bicentennial are never far from my mind.

Thomas Jefferson and his colleagues very deliberately and very daringly set out to construct a new kind of nation. They wanted to build in this beautiful land a home for equal freedom and opportunity, a haven for peace and happiness. They had blind spots in their lofty vision, and America is still not perfect. But the ideals proclaimed in their Declaration of Independence have had lasting power to create, as Abraham Lincoln said, "a new nation, conceived in Liberty and dedicated to the proposition that all men are created equal."

America's wealth is our great heritage, our freedom, and our belief in ourselves. The inspiration of the Declaration is a fixed star of freedom and justice, and will always remain a guiding light for education and study by all Americans. Jefferson's timeless truths and aspirations are ours also. We always remember that freedom is not free, and that it takes moral courage and sacrifice, without concern for the consequences.

The American adventure is a continuing process. In song and speech, in poem and letter, in essay and editorial, Americans are still refining and forging the principles proclaimed on July 4, 1776: the values of self-government, liberty and justice, equal rights, and equal opportunity. Jefferson's immortal words will remain, and they will be preserved in human hearts. As our forefathers did before us, we today can mutually pledge our lives and sacred honor to the ennobling and enduring principles of the Declaration of Independence.

Gerald R. Ford

President Gerald R. Ford

INTRODUCTION
NORMAN LEAR

O n the evening of July 4, 1776, Philadelphia printer John Dunlap carried out a rather unusual job—hand-printing 200 copies of a document declaring a new chapter in human history. His customer was the Continental Congress of the just-proclaimed United States of America. For the thirteen colonies, the purpose of the printing was to formally tell the world that they planned to break free from Great Britain; to wage war to do so, if necessary; and to begin the daunting enterprise of creating a new nation.

By 2000, only 25 of the so-called Dunlap Broadsides were known to exist. Quite by accident, my wife, Lyn, and I learned that one of them was about to be auctioned off via the Internet. The possibility of acquiring an original copy of the Declaration of Independence made me think instantly of my grandfather. From age nine to eleven, I lived with my mother's dad, Shia Seicol, 74 York Street, New Haven, Connecticut, and he was my role model for patriotism. He viewed the document as his country's birth certificate, and I came to do so as well.

There were many parades in those years—Memorial Day, July 4th, Presidents Day, and he saw all of them, with me at his side. But my grandfather's patriotism was hardly limited to parade-viewing. He was also an inveterate letter-writer-to-presidents. Every letter started the same way: "My dearest darling Mr. President, I thought you were right when . . ." Even when he disagreed the salutation was the same: "My dearest darling Mr. President . . ." But then he'd give it to the chief executive: "Didn't I tell you last time it was a mistake to . . ."

You see, my grandfather's opinion on any matter of policy was closely related to that policy's fidelity to the words and meaning in the Declaration of Independence. Did it interfere with an individual's right to life, liberty, and the pursuit of happiness? Were all men being treated equal in the eyes of a given policy? And were the politicians my grandfather helped to elect exceeding the just powers derived from *his* consent?

I worry that most of us have lost this connection to the spirit of the document on which this country was founded. After all, my grandfather's questions are relevant still. In fact, whether we realize it or not, we all have an ongoing relationship with the Declaration. That is why Lyn and I bought that rare and beautiful original copy of it. We knew at first sight that this was "The People's Document," our country's birth certificate, and that it should not hang on a wall or sit somewhere in a vault; it should travel directly to the people to whom it belonged, to towns and cities everywhere. So we founded the Declaration of Independence Road Trip to create an exhibit in which the document was the centerpiece and to keep it traveling, reuniting people everywhere with its continued importance.

The pieces in this anthology are diverse, as diverse as Americans. And just as all Americans are citizens of the same country, these speeches, letters, songs, and poems are all aspects of the same spirit—the spirit of the never-ending struggle to secure, preserve, and perfect our democracy. Many voices in this book are raised in celebration of all that we have accomplished along the way, but many are raised in protest over all that we have thus far failed to accomplish.

In this book you will hear voices that are harsh, kind, blunt, subtle, angry, yearning, grateful, wise, spirited, dispirited, and hopeful. But every voice you hear resonates with the desire to be free of disrespect, tyranny, and oppression. This book is not a flag-waving tribute for flag-wavers. It does not cater to a smug or self-congratulatory patriotism. Rather, this book is a frank exploration of the world's most powerful idea—freedom. It showcases a pantheon of patriots, famous and obscure, who have one thing in common: they are ruthlessly honest about their beloved nation and their relationships to it.

The Founding Fathers carved our democracy out of a wilderness. They fashioned it out of ideas turned into words, starting with a remarkable blueprint, the Declaration of Independence. They built a nation from this blueprint, a nation forever wrestling with questions of life, liberty, and the pursuit of happiness—a nation that often enough disappoints its own hopes and its own people but which is still the most free nation on Earth and which has not yet stopped trying to achieve its dream.

IN THE COURSE OF HUMAN EVENTS

—ESSAY—

THE ARGONAUTS OF 1776

David McCullough {July 4, 2002}

Long before David McCullough (b. 1933) became one of our great narrative historians, he was a painter, and it shows in his vividly rendered, meticulously detailed books. In works like *The Great Bridge, The Path Between the Seas, Mornings on Horseback,* and his Pulitzer Prize–winning *John Adams* and *Truman,* McCullough demonstrates that, as he himself put it, "People are the writer's real subject, after all, the mystery of human behavior."

"You will see in a few days a Declaration setting forth the causes which have impelled us to this mighty revolution. . . ."

From his boardinghouse in Philadelphia, John Adams was reporting to his wife, Abigail, in a letter dated July 3, 1776. Filled with emotion over events of the preceding day, Adams prophesied that July 2 would be celebrated for generations as a national festival. "It ought to be commemorated as the Day of Deliverance by solemn acts of devotion to God Almighty," he wrote. "It ought to be solemnized with pomp and parade, with shows, games, sports, guns, bells, bonfires, and illuminations from one end of this continent to the other from this time forward ever more."

For on July 2, after weeks of intense debate behind closed doors, the Continental Congress had voted to proceed with a declaration of independence for the "United States of America," and this to Adams and others was the crucial decision. The die was cast.

July 4, the day Congress adopted the final edited version of Thomas Jefferson's draft of the Declaration, seemed at the time to carry less historic importance. Nor was July 4 the day the document was signed. That took place a month later, on August 2, and even then not all members were present. Those who were absent would sign later still. Only the president and the secretary of Congress, John Hancock and Charles Thomson, affixed their signatures on July 4, and Congress ordered the document printed and distributed to the press and the public at large.

It was the year after, 1777, when July 4 became the national day of festival. And so we will celebrate it today, "from one end of this continent to the other," just as Adams foresaw, except that in the present national mood, in the aftermath of last September 11, there will be differences. We are at war again, and with patriotism running as strong as at almost any time in memory, our feelings will be abundantly on display, and from the heart, as perhaps never before.

But if Adams, or others of the 56 patriots who put their names on the Declaration of Independence, could imagine us celebrating what they did, how should we imagine them?

To begin with, they were not gods. Indeed, had they been they would deserve less honor and respect. Gods, after all, can do largely as they please. They were human and imperfect; each had his flaws and failings. Jefferson made the point in the very first line of the Declaration of Independence: "When in the course of human events . . . ." The key word is human.

The miracle was that imperfect mortals could so rise to the occasion, that such noble ideals and brilliant political leadership came to the fore as they did, that so few could, in the end, accomplish so much for all humankind.

With the exception of Benjamin Franklin, who was 70, and a few others, they were also younger than we usually think of them. Hancock was 39; Adams, 40; Jefferson, all of 33. The remarkable Benjamin Rush was younger still, 30. Further, the man in whom Congress had entrusted command of the fledgling American army bore little resemblance to the white-haired president with awkward teeth who looks out from the dollar bill. George Washington was 44 in 1776.

The odds against them in challenging the might of the British empire were overwhelming. None had had any experience in revolution-making. Or nation-making. And let us never forget they were setting out not only to triumph over the British Army and Navy, but to establish an entirely new nation. There was little at hand with which to fight a war—almost no gunpowder, no navy and no money to speak of. There were few trained officers. Washington himself had never commanded an army in battle.

As daunting as almost anything was the lack of popular support for independence. Though war had broken out near Boston the year before, in the spring of 1775, the Americans who fought at Lexington, Concord and Bunker Hill had been defending their rights as Englishmen, not fighting for independence. When, in late summer of 1775, Jefferson confided to a kinsman that he hoped still for a reconciliation with Great Britain, he was only expressing what was widely felt. By early 1776 about a third of the people were for independence, while another third remained adamantly opposed. The rest, in the old human way, were waiting to see who came out on top.

Had they been poll-driven, "risk-averse" politicians gathered in Philadelphia that fateful summer of 1776, they would have scrapped the whole idea of a "mighty revolution."

Those for independence argued passionately that there could be no real freedom without independence, no chance to "begin the world over again," as said in Thomas Paine's little pamphlet, "Common Sense."

We think we live in a dangerous, uncertain time, and we do. But theirs was worse, and they had no sure way of knowing how things would turn out, any more than we do. Their courage and determination, their commitment to what they called the Cause of America, were almost beyond our imagining. To sign your name to the Declaration of Independence was to declare yourself a traitor to the British Crown. If caught by enemy forces, you would almost certainly be hanged.

And consider that in that same first week of July 1776, the British fleet appeared in New York Harbor and began landing on Staten Island the largest force ever sent to crush a rebellion, fully 32,000 troops by the time they were all ashore. This was more than the entire population of Philadelphia, the largest city in America. When the signers of the Declaration pledged "our lives, our fortunes, our sacred honor," that was no mere rhetorical flourish.

The delegate Stephen Hopkins of Rhode Island, who was nearly as old as Franklin and suffered from palsy, is said to have remarked when his turn came to sign his name, "My hand trembles, but my heart does not."

When we see them in paintings, with their ruffled shirts and powdered hair, they look a little like fops, softies. But life then, at best, was tougher than we know, and they were, too, and the women no less than the men. John Adams predicted a long, costly struggle. "I am well aware of the toil and blood and treasure it will cost us to maintain their Declaration," he told

Abigail. "Yet through the gloom I can see the rays of ravishing light and glory. I can see the end is more than worth all the means."

For her part, at home in Massachusetts, raising their children, running the family farm, she had to cope with rampant inflation, shortages of all kinds, epidemic smallpox and her husband's endless absences in the service of the country. "Posterity who are to reap the blessings," she would write, "will scarcely be able to conceive the hardships and sufferings of their ancestors."

The Revolutionary War lasted eight years. Except for Vietnam it was the longest war in our history, and it was the most important. It was the birth of the nation. It made possible everything that followed. It gave us those "self-evident" truths at the heart of our whole way of life.

No one in Congress spoke for the need for a Declaration of Independence with greater force than John Adams. As is often said, Jefferson was the pen of independence; Adams, the voice.

Half a century later—amazingly, unbelievably—Jefferson and Adams died on that same day: July 4, 1826, the 50th anniversary of the Declaration of Independence. That spring, in a letter that touched Adams deeply, Jefferson had recalled how once in younger days, as "Argonauts," they had faced the perilous storms of a "heroic age." If ever there was a time to draw strength from their example, and renew our commitment to their Cause, it is now. Today's the day, their day of days. And we might well begin, as John Adams suggested, with expressions of gratitude to God Almighty.

— LETTER —

AN EXCHANGE OF LETTERS
ABIGAIL AND JOHN ADAMS
{MARCH 31, 1776 AND APRIL 14, 1776}

———

One of the most remarkable married couples in American history, Abigail Adams (1744–1818) and John Adams (1735–1826), were devoted to each other and committed to the cause of American independence. In their long, affectionate letters to one another, they alternated between news about the children and discussions of political philosophy. Among the more cautious delegates gathered in Philadelphia in 1776, John Adams was regarded as a dangerous extremist, yet Abigail Adams could be much more radical than her husband. In her letter to John, Abigail adopts a lighthearted and teasing tone, but there is an edge behind her words, and her insistence that women be given the same political and civil rights as men would have shocked virtually every man in Congress. John regarded his wife's suggestion as merely amusing. In his reply, he wrote that at the thought of women having a voice in government, "I cannot but laugh."

Abigail Adams to John Adams, March 31, 1776

I wish you would ever write me a Letter half as long as I write you; and tell me if you may where your Fleet are gone? What sort of Defence Virginia can make against our common Enemy? Whether it is so situated as to make an able Defence? Are not the Gentery Lords and the common people vassals, are they not like the uncivilized Natives Brittain represents us to be? I hope their Riffel Men who have shewen themselves very savage and even Blood thirsty; are not a specimen of the Generality of the people.

I am willing to allow the Colony great merit for having produced a Washington but they have been shamefully duped by a Dunmore.

I have sometimes been ready to think that the passion for Liberty cannot be Eaquelly Strong in the Breasts of those who have been accustomed to deprive their fellow Creatures of theirs. Of this I am certain that it is not founded upon that generous and Christian principal of doing to others as we would that others should do unto us.

Do not you want to see Boston; I am fearfull of the small pox, or I should have been in before this time. I got Mr. Crane to go to our House and see what state it was in. I find it has been occupied by one of the Doctors of a Regiment, very dirty, but no other damage has been done to it. The few things which were left in it are all gone. Cranch has the key which he never deliverd up. I have wrote to him for it and am determined to get it cleand as soon as possible and shut it up. I look upon it a new acquisition of property, a property which one month ago I did not value at a single Shilling, and could with pleasure have seen it in flames.

The Town in General is left in a better state than we expected, more oweing to a percipitate flight than any Regard to the inhabitants, tho some individuals discoverd a sense of honour and justice and have left the rent of the Houses in which they were, for the owners and the furniture unhurt, or if damaged sufficent to make it good.

Others have committed abominable Ravages. The Mansion House of your President is safe and the furniture unhurt whilst both the House and Furniture of the Solisiter General have fallen a prey to their own merciless party. Surely the very Fiends feel a Reverential awe for Virtue and patriotism, whilst they Detest the parricide and traitor.

I feel very differently at the approach of spring to what I did a month ago. We knew not then whether we could plant or sow with safety, whether when we had toild we could reap the fruits of own industery, whether we could rest in our own Cottages, or whether we should not be driven from the sea coasts to seek shelter in the wilderness, but now we feel as if we might sit under our own vine and eat the good of the land.

I feel a gaieti de Coar to which before I was a stranger. I think the Sun looks brighter, the Birds sing more melodiously, and Nature puts on a more chearfull countanance. We feel a temporary peace, and the poor fugitives are returning to their deserted habitations.

Tho we felicitate ourselves, we sympathize with those who are trembling least the Lot of Boston should be theirs. But they cannot be in similar circumstances unless pusilanimity and cowardise should take possession of them. They have time and warning given them to see the Evil and shun it.—I long to hear that you have declared independency—and by the way in the new Code of Laws which I suppose it will be necessary for you to make I desire you would Remember the Ladies, and be more generous and favourable to them than your ancestors. Do not put such unlimited power into the hand of the Husbands. Remember all Men would be tyrants if they could. If perticuliar care and attention is not paid to the Laidies we are determined to foment a Rebelion, and will not hold ourselves bound by any Laws in which we have no voice, or Representation.

That your Sex are Naturally Tyrannical is a Truth so thorougly established as to admit of no dispute, but such of you as wish to be happy willingly give up the harsh title of Master for the more tender and endearing one of Friend. Why then, not put it out of the power of the vicious and the Lawless to use us with cruelty and indignity with impunity. Men of Sense in all Ages abhor those customs which treat us only as the vassals of your Sex. Regard us then as Beings placed by providence under your protection and immitation of the Supreem Being make use of that power only for our happiness.

John Adams to Abigail Adams, April 14, 1776

You justly complain of my short Letters, but the critical State of Things and the Multiplicity of Avocations must plead my Excuse. You ask where the Fleet is. The inclosed Papers will inform you. You ask what Sort of Defence Virginia can make. I believe they will make an able Defence. Their Militia and minute Men have been some time employed in training them selves, and they have Nine Battallions of regulars as they call them, maintained among them, under good Officers, at the Continental Expence. They have set up a Number of Manufactories of Fire Arms, which are busily employed. They are tolerably supplied with Powder, and are successfull and assiduous, in making Salt Petre. Their neighbouring Sister or rather Daughter Colony of North Carolina, which is a warlike Colony, and has several Battallions at the Continental Expence, as well as a pretty good Militia, are ready to assist them, and they are in very good Spirits, and seem determined to make a brave Resistance.—The Gentry are very rich, and the common People very poor. This Inequality of Property, gives an Aristocratical Turn to all their Proceedings, and occasions a strong Aversion in their Patricians, to Common Sense. But the Spirit of these Barons, is coming down, and it must submit.

It is very true, as you observe they have been duped by Dunmore. But this is a Common Case. All the Colonies are duped, more or less, at one Time and another. A more egregious Bubble was never blown up, than the Story of Commissioners coming to treat with the Congress. Yet it has gained Credit like a Charm, not only without but against the clearest Evidence. I never shall forget the Delusion, which seized our best and most sagacious Friends the dear Inhabitants of Boston, the Winter before last. Credulity and the Want of Foresight, are Imperfections in the human Character, that no Politician can sufficiently guard against.

You have given me some Pleasure, by your Account of a certain House in Queen Street. I had burned it, long ago, in Imagination. It rises now to my View like a Phoenix.—What shall I say of the Solicitor General? I pity his pretty Children, I pity his Father, and his sisters. I wish I could be clear that it is no moral Evil to pity him and his Lady. Upon Repentance they will certainly have a large Share in the Compassions of many. But let Us take Warning and give it to our Children. Whenever Vanity, and Gaiety, a Love of Pomp and Dress, Furniture, Equipage, Buildings, great Company, expensive Diversions, and elegant Entertainments get the better of the Principles and Judgments of Men or Women there is no knowing where they will stop, nor into what Evils, natural, moral, or political, they will lead us.

Your Description of your own Gaiety de Coeur, charms me. Thanks be to God you have just Cause to rejoice—and may the bright Prospect be obscured by no Cloud.

As to Declarations of Independency, be patient. Read our Privateering Laws, and our Commercial Laws. What signifies a Word.

As to your extraordinary Code of Laws, I cannot but laugh. We have been told that our Struggle has loosened the bands of Government every where. That Children and Apprentices were disobedient—that schools and Colledges were grown turbulent—that Indians slighted their Guardians and Negroes grew insolent to their Masters. But your Letter was the first Intimation that another Tribe more numerous and powerfull than all the rest were grown discontented.— This is rather too coarse a Compliment but you are so saucy, I wont blot it out.

Depend upon it, We know better than to repeal our Masculine systems. Altho they are in full Force, you know they are little more than Theory. We dare not exert our Power in its full Latitude. We are obliged to go fair, and softly, and in Practice you know We are the subjects. We have only the Name of Masters, and rather than give up this, which would compleatly subject Us to the Despotism of the Peticoat, I hope General Washington, and all our brave Heroes would fight. I am sure every good Politician would plot, as long as he would against Despotism, Empire, Monarchy, Aristocracy, Oligarchy, or Ochlocracy.—A fine Story indeed. I begin to think the Ministry as deep as they are wicked. After stirring up Tories, Landjobbers, Trimmers, Bigots, Canadians, Indians, Negroes, Hanoverians, Hessians, Russians, Irish Roman Catholicks, Scotch Renegadoes, at last they have stimulated the [unintelligible] to demand new Priviledges and threaten to rebel.

—SPEECH—

INTRODUCTION TO DRAMATIC READING OF THE DECLARATION OF INDEPENDENCE

MORGAN FREEMAN {JULY 4, 2001}

On July 4, 2001, nearly a million people gathered near Independence Hall in Philadelphia, Pennsylvania, to hear twelve actors perform a dramatic reading of the Declaration of Independence and celebrate the 225th anniversary of its signing. The reading signified the official launch of the Declaration of Independence Road Trip, which in 2002 began bringing one of the few surviving original copies of the document around the country in order to remind people of their civic responsibility and the beliefs on which this nation was founded. Morgan Freeman (b. 1937) introduced the event, in which Michael Douglas, Whoopie Goldberg, Mel Gibson, Kathy Bates, Renée Zellweger, and others took turns reading the document that changed the world.

Picture this: a group of politicians from the thirteen American colonies come together in this building right here, to plot what turns out to be a revolution. A contentious Continental Congress needs to set forth some convincing reasons for declaring war. Congress turns to a brilliant 33-year-old aristocrat from Virginia, Thomas Jefferson. In a matter of days, the red-haired wonder writes one of the most celebrated manifestos for human freedom and self-government in the history of western civilization.

The Continental Congress authorizes Philadelphia printer John Dunlap to print 200 broadsides—poster-sized sheets. The document, unsigned, is then rushed to waiting horsemen who put it in their saddlebags and gallop throughout the colonies. You see, if this Revolutionary War is to be won, thousands of farmers and tradesmen must be persuaded to take up arms and fight. And they do.

11

Not many people realize it today, but scholars believe Jefferson intended for the Declaration to be performed, and not just read. Its words and rhythm were written to be spoken—in proud and defiant tones in grand public places.

It's a safe bet that the Continental Congress never had in mind a performer like me. That is to say . . . a black man. Thomas Jefferson was not ignorant of the problem of slavery, of course. He called it a "moral and political depravity," and in the original draft of the Declaration denounced the slave trade as "a cruel war against human nature itself."

But Congress thought better of this particular item, and deleted it. In fact, there is no mention of slavery or black people—or women, for that matter—in this preeminent statement on the equal rights of man.

So, it makes you wonder: How could a man who himself held slaves, write with such incredible passion and eloquence about human liberation and the promise of a democratic republic?

Why, some may ask, do I bring up such embarrassing truths on this glorious occasion? I answer: The real glory of the Declaration of Independence has been our nation's epic struggle throughout history to close the gap between the ideals of this remarkable document and the sometimes painful realities of American life. The Declaration symbolizes the birth of our nation, of course, but also the constant struggle to achieve its ideals.

Consider: The words of this document inspired the French Revolution in 1789, and 200 years later, the revolt of Chinese students in Tiananmen Square. It inspired Abraham Lincoln to issue the Emancipation Proclamation, Martin Luther King Jr. to fight for civil rights, and women suffragettes to fight for the vote.

This business of fulfilling the Declaration of Independence is a difficult struggle. But it is also an ennobling struggle. Jefferson called the Declaration "an expression of the American mind." It is why this nation is so great and why I am so proud to be an American. . . .

THE DECLARATION OF INDEPENDENCE

{JULY 4, 1776}

When in the Course of human Events, it becomes necessary for one People to dissolve the Political Bands which have connected them with another, and to assume among the Powers of the Earth, the separate and equal Station to which the Laws of Nature and of Nature's God entitle them, a decent Respect to the Opinions of Mankind requires that they should declare the causes which impel them to the Separation.

We hold these Truths to be self-evident, that all Men are created equal, that they are endowed by their Creator with certain unalienable Rights, that among these are Life, Liberty and the Pursuit of Happiness—That to secure these Rights, Governments are instituted among Men, deriving their just Powers from the Consent of the Governed, that whenever any Form of Government becomes destructive of these Ends, it is the Right of the People to alter or to abolish it, and to institute new Government, laying its Foundation on such Principles, and organizing its Powers in such Form, as to them shall seem most likely to effect their Safety and Happiness. Prudence, indeed, will dictate that Governments long established should not be changed for light and transient Causes; and accordingly all Experience hath shewn, that Mankind are more disposed to suffer, while Evils are sufferable, than to right themselves by abolishing the Forms to which they are accustomed. But when a long Train of Abuses and Usurpations, pursuing invariably the same Object, evinces a Design to reduce them under absolute Despotism, it is their Right, it is their Duty, to throw off such Government, and to provide new Guards for their future Security. Such has been the patient Sufferance of these Colonies; and such is now the Necessity which constrains them to alter their former Systems of Government. The History of the present King of Great-Britain is a History of repeated Injuries and Usurpations, all having in direct Object the Establishment of an absolute Tyranny over these States. To prove this, let Facts be submitted to a candid World.

∞ He has refused his Assent to Laws, the most wholesome and necessary for the public Good.

∞ He has forbidden his Governors to pass Laws of immediate and pressing Importance, unless suspended in their Operation till his Assent should be obtained; and when so suspended, he has utterly neglected to attend to them.

∞ He has refused to pass other Laws for the Accommodation of large Districts of People, unless those People would relinquish the Right of Representation in the Legislature, a Right inestimable to them, and formidable to Tyrants only.

∞ He has called together Legislative Bodies at Places unusual, uncomfortable, and distant from the Depository of their public Records, for the sole Purpose of fatiguing them into Compliance with his Measures.

∞ He has dissolved Representative Houses repeatedly, for opposing with manly Firmness his Invasions on the Rights of the People.

∞ He has refused for a long Time, after such Dissolutions, to cause others to be elected; whereby the Legislative Powers, incapable of the Annihilation, have returned to the People at large for their exercise; the State remaining in the mean time exposed to all the Dangers of Invasion from without, and the Convulsions within.

∞ He has endeavoured to prevent the Population of these States; for that Purpose obstructing the Laws for Naturalization of Foreigners; refusing to pass others to encourage their Migrations hither, and raising the Conditions of new Appropriations of Lands.

∞ He has obstructed the Administration of Justice, by refusing his Assent to Laws for establishing Judiciary Powers.

∞ He has made Judges dependent on his Will alone, for the Tenure of their Offices, and the Amount and Payment of their Salaries.

∞ He has erected a Multitude of new Offices, and sent hither Swarms of Officers to harrass our People, and eat out their Substance.

∞ He has kept among us, in Times of Peace, Standing Armies, without the consent of our Legislatures.

∞ He has affected to render the Military independent of and superior to the Civil Power.

∽ He has combined with others to subject us to a Jurisdiction foreign to our Constitution, and unacknowledged by our Laws; giving his Assent to their Acts of pretended Legislation:

> For quartering large Bodies of Armed Troops among us;
>
> For protecting them, by a mock Trial, from Punishment for any Murders which they should commit on the Inhabitants of these States:
>
> For cutting off our Trade with all Parts of the World:
>
> For imposing Taxes on us without our Consent:
>
> For depriving us, in many Cases, of the Benefits of Trial by Jury:
>
> For transporting us beyond Seas to be tried for pretended Offences:
>
> For abolishing the free System of English Laws in a neighbouring Province, establishing therein an arbitrary Government, and enlarging its Boundaries, so as to render it at once an Example and fit Instrument for introducing the same absolute Rules into these Colonies:
>
> For taking away our Charters, abolishing our most valuable Laws, and altering fundamentally the Forms of our Governments:
>
> For suspending our own Legislatures, and declaring themselves invested with Power to legislate for us in all Cases whatsoever.

∽ He has abdicated Government here, by declaring us out of his Protection and waging War against us.

∽ He has plundered our Seas, ravaged our Coasts, burnt our Towns, and destroyed the Lives of our People.

∽ He is, at this Time, transporting large Armies of foreign Mercenaries to compleat the Works of Death, Desolation, and Tyranny, already begun with circumstances of Cruelty and Perfidy, scarcely paralleled in the most bar-barous Ages, and totally unworthy of the Head of a civilized Nation.

∽ He has constrained our fellow Citizens taken Captive on the high Seas to bear Arms against their Country, to become the Executioners of their Friends and Brethren, or to fall themselves by their Hands.

∽ He has excited domestic Insurrections amongst us, and has endeavoured to bring on the Inhabitants of our Frontiers, the merciless Indian Savages, whose known Rule of Warfare, is an undistinguished Destruction, of all Ages, Sexes and Conditions.

In every stage of these Oppressions we have Petitioned for Redress in the most humble Terms: Our repeated Petitions have been answered only by repeated Injury. A Prince, whose Character is thus marked by every act which may define a Tyrant, is unfit to be the Ruler of a free People.

Nor have we been wanting in Attentions to our British Brethren. We have warned them from Time to Time of Attempts by their Legislature to extend an unwarrantable Jurisdiction over us. We have reminded them of the Circumstances of our Emigration and Settlement here. We have appealed to their native Justice and Magnanimity, and we have conjured them by the Ties of our common Kindred to disavow these Usurpations, which, would inevitably interrupt our Connections and Correspondence. They too have been deaf to the Voice of Justice and of Consanguinity. We must, therefore, acquiesce in the Necessity, which denounces our Separation, and hold them, as we hold the rest of Mankind, Enemies in War, in Peace, Friends.

We, therefore, the Representatives of the United States of America, in General Congress, Assembled, appealing to the Supreme Judge of the World for the Rectitude of our Intentions, do, in the Name, and by Authority of the good People of these Colonies, solemnly Publish and Declare, That these United Colonies are, and of Right ought to be, Free and Independent States; that they are absolved from all Allegiance to the British Crown, and that all political Connection between them and the State of Great-Britain, is and ought to be totally dissolved; and that as Free and Independent States, they have full Power to levy War, conclude Peace, contract Alliances, establish Commerce, and to do all other Acts and Things which Independent States may of right do. And for the support of this Declaration, with a firm Reliance on the Protection of divine Providence, we mutually pledge to each other our Lives, our Fortunes, and our sacred Honor.

Signed by ORDER and in BEHALF of the CONGRESS,
John Hancock, PRESIDENT

Attest.
Charles Thomson, Secretary

— POEM —

THE GIFT OUTRIGHT

ROBERT FROST {1942}

Robert Frost (1874–1963) was a Dartmouth College dropout, schoolteacher, millworker, journalist, and dairy farmer before devoting himself to poetry at the age of thirty-eight. His verse, which won him four Pulitzer Prizes and a place in virtually every anthology of American poetry, often uses simple rural settings and colloquial language to invoke the rich ambiguities of universal questions. Here, in sixteen unrhymed lines, Frost examines the idea of destiny and the salvation to be found in surrendering to what may already be yours.

The land was ours before we were the land's.
She was our land more than a hundred years
Before we were her people. She was ours
In Massachusetts, in Virginia,
But we were England's, still colonials,
Possessing what we still were unpossessed by,
Possessed by what we now no more possessed.
Something we were withholding made us weak
Until we found out that it was ourselves
We were withholding from our land of living,
And forthwith found salvation in surrender.
Such as we were we gave ourselves outright
(The deed of gift was many deeds of war)
To the land vaguely realizing westward,
But still unstoried, artless, unenhanced,
Such as she was, such as she would become.

—SPEECH—

PUBLIC SPEECH

CHIEF SEATTLE {CIRCA 1854}

The land may have been ours before we were the land's, but before it was the white man's it belonged to the American Indians. A long-standing legend tells us that Seattle (1787–1866), chief of the Duwamish and Suquamish tribes of Puget Sound, delivered this speech in 1854 or 1855 in what is now downtown Seattle to Isaac Ingalls Stevens, governor of the Washington Territory. From a historian's point of view, however, the documentation for this heart-wrenching oration is meager. Nonetheless, it is a powerful indictment of the wrongs done to the Native American tribes and to the American landscape since the arrival of the Europeans.

Yonder sky that has wept tears of compassion upon my people for centuries untold, and which to us appears changeless and eternal, may change. Today is fair. Tomorrow it may be overcast with clouds. My words are like the stars that never change. Whatever Seattle says, the great chief at Washington can rely upon with as much certainty as he can upon the return of the sun or the seasons. The white chief says that Big Chief at Washington sends us greetings of friendship and goodwill. This is kind of him for we know he has little need of our friendship in return. His people are many. They are like the grass that covers vast prairies. My people are few. They resemble the scattering trees of a storm-swept plain. The great, and I presume also good, White Chief sends us word that he wishes to buy our land but is willing to allow us enough to live comfortably. This indeed appears just, even generous, for the Red Man no longer has rights that he need respect, and the offer may be wise, also, as we are no longer in need of an extensive country.

There was a time when our people covered the land as the waves of a wind-ruffled sea cover its shell-paved floor, but that time long since passed away with the greatness of tribes that are now but a mournful memory. I will not dwell on, nor mourn over, our untimely decay, nor reproach my paleface brothers with hastening it, as we too may have been somewhat to blame.

Youth is impulsive. When our young men grow angry at some real or imaginary wrong, and disfigure their faces with black paint, it denotes that their hearts are black, and that they are often cruel and relentless, and our old men and old women are unable to restrain them. Thus it has ever been. Thus it was when the white man began to push our forefathers ever westward. But let us hope that the hostilities between us may never return. We would have everything to lose and nothing to gain. Revenge by young men is considered gain, even at the cost of their own lives, but old men who stay at home in times of war, and mothers who have sons to lose, know better.

Our great father in Washington, for I presume he is now our father as well as yours, since King George has moved his boundaries further north; our great and good father, I say, sends us word that if we do as he desires he will protect us. His brave warriors will be to us a bristling wall of strength, and his wonderful ships of war will fill our harbors, so that our ancient enemies far to the northward—the Haidas and Tsimshians—will cease to frighten our women, children, and old men. Then in reality he will be our father and we his children. But can that ever be? Your God is not our God! Your God loves your people and hates mine; he folds his strong protecting arms lovingly about the paleface and leads him by the hand as a father leads an infant son. But, He has forsaken His Red children, if they really are His. Our God, the Great Spirit, seems also to have forsaken us. Your God makes your people wax stronger every day. Soon they will fill all the land. Our people are ebbing away like a rapidly receding tide that will never return. The white man's God cannot love our people or He would protect them. They seem to be orphans who can look nowhere for help. How then can we be brothers? How can your God become our God and renew our prosperity and awaken in us dreams of returning greatness? If we have a common Heavenly Father, He must be partial, for He came to His paleface children. We never saw Him. He gave you laws but had no word for His red children whose teeming multitudes once filled this vast continent as stars fill the firmament. No, we are two distinct races with separate origins and separate destinies. There is little in common between us.

To us the ashes of our ancestors are sacred and their resting place is hallowed ground. You wander far from the graves of your ancestors and seemingly without regret. Your religion was written upon tablets of stone by

19

the iron finger of your God so that you could not forget. The Red Man could never comprehend or remember it. Our religion is the traditions of our ancestors—the dreams of our old men, given them in solemn hours of the night by the Great Spirit; and the visions of our sachems, and is written in the hearts of our people.

Your dead cease to love you and the land of their nativity as soon as they pass the portals of the tomb and wander away beyond the stars. They are soon forgotten and never return. Our dead never forget this beautiful world that gave them being. They still love its verdant valleys, its murmuring rivers, its magnificent mountains, sequestered vales and verdant lined lakes and bays, and ever yearn in tender fond affection over the lonely hearted living, and often return from the happy hunting ground to visit, guide, console, and comfort them.

Day and night cannot dwell together. The Red Man has ever fled the approach of the White Man, as the morning mist flees before the morning sun. However, your proposition seems fair and I think that my people will accept it and will retire to the reservation you offer them. Then we will dwell apart in peace, for the words of the Great White Chief seem to be the words of nature speaking to my people out of dense darkness.

It matters little where we pass the remnant of our days. They will not be many. The Indian's night promises to be dark. Not a single star of hope hovers above his horizon. Sad-voiced winds moan in the distance. Grim fate seems to be on the Red Man's trail, and wherever he will hear the approaching footsteps of his fell destroyer and prepare stolidly to meet his doom, as does the wounded doe that hears the approaching footsteps of the hunter.

A few more moons, a few more winters, and not one of the descendants of the mighty hosts that once moved over this broad land or lived in happy homes, protected by the Great Spirit, will remain to mourn over the graves of a people once more powerful and hopeful than yours. But why should I mourn at the untimely fate of my people? Tribe follows tribe, and nation follows nation, like the waves of the sea. It is the order of nature, and regret is useless. Your time of decay may be distant, but it will surely come, for even the White Man whose God walked and talked with him as friend to friend, cannot be exempt from the common destiny. We may be brothers after all. We will see.

We will ponder your proposition and when we decide we will let you know. But should we accept it, I here and now make this condition that we will not be denied the privilege without molestation of visiting at any time the tombs of our ancestors, friends, and children. Every part of this soil is sacred in the estimation of my people. Every hillside, every valley, every plain and grove, has been hallowed by some sad or happy event in days long vanished. Even the rocks, which seem to be dumb and dead as they swelter in the sun along the silent shore, thrill with memories of stirring events connected with the lives of my people, and the very dust upon which you now stand responds more lovingly to their footsteps than yours, because it is rich with the blood of our ancestors, and our bare feet are conscious of the sympathetic touch. Our departed braves, fond mothers, glad, happy hearted maidens, and even the little children who lived here and rejoiced here for a brief season, will love these somber solitudes and at eventide they greet shadowy returning spirits. And when the last Red Man shall have perished, and the memory of my tribe shall have become a myth among the White Men, these shores will swarm with the invisible dead of my tribe, and when your children's children think themselves alone in the field, the store, the shop, upon the highway, or in the silence of the pathless woods, they will not be alone. In all the earth there is no place dedicated to solitude. At night when the streets of your cities and villages are silent and you think them deserted, they will throng with the returning hosts that once filled them and still love this beautiful land. The White Man will never be alone.

Let him be just and deal kindly with my people, for the dead are not altogether powerless.

—SONG—

GOD BLESS AMERICA

IRVING BERLIN {1918}

Irving Berlin (1888–1989), born Israel Baline, inherited his love of music from his father, the cantor in their synagogue. In 1918, he wrote "God Bless America" for a musical called *Yip, Yip, Yaphank*, but the producers cut it. When popular singer Kate Smith asked Berlin for a new patriotic song, he dusted off "God Bless America." After Smith sang it on her radio program on November 10, 1938, it became an instant hit. Before handing over the song to Smith, Berlin made a few revisions, adding "From the mountains, to the prairies/To the oceans white with foam" in place of the more provincial original lines, which read, "From the green fields of Virginia/To the gold fields out in Nome."

> While the storm clouds gather
> Far across the sea,
> Let us swear allegiance
> To a land that's free;
> Let us all be grateful
> For a land so fair,
> As we raise our voices
> In a solemn prayer:
>
> God Bless America,
> Land that I love.
> Stand beside her and guide her
> Through the night with a light from above.
> From the mountains, to the prairies,
> To the oceans white with foam,
> God bless America,
> My home sweet home.

— SONG —

THIS LAND IS YOUR LAND

WOODY GUTHRIE {1940}

Though most Americans sing Woody Guthrie's rousing "This Land is Your Land" as schoolchildren, Guthrie (1912–1967) actually wrote the song as a socialist response to Irving Berlin's "God Bless America." School songbooks censor the two verses most critical of capitalism— about the relief office and walking on private property. It would have been impossible for Guthrie to write an American anthem that left out the poor; he had traveled around the country during the Great Depression, and everywhere he went, he sang of the destitute and their struggles.

This land is your land, This land is my land,
From California to the New York Island;
From the redwood forest to the Gulf Stream waters:
This land was made for you and me.

As I was walking that ribbon of highway,
I saw above me that endless skyway:
I saw below me that golden valley:
This land was made for you and me.

I've roamed and rambled and I followed my footsteps
To the sparkling sands of her diamond deserts;
All around me a voice was sounding:
This land was made for you and me.

When the sun came shining, and I was strolling,
And the wheat fields waving and the dust clouds rolling,
As the fog was lifting a voice was chanting:
This land was made for you and me.

As I went walking, I saw a sign there,
And on the sign it said "No Trespassing."
But on the other side it didn't say nothing,
That side was made for you and me.

In the shadow of the steeple I saw my people,
By the relief office I seen my people;
As they stood there hungry, I stood there asking
Is this land made for you and me?

Nobody living can ever stop me,
As I go walking my freedom highway;
Nobody living can make me turn back,
This land was made for you and me.

— SPEECH —

BICENTENNIAL SPEECH

GERALD R. FORD {JULY 4, 1976}

If all had gone as planned, Richard Nixon would have been addressing the nation on the 200th anniversary of American independence. But Nixon had been brought down by the Watergate scandal and threatened with impeachment. When he resigned in 1974, Gerald R. Ford (b. 1913) succeeded to the presidency. The fresh memory of the Watergate debacle may explain why, in his Bicentennial Speech in Philadelphia, Ford touched on the theme of America's faith in the rule of law.

The American Revolution was unique and remains unique in that it was fought in the name of the law as well as liberty. At the start, the Declaration of Independence proclaimed the divine source of individual rights and the purpose of human government as Americans understood it.

That purpose is to secure the rights of the individuals against even government itself. But the Declaration did not tell us how to accomplish this purpose or what kind of government to set up. . . .

The Constitution was created to make the promise of the Declaration come true. The Declaration was not a protest against government but against the excesses of government. It prescribed the proper role of government to secure the rights of individuals and to effect their safety and their happiness. In modern society, no individual can do this all alone, so government is not necessarily evil but a necessary good.

The Framers of the Constitution feared a central government that was too strong, as many Americans rightly do today. The Framers of the Constitution, after their experience under the Articles, feared a central government that was too weak, as many Americans rightly do today. They spent days studying all of the contemporary governments of Europe and concluded with Dr. Franklin that all contained the seeds of their own destruction. So the Framers built something new, drawing upon their English traditions, on the Roman Republic, on the uniquely American institution of the town meeting. To reassure those who felt the original Constitution did not sufficiently spell out the inalienable rights of the Declaration, the First United States Congress added—and the States ratified—the first 10 amendments, which we call the Bill of Rights.

Later, after a tragic, fraternal war, those guarantees were expanded to include all Americans. Later still, voting rights were assured for women and for younger citizens 18 to 21 years of age.

It is good to know that in our own lifetime we have taken part in the growth of freedom and in the expansion of equality which began here so long ago. This union of corrected wrongs and expanded rights has brought the blessings of liberty to the 215 million Americans, but the struggle for life, liberty, and the pursuit of happiness is never truly won. Each generation of Americans, indeed of all humanity, must strive to achieve these aspirations anew. Liberty is a living flame to be fed, not dead ashes to be revered, even in a Bicentennial Year.

It is fitting that we ask ourselves hard questions even on a glorious day like today. Are the institutions under which we live working the way they should? Are the foundations laid in 1776 and 1789 still strong enough and sound enough to resist the tremors of our times? Are our God-given rights secure, our hard-won liberties protected?

The very fact that we can ask these questions, that we can freely examine and criticize our society, is cause for confidence itself. Many of the voices raised in doubt 200 years ago served to strengthen and improve the decisions finally made.

The American adventure is a continuing process. As one milestone is passed, another is sighted. As we achieve one goal—a longer lifespan, a literate population, a leadership in world affairs—we raise our sights.

As we begin our third century, there is still so much to be done. We must increase the independence of the individual and the opportunity of all Americans to attain their full potential. We must ensure each citizen's right to privacy. We must create a more beautiful America, making human works conform to the harmony of nature. We must develop a safer society, so ordered that happiness may be pursued without fear of crime or man-made hazards. We must build a more stable international order, politically, economically, and legally. We must match the great breakthroughs of the past century by improving health and conquering disease. We must continue to unlock the secrets of the universe beyond our planet as well as within ourselves. We must work to enrich the quality of American life at work, at play, and in our homes.

It is right that Americans are always improving. It is not only right, it is necessary. From need comes action, as it did here in Independence Hall. Those fierce political rivals—John Adams and Thomas Jefferson—in their later years carried out a warm correspondence. Both died on the Fourth of July of 1826, having lived to see the handiwork of their finest hour endure a full 50 years.

They had seen the Declaration's clear call for human liberty and equality arouse the hopes of all mankind. Jefferson wrote to Adams that "even should the cloud of barbarism and despotism again obscure the science and libraries of Europe, this country remains to preserve and restore life [light] and liberty to them."

Over a century later, in 1936, Jefferson's dire prophesy seemed about to come true. President Franklin D. Roosevelt, speaking for a mighty nation, reinforced by millions and millions of immigrants who had joined the

American adventure, was able to warn the new despotisms: "We too, born to freedom, and believing in freedom, are willing to fight to maintain freedom. We, and all others who believe as deeply as we do, would rather die on our feet than live on our knees."

The world knows where we stand. The world is ever conscious of what Americans are doing for better or for worse, because the United States today remains the most successful realization of humanity's universal hope.

The world may or may not follow, but we lead because our whole history says we must. Liberty is for all men and women as a matter of equal and inalienable right. The establishment of justice and peace abroad will in large measure depend upon the peace and justice we create here in our own country, where we still show the way.

The American adventure began here with a firm reliance on the protection of Divine Providence. It continues in a common conviction that the source of our blessings is a loving God, in whom we trust. Therefore, I ask all the members of the American family, our guests and friends, to join me now in a moment of silent prayer and meditation in gratitude for all that we have received and to ask continued safety and happiness for each of us and for the United States of America.

Thank you, and God bless you.

— SPEECH —

SPEECH AT INDEPENDENCE HALL
ABRAHAM LINCOLN {FEBRUARY 22, 1861}

En route to his inauguration as president on February 22, 1861, Abraham Lincoln (1809–1865) stopped at Independence Hall in Philadelphia, where the Declaration of Independence had been signed, and delivered this impromptu speech. Four years and a Civil War later, Lincoln would return to Independence Hall, this time in an open casket, as hundreds of thousands of mourners filed past the body of the assassinated sixteenth President.

I am filled with deep emotion at finding myself standing here, in this place, where were collected together the wisdom, the patriotism, the devotion to principle, from which sprang the institutions under which we live. You have kindly suggested to me that in my hands is the task of restoring peace to the present distracted condition of the country. I can say in return, Sir, that all the political sentiments I entertain have been drawn, so far as I have been able to draw them, from the sentiments which originated and were given to the world from this hall. I have never had a feeling politically that did not spring from the sentiments embodied in the Declaration of Independence. I have often pondered over the dangers which were incurred by the men who assembled here, and framed and adopted that Declaration of Independence. I have pondered over the toils that were endured by the officers and soldiers of the army who achieved that Independence. I have often inquired of myself what great principle of idea it was that kept this Confederacy so long together. It was not the mere matter of the separation of the Colonies from the motherland; but that sentiment in the Declaration of Independence which gave liberty, not alone to the people of this country, but, I hope, to the world, for all future time. It was that which gave promise that in due time the weight would be lifted from the shoulders of all men. This is a sentiment embodied in the Declaration of Independence. Now, my friends, can this country be saved upon that basis? If it can, I will consider myself one of the happiest men in the world, if I can help to save it. If it cannot be saved upon that principle, it will be truly awful. But if this country cannot be saved without giving up that principle, I was about to say I would rather be assassinated on this spot than surrender it. Now, in my view of the present aspect of affairs, there need be no bloodshed or war. There is no necessity for it. I am not in favor of such a course, and I may say, in advance, that there will be no bloodshed unless it be forced upon the Government, and then it will be compelled to act in self-defence.

My friends, this is wholly an unexpected speech, and I did not expect to be called upon to say a word when I came here. I supposed it was merely to do something toward raising the flag. I may, therefore, have said something indiscreet. I have said nothing but what I am willing to live by and, if it be the pleasure of Almighty God, die by.

—POEM—

LET AMERICA BE AMERICA AGAIN

LANGSTON HUGHES {1935}

At age 19, Langston Hughes (1902–1967) had a hard time forcing himself to go to classes at Columbia University. The lure of the Harlem Renaissance just a few blocks away was too strong for Hughes to resist. By 1923, he was recognized as an important young poet who wrote on African-American themes in rhythms reminiscent of jazz. Like W.E.B. Du Bois, Hughes vigorously embraced his identity as an African American. He didn't want his poetry to "pass" as the work of a white man; he wanted people to know they were reading the work of a black poet. And he didn't care if his style offended his readers, black or white. "We build our temples for tomorrow, as strong as we know how," he said of African-American artists, "and we stand on the top of the mountain, free within ourselves."

Let America be America again.
Let it be the dream it used to be.
Let it be the pioneer on the plain
Seeking a home where he himself is free.

(America never was America to me.)

Let America be the dream the dreamers dreamed—
Let it be that great strong land of love
Where never kings connive nor tyrants scheme
That any man be crushed by one above.

(It never was America to me.)

O, let my land be a land where Liberty
Is crowned with no false patriotic wreath,
But opportunity is real, and life is free,
Equality is in the air we breathe.

(There's never been equality for me,
Nor freedom in this "homeland of the free.")

Say, who are you that mumbles in the dark?
And who are you that draws your veil across the stars?

I am the poor white, fooled and pushed apart,
I am the Negro bearing slavery's scars.
I am the red man driven from the land,
I am the immigrant clutching the hope I seek—
    And finding only the same old stupid plan
Of dog eat dog, of mighty crush the weak.

I am the young man, full of strength and hope,
Tangled in that ancient endless chain
Of profit, power, gain, of grab the land!
Of grab the gold! Of grab the ways of satisfying need!
Of work the men! Of take the pay!
Of owning everything for one's own greed!

I am the farmer, bondsman to the soil.
I am the worker sold to the machine.
I am the Negro, servant to you all.
I am the people, humble, hungry, mean—
Hungry yet today despite the dream.
Beaten yet today—O, Pioneers!
I am the man who never got ahead,
The poorest worker bartered through the years.

Yet I'm the one who dreamt our basic dream
In the Old World while still a serf of kings,
Who dreamt a dream so strong, so brave, so true,
That even yet its mighty daring sings
In every brick and stone, in every furrow turned
That's made America the land it has become.

O, I'm the man who sailed those early seas
In search of what I meant to be my home—
For I'm the one who left dark Ireland's shore,
And Poland's plain, and England's grassy lea,
And torn from Black Africa's strand I came
To build a "homeland of the free."

The free?

Who said the free? Not me?
Surely not me? The millions on relief today?
The millions shot down when we strike?
The millions who have nothing for our pay?
For all the dreams we've dreamed
And all the songs we've sung
And all the hopes we've held
And all the flags we've hung,
The millions who have nothing for our pay—
Except the dream that's almost dead today.

O, let America be America again—
The land that never has been yet—
And yet must be—the land where *every* man is free.
The land that's mine—the poor man's, Indian's,
    Negro's, ME—
Who made America,
Whose sweat and blood, whose faith and pain,
Whose hand at the foundry, whose plow in the rain,
Must bring back our mighty dream again.

Sure, call me any ugly name you choose—
The steel of freedom does not stain.
From those who live like leeches on the people's lives,
We must take back our land again,
America!

O, yes,
I say it plain,
America never was America to me,
And yet I swear this oath—
America will be!

Out of the rack and ruin of our gangster death,
The rape and rot of graft, and stealth, and lies,
We, the people, must redeem
The land, the mines, the plants, the rivers.
The mountains and the endless plain—
All, all the stretch of these great green states—
And make America again!

—SPEECH—

THE AMERICAN DREAM
MARTIN LUTHER KING JR. {JULY 4, 1965}

Martin Luther King Jr. (1929–1968), one of the pivotal figures in the Civil
Rights Movement, was ordained as a minister at the Ebenezer Baptist
Church in Atlanta at the age of 19. Although Reverend King went on to
preach the gospel of nonviolent resistance to millions around the world—he
was named *Time's* "Man of the Year" in 1963 and awarded the Nobel Peace
Prize a year later—he remained loyal to his home church. It was from the pulpit there that he delivered this sermon.

I planned to use for the textual basis for our thinking together that passage
from the prologue of the book of Job where Satan is pictured as asking God,
"Does Job serve thee for nought?" And I'd like to ask you to allow me to hold
that sermon "Why Serve God?" in abeyance and preach it the next time I am
in the pulpit in order to share with you some other ideas. This morning I was

riding to the airport in Washington, D.C., and on the way to the airport the lim-
ousine passed by the Jefferson Monument, and Reverend Andrew Young, my
executive assistant, said to me, "It's quite coincidental that we would be passing by the Jefferson Monument on Independence Day." You can get so busy in
life that you forget holidays and other days, and it had slipped my mind altogether that today was the Fourth of July. And I said to him, "It is coincidental
and quite significant, and I think when I get to Atlanta and go to my pulpit, I
will try to preach a sermon in the spirit of the Founding Fathers of our nation
and in the spirit of the Declaration of Independence." And so this morning I
would like to use as a subject from which to preach: "The American Dream."

It wouldn't take us long to discover the substance of that dream. It is
found in those majestic words of the Declaration of Independence, words
lifted to cosmic proportions: "We hold these truths to be self-evident, that all
men are created equal, that they are endowed by God, their Creator, with certain inalienable Rights, that among these are Life, Liberty, and the pursuit of
Happiness." This is a dream. It's a great dream.

The first saying we notice in this dream is an amazing universalism. It
doesn't say "some men," it says "all men." It doesn't say "all white men,"
it says "all men," which includes black men. It does not say "all Gentiles," it
says "all men," which includes Jews. It doesn't say "all Protestants," it says "all
men," which includes Catholics. It doesn't even say "all theists and believers,"
it says "all men," which includes humanists and agnostics.

Then that dream goes on to say another thing that ultimately distinguishes
our nation and our form of government from any totalitarian system in the
world. It says that each of us has certain basic rights that are neither derived
from or conferred by the state. In order to discover where they came from, it is
necessary to move back behind the dim mist of eternity. They are God-given,
gifts from His hands. Never before in the history of the world has a sociopolit-
ical document expressed in such profound, eloquent, and unequivocal language the dignity and the worth of human personality. The American Dream
reminds us, and we should think about it anew on this Independence Day, that
every man is an heir of the legacy of dignity and worth.

Now ever since the Founding Fathers of our nation dreamed this dream
in all of its magnificence—to use a big word that the psychiatrists use—

America has been something of a schizophrenic personality, tragically divided against herself. On the one hand we have proudly professed the great principles of democracy, but on the other hand we have sadly practiced the very opposite of those principles.

But now more than ever before, America is challenged to realize its dream, for the shape of the world today does not permit our nation the luxury of an anemic democracy. And the price that America must pay for the continued oppression of the Negro and other minority groups is the price of its own destruction. For the hour is late. And the clock of destiny is ticking out. We must act now before it is too late.

And so it is marvelous and great that we do have a dream, that we have a nation with a dream; and to forever challenge us; to forever give us a sense of urgency; to forever stand in the midst of the "isness" of our terrible injustices; to remind us of the "oughtness" of our noble capacity for justice and love and brotherhood.

This morning I would like to deal with some of the challenges that we face today in our nation as a result of the American dream. First, I want to reiterate the fact that we are challenged more than ever before to respect the dignity and the worth of all human personality. We are challenged to really believe that all men are created equal. And don't misunderstand that. It does not mean that all men are created equal in terms of native endowment, in terms of intellectual capacity—it doesn't mean that. There are certain bright stars in the human firmament in every field. It doesn't mean that every musician is equal to a Beethoven or Handel, a Verdi or a Mozart. It doesn't mean that every physicist is equal to an Einstein. It does not mean that every literary figure in history is equal to Aeschylus and Euripides, Shakespeare and Chaucer. It does not mean that every philosopher is equal to Plato, Aristotle, Immanuel Kant, and Friedrich Hegel. It doesn't mean that. There are individuals who do excel and rise to the heights of genius in their areas and in their fields. What it does mean is that all men are equal in intrinsic worth.

You see, the Founding Fathers were really influenced by the Bible. The whole concept of the *imago dei*, as it is expressed in Latin, the "image of God," is the idea that all men have something within them that God injected. Not that they have substantial unity with God, but that every man has a capacity to have fellowship with God. And this gives him a uniqueness, it gives him worth, it gives him dignity. And we must never forget this as a nation: there are no gradations in the image of God. Every man from a treble white to a bass black is significant on God's keyboard, precisely because every man is made in the image of God. One day we will learn that. We will know one day that God made us to live together as brothers and to respect the dignity and worth of every man.

This is why we must fight segregation with all of our nonviolent might. Segregation is not only inconvenient—that isn't what makes it wrong. Segregation is not only sociologically untenable—that isn't what makes it wrong. Segregation is not only politically and economically unsound—that is not what makes it wrong. Ultimately, segregation is morally wrong and sinful. To use the words of a great Jewish philosopher that died a few days ago, Martin Buber, "It's wrong because it substitutes an 'I–It' relationship for the 'I–Thou' relationship and relegates persons to the status of things." That's it.

I remember when Mrs. King and I were in India, we journeyed down one afternoon to the southernmost part of India, the state of Kerala, the city of Trivandrum. That afternoon I was to speak in one of the schools, what we would call high schools in our country, and it was a school attended by and large by students who were the children of former untouchables. Now you know in India, there was the caste system—and India has done a marvelous job in grappling with this problem—but you had your full caste and individuals were in one of the castes. And then you had some sixty or seventy million people who were considered outcasts. They were the untouchables; they could not go places that other people went; they could not do certain things. And this was one of the things that Mahatma Gandhi battled—along with his struggle to end the long night of colonialism—also to end the long night of the caste system and caste untouchability. You remember some of his great fasts were around the question of making equality a reality for the Harijans, as they were called, the "untouchables." He called them the children of God, and he even adopted an untouchable as his daughter. He demonstrated in his own personal life and in his family that he was going to revolt against a whole idea. And I remember that afternoon when I stood up in that school. The principal introduced me and then as he came to the conclusion of his introduction, he says, "Young people, I would like to present to you a fellow untouchable from the United States of America." And for the moment I was a bit shocked and peeved that I would be referred to as an untouchable.

Pretty soon my mind dashed back across the mighty Atlantic. And I started thinking about the fact that at that time no matter how much I needed to rest my tired body after a long night of travel, I couldn't stop in the average motel of the highways and the hotels of the cities of the South. I started thinking about the fact that no matter how long an old Negro woman had been shopping downtown and got a little tired and needed to get a hamburger or a cup of coffee at a lunch counter, she couldn't get it there. I started thinking about the fact that still in too many instances, Negroes have to go to the back of the bus and have to stand up over empty seats. I started thinking about the fact that my children and the other children that would be born would have to go to segregated schools. I started thinking about the fact: twenty million of my brothers and sisters were still smothering in an airtight cage of poverty in an affluent society. I started thinking about the fact: these twenty million brothers and sisters were still by and large housed in rat-infested, unendurable slums in the big cities of our nation, still attended inadequate schools faced with improper recreational facilities. And I said to myself, "Yes, I am an untouchable, and every Negro in the United States of America is an untouchable." And this is the evilness of segregation: it stigmatizes the segregated as an untouchable in a caste system. We hold these truths to be self-evident, if we are to be a great nation, that all men are created equal. God's black children are as significant as his white children. "We hold these truths to be self-evident." One day we will learn this.

The other day Mrs. King and I spent about ten days down in Jamaica. I'd gone down to deliver the commencement address at the University of the West Indies. I always love to go to that great island which I consider the most beautiful island in all the world. The government prevailed upon us to be their guests and spend some time and try to get a little rest while there on the speaking tour. And so for those days we traveled all over Jamaica. And over and over again I was impressed by one thing. Here you have people from many national backgrounds: Chinese, Indians, so-called Negroes, and you can just go down the line, Europeans, and people from many, many nations. Do you know they all live there and they have a motto in Jamaica, "Out of many people, one people." And they say, "Here in Jamaica we are not Chinese, we are not Japanese, we are not Indians, we are not Negroes, we are not Englishmen, we are not Canadians. But we are all one big family of Jamaicans." One day, here in America, I hope that we will see this and we will become one big family of Americans. Not white Americans, not black Americans, not Jewish or Gentile Americans, not Irish or Italian Americans, not Mexican Americans, not Puerto Rican Americans, but just Americans. One big family of Americans.

And I tell you this morning, my friends, the reason we got to solve this problem here in America: Because God somehow called America to do a special job for mankind and the world. Never before in the history of the world have so many racial groups and so many national backgrounds assembled together in one nation. And somehow if we can't solve the problem in America, the world can't solve the problem, because America is the world in miniature and the world is America writ large. And God set us out with all of the opportunities. He set us between two great oceans; made it possible for us to live with some of the great natural resources of the world. And there he gave us through the minds of our forefathers a great creed: "We hold these truths to be self-evident, that all men are created equal."

Now that doesn't only apply on the race issue, it applies on the class question. You know, sometimes a class system can be as vicious and evil as a system based on racial injustice. When we say, "We hold these truths to be self-evident, that all men are created equal," and when we live it out, we know as I say so often that the "no D." is as significant as the "Ph.D." And the man who has been to "No House" is as significant as the man who's been to Morehouse. We build our little class systems, and you know you got a lot of Negroes with classism in their veins. You know that they don't want to be bothered with certain other Negroes and they try to separate themselves from them.

I remember when I was in theological school, and we were coming to the end of our years there, a classmate—he came to me to talk with me—said that he wanted to invite his mother up. And she'd struggled in order to help him get through school. He wanted to invite his mother up, but he said,

"You know, the problem is I don't know if she would quite fit in this atmosphere. You know, her verbs aren't quite right; and she doesn't know how to dress too well; she lives in a rural area." And I wanted to say to him so bad that you aren't fit to finish this school. If you cannot acknowledge your mother, if you cannot acknowledge your brothers and sisters, even if they have not risen to the heights of educational attainment, then you aren't fit to go out and try to preach to men and women.

Oh, I'll tell you this morning, and you learn this and you discover the meaning of "God's image." You'll know what the New Testament means when it says that "I revealed it to babes and so often withheld it from the wise." And I have learned a great deal in my few years, not only from the philosophers that I have studied with in the universities, not only from the theologians and the psychologists and the historians, but so often from that humble human being who didn't have the opportunity to get an education but who had something basic deep down within. Sometimes Aunt Jane on her knees can get more truth than the philosopher on his tiptoes. And this is what "all men are made in the image of God" tells us. We must believe this and we must live by it.

This is why we must join the war against poverty and believe in the dignity of all work. What makes a job menial? I'm tired of this stuff about menial labor. What makes it menial is that we don't pay folk anything. Give somebody a job and pay them some money so they can live and educate their children and buy a home and have the basic necessities of life. And no matter what the job is it takes on dignity.

I submit to you when I took off on that plane this morning, I saw men go out there in their overalls. I saw them working on things here and there, and saw some more going out there to put the breakfast on there so that we could eat on our way to Atlanta. And I said to myself that these people who constitute the ground crew are just as significant as the pilot, because this plane couldn't move if you didn't have the ground crew. I submit to you that in Hugh Spaulding or Grady Hospital, the woman or the man who goes in there to sweep the floor is just as significant as the doctor, because if he doesn't get that dust off the floor, germs will begin to circulate. And those same germs can do injury and harm to the human being. I submit to you this morning that there is dignity in all work when we learn to pay people decent wages. Whoever cooks in your house, whoever sweeps the floor in your house is just as significant as anybody who lives in that house. And everybody that we call a maid is serving God in a significant way. And I love the maids, I love the people who have been ignored, and I want to see them get the kind of wages that they need. And their job is no longer a menial job, for you come to see its worth and its dignity.

Are we really taking this thing seriously? "All men are created equal." And that means that every man who lives in a slum today is just as significant as John D., Nelson, or any other Rockefeller. Every man who lives in the slum is just as significant as Henry Ford. All men are created equal, and they are endowed by their Creator with certain inalienable rights, rights that can't be separated from you. Go down and tell them, "You may take my life, but you can't take my right to life. You may take liberty from me, but you can't take my right to liberty. You may take from me the desire, you may take from me the propensity to pursue happiness, but you can't take from me my right to pursue happiness." "We hold these truths to be self-evident that all men are created equal and endowed by their Creator with certain inalienable Rights and among these are Life, Liberty, and the pursuit of Happiness."

Now there's another thing that we must never forget. If we are going to make the American dream a reality, we are challenged to work in an action program to get rid of the last vestiges of segregation and discrimination. This problem isn't going to solve itself, however much people tell us this. However much the Uncle Toms and Nervous Nellies in the Negro communities tell us this, this problem isn't just going to work itself out. History is the long story of the fact that privileged groups seldom give up their privileges without strong resistance, and they seldom do it voluntarily. And so if the American dream is to be a reality, we must work to make it a reality and realize the urgency of the moment. And we must say now is the time to make real the promises of democracy. Now is the time to get rid of segregation and discrimination. Now is the time to make Georgia a better state. Now is the time to make the United States a better nation. We must live with that, and we must believe that.

And I would like to say to you this morning what I've tried to say all over this nation, what I believe firmly: that in seeking to make the dream a reality we must use and adopt a proper method. I'm more convinced than ever before that nonviolence is the way. I'm more convinced than ever before that violence is impractical as well as immoral. If we are to build right here a better America, we have a method as old as the insights of Jesus of Nazareth and as modern as the techniques of Mohandas K. Gandhi. We need not hate; we need not use violence. We can stand up before our most violent opponent and say: We will match your capacity to inflict suffering by our capacity to endure suffering. We will meet your physical force with soul force. Do to us what you will and we will still love you. We cannot in all good conscience obey your unjust laws, because noncooperation with evil is as much a moral obligation as is cooperation with good, and so throw us in jail. We will go in those jails and transform them from dungeons of shame to havens of freedom and human dignity. Send your hooded perpetrators of violence into our communities after midnight hours and drag us out on some wayside road and beat us and leave us half-dead, and as difficult as it is, we will still love you. Somehow go around the country and use your propaganda agents to make it appear that we are not fit culturally, morally, or otherwise for integration, and we will still love you. Threaten our children and bomb our homes, and as difficult as it is, we will still love you.

But be assured that we will ride you down by our capacity to suffer. One day we will win our freedom, but we will not only win freedom for ourselves, we will so appeal to your heart and your conscience that we will win you in the process. And our victory will be a double victory.

Oh yes, love is the way. Love is the only absolute. More and more I see this. I've seen too much hate to want to hate myself; hate is too great a burden to bear. I've seen it on the faces of too many sheriffs of the South—I've seen hate. In the faces and even the walk of too many Klansmen of the South, I've seen hate. Hate distorts the personality. Hate does something to the soul that causes one to lose his objectivity. The man who hates can't think straight; the man who hates can't reason right; the man who hates can't see right; the man who hates can't walk right. And I know now that Jesus is right, that love is the way. And this is why John said, "God is love," so that he who hates does not know God, but he who loves at that moment has the key that opens the door to the meaning of ultimate reality. So this morning there is so much that we have to offer to the world.

40

We have a great dream. It started way back in 1776, and God grant that America will be true to her dream.

About two years ago now, I stood with many of you who stood there in person and all of you who were there in spirit before the Lincoln Monument in Washington. As I came to the end of my speech there, I tried to tell the nation about a dream I had. I must confess to you this morning that since that sweltering August afternoon in 1963, my dream has often turned into a nightmare; I've seen it shattered. I saw it shattered one night on Highway 80 in Alabama when Mrs. Viola Liuzzo was shot down. I had a nightmare and saw my dream shattered one night in Marion, Alabama, when Jimmie Lee Jackson was shot down. I saw my dream shattered one night in Selma when Reverend Reeb was clubbed to the ground by a vicious racist and later died. And oh, I continue to see it shattered as I walk through the Harlems of our nation and see sometimes ten and fifteen Negroes trying to live in one or two rooms. I've been down to the Delta of Mississippi since then, and I've seen my dream shattered as I met hundreds of people who didn't earn more than six or seven hundred dollars a week. I've seen my dream shattered as I've walked the streets of Chicago and seen Negroes, young men and women, with a sense of utter hopelessness because they can't find any jobs. And they see life as a long and desolate corridor with no exit signs. And not only Negroes at this point. I've seen my dream shattered because I've been through Appalachia, and I've seen my white brothers along with Negroes living in poverty. And I'm concerned about white poverty as much as I'm concerned about Negro poverty.

So yes, the dream has been shattered, and I have had my nightmarish experiences, but I tell you this morning once more that I haven't lost the faith. I still have a dream that one day all of God's children will have food and clothing and material well-being for their bodies, culture and education for their minds, and freedom for their spirits.

I still have a dream this morning: one day all of God's black children will be respected like his white children.

I still have a dream this morning that one day the lion and the lamb will lie down together, and every man will sit under his own vine and fig tree and none shall be afraid.

I still have a dream this morning that one day all men everywhere will recognize that out of one blood God made all men to dwell upon the face of the earth.

I still have a dream this morning that one day every valley shall be exalted, and every mountain and hill will be made low; the rough places will be made plain, and the crooked places straight; and the glory of the Lord shall be revealed, and all flesh shall see it together.

I still have a dream this morning that truth will reign supreme and all of God's children will respect the dignity and worth of human personality. And when this day comes the morning stars will sing together and the sons of God will shout for joy.

"We hold these truths to be self-evident that all men are created equal, that they are endowed by their Creator with certain inalienable Rights, that among these are Life, Liberty, and the pursuit of Happiness."

— S O N G —

I AM A PATRIOT

STEVEN VAN ZANDT {1984}

Steven Van Zandt (b. 1950) is famous for being a long-time producer, song writer, and guitarist for Bruce Springsteen's E Street Band and for his role as Silvio Dante on the hit series *The Sopranos*. Although far less well known for his political activism, the outspoken Van Zandt twice has been honored by the United Nations for his work on human rights. The New Jersey-born native wrote "I Am a Patriot" for his 1984 *Voice of America* album as a way to express love for his country but also confusion over its foreign policy.

And the river opens for the righteous
Someday

I was walking with my brother
And he wondered what's on my mind
I said what I believe in my soul
Ain't what I see with my eyes
And we can't turn our backs this time

I am a patriot
And I love my county
Because my country is all I know
I want to be with my family
The people who understand me
I've got nowhere else to go

And the river opens for the righteous
Someday

And I was talking with my sister
She looked so fine
I said, Baby, what's on your mind?
She said, I want to run like the lion
Released from the cages
Released from the rages
Burning in my heart tonight

And I ain't no communist
And I ain't no capitalist
And I ain't no socialist
And I ain't no imperialist
And I ain't no democrat
And I ain't no republican
I only know one party
And its name is freedom

I am, I am, I am
I am a patriot

And the river opens for the righteous
Someday

— SPEECH —

SPEECH ON THE DRED SCOTT DECISION

ABRAHAM LINCOLN {JUNE 26, 1857}

Like many Northern whites before the Civil War, Abraham Lincoln wanted to halt the spread of slavery, but still held some racist views that seem shocking today. He opposed the Dred Scott decision of 1857, in which the Supreme Court ruled that slaves were not citizens and that a slave's residence on free soil did not make him free upon his return to slave territory. During the 1858 Lincoln–Douglas debates in their race for a U.S. Senate seat from Illinois, Stephen Douglas forced Lincoln to defend his opposition to the decision, which Lincoln did by distinguishing between wanting blacks to be free and wanting them to have complete equality. Lincoln counterattacked by accusing Douglas of avoiding the moral aspect of slavery altogether. What he saw as moderation, we now see as impossibly inconsistent.

He finds the Republicans insisting that the Declaration of Independence includes ALL men, black as well as white; and forthwith he boldly denies that it includes Negroes at all, and proceeds to argue gravely that all who contend it does, do so only because they want to vote, and eat, and sleep, and marry with Negroes! He will have it that they cannot be consistent else. Now I protest against that counterfeit logic which concludes that, because I do not want a black woman for a *slave* I must necessarily want her for a *wife*. I need not have her for either, I can just leave her alone. In some respects she certainly is not my equal; but in her natural right to eat the bread she earns with her own hands without asking leave of any one else, she is my equal, and the equal of all others. . . .

I think the authors of that notable instrument intended to include all men, but they did not intend to declare all men equal in all respects. They did not mean to say all were equal in color, size, intellect, moral developments, or social capacity. They defined with tolerable distinctness, in what respects they did consider all men created equal—equal in "certain inalienable rights, among which are life, liberty, and the pursuit of happiness." This they said, and this meant. They did not mean to assert the obvious untruth, that all were then actually enjoying that equality, nor yet, that they were about to confer it immediately upon them. In fact they had no power to confer such a boon. They meant simply to declare the *right*, so that the *enforcement* of it might follow as fast as circumstances should permit. They meant to set up a standard maxim for free society, which should be familiar to all, and revered by all; constantly looked to, constantly labored for, and even though never perfectly attained, constantly approximated, and thereby constantly spreading and deepening its influence, and augmenting the happiness and value of life to all people of all colors everywhere. The assertion that "All men are created equal" was of no practical use in effecting our separation from Great Britain; and it was placed in the Declaration, not for that, but for future use. Its authors meant it to be, thank God, it is now proving itself, a stumbling block to those who in [after] times might seek to turn a free people back into the hateful paths of despotism. They knew the proneness of prosperity to breed tyrants, and they meant when such should re-appear in this fair land and commence their vocation they should find left for them at least one hard nut to crack . . .

—NOVEL—

THE KILLER ANGELS

MICHAEL SHAARA {1975}

In his extensively researched, Pulitzer Prize–winning novel about the battle of Gettysburg, Michael Shaara (1928–1988) describes the predicament of 34-year-old Lieutenant Joshua Chamberlain of the 20th Maine regiment on the morning of Monday, June 29, 1863. He has been sent 120 mutinous Union soldiers—also, as it happens, from Maine—with orders to shoot them if he can't get them to fight in a battle brewing nearby in a little Pennsylvania crossroads called Gettysburg, a crucial battle he will be instrumental in helping the North to win. Since Chamberlain knows he won't shoot these men from his own state, this former professor of rhetoric at Bowdoin College has no choice but to persuade them to take up arms once again for ideals they may only dimly understand.

He walked slowly toward the dark grove. He had a complicated brain and there were things going on back there from time that he only dimly understood, so he relied on his instincts, but he was learning all the time. The faith itself was simple: he believed in the dignity of man. His ancestors were Huguenots, refugees of a chained and bloody Europe. He had learned their stories in the cradle. He had grown up believing in America and the individual and it was a stronger faith than his faith in God. This was the land where no man had to bow. In this place at last a man could stand up free of the past, free of tradition and blood ties and the curse of royalty and become what he wished to become. This was the first place on earth where the man mattered more than the state. True freedom had begun here and it would spread eventually over all the earth. But it had begun *here*. The fact of slavery upon this incredibly beautiful new clean earth was appalling, but more even than that was the horror of old Europe, the curse of nobility, which the South was transplanting to new soil. They were forming a new aristocracy, a new breed of glittering men, and Chamberlain had come to crush it. But he was fighting for the dignity of man and in that way he was fighting for himself. If men were equal in America, all these former Poles and English and Czechs and blacks, then they were equal everywhere, and there was really no such thing as a foreigner; there were only free men and slaves. And so it was not even patriotism but a new faith. The Frenchman may fight for France, but the American fights for mankind, for freedom; for the people, not the land.

Yet the words had been used too often and the fragments that came to Chamberlain now were weak. A man who has been shot at is a new realist, and what do you say to a realist when the war is a war of ideals? He thought finally, Well, I owe them the truth at least. Might's well begin with that.

The Regiment had begun to form. Chamberlain thought: At least it'll be a short speech. He walked slowly toward the prisoners.

Glazier Estabrook was standing guard, leaning patiently on his rifle. He was a thick little man of about forty. Except for Kilrain he was the oldest man in the Regiment, the strongest man Chamberlain had ever seen. He waved happily as Chamberlain came up but went on leaning on the rifle. He pointed at one of the prisoners.

"Hey, Colonel, you know who this is? This here is Dan Burns from Orono. I know his daddy. Daddy's a preacher. You really ought to hear him. Best damn cusser I ever heard. Knows more fine swear words than any man in Maine, I bet. Hee."

Chamberlain smiled. But the Burns boy was looking at him with no expression. Chamberlain said, "You fellas gather round. "

He stood in the shade, waited while they closed in silently, watchfully around him. In the background the tents were coming down, the wagons were hitching, but some of the men of the Regiment had come out to watch and listen. Some of the men here were still chewing. But they were quiet, attentive.

Chamberlain waited a moment longer. Now it was quiet in the grove and the clink of the wagons was sharp in the distance. Chamberlain said, "I've been talking with Bucklin. He's told me your problem."

Some of the men grumbled. Chamberlain heard no words clearly. He went on speaking softly so that they would have to quiet to hear him.

"I don't know what I can do about it. I'll do what I can. I'll look into it as soon as possible. But there's nothing I can do today. We're moving out in a few minutes and we'll be marching all day and we may be in a big fight before nightfall. But as soon as I can, I'll do what I can."

They were silent, watching him. Chamberlain began to relax. He had made many speeches and he had a gift for it. He did not know what it was, but when he spoke most men stopped to listen. Fanny said it was something in his voice. He hoped it was there now.

"I've been ordered to take you men with me. I've been told that if you don't come I can shoot you. Well, you know I won't do that. Not Maine men. I won't shoot any man who doesn't want this fight. Maybe someone else will, but I won't. So that's that."

He paused again. There was nothing on their faces to lead him.

"Here's the situation. I've been ordered to take you along, and that's what I'm going to do. Under guard if necessary. But you can have your rifles if you want them. The whole Reb army up the road a ways waiting for us and this is no time for an argument like this. I tell you this: we sure can use you. We're down below half strength and we need you, no doubt of that. But whether you fight or not is up to you. Whether you come along, well, you're coming."

Tom had come up with Chamberlain's horse. Over the heads of the prisoners Chamberlain could see the Regiment falling into line out in the flaming road. He took a deep breath.

"Well, I don't want to preach to you. You know who we are and what we're doing here. But if you're going to fight alongside us there's a few things I want you to know."

He bowed his head, not looking at eyes. He folded his hands together.

"This Regiment was formed last fall, back in Maine. There were a thousand of us then. There's not three hundred of us now." He glanced up briefly. "But what is left is choice."

He was embarrassed. He spoke very slowly, staring at the ground.

"Some of us volunteered to fight for Union. Some came in mainly because we were bored at home and this looked like it might be fun. Some came because we were ashamed not to. Many of us came . . . because it was the right thing to do. All of us have seen men die. Most of us never saw a black man back home. We think on that, too. But freedom . . . is not just a word."

He looked up in to the sky, over silent faces.

"This is a different kind of army. If you look at history you'll see men fight for pay, or women, or some other kind of loot. They fight for land, or because a king makes them, or just because they like killing. But we're here for something new. I don't . . . this hasn't happened much in the history of the world. We're an army going out to set other men free."

He bent down, scratched the black dirt into his fingers. He was beginning to warm to it; the words were beginning to flow. No one in front of him was moving. He said, "This is free ground. All the way from here to the Pacific Ocean. No man has to bow. No man born to royalty. Here we judge you by what *you* do, not by what your father was. Here you can be *something*. Here's a place to build a home. It isn't the land—there's always more land. It's the idea that we all have value, you and me, we're worth something more than the dirt. I never saw dirt I'd die for, but I'm not asking you to come join us and fight for dirt. What we're all fighting for, in the end, is each other."

Once he started talking he broke right through the embarrassment and there was suddenly no longer a barrier there. The words came out of him in a clear river, and he felt himself silent and suspended in the grove listening to himself speak, carried outside himself and looking back down on the silent faces and himself speaking, and he felt the power in him, the power of his cause. For an instant he could see black castles in the air; he could create centuries of screaming, eons of torture. Then he was back in sunlit Pennsylvania. The bugles were blowing and he was done.

He had nothing else to say. No one moved. He felt the embarrassment return. He was suddenly enormously tired. The faces were staring up at him like white stones. Some heads were down. He said, "Didn't mean to preach. Sorry. But I thought . . . you should know who we are." He had forgotten how tiring it was just to speak. "Well, this is still the army, but you're as free as I can make you. Go ahead and talk for a while. If you want your rifles for this fight you'll have them back and nothing else will be said. If you won't join us you'll come along under guard. When this is over I'll do what I can to see that you get fair treatment. Now we have to move out." He stopped, looked at them. The faces showed nothing. He said slowly, "I think if we lose this fight the war will be over. So if you choose to come with us I'll be personally grateful. Well. We have to move out."

He turned, left silence behind him. Tom came up with the horse—a pale-gray lightfooted animal. Tom's face was shiny red.

"My, Lawrence, you sure talk pretty."

Chamberlain grunted. He was really tired. Rest a moment. He paused with his hands on the saddle horn. There was a new vague doubt stirring in his brain. Something troubled him; he did not know why.

"You ride today, Lawrence. You look weary." Chamberlain nodded. Ellis Spear was up. He was Chamberlain's ranking officer, an ex-teacher from Wiscasset who was impressed with Chamberlain's professorship. A shy man, formal, but very competent. He gestured toward the prisoners.

"Colonel, what do you suggest we do with them?"

"Give them a moment. Some of them may be willing to fight. Tom, you go back and see what they say. We'll have to march them under guard. Don't know what else to do. I'm not going to shoot them. We can't leave them here."

The Regiment had formed out in the road, the color bearers in front. Chamberlain mounted, put on the wide-brimmed hat with the emblem of the infantry, began walking his horse slowly across the field toward the road. The uneasiness still troubled him. He had missed something, he did not know what. Well, he was an instinctive man; the mind would tell him sooner or later. Perhaps it was only that when you try to put it into words you cannot express it truly, it never sounds as you dream it. But then . . . you were asking them to die.

Ellis Spear was saying, "How far are we from Pennsylvania, Colonel, you have any idea?"

"Better than twenty miles." Chamberlain squinted upward. "Going to be another hot day."

He moved to the head of the column. The troops were moving slowly, patiently, setting themselves for the long march. After a moment Tom came riding up. His face was delighted. Chamberlain said, "How many are going to join us?"

Tom grinned hugely. "Would you believe it? All but six."

"*How many?*"

"I counted, by actual count, one hundred and fourteen."

"Well." Chamberlain rubbed his nose, astounded.

Tom said, still grinning, "Brother, you did real good."

"They're all marching together?"

"Right. Glazier's got the six hardheads in tow."

"Well, get all the names and start assigning them to different companies. I don't want them bunched up, spread them out. See about their arms."

"Yes, sir, Colonel, sir."

Chamberlain reached the head of the column. The road was long and straight, rising toward a ridge of trees. He turned in his saddle, looked back, saw the entire Fifth Corps forming behind him. He thought: 120 new men. Hardly noticeable in such a mass. And yet . . . he felt a moment of huge joy. He called for road guards and skirmishers and the Twentieth Maine began to move toward Gettysburg.

—SCREENPLAY—

THE REMARKABLE ANDREW

Dalton Trumbo {1942}

Author and screenwriter Dalton Trumbo (1905–1976) is best remembered for his anti-war novel *Johnny Got His Gun*, in part because his name was not on many of the other fine movies he wrote. In 1947, he was blacklisted with the rest of the "Hollywood Ten," a group of producers, writers, and actors who refused to answer questions before the House Un-American Activities Committee (HUAC). Like many of those blacklisted by the industry for their Socialist and Communist sympathies, Trumbo worked under a pseudonym until the 1960s, winning Oscars for *Roman Holiday* and *The Brave One*. There are hints of Trumbo's impassioned speeches before HUAC in this monologue he wrote for the 1942 film, *The Remarkable Andrew*, in which a wrongly imprisoned accountant claims to be visited by the ghosts of the Founding Fathers.

Everybody now seems to be talking about democracy. I don't understand this. As I think of it, democracy isn't like a Sunday suit to be brought out and worn only for parades. It's the kind of a life a decent man leads, it's something to live for and to die for. . . . Democracy means that people can say what they want to. All the people. It means that they can vote as they wish. All the people. It means that they can worship God in any way they feel right, and that includes Christians and Jews and voodoo doctors as well. It means that everybody should have a job, if he's willing to work, and an education, and the right to bring up his children without fear of the future. And it means that the old shall be provided for, without shame to themselves or to their families. It means do unto others as you would have others do unto you. It also means the prayers of the pilgrim fathers in the wilderness, and the Declaration of Independence, and the Constitution of the United States, and the Bill of Rights, and the Emancipation Proclamation, and the dreams of an immigrant mother for her children. And that's what I believe in.

—SPEECH—

WHAT JULY FOURTH MEANS TO ME

RONALD REAGAN {1981}

Voters responded warmly to Ronald Reagan's optimism and patriotism. During his years in Hollywood, Reagan (b. 1911) had learned how to communicate to a mass audience. As president, he sold himself with an upbeat, seemingly informal speaking style that a broad segment of the American public found irresistible. Even his critics had to admire it. This Fourth of July speech is vintage Reagan: a little nostalgia, a little history, and finally, a ringing summons to defend and cherish nature's most precious gift to humankind—individual liberty.

For one who was born and grew up in the small towns of the Midwest, there is a special kind of nostalgia about the Fourth of July.

I remember it as a day almost as long anticipated as Christmas. This was helped along by the appearance in store windows of all kinds of fireworks and colorful posters advertising them with vivid pictures.

No later than the third of July—sometimes earlier—Dad would bring home what he felt he could afford to see go up in smoke and flame. We'd count and recount the number of firecrackers, display pieces and other things and go to bed determined to be up with the sun so as to offer the first, thunderous notice of the Fourth of July.

I'm afraid we didn't give too much thought to the meaning of the day. And, yes, there were tragic accidents to mar it, resulting from careless handling of the fireworks. I'm sure we're better off today with fireworks largely handled by professionals. Yet there was a thrill never to be forgotten in seeing a tin can blown 30 feet in the air by a giant "cracker"—giant meaning it was about 4 inches long.

But enough of nostalgia. Somewhere in our growing up we began to be aware of the meaning of days and with that awareness came the birth of patriotism. July Fourth is the birthday of our nation. I believed as a boy, and believe even more today, that it is the birthday of the greatest nation on earth.

There is a legend about the day of our nation's birth in the little hall in Philadelphia, a day on which debate had raged for hours. The men gathered there were honorable men hard-pressed by a king who had flouted the very laws they were willing to obey. Even so, to sign the Declaration of Independence was such an irretrievable act that the walls resounded with the words "treason, the gallows, the headsman's axe," and the issue remained in doubt.

The legend says that at that point a man rose and spoke. He is described as not a young man, but one who had to summon all his energy for an impassioned plea. He cited the grievances that had brought them to this moment and finally, his voice falling, he said, "They may turn every tree into a gallows, every hole into a grave, and yet the words of that parchment can never die. To the mechanic in the workshop, they will speak hope; to the slave in the mines, freedom. Sign that parchment. Sign if the next moment the noose is around your neck, for that parchment will be the textbook of freedom, the Bible of the rights of man forever."

He fell back exhausted. The 56 delegates, swept up by his eloquence, rushed forward and signed that document destined to be as immortal as a work of man can be. When they turned to thank him for his timely oratory, he was not to be found, nor could any be found who knew who he was or how he had come in or gone out through the locked and guarded doors.

Well, that is the legend. But we do know for certain that 56 men, a little band so unique we have never seen their like since, had pledged their lives, their fortunes and their sacred honor. Some gave their lives in the war that followed, most gave their fortunes, and all preserved their sacred honor.

What manner of men were they? Twenty-four were lawyers and jurists, 11 were merchants and tradesmen, and nine were farmers. They were soft-spoken men of means and education; they were not an unwashed rabble. They had achieved security but valued freedom more. Their stories have not been told nearly enough.

John Hart was driven from the side of his desperately ill wife. For more than a year he lived in the forest and in caves before he returned to find his wife dead, his children vanished, his property destroyed. He died of exhaustion and a broken heart.

Carter Braxton of Virginia lost all his ships, sold his home to pay his debts, and died in rags. And so it was with Ellery, Clymer, Hall, Walton, Gwinnett, Rutledge, Morris, Livingston and Middleton.

Nelson personally urged Washington to fire on his home and destroy it when it became the headquarters for General Cornwallis. Nelson died bankrupt.

But they sired a nation that grew from sea to shining sea. Five million farms, quiet villages, cities that never sleep, 3 million square miles of forest, field, mountain and desert, 227 million people with a pedigree that includes the bloodlines of all the world.

In recent years, however, I've come to think of that day as more than just the birthday of a nation.

It also commemorates the only true philosophical revolution in all history.

Oh, there have been revolutions before and since ours. But those revolutions simply exchanged one set of rules for another. Ours was a revolution that changed the very concept of government.

Let the Fourth of July always be a reminder that here in this land, for the first time, it was decided that man is born with certain God-given rights; that government is only a convenience created and managed by the people, with no powers of its own except those voluntarily granted to it by the people.

We sometimes forget that great truth, and we never should.

Happy Fourth of July.

———————

—ESSAY—

REASONING THE FOURTH

The New York Times Editorial {July 4, 1999}

The Fourth of July is everybody's favorite day for flag-waving. But flag-waving tends to be about emotion and sentiment. The author of this *New York Times* editorial decides to wave around an idea instead: that it is not sentiment that lies at the true heart of the Declaration of Independence, but a rational, pragmatic ideal.

It has been 223 years since the first Fourth, the one commemorated on this anniversary, and in that time Independence Day has been celebrated in just about every possible way, with emotions ranging from a throb of sanctity to irate mockery, with fireworks, parades, doubleheaders, hot dogs, speeches, demonstrations, John Philip Sousa and long afternoon naps on what feels delightfully like the second Saturday in the week. This is still the least commercial holiday in the American holiday roster. No one has figured out a way to sell the public on exchanging Independence Day presents, and you can only use so much red, white and blue bunting before the front porch and the leaves start to look overdressed. The few things that always sell well for the Fourth—explosives—are illegal in most states. One good flag lasts a very long time.

In some celebrations of the Fourth—not many—there still exists an attractive vein of rationalism, a recognition that what is being celebrated is both an event and an idea. Rationalism does not sound like a very patriotic emotion, or much like an emotion at all, but it is the spirit in which the Declaration of Independence was written, and it reflects a historic part of the American character, a brusque, native skepticism that is rarely honored enough these days. In the phrasing of the document, in the way it was promulgated, there was an assurance that reason was preferable to sentiment and that the reason embodied in the Declaration of Independence would be sufficient to dissolve whatever feeling still bound Americans in that era to England.

55

You hear it said repeatedly that the Fourth is America's birthday, which is true but not true enough. The emotion the holiday most often summons is patriotism, love of country, which is good but not good enough. A sequined rodeo queen races into the arena in a Western town, circling the crowd on a fast horse, standing in her stirrups, the American flag she holds snapping in the wind while the announcer lets his voice overflow with feeling. All the people in the grandstand rise and their hearts rise too, mostly. This is a fine thing, but it is not what has carried us all these years, not this alone, no matter what form it takes.

By now, 223 years later, it is almost impossible to read the words of the Declaration of Independence—especially the unequivocal statement of self-evident truths—without emotion, without, at least, acknowledging that the rhythms ring with a familiarity next door to emotion. But the Declaration does not adjure its signers or the people they represented to strong feeling or, for that matter, to patriotism. It adjures them to a sober consideration of causes and first principles based on the laws of nature. It speaks not only to the idealism of its first audience, but also to its pragmatism, its sense of justice. These are the qualities, arid though they may sound, that have preserved the fundamental idea with which this country began. We speak as though conviction were always an emotion and as though emotion were the deepest experience a human could know. The authors of our freedom knew better.

LIFE

—LETTER—

LETTER TO AUNT FANNIE ADOUE

MARION LEE KEMPNER {OCTOBER 20, 1966}

This short letter that Marion Lee "Sandy" Kempner (1942–1966) wrote to his great-aunt from the jungles of Vietnam hauntingly captures life's fragility. Kempner, a good student and Peace Corps volunteer who came from a well-to-do family in Galveston, Texas, could easily have avoided the Vietnam War by going to graduate school. Instead he enlisted in the Marines, rose to the rank of second lieutenant, and was awarded two purple hearts. On November 11, 1966, three weeks after composing this letter, Sandy Kempner was killed in Quang Tin, South Vietnam. He was 24 years old.

Dear Aunt Fannie,

This morning, my platoon and I were finishing up a three-day patrol. Struggling over steep hills covered with hedgerows, trees, and generally impenetrable jungle, one of my men turned to me and pointed a hand, filled with cuts and scratches, at a rather distinguished-looking plant with soft red flowers waving gaily in the downpour (which had been going on ever since the patrol began) and said, "That is the first plant I have seen today which didn't have thorns on it." I immediately thought of you.

The plant, and the hill upon which it grew, was also representative of Vietnam. It is a country of thorns and cuts, of guns and marauding, of little hope and of great failure. Yet in the midst of it all, a beautiful thought, gesture, and even person can arise among it waving bravely at the death that pours down upon it. Some day this hill will be burned by napalm, and the red flower will crackle up and die among the thorns. So what was the use of it living and being a beauty among the beasts, if it must, in the end, die because of them, and with them? This is a question which is answered by Gertrude Stein's "A rose is a rose is a rose." You are what you are what you are. Whether you believe in God, fate, or the crumbling cookie, elements are so mixed in a being that make him what he is; his salvation from the thorns around him lies in the fact that he existed at all, in his very own personality. There once was a time with the Jewish idea of heaven and hell was the thoughts and opinions people had of you after you died. But what if the plant was on an isolated hill and was never seen by anyone? That is like the question of whether the falling tree makes a sound in the forest primeval when no one is there to hear it. It makes a sound, and the plant was beautiful and the thought was kind, and the person was humane, and distinguished and brave, not merely because other people recognized it as such, but because it is, and it is, and it is.

The flower will always live in the memory of a tired, wet Marine, and thus has achieved a sort of immortality. But even if we had never gone on that hill, it would still be a distinguished, soft, red, thornless flower growing among the cutting, scratching plants, and that in itself is its own reward.

Love,
Sandy

—LETTER—

PROLOGUE:
A LETTER TO THOREAU
E.O. WILSON {2002}

Dr. Edward O. Wilson (b. 1929), the Pellegrino Research Professor in Entomology at Harvard University, is famous for alerting the world to the planet's rapid loss of animal and plant species, but he still sees the future of life on earth through a rose-colored magnifying glass. Although Wilson

59

spends a significant amount of time on his knees, it's not because he's praying for conservation (despite being known as an ardent scientist-conservationist); he's merely studying ants. His 1990 tome on ants—730 pages long—won the Pulitzer Prize, as did his 1978 work, *On Human Nature*. Wilson is often compared to Henry David Thoreau, to whom he writes this letter in his book, *The Future of Life*.

Henry!

May I call you by your Christian name? Your words invite familiarity and make little sense otherwise. How else to interpret your insistent use of the first personal pronoun? *I* wrote this account, you say, here are *my* deepest thoughts, and no third person placed between us could ever be so well represented. Although *Walden* is sometimes oracular in tone, I don't read it, the way some do, as an oration to the multitude. Rather, it is a work of art, the testament of a citizen of Concord, in New England, from one place, one time, and one writer's personal circumstance that manages nevertheless to reach across five generations to address accurately the general human condition. Can there be a better definition of art?

You brought me here. Our meeting could have just as well been a woodlot in Delaware, but here I am at the site of your cabin on the edge of Walden Pond. I came because of your stature in literature and the conservation movement, but also—less nobly, I confess—because my home is in Lexington, two towns over. My pilgrimage is a pleasant afternoon's excursion to a nature reserve. But mostly I came because of all your contemporaries you are the one I most need to understand. As a biologist with a modern scientific library, I know more than Darwin knew. I can imagine the measured responses of that country gentleman to a voice a century and a half beyond his own. It is not a satisfying fantasy: the Victorians have for the most part settled into a comfortable corner of our remembrance. But I cannot imagine your responses, at least not all of them. Too many shadowed residues there in your text, too many emotional trip wires. You left too soon, and your restless spirit haunts us still.

Is it so odd to speak apostrophically across 150 years? I think not. Certainly not if the subject is natural history. The wheels of organic evolution turn at a millennial pace, too slowly for evolution to have transformed species from your time to mine. The natural habitats they compose also remain mostly unchanged. Walden Woods around the pond, having been only partly cut and never plowed, looks much the same in my time as in yours, although now more fully wooded. Its ambience can be expressed in similar language.

Anyway, the older I become, the more it makes sense to measure history in units of life span. That pulls us closer together in real time. Had you lived to eighty instead of just forty-four, we might today have a film clip of you walking on Walden Pond beach through a straw-hatted and parasoled crowd on holiday. We could listen to your recorded voice from one of Mr. Edison's wax cylinders. Did you speak with a slight burr, as generally believed? I am seventy-two now, old enough to have had tea with Darwin's last surviving grand-daughter at the University of Cambridge. While a Harvard graduate student I discussed my first articles on evolution with Julian Huxley, who as a little boy sat on the knee of his grandfather Thomas Henry Huxley, Darwin's "bulldog" disciple and personal friend. You will know what I am talking about. You still had three years to live when in 1859 *The Origin of Species* was published. It was the talk of Harvard and salons along the Atlantic seaboard. You purchased one of the first copies available in America and annotated it briskly. And here is one more circumstance on which I often reflect: as a child I could in theory have spoken to old men who visited you at Walden Pond when they were children of the same age. Thus only one living memory separates us. At the cabin site even that seems to vanish.

Forgive me, I digress. I am here for a purpose: to become more a Thoreauvian, and with that perspective better to explain to you, and in reality to others and not least to myself, what has happened to the world we both have loved.

The landscape away from Walden Pond, to start, has changed drastically. In your time the forest was almost gone. The tallest white pines had been cut long before and hauled away to Boston to be trimmed into ship masts. Other timber was harvested for houses, railroad ties, and fuel. Most of the swamp cedars had become roof shingles. America, still a wood-powered nation, was approaching its first energy crisis as charcoal and cordwood ran short. Soon everything would change. Then coal would fill the breach and catapult the industrial revolution forward at an even more furious pace.

When you built your little house from the dismantled planks of James Collins's shanty in 1845, Walden Woods was a threatened oasis in a mostly treeless terrain. Today it is pretty much the same, although forest has grown up to fill the farmland around it. The trees are still scraggly second-growth descendants of the primeval giants that clothed the lake banks until the mid-1700s. Around the cabin site, beech, hickory, red maple, and scarlet and white oak push up among half-grown white pines in a bid to reestablish the rightful hardwood domination of southern New England forests. Along the path from your cabin on down to the nearest inlet—now called Thoreau's Cove—these trees give way to an open stand of larger white pines, whose trunks are straight and whose branches are evenly spread and high off the ground. The undergrowth consists of a sparse scattering of saplings and huckleberry. The American chestnut, I regret to report, is gone, done in by an overzealous European fungus. Only a few sprouts still struggle up from old stumps here and there, soon to be discovered by the fungus and killed back. Sprouting their serrate leaves, the doomed saplings are faint reminders of the mighty species that once composed a full quarter of the eastern virgin forest. But all the other trees and shrubs you knew so well still flourish. The red maple is more abundant than in your day. It is more than ever both the jack-of-all-trades in forest regeneration and the crimson glory of the New England autumn.

I can picture you clearly as your sister Sophia sketched you, sitting here on the slightly raised doorstep. It is a cool morning in June, by my tastes the best month of the year in New England. In my imagination I have settled beside you. We gaze idly across this spring-fed lake of considerable size that New Englanders perversely call a pond. Today in this place we speak a common idiom, breathe the same clean air, listen to the whisper of the pines. We scruff the familiar leaf litter with our shoes, pause, look up to watch a circling red-tailed hawk pass overhead. Our talk drifts from here to there but never so far from natural history as to break the ghostly spell and never so intimate as to betray the childish sources of our common pleasure. A thousand years will pass and Walden Woods will stay the same, I think, a flickering equilibrium that works its magic on human emotion in variations with each experience.

We stand up to go a-sauntering. We descend the cordwood path to the lake shore, little changed in contour from the sketch you made in 1846, follow it around, and coming to a rise climb to the Lincoln Road, then circle back to the Wyman Meadow and on down to Thoreau's Cove, completing a round-trip of two miles. We search along the way for the woods least savaged by axe and and crosscut saw. It is our intention to work not around but *through* these remains. We stay within a quarter-mile or so of the lake, remembering that in your time almost all the land outside the perimeter woods was cultivated.

Mostly we talk in alternating monologues, because the organisms we respectively favor are different enough to require cross explanation. There are two kinds of naturalists, you will agree, defined by the search images that guide them. The first—your tribe—are intent on finding big organisms: plants, birds, mammals, reptiles, amphibians, perhaps butterflies. Big-organism people listen for animal calls, peer into the canopy, poke into tree hollows, search mud banks for scat and spoor. Their line of sight vacillates around the horizontal, first upward to scan the canopy, then down to peer at the ground. Big-organism people search for a single find good enough for the day. You, I recall, thought little of walking four miles or more to see if a certain plant had begun to flower.

I am a member of the other tribe—a lover of little things, a hunter also, but more the snuffling opossum than the questing panther. I think in millimeters and minutes, and am nowhere near patient as I prowl, having been spoiled forever by the richness of invertebrates and quick reward for little effort. Let me enter a tract of rich forest and I seldom walk more than a few hundred feet. I halt before the first promising rotten log I encounter. Kneeling, I roll it over, and always there is instant gratification from the little world hidden beneath. Rootlets and fungal strands pull apart, adhering flakes of bark fall back to earth. The sweet damp musty scent of healthy soil rises like a perfume to the nostrils that love it. The inhabitants exposed are like deer jacklighted on a country road, frozen in a moment of their secret lives. They quickly scatter to evade the light and desiccating air, each maneuvering in the manner particular to its species. A female wolf spider sprints headlong for several body lengths and, finding no shelter, stops and stands rigid. Her brindled integument provides camouflage, but the white silken egg case she carries between her pedipalps and fangs gives her away. Close by, julid millipedes, which were browsing on mold when the cataclysm struck, coil their bodies in defensive spirals. At the far end of the exposed surface a large scolopendrid centipede lies partly concealed beneath decayed bark fragments. Its sclerites are a glistening brown armor, its jaws poison-filled hypodermic needles, its legs downward-curving scythes. The scolopendrid offers no threat unless you pick it up. But who would dare touch this miniature dragon? Instead I poke it with the tip of a twig. *Get out of there!* It writhes, spins around, and is gone in a flash. Now I can safely rake my fingers through the humus in search of less threatening species.

These arthropods are the giants of the microcosm (if you will allow me to continue what has turned into a short lecture). Creatures their size are present in dozens—hundreds, if an ant or termite colony is present. But these are comparatively trivial numbers. If you focus down by a power of ten in size, enough to pick out animals barely visible to the naked eye, the numbers jump to thousands. Nematode and enchytraeid pot worms, mites, springtales, pauropods, diplurans, symphylans, and tardigrades seethe in the underground. Scattered out on a white ground cloth, each crawling speck becomes a full-blown animal. Together they are far more striking and diverse in appearance than snakes, mice, sparrows, and all the other vertebrates hereabouts combined. Their home is a labyrinth of miniature caves and walls of rotting vegetable debris crossstrung with ten yards of fungal threads. And they are just the surface of the fauna and flora at our feet. Keep going, keep magnifying until the eye penetrates microscopic water films on grains of sand, and there you will find ten billion bacteria in a thimbleful of soil and grass. You will have reached the energy base of the decomposed world as we understand it 150 years after your sojourn in Walden Woods.

Untrammeled nature exists in the dirt and rotting vegetation beneath our shoes. The wilderness of ordinary vision may have vanished—wolf, puma, and wolverine no longer exist in the tamed forests of Massachusetts. But another, even more ancient wilderness lives on. The microscope can take you there. We need only narrow the scale of vision to see a part of these woods as they were a thousand years ago. This is what, as a small-organism naturalist, I can tell you.

"Thó-reau." Your family put the emphasis on the first syllable, as in "thorough," did it not? At least that is what your close friend Ralph Waldo Emerson scribbled on a note found among his papers. Thoreau, thorough naturalist, you would have liked the Biodiversity Day we held in your honor here recently. It was conceived by Peter Alden, a Concord resident and international wildlife tour guide. (Easy name to remember; he is a descendant of John Alden of Pilgrim fame.) On July 4, 1998, the anniversary of the day in 1845 you moved furniture into the Walden cabin, Peter and I were joined by more than a hundred other naturalists from around New England. We set out to list all the wild species of organisms—plants, animals, and fungi—we could find in one day with unaided vision or hand lens within a broad section of Concord and Lincoln around Walden Pond. We aimed for a thousand. The final tally, announced to the thorn-scratched, mosquito-bitten group assembled at an outdoor meal that evening, was 1,904. Well, actually 1,905, to stretch the standards a bit, because the next day a moose (*Alces alces*) came from somewhere and strolled into Concord Center. It soon strolled out again, and evidently departed the Concord area, thus lowering the biodiversity back to the July 4 level.

If you could have come back that Biodiversity Day you might have joined us unnoticed (that is, if you refrained from bringing up President Polk and the Mexican question). Even the 1840s clothing would not have betrayed you, given our own scruffy and eclectic field wear. You would have understood our purpose too. From your last two books, *Faith in a Seed* and *Wild Fruits* (finally rescued from your almost indecipherable notes and published in the 1990s), it is apparent that you were moving toward scientific natural history when your life prematurely ended. It was logical for you to take that turn: the beginning of every science is the description and naming of phenomena. Human beings seem to have an instinct to master their surroundings that way. We cannot think clearly about a plant or animal until we have a name for it; hence the pleasure of bird watching with a field guide in hand. Alden's idea quickly caught on. As I write, in 2001, Biodiversity Days, or "bioblitzes" as they are also called, are being held or planned elsewhere in the United States as well as in Austria, Germany, Luxembourg, and Switzerland. In June 2001 we were joined for a third event in Massachusetts by students from 260 towns over the entire state.

At Walden Pond that first day I met Brad Parker, one of the character actors who play you while giving tours around the reconstructed cabin. He is steeped in Thoreauviana, and eerily convincing. He refused to deviate even one second from your persona as we talked, bless him, and for a pleasant hour I lived in the virtual 1840s he created. Of course, to reciprocate I invited him to peer with me at insects and other invertebrates beneath nearby stones and fallen dead branches. We moved on to a clump of bright yellow mushrooms. Then Neo-Thoreau mentioned a singing wood thrush in the canopy above us, which my deafness in the upper registers prevented me from hearing. We went on like this for a while, with his making nineteenth-century sallies and responses and my struggling to play the part of a time-warped visitor. No mention was made of the thunder of aircraft above us on their approach to Hanscom Field. Nor did I think it anomalous that at sixty-nine I was speaking to a reanimation of you, Henry Real-Thoreau, at thirty. In one sense it was quite appropriate. The naturalists of my generation are you grown older and more knowledgeable, if not wiser.

A case in point on the growth of knowledge. Neo-Thoreau and I talked about the ant war you described in *Walden*. One summer day you found red ants locked in mandible-to-mandible combat with black ants all around your cabin. The ground was littered with the dead and dying, and the ambulatory maimed fought bravely on. It was an ant-world Austerlitz, as you said, a conflict dwarfing the skirmish on the Concord

Bridge that started the American Revolution a rifle shot from Walden Pond. May I presume to tell you what you saw? It was a slave raid. The slavers were the red ants, most likely *Formica subintegra*, and the victims were the black ants, probably *Formica subsericea*. The red ants capture the infants of their victims, or more precisely, their cocoon-clad pupae. Back in the red-ant nest the kidnapped pupae complete their development and emerge from their cocoons as adult workers. Then, because they instinctively accept the first workers they meet as nestmates, they enter into voluntary servitude to their captors. Imagine that! A slave raid at the doorstep of one of America's most ardent abolitionists. For millions of years this harsh Darwinian strategy has prevailed, and so will it ever be, with no hope that a Lincoln, a Thoreau, or an Underground Railroad might arise in the formicid world to save the victim colonies.

Now, prophet of the conservation movement, mentor of Gandhi and Martin Luther King Jr., accept this tribute tardily given. Keen observer of the human condition, scourge of the philistine culture, Greek stoic adrift in the New World, you are reborn in each generation and vested with new meaning and nuance. Sage of Concord—Saint Henry, they sometimes call you—you've fairly earned your place in history.

On the other hand, you were not a great naturalist. (Forgive me!) Even had you kept entirely to natural history during your short life, you would have ranked well below William Bartram, Louis Agassiz, and that prodigious collector of North American plants John Torrey, and be scarcely remembered today. With longer life it would likely have been different, because you were building momentum in natural history rapidly when you left us. And to give you full credit, your ideas on succession and other properties of living communities pointed straight toward the modern science of ecology.

That doesn't matter now. I understand why you came to Walden Pond; your words are clear enough on that score.

Granted, you chose this spot primarily to study nature. But you could have done that as easily and far more comfortably on daily excursions from your mother's house in Concord Center, half an hour's walk away, where in fact you did frequently repair for a decent meal. Nor was your little cabin meant to be a wilderness hermitage. No wilderness lay within easy reach anyway, and even the woods around Walden Pond had shrunk to their final thin margins by the 1840s. You called solitude your favorite companion. You were not afraid, you said, to be left to the mercy of your own thoughts. Yet you craved humanity passionately, and your voice is anthropocentric in mood and philosophy. Visitors to the Walden cabin were welcomed. Once a group of twenty-five or more crowded into the solitary room of the tiny house, shoulder to shoulder. You were not appalled by so much human flesh pressed together (but I am). You were lonely at times. The whistle of a passing train on the Fitchburg track and the distant rumble of oxcarts crossing a bridge must have given you comfort on cold, rainy days. Sometimes you went out looking for someone, anyone, in spite of your notorious shyness, just to have a conversation. You fastened on them, as you put it, like a bloodsucker.

In short, you were far from the hard-eyed frontiersman bearing pemmican and a long rifle. Frontiersmen did not saunter, botanize, and read Greek. So how did it happen that an amateur naturalist perched in a toy house on the edge of a ravaged woodland became the founding saint of the conservation movement? Here is what I believe happened. Your spirit craved an epiphany. You sought enlightenment and fulfillment the Old Testament way, by reduction of material existence to the fundamentals. The cabin was your cave on the mountainside. You used poverty to purchase a margin of free existence. It was the only method you could devise to seek the meaning in a life otherwise smothered by quotidian necessity and haste. You lived at Walden, as you said (I dare not paraphrase),

*to front only the essential facts of life, and see if I could not
learn what it had to teach, and not, when I came to die, discover that I had not lived . . . to live deep and suck out all the
marrow of life, to live so sturdily and Spartan-like as to put
to rout all that was not life, to cut a broad swath and shave
close, to drive life into a corner, and reduce it to its lowest
terms, and, if it proved to be mean, why then to get the whole
and genuine meanness of it, and publish its meanness to the
world; or if it were sublime, to know it by experience, and be
able to give a true account of it in my next excursion.*

You were mistaken, I think, to suppose that there are as
many ways of life possible as radii that can be drawn from the
center of a circle, and your choice just one of them. On the
contrary, the human mind can develop along only a very few
pathways imaginable. They are selected by satisfactions we
instinctively seek in common. The sturdiness of human nature
is the reason people plant flowers, gods live on high mountains, and a lake is the eye of the world through which—your
metaphor—we can measure our own souls.

It is exquisitely human to search for wholeness and richness of experience. When these qualities are lost among the
distracting schedules of everyday life, we seek them elsewhere.
When you stripped your outside obligations to the survivable
minimum, you placed your trained and very active mind in an
unendurable vacuum. And this is the essence of the matter: in
order to fill the vacuum, you discovered the human proclivity
to embrace the natural world.

Your childhood experience told you exactly where to go. It
could not be a local cornfield or gravel pit. Nor the streets of
Boston, which, however vibrant as the hub of a growing
nation, might cost a layabout his dignity and even his life. It
had to be a world both tolerant of poverty and rich and beautiful enough to be spiritually rewarding. Where around
Concord could that possibly be but a woodlot next to a lake?

You traded most of the richness of social existence for an equivalent richness of the natural world. The choice was entirely logical, for the following reason. Each of us finds a comfortable position somewhere along the continuum that ranges from complete withdrawal and self-absorption at one end to full civic engagement and reciprocity at the other. The position is never fixed. We fret, vacillate, and steer our lives through the riptide of countervailing instincts that press from both ends of the continuum. The uncertainty we feel is not a curse. It is not a confusion on the road out of Eden. It is just the human condition. We are intelligent mammals, fitted by evolution—by God, if you prefer—to pursue personal ends through cooperation. Our priceless selves and family first, society next. In this respect we are the polar opposite of your cabinside ants, bound together as replaceable parts of a super-organism. Our lives are therefore an insoluble problem, a dynamic process in search of an indefinable goal. They are neither a celebration nor a spectacle but rather, as a later philosopher put it, a predicament. Humanity is the species forced by its nature to make moral choices and seek fulfillment in a changing world by any means it can devise.

You searched for essence at Walden and, whether successful in your own mind or not, you hit upon an ethic with a solid feel to it: nature is ours to explore forever; it is our crucible and refuge; it is our natural home; it is all these things. Save it, you said: in wilderness is the preservation of the world.

Now, in closing this letter, I am forced to report bad news. (I put it off till the end.) The natural world in the year 2001 is everywhere disappearing before our eyes—cut to pieces, mowed down, plowed under, gobbled up, replaced by human artifacts.

No one in your time could imagine a disaster of this magnitude. Little more than a billion people were alive in the 1840s. They were overwhelmingly agricultural, and few families needed more than two or three acres to survive. The

American frontier was still wide open. And far away on continents to the south, up great rivers, beyond unclimbed mountain ranges, stretched unspoiled equatorial forests brimming
with the maximum diversity of life. These wildernesses
seemed as unattainable and timeless as the planets and stars.
That could not last, because the mood of Western civilization
is Abrahamic. The explorers and colonists were guided by a
biblical prayer: May we take possession of this land that God
has provided and let it drip milk and honey into our mouths
forever.

Now more than six billion people fill the world. The great
majority are very poor; nearly one billion exist on the edge of
starvation. All are struggling to raise the quality of their lives
any way they can. That unfortunately includes the conversion
of the surviving remnants of the natural environment. Half of
the great tropical forests have been cleared. The last frontiers
of the world are effectively gone. Species of plants and animals
are disappearing a hundred or more times faster than before
the coming of humanity, and as many as half may be gone by
the end of this century. An Armageddon is approaching at the
beginning of the third millennium. But it is not the cosmic war
and fiery collapse of mankind foretold in sacred scripture. It is
the wreckage of the planet by an exuberantly plentiful and
ingenious humanity.

The race is now on between the technoscientific forces that
are destroying the living environment and those that can be
harnessed to save it. We are inside a bottleneck of overpopulation and wasteful consumption. If the race is won, humanity
can emerge in far better condition than when it entered, and
with most of the diversity of life still intact.

The situation is desperate—but there are encouraging
signs that the race can be won. Population growth has slowed,
and, if the present trajectory holds, is likely to peak between
eight and ten billion people by century's end. That many
people, experts tell us, can be accommodated with a decent

standard of living, but just barely: the amount of arable land and water available per person, globally, is already declining. In solving the problem, other experts tell us, it should also be possible to shelter most of the vulnerable plant and animal species.

In order to pass through the bottleneck, a global land ethic is urgently needed. Not just any land ethic that might happen to enjoy agreeable sentiment, but one based on the best understanding of ourselves and the world around us that science and technology can provide. Surely the rest of life matters. Surely our stewardship is its only hope. We will be wise to listen carefully to the heart, then act with rational intention and all the tools we can gather and bring to bear.

Henry, my friend, thank you for putting the first element of that ethic in place. Now it is up to us to summon a more encompassing wisdom. The living world is dying; the natural economy is crumbling beneath our busy feet. We have been too self-absorbed to foresee the long-term consequences of our actions, and we will suffer a terrible loss unless we shake off our delusions and move quickly to a solution. Science and technology led us into this bottleneck. Now science and technology must help us find our way through and out.

You once said that old deeds are for old people, and new deeds are for new. I think that in historical perspective it is the other way around. You were the new and we are the old. Can we now be the wiser? For you, here at Walden Pond, the lamentation of the mourning dove and the green frog's *t-r-r-oonk!* across the predawn water were the true reason for saving this place. For us, it is an exact knowledge of what that truth is, all that it implies, and how to employ it to best effect. So, two truths. We will have them both, you and I and all those now and forever to come who accept the stewardship of nature.

Affectionately yours,
Edward

—POEM—

OCTOBER FULLNESS

PABLO NERUDA {1964}

In 1923, Pablo Neruda (1904–1973) sold all of his possessions to finance the publication of his first book of poetry, *Crepusculario* ("Twilight"). But by the end of his successful career, Neruda (real name: Neftali Ricardo Reyes Basoalto) had made up for the loss; his beach house in Isla Negra, Chile, was filled with a lifetime of objects collected from years of traveling as a political diplomat for Chile. In 1971, he collected Latin America's first Nobel Prize for Literature to go with his many other prestigious awards. However, Neruda's greatest collection was of life's wonderful experiences, which he transmuted into some of the world's most beautiful, touching poems. He died of leukemia in 1973, but friends say he died of a broken heart—just twelve days after a bloody coup removed Chile's democratically elected president, Salvador Allende, who was either murdered or committed suicide.

> Little by little, and also in great leaps,
> life happened to me,
> and how significant this business is.
> These veins carried
> my blood, which I scarcely ever saw,
> I breathed the air of so many places
> without keeping a sample of any.
> In the end, everyone is aware of this:
> nobody keeps any of what he has,
> and life is only a borrowing of bones.
> The best thing was learning not to have too much
> either of sorrow or of joy,
> to hope for the chance of a last drop,
> to ask more from honey and from twilight.

Perhaps it was my punishment.
Perhaps I was condemned to be happy.
Let it be known that nobody
crossed my path without sharing my being.
I plunged up to the neck
into adversities that were not mine,
into all the sufferings of others.
It wasn't a question of applause or profit.
Much less. It was not being able
to live or breathe in this shadow,
the shadow of others like towers,
like bitter trees that bury you,
like cobblestones on the knees.

Our own wounds heal with weeping,
our own wounds heal with singing,
but in our own doorway lie bleeding
widows, Indians, poor men, fishermen.
The miner's child doesn't know his father
amidst all that suffering.

So be it, but my business
was the fullness of the spirit:
a cry of pleasure choking you,
a sigh from an uprooted plant,
the sum of all action.

It pleased me to grow with the morning,
to bathe in the sun, in the great joy
of sun, salt, sea-light and wave,
and in that unwinding of the foam
my heart began to move,
growing in that essential spasm,
and dying away as it seeped into the sand.

—DIARY—

THE CELL DOOR CLOSES

ARTHUR KOESTLER {1937}

Arthur Koestler (1905–1983) experienced first-hand every modern European ideology through the end of World War II. He was born into a Jewish family in Budapest during the final years of the Austro-Hungarian Empire; at age 21 he moved to a Zionist collective in Palestine; he then joined the Communist Party and traveled to the Soviet Union to see "the workers' paradise," but Stalin's brutality so disgusted him he returned to Europe. While on assignment covering the Spanish Civil War for a London newspaper, he was arrested, tried, and sentenced to death by Francisco Franco's regime. On his reprieve, Koestler went to France. He was still there when the Nazis occupied the country in 1940, and once again he was imprisoned. This time he escaped, and made his way to England. "The Cell Door Closes" comes from Koestler's book, *Dialogue with Death*, and is based on his own experiences as a political prisoner.

It is a unique sound. A cell door has no handle, either outside or inside. It cannot be shut except by being slammed. It is made of massive steel and concrete, about four inches thick, and every time it falls to there is a resounding crash just as though a shot has been fired. But this report dies away without an echo. Prison sounds are echo-less and bleak.

When the door has been slammed behind him for the first time, the prisoner stands in the middle of the cell and looks round. I fancy that everyone must behave in more or less the same way.

First of all he gives a fleeting look round the walls and takes a mental inventory of all the objects in what is now to be his domain:

the iron bedstead
the wash-basin
the WC
the barred window

His next action is invariably to try to pull himself up by the iron bars of the window and look out. He fails and his suit is covered with white from the plaster on the wall against which he pressed himself. He desists but decides to practice and master the art of pulling himself up by his hands. Indeed, he makes all sorts of laudable resolutions; he will do exercises every morning and learn a foreign language, and he simply won't let his spirit be broken. He dusts his suit and continues his voyage of exploration round his puny realm—five paces long by four paces broad. He tries the iron bedstead. The springs are broken, the wire mattress sags and cuts into the flesh; it's like lying in a hammock made of steel wire. He pulls a face, being determined to prove that he is full of courage and confidence. Then his gaze rests on the cell door, and he sees that an eye is glued to the spy-hole and is watching him.

The eye goggles at him glassily, its pupil unbelievably big. It is an eye without a man attached to it and for a few moments the prisoner's heart stops beating.

The eye disappears and the prisoner takes a deep breath and presses his hand against the left side of his chest.

"Now then," he says to himself encouragingly, "how silly to go and get so frightened. You must get used to that. After all the official's only doing his duty by peeping in. That's part of being in prison. But they won't get me down, they'll never get me down. I'll stuff paper in the spy-hole at night . . . ."

As a matter of fact there's no reason why he shouldn't do so straight away. The idea fills him with genuine enthusiasm. For the first time he experiences that almost maniac desire for activity that from now on will alternate continually—up and down in a never-ending zig-zag—with melancholia and depression.

Then he realizes that he has no paper on him, and his next impulse is— according to his social status—either to ring or to run over to the stationer's at the corner. This impulse lasts only the fraction of a second. The next moment he becomes conscious for the first time of the true significance of his situation. For the first time he grasps the full reality of being behind a door which is locked from outside, grasps it in all its searing, devastating poignancy. . . .

And this is how things are to go on—in the coming minutes, hours, days, weeks, years.

How long has he already been in the cell?

He looks at his watch: exactly three minutes.

—LETTER—

LETTER TO OLGA

VÁCLAV HAVEL {AUGUST 29, 1981}

The life of Václav Havel (b. 1936) bears a striking resemblance to that of Thomas Jefferson. Both men of letters, they used their pens to champion democracy and denounce repressive ruling governments. Both became president after the revolutions they helped engender were over. In Havel's case, the government was the Communist dictatorship of Czechoslovakia, which he fought to overthrow in the nonviolent "Velvet Revolution" of 1989. Before the revolution, Havel had been a radical playwright and activist, spending a number of years in jail for his beliefs. From prison, he wrote weekly letters to his wife, Olga, but the letters had to adhere to strict guidelines: no talk of prison conditions, no quotes or underlined words, no jokes.

Dear Olga,

Today I have served half my sentence and so I've written a request for parole, and also a letter to my lawyer in which I've asked him, among other things, to visit me sometime. Please let him know about any eventual moves I may have to make.

*

When I was still in Heřmanice, something happened to me that superficially was in no way remarkable, but was nevertheless very profoundly important to me internally: I had an afternoon shift, it was wonderful summer weather, I was sitting on a pile of iron, resting, thinking over my own affairs and at the same time, gazing at the crown of a single tree some distance beyond the fence. The sky was a dark blue, cloudless, the air was hot and still, the leaves of the tree shimmered and trembled slightly. And slowly but surely, I found myself in a very strange and wonderful state of mind: I imagined I was lying somewhere in the grass beneath a tree, doing nothing, expecting nothing, worrying about nothing, simply letting the intoxication of a hot summer day possess me. Suddenly, it seemed to me that all the beautiful summer days I had ever experienced and would yet experience were present in that moment; I had direct, physical memories of the summers I spent in Žďárec as a child; I could smell the hay, the pond, and I don't know what else (as I write this, it seems like a parody of a passage from one of my plays—but what can I do? And anyway, isn't parody often merely an attempt at self-control by stepping back a little from oneself and one's secret emotions?). I seemed to be experiencing, in my mind, a moment of supreme bliss, of infinite joy (all the other important joys, such as the presence of those I love, seemed latent in that moment), and though I felt physically intoxicated by it, there was far more to it than that: it was a moment of supreme self-awareness, a supremely elevating state of the soul, a total and totally harmonic merging of existence with itself and with the entire world.

So far, there was nothing especially unusual about this. The important thing was that because of this experience, which contrasted so entirely with my prison-house/ironworks reality, was more sudden and urgent than usual, I realized more clearly something I had felt only dimly in such moments before, which is that this state of supreme bliss inevitably contains the hint of a vaguely constricting anxiety, the faint echo of an infinite yearning, the strange undertone of a deep and inconsolable sense of futility. One is exhilarated, one has everything imaginable, one neither needs nor wants anything any longer—and yet simultaneously it seems as though one had nothing, that one's happiness were no more than a tragic mirage, with no purpose and leading nowhere. In short, the more wonderful the moment, the more clearly the telltale question arises: and then what? What more? What else? What next? What is to be done with it and what will come of it? It is, I would say, an experience of the limits of the finite; one has approached the outermost limits of the meaning that his finite, worldly existence can offer him (that "spontaneous" and "unmetaphysical" meaning) and for this very reason, he is suddenly given a glimpse into the abyss of the infinite, of uncertainty, of mystery. There is simply nowhere to go—except into emptiness, into the abyss itself.

This is the familiar dialectic of life and death. The more intensely and more fully one lives and is aware of one's life, the more powerfully there comes to meet him, from the bowels of his experience, that which makes Being, life and meaning what they are, their opposite: non-Being, death and nothingness, the only background against which they can be measured and defined. I think everyone must have experienced this at some time: in a moment of supreme happiness, it suddenly occurs to you that there is nothing left now but death (a feeling, by the way, that has entered into common speech, for we say, "I love you to death," "See Naples and die," etc.).

This vague anxiety, this breath of infinite nonfulfillment emanating from an experience of the greatest fulfillment, this sensation of terrifying incomprehensibility that blooms in a moment of firmest comprehension, can always be brushed aside like a bothersome piece of fluff. You may wait till the cloud temporarily covering the sun passes by and go on living in peace and delight without asking troublesome questions. But you may also do the opposite: forget all about the "spontaneous meaningfulness" that gave you such intense pleasure, forget about the answer given before the question was posed and stop precisely at the point where the cold air from the abyss struck you most powerfully—when you felt most intensely that in fact you have nothing, know nothing and worst of all, do not even know what you want—and bravely confront the question that comes to mind in such moments. That is, the genuine, profound and essentially metaphysical question of the meaning of life.

There it is: I'm trying to write about the meaning of life and so far, I've done no more than make repeated efforts to define the questions more precisely, or rather the existential circumstances in which it takes hold of one.

But there's no hurry—I still have quite enough prison Saturdays and Sundays ahead of me (at least as many before me as behind me).

*

Today I watched a variety show put on by prisoners for other prisoners. I enjoyed it a lot, and was even quite moved. It's hard to explain why, but these things moved me a lot back in Heřmanice too; its entire human context makes it something strange and unrepeatable, something scarcely to be found on any stage "outside." I don't suppose many playwrights have had this experience; it's difficult to know what to make of it. I've long since put out of my mind any thought of what I'll write once I'm free.

*

Looking forward to seeing you, and kisses—
Vašek

—LETTER—
LETTER TO PRESIDENT FRANKLIN D. ROOSEVELT
ARTHUR W. MITCHELL {OCTOBER 12, 1938}

Arthur W. Mitchell (1883–1968), the son of freed slaves, was born on a farm in Chamber County, Alabama. At Tuskegee Institute, he worked as an office boy for Booker T. Washington before going on to study at Columbia University and Harvard University. Mitchell settled in Chicago, where in 1935 he became the first African-American Democrat ever elected to the U.S. Congress. In spite of his high office, Mitchell was once expelled from a Pullman car because of his race; he took his case to the U.S. Supreme Court, and won. In 1938, as the Nazi persecution of the Jews intensified, Congressman Mitchell wrote this appeal to President Franklin D. Roosevelt.

As a representative of a minority group in America, an underprivileged group which has been subjected to prejudice and mistreatment from time to time, we are interested in the attitude of majority groups throughout the world toward minority groups. At the present time we are greatly disturbed because of the intolerance of certain major groups toward the Jewish people residing in European countries and wish to have our voice heard in the interest of justice and fair play for all racial groups. We believe that the same spirit of intolerance which is working so tremendously against the safety and sacred rights of the Jewish people, if permitted to go unchallenged, will manifest itself sooner or later against all minority groups, perhaps in all parts of the world. [We] request you, the highest representative of our Government, to use every reasonable and peaceable means at your command in securing protection for the Jewish people in this hour of sad calamity.

—DIARY—

THE DIARY OF A YOUNG GIRL
ANNE FRANK {JULY 15, 1944}

On July 6, 1942, as the Nazis began their roundup of Holland's Jews, the Frank family—Otto, Edith, Margot, and Anne (1929–1945)—left their home and moved into a hiding place in the annex of Otto Frank's warehouse. Soon they were joined by the three-member Van Pels family and Fritz Pfeffer. These eight people lived together in four small rooms for twenty-five months. The diary Anne kept became one of the most intimate records we have of the day-to-day experiences of Jewish men, women, and children in hiding from the Holocaust. Twenty days after Anne made this entry, the Nazis broke into the hiding place and shipped everyone to Auschwitz. Of the eight people in the annex, only Otto Frank survived.

Anyone who claims that the older ones have a more difficult time here doesn't realize to what extent our problems weigh down on us, problems for which we are probably much too young, but which thrust themselves upon us constantly, until, after a long time, we think we've found a solution, but the solution doesn't seem able to resist the facts which reduce it to nothing again. That's the difficulty in these times: ideals, dreams, and cherished hopes rise within us, only to meet the horrible truth and be shattered.

It's really a wonder that I haven't dropped all my ideals, because they seem so absurd and impossible to carry out. Yet I keep them, because in spite of everything, I still believe that people are really good at heart. I simply can't build up my hopes on a foundation consisting of confusion, misery, and death. I see the world gradually being turned into a wilderness, I hear the ever-approaching thunder, which will destroy us too, I can feel the sufferings of millions and yet, if I look up into the heavens, I think that it will all come right, that this cruelty too will end, and that peace and tranquility will return again.

In the meantime, I must uphold my ideals, for perhaps, the time will come when I shall be able to carry them out!

— SPEECH —

THE FOUR FREEDOMS

FRANKLIN D. ROOSEVELT {JANUARY 6, 1941}

When Franklin Delano Roosevelt (1882–1945) took office as president in 1932, the United States and much of the industrialized world was in the midst of a devastating economic depression. Roosevelt had barely weathered that storm when the Nazis swept across Europe. Suddenly, the United States was called upon to act as "the great arsenal of democracy." On January 6, 1941, FDR went before Congress and the American people to urge the production of weapons that England and the other beleaguered nations of Europe needed to defeat Hitler. But while he called the nation to a spirit of sacrifice, FDR also promised a brighter day when all the people of the world would enjoy four essential freedoms. To freedom of speech and freedom of worship, rights that Americans knew and cherished, FDR added two other freedoms—freedom from want and freedom from fear—and Americans embraced them as eagerly as any listed in the Bill of Rights.

The nation takes great satisfaction and much strength from the things which have been done to make its people conscious of their individual stake in the preservation of democratic life in America. Those things have toughened the fiber of our people, have renewed their faith and strengthened their devotion to the institutions we make ready to protect.

Certainly this is no time for any of us to stop thinking about the social and economic problems which are the root cause of the social revolution which is today a supreme factor in the world.

There is nothing mysterious about the foundations of a healthy and strong democracy.

The basic things expected by our people of their political and economic systems are simple. They are:

Equality of opportunity for youth and for others.

Jobs for those who can work.

Security for those who need it.

The ending of special privilege for the few.

The preservation of civil liberties for all.

The enjoyment of the fruits of scientific progress in a wider and constantly rising standard of living.

These are the simple, the basic things that must never be lost sight of in the turmoil and unbelievable complexity of our modern world. The inner and abiding straight of our economic and political systems is dependent upon the degree to which they fulfill these expectations.

Many subjects connected with our social economy call for immediate improvement. As examples:

We should bring more citizens under the coverage of old-age pensions and unemployment insurance.

We should widen the opportunities for adequate medical care.

We should plan a better system by which persons deserving or needing gainful employment may obtain it.

I have called for personal sacrifice. I am assured of the willingness of almost all Americans to respond to that call.

A part of the sacrifice means the payment of more money in taxes. In my Budget message I will recommend that a greater portion of this great defense program be paid for from taxation than we are paying for today. No person should try, or be allowed to get rich out of the program; and the principle of tax payments in accordance with ability to pay should be constantly before our eyes to guide our legislation.

If the congress maintains these principles the voters, putting patriotism ahead of pocketbooks, will give you their applause.

In the future days which we seek to make secure, we look forward to a world founded upon four essential human freedoms.

The first is freedom of speech and expression—everywhere in the world.

The second is freedom of every person to worship God in his own way—everywhere in the world.

The third is freedom from want, which, translated into world terms, means economic understandings which will secure to every nation a healthy peacetime life for its inhabitants—everywhere in the world.

The fourth is freedom from fear, which, translated into world terms, means a world-wide reduction of armaments to such a point and in such a thorough fashion that no nation will be in a position to commit an act of physical aggression against any neighbor—anywhere in the world.

That is no vision of a distant millennium. It is a definite basis for a kind of world attainable in our own time and generation. That kind of world is the very antithesis of the so-called "new order" of tyranny which the dictators seek to create with the crash of a bomb.

To that new order we oppose the greater conception—the moral order. A good society is able to face schemes of world domination and foreign revolutions alike without fear.

Since the beginning of our American history we have been engaged in change—in a perpetual, peaceful revolution—a revolution which goes on steadily, quietly, adjusting itself to changing conditions without the concentration camp or the quicklime in the ditch. The world order which we seek is the cooperation of free countries, working together in a friendly, civilized society.

This nation has placed its destiny in the hands, heads and hearts of its millions of free men and women; and its faith in freedom under the guidance of God. Freedom means the supremacy of human rights everywhere. Our support goes to those who struggle to gain those rights and keep them. Our strength is our unity of purpose.

To that high concept there can be no end save victory.

— SPEECH —

THE PERILS OF INDIFFERENCE

ELIE WIESEL {APRIL 12, 1999}

The 1996 winner of the Nobel Peace Prize and author of over fifty books, Elie Wiesel (b. 1928) is recognized as a champion for oppressed people around the world. Born and raised in a small town in Romania, Wiesel lived the quiet life of a religion student until he was 14, when his village was occupied by the Nazis and his entire family was shipped off to concentration camps. Wiesel survived Auschwitz, Buna, Buchenwald, and Gleiwitz, but could neither speak nor write about the experience for ten years before producing a 900-page memoir in Yiddish, which he later compressed into *Night*. Among Wiesel's many honors: In 1978, President Jimmy Carter appointed him Chairman of the United States Holocaust Memorial Council; in 1985, President Ronald Reagan presented him with the Congressional Gold Medal. He delivered the following speech at a White House Symposium.

Fifty-four years ago to the day, a young Jewish boy from a small town in the Carpathian Mountains woke up, not far from Goethe's beloved Weimar, in a place of eternal infamy called Buchenwald. He was finally free, but there was no joy in his heart. He thought there never would be again.

Liberated a day earlier by American soldiers, he remembers their rage at what they saw. And even if he lives to be a very old man, he will always be grateful to them for that rage, and also for their compassion. Though he did not understand their language, their eyes told him what he needed to know—that they, too, would remember, and bear witness.

And now, I stand before you, Mr. President, the Commander-in-Chief of the army that freed me and tens of thousands of others, and I am filled with a profound and abiding gratitude to the American people.

Gratitude is a word that I cherish. Gratitude is what defines the humanity of the human being. . . .

We are on the threshold of a new century, a new millennium. What will the legacy of this vanishing century be? How will it be remembered in the new millennium? Surely it will be judged, and judged severely, in both moral and metaphysical terms. These failures have cast a dark shadow over humanity: two World Wars, countless civil wars, the senseless chain of assassinations—Gandhi, the Kennedys, Martin Luther King, Sadat, Rabin—bloodbaths in Cambodia and Nigeria, India and Pakistan, Ireland and Rwanda, Eritrea and Ethiopia, Sarajevo and Kosovo; the inhumanity in the gulag and the tragedy of Hiroshima. And, on a different level, of course, Auschwitz and Treblinka. So much violence, so much indifference.

What is indifference? Etymologically, the word means "no difference." A strange and unnatural state in which the lines blur between light and darkness, dusk and dawn, crime and punishment, cruelty and compassion, good and evil.

What are its courses and inescapable consequences? Is it a philosophy? Is there a philosophy of indifference conceivable? Can one possibly view indifference as a virtue? Is it necessary at times to practice it simply to keep one's sanity, live normally, enjoy a fine meal and a glass of wine, as the world around us experiences harrowing upheavals?

Of course, indifference can be tempting—more than that, seductive. It is so much easier to look away from victims. It is so much easier to avoid such rude interruptions to our work, our dreams, our hopes. It is, after all, awkward, troublesome, to be involved in another person's pain and despair. Yet, for the person who is indifferent, his or her neighbors are of no consequence. And, therefore, their lives are meaningless. Their hidden or even visible anguish is of no interest. Indifference reduces the other to an abstraction.

Over there, behind the black gates of Auschwitz, the most tragic of all prisoners were the "Muselmanner," as they were called. Wrapped in their torn blankets, they would sit or lie on the ground, staring vacantly into space, unaware of who or where they were, strangers to their surroundings. They no longer felt pain, hunger, thirst. They feared nothing. They felt nothing. They were dead and did not know it.

Rooted in our tradition, some of us felt that to be abandoned by humanity then was not the ultimate. We felt that to be abandoned by God was worse than to be punished by Him. Better an unjust God than an indifferent one. For us to be ignored by God was a harsher punishment than to be a victim of His anger. Man can live far from God—not outside God. God is wherever we are. Even in suffering? Even in suffering.

In a way, to be indifferent to that suffering is what makes the human being inhuman. Indifference, after all, is more dangerous than anger and hatred. Anger can at times be creative. One writes a great poem, a great symphony, having done something special for the sake of humanity because one is angry at the injustice that one witnesses. But indifference is never creative. Even hatred at times may elicit a response. You fight it. You denounce it. You disarm it. Indifference elicits no response. Indifference is not a response.

Indifference is not a beginning, it is an end. And, therefore, indifference is always the friend of the enemy, for it benefits the aggressor—never his victim, whose pain is magnified when he or she feels forgotten. The political prisoner in his cell, the hungry children, the homeless refugees—not to respond to their plight, not to relieve their solitude by offering them a spark of hope is to exile them from human memory. And in denying their humanity we betray our own.

Indifference, then, is not only a sin, it is a punishment. And this is one of the most important lessons of this outgoing century's wide-ranging experiments in good and evil.

In the place that I come from, society was composed of three simple categories: the killers, the victims, and the bystanders. During the darkest of times, inside the ghettoes and death camps . . . we felt abandoned, forgotten. All of us did.

And our only miserable consolation was that we believed that Auschwitz and Treblinka were closely guarded secrets; that the leaders of the free world did not know what was going on behind those black gates and barbed wire; that they had no knowledge of the war against the Jews that Hitler's armies and their accomplices waged as part of the war against the Allies.

If they knew, we thought, surely those leaders would have moved heaven and earth to intervene. They would have spoken out with great outrage and conviction. They would have bombed the railways leading to Birkenau, just the railways, just once.

And now we knew, we learned, we discovered that the Pentagon knew, the State Department knew. And the illustrious occupant of the White House then, who was a great leader—and I say it with some anguish and pain, because, today is exactly 54 years marking his death—Franklin Delano Roosevelt died on April the 12th, 1945, so he is very much present to me and to us.

No doubt, he was a great leader. He mobilized the American people and the world, going into battle, bringing hundreds and thousands of valiant and brave soldiers in America to fight fascism, to fight dictatorship, to fight Hitler. And so many of the young people fell in battle. And, nevertheless, his image in Jewish history—I must say it—his image in Jewish history is flawed.

The depressing tale of the *St. Louis* is a case in point. Sixty years ago, its human cargo—maybe 1,000 Jews—was turned back to Nazi Germany. And that happened after the *Kristallnacht*, after the first state-sponsored pogrom, with hundreds of Jewish shops destroyed, synagogues burned, thousands of people put in concentration camps. And that ship, which was already on the shores of the United States, was sent back.

I don't understand. Roosevelt was a good man, with a heart. He understood those who needed help. Why didn't he allow these refugees to disembark? A thousand people—in America, a great country, the greatest democracy, the most generous of all new nations in modern history. What happened? I don't understand. Why the indifference, on the highest level, to the suffering of the victims?

But then, there were human beings who were sensitive to our tragedy. Those non-Jews, those Christians, that we called the "Righteous Gentiles," whose selfless acts of heroism saved the honor of their faith. Why were they so few? Why was there a greater effort to save SS murderers after the war than to save their victims during the war?

Why did some of America's largest corporations continue to do business with Hitler's Germany until 1942? It has been suggested, and it was documented, that the Wehrmacht could not have conducted its invasion of France without oil obtained from American sources. How is one to explain their indifference?

And yet, my friends, good things have also happened in this traumatic century: the defeat of Nazism, the collapse of communism, the rebirth of Israel on its ancestral soil, the demise of apartheid, Israel's peace treaty with Egypt, the peace accord in Ireland. And let us remember the meeting, filled with drama and emotion, between Rabin and Arafat that you, Mr. President, convened in this very place. I was here and I will never forget it.

And then, of course, the joint decision of the United States and NATO to intervene in Kosovo and save those victims, those refugees, those who were uprooted by a man whom I believe that because of his crimes, should be charged with crimes against humanity. But this time, the world was not silent. This time, we do respond. This time, we intervene.

Does it mean that we have learned from the past? Does it mean that society has changed? Has the human being become less indifferent and more human? Have we really learned from our experiences? Are we less insensitive to the plight of victims of ethnic cleansing and other forms of injustices in places near and far? Is today's justified intervention in Kosovo . . . a lasting warning that never again will the deportation, the terrorization of children and their parents be allowed anywhere in the world? Will it discourage other dictators in other lands to do the same?

What about the children? Oh, we see them on television, we read about them in the papers, and we do so with a broken heart. Their fate is always the most tragic, inevitably. When adults wage war, children perish. We see their faces, their eyes. Do we hear their pleas? Do we feel their pain, their agony? Every minute one of them dies of disease, violence, famine. Some of them— so many of them—could be saved.

And so, once again, I think of the young Jewish boy from the Carpathian Mountains. He has accompanied the old man I have become throughout these years of quest and struggle. And together we walk towards the new millennium, carried by profound fear and extraordinary hope.

—ESSAY—

FREEDOM FROM FEAR

Aung San Suu Kyi {1991}

In 1988, General Ne Win, the brutal dictator of Burma (now Myanmar), resigned from office and a massive pro-democracy movement swept across the country. Aung San Suu Kyi (b. 1945) joined in, speaking out for freedom at hundreds of rallies. When the military regained control of the government, Suu Kyi was placed under house arrest. Her commitment to nonviolence won Suu Kyi the 1991 Nobel Peace Prize. The Nobel Committee said it wanted "to show its support for the many people throughout the world who are striving to attain democracy, human rights, and ethnic conciliation by peaceful means." The struggle continues; she was released from house arrest in 1995, rearrested in 2000, and thrown in one of the country's most notorious jails in May 2003, prompting international protests.

It is not power that corrupts but fear. Fear of losing power corrupts those who wield it and fear of the scourge of power corrupts those who are subject to it. Most Burmese are familiar with the four *a-gati*, the four kinds of corruption. *Chanda-gati*, corruption induced by desire, is deviation from the right path in pursuit of bribes or for the sake of those one loves. *Dosa-gati* is taking the wrong path to spite those against whom one bears ill will, and *moga-gati* is aberration due to ignorance. But perhaps the worst of the four is *bhaya-gati*, for not only does *bhaya*, fear, stifle and slowly destroy all sense of right and wrong, it so often lies at the root of the other three kinds of corruption.

Just as *chanda-gati*, when not the result of sheer avarice, can be caused by fear of want or fear of losing the goodwill of those one loves, so fear of being surpassed, humiliated or injured in some way can provide the impetus for ill will. And it would be difficult to dispel ignorance unless there is freedom to pursue the truth unfettered by fear. With so close a relationship between fear and corruption it is little wonder that in any society where fear is rife corruption in all forms becomes deeply entrenched.

Public dissatisfaction with economic hardships has been seen as the chief cause of the movement for democracy in Burma, sparked off by the student demonstrations of 1988. It is true that years of incoherent policies, inept official measures, burgeoning inflation and falling real income had turned the country into an economic shambles. But it was more than the difficulties of eking out a barely acceptable standard of living that had eroded the patience of a traditionally good-natured, quiescent people—it was also the humiliation of a way of life disfigured by corruption and fear. The students were protesting not just against the death of their comrades but against the denial of their right to life by a totalitarian regime which deprived the present of meaningfulness and held out no hope for the future. And because the students' protests articulated the frustrations of the people at large, the demonstrations quickly grew into a nationwide movement. Some of its keenest supporters were businessmen who had developed the skills and the contacts necessary not only to survive but to prosper within the system. But their affluence offered them no genuine sense of security or fulfillment, and they could not but see that if they and their fellow citizens, regardless of economic status, were to achieve a worthwhile existence, an accountable administration was at least a necessary if not a sufficient condition. The people of Burma had wearied of a precarious state of passive apprehension where they were "as water in the cupped hands" of the powers that be.

> Emerald cool we may be
> As water in cupped hands
> But oh that we might be
> As splinters of glass
> In cupped hands.

Glass splinters, the smallest with its sharp, glinting power to defend itself against hands that try to crush, could be seen as a vivid symbol of the spark of courage that is an essential attribute of those who would free themselves from the grip of oppression. Bogyoke Aung San regarded himself as a revolutionary and searched tirelessly for answers to the problems that beset Burma during her times of trial. He exhorted the people to develop courage: "Don't just depend on the courage and intrepidity of others. Each and every one of you must make sacrifices to become a hero possessed of courage and intrepidity. Then only shall we all be able to enjoy true freedom."

The effort necessary to remain uncorrupted in an environment where fear is an integral part of everyday existence is not immediately apparent to those fortunate enough to live in states governed by the rule of law. Just laws do not merely prevent corruption by meting out impartial punishment to offenders. They also help to create a society in which people can fulfill the basic requirements necessary for the preservation of human dignity without recourse to corrupt practices. Where there are no such laws, the burden of upholding the principles of justice and common decency falls on the ordinary people. It is the cumulative effect on their sustained effort and steady endurance which will change a nation where reason and conscience are warped by fear into one where legal rules exist to promote man's desire for harmony and justice while restraining the less desirable destructive traits in his nature.

In an age when immense technological advances have created lethal weapons which could be, and are, used by the powerful and the unprincipled to dominate the weak and the helpless, there is a compelling need for a closer relationship between politics and ethics at both the national and international levels. The Universal Declaration of Human Rights of the United Nations proclaims that "every individual and every organ of society" should strive to promote the basic rights and freedoms to which all human beings regardless of race, nationality or religion are entitled. But as long as there are governments whose authority is founded on coercion rather than on the mandate of the people, and interest groups which place short-term profits above long-term peace and prosperity, concerted international action to protect and promote human rights will remain at best a partially realized struggle. There will continue to be arenas of struggle where victims of oppression have to draw on their own inner resources to defend their inalienable rights as members of the human family.

The quintessential revolution is that of the spirit, born of an intellectual conviction of the need for change in those mental attitudes and values which shape the course of a nation's development. A revolution which aims merely at changing official policies and institutions with a view to an improvement in material conditions has little chance of genuine success. Without a revolution of the spirit, the forces which produced the iniquities of the old order would continue to be operative, posing a constant threat to the process of reform and regeneration. It is not enough merely to call for freedom, democracy and human rights. There has to be a united determination to persevere in the struggle, to make sacrifices in the name of enduring truths, to resist the corrupting influences of desire, ill will, ignorance and fear.

Saints, it has been said, are the sinners who go on trying. So free men are the oppressed who go on trying and who in the process make themselves fit to bear the responsibilities and to uphold the disciplines which will maintain a free society. Among the basic freedoms to which men aspire that their lives might be full and uncramped, freedom from fear stands out as both a means and an end. A people who would build a nation in which strong, democratic institutions are firmly established as a guarantee against state-induced power must first learn to liberate their own minds from apathy and fear.

Always one to practice what he preached, Aung San himself constantly demonstrated courage—not just the physical sort but the kind that enabled him to speak the truth, to stand by his word, to accept criticism, to admit his faults, to correct his mistakes, to respect the opposition, to parley with the enemy and to let people be the judge of his worthiness as a leader. It is for such moral courage that he will always be loved and respected in Burma— not merely as a warrior hero but as the inspiration and conscience of the nation. The words used by Jawaharlal Nehru to describe Mahatma Gandhi could well be applied to Aung San: "The essence of his teaching was fearlessness and truth, and action allied to these, always keeping the welfare of the masses in view."

Gandhi, that great apostle of nonviolence, and Aung San, the founder of a national army, were very different personalities, but as there is an inevitable sameness about the challenges of authoritarian rule anywhere at any time, so there is a similarity in the intrinsic qualities of those who rise up to meet the challenge. Nehru, who considered the instillation of courage in the people of India one of Gandhi's greatest achievements, was a political modernist, but as he assessed the needs for a twentieth-century movement for independence, he found himself looking back to the philosophy of ancient India: "The greatest gift for an individual or a nation . . . was *abhaya*, fearlessness, not merely bodily courage but absence of fear from the mind."

Fearlessness may be a gift but perhaps more precious is the courage acquired through endeavour, courage that comes from cultivating the habit of refusing to let fear dictate one's actions, courage that could be described as "grace under pressure"—grace which is renewed repeatedly in the face of harsh, unremitting pressure.

Within a system which denies the existence of basic human rights, fear tends to be the order of the day. Fear of imprisonment, fear of torture, fear of death, fear of losing friends, family, property or means of livelihood, fear of poverty, fear of isolation, fear of failure. A most insidious form of fear is that which masquerades as common sense or even wisdom, condemning as foolish, reckless, insignificant or futile the small, daily acts of courage which help to preserve man's self-respect and inherent human dignity. It is not easy for a people conditioned by fear under the iron rule of the principle that might is right to free themselves from the enervating miasma of fear. Yet even under the most crushing state machinery courage rises up again and again, for fear is not the natural state of civilized man.

The wellspring of courage and endurance in the face of unbridled power is generally a firm belief in the sanctity of ethical principles combined with a historical sense that despite all setbacks the condition of man is set on an ultimate course for both spiritual and material advancement. It is his capacity for self-improvement and self-redemption which most distinguishes man from the mere brute. At the root of human responsibility is the concept of perfection, the urge to achieve it, the intelligence to find a path towards it, and the will to follow that path if not to the end at least the distance needed to rise above individual limitations and environmental impediments. It is man's vision of a world fit for rational, civilized humanity which leads him to dare and to suffer to build societies free from want and fear. Concepts such as truth, justice and compassion cannot be dismissed as trite when these are often the only bulwarks which stand against ruthless power.

—SONG—

OH FREEDOM

TRADITIONAL NEGRO SPIRITUAL {CIRCA 1830}

When Rosa Parks was young, "Oh Freedom" was the song that instilled in her a deep love of the Negro spiritual. The first truly American musical form, Negro spirituals gave Blacks a better means than hymns and psalms for expressing the pain of slavery and the hope for freedom. Spirituals were often coded as well, communicating messages of support and unity—and even directions to the Underground Railroad. "Oh Freedom" was sung during the Civil War by black Union soldiers, some of whom had just been given their own freedom by President Lincoln's Emancipation Proclamation, and nearly 100 years later became a rallying cry for the Civil Rights Movement.

Oh freedom, oh freedom, oh freedom over me!
And before I'd be a slave, I'll be buried in my grave
And go home to my Lord and be free.

No more mourning, no more mourning, no more mourning over me!
And before I'd be a slave, I'll be buried in my grave
And go home to my Lord and be free.

No more shouting, no more shouting, no more shouting over me!
And before I'd be a slave, I'll be buried in my grave
And go home to my Lord and be free.

No more crying, no more crying, no more crying over me!
And before I'd be a slave, I'll be buried in my grave
And go home to my Lord and be free.

Oh freedom, oh freedom, oh freedom over me!
And before I'd be a slave, I'll be buried in my grave
And go home to my Lord and be free.

There'll be singin', there'll be singin', there'll be singin' over me!
And before I'd be a slave, I'll be buried in my grave
And go home to my Lord and be free.

Oh freedom, oh freedom, oh freedom over me!
And before I'd be a slave, I'll be buried in my grave
And go home to my Lord and be free.

— SPEECH —

INAUGURAL ADDRESS

JOHN F. KENNEDY {JANUARY 20, 1961}

On a bitterly cold January afternoon in 1961, 43-year-old John Fitzgerald Kennedy (1917–1963), the newly elected President of the United States, removed his top hat and topcoat and proceeded to give one of the most inspiring inaugural addresses in American history. Its most memorable line— "Ask not what your country can do for you—ask what you can do for your country"—is an example of chiasmus, a popular oratorical device in which the order of words in two otherwise parallel phrases are reversed. Kennedy and his speechwriters, Theodore Sorenson and Arthur Schlesinger Jr., were probably aware of the device's rich history. One earlier example comes from a popular turn-of-the-century writing professor at Harvard, John Kennedy's alma mater, who used to urge his students to think of Harvard and always "ask not 'What can she do for me?' but 'What can I do for her?'" Even if this speech's most famous turn of phrase is less than completely original, it did the trick in setting a patriotic tone for Kennedy's administration.

We observe today not a victory of party, but a celebration of freedom— symbolizing an end as well as a beginning—signifying renewal as well as change. For I have sworn before you and Almighty God the same solemn oath our forbears prescribed nearly a century and three-quarters ago.

The world is very different now. For man holds in his mortal hands the power to abolish all forms of human poverty and all forms of human life. And yet the same revolutionary beliefs for which our forebears fought are still at issue around the globe—the belief that the rights of man come not from the generosity of the state but from the hand of God.

We dare not forget today that we are the heirs of that first revolution. Let the word go forth from this time and place, to friend and foe alike, that the torch has been passed to a new generation of Americans—born in this century, tempered by war, disciplined by a hard and bitter peace, proud of our ancient heritage—and unwilling to witness or permit the slow undoing of those human rights to which this Nation has always been committed, and to which we are committed today at home and around the world.

Let every nation know, whether it wishes us well or ill, that we shall pay any price, bear any burden, meet any hardship, support any friend, oppose any foe to assure the survival and the success of liberty.

This much we pledge—and more.

To those old allies whose cultural and spiritual origins we share, we pledge the loyalty of faithful friends. United there is little we cannot do in a host of cooperative ventures. Divided there is little we can do—for we dare not meet a powerful challenge at odds and split asunder.

To those new States whom we welcome to the ranks of the free, we pledge our word that one form of colonial control shall not have passed away merely to be replaced by a far more iron tyranny. We shall not always expect to find them supporting our view. But we shall always hope to find them strongly supporting their own freedom—and to remember that, in the past, those who foolishly sought power by riding the back of the tiger ended up inside.

To those people in the huts and villages of half the globe struggling to break the bonds of mass misery, we pledge our best efforts to help them help themselves, for whatever period is required—not because the Communists may be doing it, not because we seek their votes, but because it is right. If a free society cannot help the many who are poor, it cannot save the few who are rich.

To our sister republics south of our border, we offer a special pledge—to convert our good words into good deeds—in a new alliance for progress—

to assist free men and free governments in casting off the chains of poverty. But this peaceful revolution of hope cannot become the prey of hostile powers. Let all our neighbors know that we shall join with them to oppose aggression or subversion anywhere in the Americas. And let every other power know that this Hemisphere intends to remain the master of its own house.

To that world assembly of sovereign states, the United Nations, our last best hope in an age where the instruments of war have far outpaced the instruments of peace, we renew our pledge of support—to prevent it from becoming merely a forum for invective—to strengthen its shield of the new and the weak—and to enlarge the area in which its writ may run.

Finally, to those nations who would make themselves our adversary, we offer not a pledge but a request: that both sides begin anew the quest for peace, before the dark powers of destruction unleashed by science engulf all humanity in planned or accidental self-destruction.

We dare not tempt them with weakness. For only when our arms are sufficient beyond doubt can we be certain beyond doubt that they will never be employed.

But neither can two great and powerful groups of nations take comfort from our present course—both sides overburdened by the cost of modern weapons, both rightly alarmed by the steady spread of the deadly atom, yet both racing to alter that uncertain balance of terror that stays the hand of mankind's final war.

So let us begin anew—remembering on both sides that civility is not a sign of weakness, and sincerity is always subject to proof. Let us never negotiate out of fear. But let us never fear to negotiate.

Let both sides explore what problems unite us instead of belaboring those problems which divide us.

Let both sides, for the first time, formulate serious and precise proposals for the inspection and control of arms—and bring the absolute power to destroy other nations under the absolute control of all nations.

Let both sides seek to invoke the wonders of science instead of its terrors. Together let us explore the stars, conquer the deserts, eradicate disease, tap the ocean depths and encourage the arts and commerce.

Let both sides unite to heed in all corners of the earth the command of Isaiah—to "undo the heavy burdens . . . and to let the oppressed go free."

And if a beachhead of cooperation may push back the jungle of suspicion, let both sides join in creating a new endeavor, not a new balance of power, but a new world of law, where the strong are just and the weak secure and the peace preserved.

All this will not be finished in the first 100 days. Nor will it be finished in the first 1,000 days, nor in the life of this Administration, nor even perhaps in our lifetime on this planet. But let us begin.

In your hands, my fellow citizens, more than mine, will rest the final success or failure of our course. Since this country was founded, each generation of Americans has been summoned to give testimony to its national loyalty. The graves of young Americans who answered the call to service surround the globe.

Now the trumpet summons us again—not as a call to bear arms, though arms we need—not as a call to battle, though embattled we are—but a call to bear the burden of a long twilight struggle, year in and year out, "rejoicing in hope, patient in tribulation"—a struggle against the common enemies of man: tyranny, poverty, disease and war itself.

Can we forge against these enemies a grand and global alliance, North and South, East and West, that can assure a more fruitful life for all mankind? Will you join in that historic effort?

In the long history of the world, only a few generations have been granted the role of defending freedom in its hour of maximum danger. I do not shrink from this responsibility—I welcome it. I do not believe that any of us would exchange places with any other people or any other generation. The energy, the faith, the devotion which we bring to this endeavor will light our country and all who serve it—and the glow from that fire can truly light the world.

And so, my fellow Americans: Ask not what your country can do for you—ask what you can do for your country.

My fellow citizens of the world: ask not what America will do for you, but what together we can do for the freedom of man.

Finally, whether you are citizens of America or citizens of the world, ask of us here the same high standards of strength and sacrifice which we ask of you. With a good conscience our only sure reward, with history the final judge of our deeds, let us go forth to lead the land we love, asking His blessing and His help, but knowing that here on earth God's work must truly be our own.

NOBEL PRIZE ACCEPTANCE SPEECH: TO ENDURE AND TO PREVAIL

WILLIAM FAULKNER {DECEMBER 10, 1950}

When William Faulkner (1897–1962) won the 1950 Nobel Prize for Literature, he had to be coaxed to make the trip to Stockholm to accept it. But the author of such books as *The Sound and the Fury* and *As I Lay Dying* rose magnificently to the occasion, delivering an acceptance speech that affirmed humankind's endurance, even in the shadow of Hiroshima and Nagasaki.

I feel that this award was not made to me as a man, but to my work—a life's work in the agony and sweat of the human spirit, not for glory and least of all for profit, but to create out of the materials of the human spirit something which did not exist before. So this award is only mine in trust. It will not be difficult to find a dedication for the money part of it commensurate with the purpose and significance of its origin. But I would like to do the same with the acclaim, too, by using this moment as a pinnacle from which I might be listened to by young men and women already dedicated to the same anguish and travail, among whom is already that one who will some day stand where I am standing.

Our tragedy today is a general and universal fear so long sustained by now that we can even bear it. There are no longer problems of the spirit. There is only the question: When will I be blown up? Because of this, the young man or woman writing today has forgotten the problems of the human heart in conflict with itself which alone can make good writing because only that is worth writing about, worth the agony and the sweat.

He must learn them again. He must teach himself that the basest of all things is to be afraid; and, teaching himself that, forget it forever, leaving no room in his workshop for anything but the old verities and truths of the heart, the old universal truths lacking which any story is ephemeral and doomed—love and honor and pity and pride and compassion and sacrifice. Until he does, he labors under a curse. He writes not of love but of lust, of defeats in which nobody loses anything of value, of victories without hope and, worst of all, without pity or compassion. His griefs grieve on no universal bones, leaving no scars. He writes not of the heart but of the glands.

Until he learns these things, he will write as though he stood among and watched the end of man. I decline to accept the end of man. It is easy enough to say that man is immortal simply because he will endure: that when the last dingdong of doom has clanged and faded from the last worthless rock hanging tideless in the last red and dying evening, that even then there will still be one more sound: that of his puny inexhaustible voice, still talking. I refuse to accept this. I believe that man will not merely endure; he will prevail. He is immortal, not because he alone among creatures has an inexhaustible voice, but because he has a soul, a spirit capable of compassion and sacrifice and endurance. The poet's, the writer's, duty is to write about these things. It is his privilege to help man endure by lifting his heart, by reminding him of the courage and honor and hope and pride and compassion and pity and sacrifice which have been the glory of his past. The poet's voice need not merely be the record of man, it can be one of the props, the pillars to help him endure and prevail.

—POEM—

SONG OF MYSELF

WALT WHITMAN {1855}

When Walt Whitman (1819–1892), perhaps America's greatest poet of the people, self-published his first book of poetry, *Leaves of Grass*, in 1855, it was generally ignored, although a select few, such as Ralph Waldo Emerson, immediately recognized the author's talent. The first untitled poem in the collection was retitled *Poem of Walt Whitman, An American* in the book's second edition. It wasn't until the book's third edition in 1882 that the reworked poem became "Song of Myself." In this masterpiece by the "Great Grey Poet of Long Island," it's of all humanity that he sings.

I celebrate myself, and sing myself,
And what I assume you shall assume,
For every atom belonging to me as good belongs to you.

I loafe and invite my soul,
I lean and loafe at my ease observing a spear of summer grass.

My tongue, every atom of my blood, form'd from this soil, this air,
Born here of parents born here from parents the same, and their
    parents the same, parents the same, I, now thirty-seven years old
    in perfect health begin,
Hoping to cease not till death.

Creeds and schools in abeyance,
Retiring back a while sufficed at what they are, but never forgotten,
I harbor for good or bad, I permit to speak at every hazard,
Nature without check with original energy.

Houses and rooms are full of perfumes, the shelves are crowded
   with perfumes,
I breathe the fragrance myself and know it and like it,
The distillation would intoxicate me also, but I shall not let it.

The atmosphere is not a perfume, it has no taste of the
   distillation, it is odorless,
It is for my mouth forever, I am in love with it,
I will go to the bank by the wood and become undisguised
   and naked,
I am mad for it to be in contact with me.

The smoke of my own breath,
Echoes, ripples, buzz'd whispers, love-root, silk-thread,
   crotch and vine
My respiration and inspiration, the beating of my heart,
   the passing of blood and air through my lungs,
The sniff of green leaves and dry leaves, and of the shore and
   dark color'd sea-rocks, and of hay in the barn,
The sound of the belch'd words of my voice loos'd
   to the eddies of the wind,
A few light kisses, a few embraces, a reaching around of arms,
The play of shine and shade on the trees as the supple boughs wag,
The delight alone or in the rush of the streets, or along the fields
   and hill-sides.
The feeling of health, the full-noon trill, the song of me rising from
   bed and meeting the sun.

Have you reckon'd a thousand acres much?
   have you reckon'd the earth much?
Have you practis'd so long to learn to read?
Have you felt so proud to get at the meaning of poems?
Stop this day and night with me and you shall possess
   the origin of all poems,

You shall possess the good of the earth and sun,
    (there are millions of suns left,)
You shall no longer take things at second or third hand, nor look
    through the eyes of the dead, nor feed on the spectres in books,
You shall not look through my eyes either, nor take things from me,
You shall listen to all sides and filter them from your self. . . .

— POEM —

THE NEW COLOSSUS

EMMA LAZARUS {1883}

The Statue of Liberty, created to commemorate the centennial of the signing
of the Declaration of Independence in 1876, was a joint project of France,
which made a gift of the statue, and the United States, which was responsible for the pedestal. Both countries worked valiantly to raise funds to complete the project before the 1876 centennial, but the statue wasn't dedicated
until ten years later. And it wasn't until 1903 that an art patron stumbled on
"The New Colossus," a sonnet that Jewish poet and political activist Emma
Lazarus (1849–1887) had composed and donated to a fund-raising auction
for the pedestal twenty years earlier. Sixteen years after the poet's death, the
last five lines were engraved on the statue. In 1945, the sonnet's other nine
lines joined them on a bronze plaque inside the pedestal. Today, over five
million people a year read Lazarus's ornate ode to exile, freedom, and the
United States of America.

    Not like the brazen giant of Greek fame,
    With conquering limbs astride from land to land;
    Here at the sea-washed, sunset gates shall stand
    A mighty woman with a torch, whose flame
    Is the imprisoned lightning, and her name
    Mother of Exiles. From her beacon-hand

Glows world-wide welcome; her mild eyes command
The air-bridged harbor that twin cities frame

"Keep ancient lands, your storied pomp!" cries she
With silent lips. "Give me your tired, your poor,
Your huddled masses yearning to breathe free,
The wretched refuse of your teeming shore.
Send these, the homeless, tempest-tost, to me,
I lift my lamp beside the golden door!"

—SONG—

CHIMES OF FREEDOM

BOB DYLAN {1964}

In February 1964, 22-year-old singer/songwriter Bob Dylan (b. 1941) hit the road in a station wagon on a twenty-day, cross-country concert tour. While folksinger Paul Clayton, road manager Victor Maymudes, and Peter Karman (a close friend of Dylan's then-girlfriend Suze Rotolo) took turns driving, Dylan, whom no one trusted behind the wheel, sat in the back banging out lyrics on a manual typewriter. The journey was motivated by Dylan's desire to transcend the folk-song form, and transcend it he did on the way to New Orleans by writing "Chimes of Freedom," a song that eerily echoes—the song's chimes are "Flashing for the refugees on the unarmed road of flight" —the sentiments of Emma Lazarus's "The New Colossus."

Far between sundown's finish an' midnight's broken toll
We ducked inside the doorway, thunder crashing
As majestic bells of bolts struck shadows in the sounds
Seeming to be the chimes of freedom flashing
Flashing for the warriors whose strength is not to fight
Flashing for the refugees on the unarmed road of flight

An' for each an' ev'ry underdog soldier in the night
An' we gazed upon the chimes of freedom flashing.

In the city's melted furnace, unexpectedly we watched
With faces hidden while the walls were tightening
As the echo of the wedding bells before the blowin' rain
Dissolved into the bells of the lightning
Tolling for the rebel, tolling for the rake
Tolling for the luckless, the abandoned an' forsaked
Tolling for the outcast, burnin' constantly at stake
An' we gazed upon the chimes of freedom flashing.

Through the mad mystic hammering of the wild ripping hail
The sky cracked its poems in naked wonder
That the clinging of the church bells blew far into the breeze
Leaving only bells of lightning and its thunder
Striking for the gentle, striking for the kind
Striking for the guardians and protectors of the mind
An' the unpawned painter behind beyond his rightful time
An' we gazed upon the chimes of freedom flashing.

Through the wild cathedral evening the rain unraveled tales
For the disrobed faceless forms of no position
Tolling for the tongues with no place to bring their thoughts
All down in taken-for-granted situations
Tolling for the deaf an' blind, tolling for the mute
Tolling for the mistreated, mateless mother, the mistitled prostitute
For the misdemeanor outlaw, chased an' cheated by pursuit
An' we gazed upon the chimes of freedom flashing.

Even though a cloud's white curtain in a far-off corner flashed
An' the hypnotic splattered mist was slowly lifting
Electric light still struck like arrows, fired but for the ones
Condemned to drift or else be kept from drifting
Tolling for the searching ones, on their speechless, seeking trail

For the lonesome-hearted lovers with too personal a tale
An' for each unharmful, gentle soul misplaced inside a jail
An' we gazed upon the chimes of freedom flashing.

Starry-eyed an' laughing as I recall when we were caught
Trapped by no track of hours for they hanged suspended
As we listened one last time an' we watched with one last look
Spellbound an' swallowed 'til the tolling ended
Tolling for the aching ones whose wounds cannot be nursed
For the countless confused, accused, misused, strung-out ones an' worse
An' for every hung-up person in the whole wide universe
An' we gazed upon the chimes of freedom flashing.

—ESSAY—

PROLOGUE FROM WOMEN IN EXILE

Mahnaz Afkhami {1994}

After the Islamic fundamentalists took over Iran in 1978, Mahnaz Afkhami, then Minister of State for Women's Affairs and the leading advocate for women's rights, knew she was no longer safe in her country. Afkhami (b. 1941) fled to the United States, where she has spent the last twenty-five years running international women's organizations and writing books. *Women in Exile* told the stories of twelve women exiled from their native lands, and how their identities shifted and changed in the United States.

I am an exile. I have been in exile for twenty years. I have been forced to stay out of my own country, Iran, because of my work for women's rights. I recognized no limits, ends, or framework in this work outside those set by women themselves in their capacity as independent human beings.

The charges against me are "corruption on earth" and "warring with God." Being charged in the Islamic Republic of Iran is being convicted. There is no defense or appeal, although I would not have known how to defend myself against such a grand accusation as warring with God anyway. There has not been a trial, not even in absentia, and no formal conviction. Nevertheless, my home in Tehran has been ransacked and confiscated, my books, pictures, and mementos taken, my passport invalidated, and my life threatened repeatedly.

My life in exile began at dawn on November 27, 1978. I was awakened by the ringing of the telephone. My husband's voice sounded very near. It took me a while to remember he was calling from Tehran. He had just spoken with Queen Farah who had suggested I cancel my return trip from New York scheduled for the following day. The government was trying to appease the opposition by making scapegoats of its own high-ranking officials. Feminists were primary targets for the fundamentalist revolutionaries. I had recently lost my cabinet post as minister of state for women's affairs as the regime's gesture of appeasement to the mullahs. It was very likely, my husband was saying, that as the most visible feminist in the country I would be arrested on arrival at the airport.

I searched for my glasses on the table by the bed and turned on the light, still clutching the receiver. I looked out the window at the black asphalt, glistening under the street lights. It must have rained earlier, I thought as I listened to my husband's voice, tinged with despair, yet somehow aloof and impersonal, as if this had little to do with him. Two months later when I would call to discuss the deteriorating situation and the need for him to get away, I would sound the same to him. The ties between a person and her home are such that even those nearest fear to intervene directly.

When I said good-bye I was wide awake but not clear-headed. What will I do here, I wondered. During the past few weeks my days had been spent negotiating with the United Nations' lawyers the terms of an agreement between the government of Iran and the UN, setting up the International Research and Training Institute for the Advancement of Women in Tehran. Evenings had been spent in meetings with groups and individuals trying desperately to affect the outcome of events in Iran.

Now it was suddenly all over for me. I could not go back home. I was left with a temporary visa, less than $1,000 in cash, and no plans whatsoever. I crossed the small room and automatically turned on the television to the Reuters news channel. The moving lines of the news tape were a familiar sight. In the last few weeks I had spent many hours staring at the screen, following the latest news, waiting for the inevitable items on Iran. When I looked up, the sun was streaming through the room.

Where would I go, I wondered as I dressed. I remembered I had planned to buy a coat that day. "What sort of a coat?" I asked myself. What sort of life will I be leading and what kind of a coat will that life require? Who am I going to be now that I am no longer who I was a few hours ago? I smiled at my reflection in the mirror. Need there be such existential probing connected to the buying of a winter coat? Even though I was far from the realization of the dimensions and the meaning of what had happened to me, my identity was already becoming blurred. The "I" of me no longer had clear outlines, no longer cast a definite shadow.

For a decade I had defined myself by my place within the Iranian women's movement. The question "Who am I?" was answered not by indicating gender, religion, nationality, or family ties but by my position as the secretary general of the Women's Organization of Iran, a title that described my profession, indicated my cause, and defined the philosophic framework for my essence. On that November morning in 1978, I realized that an immediate and formal severance of my connection to WOI was absolutely necessary. In those days of turmoil, when the movement's very existence was threatened, WOI did not need a secretary general who had become persona non grata to the system and its opposition. I sat at the desk in my hotel room and began to write a letter of resignation.

During the next days I lived a refusal to believe, a denial of the event, an inability to mourn—a state of mind which for me continued for years to come. A flurry of activity related to making arrangements concerning the death of a loved one is the surest means of keeping full realization of the fact of it at bay. So I plunged myself into a series of actions aimed at ensuring survival in the new setting. The first priority was obtaining permission to stay in the United States. You need this to get a job although sometimes you can't

110

get it without having a job—one of the many vicious circles encountered in the life of exiles. Those who enter the country as exiles discover that what had been their natural birthright at home will now depend on the decision of an official who may, for any reason at all or none, deny permission. A process from which there is no recourse.

As soon as possible, I was told, one must get the necessary cards—a driver's license, social security, credit card. These are to help one to assure the community that one exists and will continue to exist for the foreseeable future and can be trusted to handle a car and pay a bill. There is a certain excitement involved in all this. Finding a place to live, learning new routines, looking for a job, establishing new relationships—all within a separate reality, outside the framework of one's customary existence. It is possible to once again ask, "What do I want to be?" I contemplated whole new careers, from real estate to law, from teaching to opening a small business. They all seemed equally possible yet uniformly improbable.

All of this activity buys one time to assimilate the fact of loss and time to prepare to face it. You are told often that you must distance yourself from the past, that you must start a new life. But as in the case of death of kin you don't want to move away, close his room, give away his clothes. You want to talk about him, look at pictures, exchange memories. You shun contact with all those healthy, normal natives who are going about their business as if the world is a safe, secure, and permanent place, a piece of which belongs to them by birthright. You work frantically to retain the memory and to reconstruct the past.

When you mourn a loved one, you wish more than anything to be either alone or with others who share your sense of loss. I sought mostly the company of other exiled Iranians. Together we listened to Persian music, exchanged memories, recalled oft-repeated stories and anecdotes, and allowed ourselves inordinate sentimentality. We remembered tastes, smells, sounds. We knew that no fruit would ever have the pungent aroma and the luscious sweetness of the fruit in Iran, that the sun would never shine so bright, nor the moon shed such light as we experienced under the desert sky in Kerman. The green of the vegetation on the road to the Caspian has no equal, the jasmine elsewhere does not smell as sweet.

Like children who need to hear a story endless times, we repeated for each other scenes from our collective childhood experiences. We recalled the young street vendors sitting in front of round trays on which they had built a mosaic of quartets of fresh walnuts positioned neatly at one inch intervals. We recalled the crunchy, salty taste of the walnuts we carried with us in a small brown bag as we walked around Tajrish Square, taking in the sounds and sights of an early evening in summer. We recalled the smell of corn sizzling on makeshift grills on the sidewalk. We remembered our attempts to convince the ice cream vendor, a young boy not much older than ourselves, to give us five one-rial portions of the creamy stuff smelling of rose water, each of which he carefully placed between two thin wafers. We knew that any combination of sizes would get us more than the largest—the five-rial portion. But the vendor, in possession of the facts and in command of the situation, sometimes refused to serve more than one portion to each child. We remembered walking past families who were picnicking, sitting on small rugs spread by the narrow waterways at the edge of the avenue, laughing and clapping to the music which blared from their radios, oblivious to the traffic a few feet away. We laughed about our grandmothers or aunts who sat in front of the television enjoying images from faraway places, around which they constructed their own stories, independently of the original creator's intention.

During the early years I kept myself frantically busy with phone calls, lectures, and meetings. Slowly, the life I had fashioned for myself in the new surroundings began to take shape. I now had a home in a suburb of Washington, D.C. Artist friends helped me collect a small selection of the works of Iranian women painters. A growing library of my old favorite books of poetry and fiction found a place in my room. The Foundation for Iranian Studies, a cultural institution that I helped create and managed with the aid of former colleagues, began to expand its activities. My family survived the travails and threats against them and all gathered near each other around Washington. Iran as a physical entity grew dimmer in our memory and more distant. But we remained obsessed with the events and processes that had led to our exile. All conversations, social occasions, and readings centered around what happened to us and more often than not ended in assigning blame. As I went about building a life for myself in America, I learned through many encounters to simplify the spelling of my name, to mispronounce it to make it more easily comprehensible for my new contacts. I made small changes in my walk, posture, way of dressing to approach the new environment's expectations. In the process I drifted farther away from my self. The woman exclaiming about the weather to the sales girl at Macy's, calling herself Menaaz was not me. The original word, *Mahnaz*, had a meaning—*Mah,* moon; *Naz,* grace. Translating myself into the new culture made me incomprehensible to myself. I barely recognized this altered version of my personality. Frost once said, "Poetry is what is lost in translation." I realized that whatever poetry exists in the nuances which give subtlety to one's personality is lost in the new culture. What remains is dull prose—a rougher version, sometimes a caricature of one's real self. This smiling, mushy person was not me. It was my interpretation of the simplicity and friendliness of American social conduct. I embarrassed myself with it.

In public places I acted as if I were alone. In Iran, even in places where I was unlikely to meet someone I knew, I always acted "socially"—as if the people I met were potentially people I might come to know, people I might see again. I conducted myself with a consciousness of this assumption of possible further acquaintance, of a reasonable continuity of events. In America I acted totally isolated and separate, as if there were no chance that someone on the street might ever relate to me in any other way than as a total stranger. I caught glimpses of my American friends in a neighborhood restaurant chatting with the owner, greeting friends at other tables, talking about their plans, their homes, their professions, discussing the variations in the menu with the waiter, amazed that life went on as if nothing much had happened. I longed for this elemental sense of connection with my environment.

I kept on searching for the effects of dislocation on my feelings and reactions and spent much of my time studying my own mental state. The preoccupation had come close to neurotic proportions. Fortunately, in my work with the Sisterhood Is Global Institute, an international feminist think tank, I had become acquainted with a number of women from various countries who, like myself, were in exile. Gradually, through our conversations, I began to see that the only way to understand myself was to stand back from my own experiences and focus on someone else, that the best way to see inside my mind was to concentrate on another as she looked inside hers. It was in talking with them that I began to reappropriate myself.

My conversations with twelve of these women led to the publications of *Women In Exile,* a project that became a cathartic and healing experience for me. I learned through writing their stories that although my past was mine in the specifics of my experiences, I shared so much of its deeper meaning with other women in exile. Working with them I began to see the fine thread that wove through all our varied lives and backgrounds. The narratives all followed the same pattern.

Our stories begin with descriptions of a society's disingenuous ways of shaping the woman's personality to fit the patriarchal mold. Even those who are active participants in political movements are often outsiders without the power to influence the decision-making process in their society. Political events beyond our control lead to upheaval. We are vulnerable and as caretakers of families our lives are most affected by disruptive and cataclysmic events. There comes a time when our own safety or that of our children requires us to take charge of our lives and make the decision to escape. Many of us are forced to undertake journeys of turbulence and danger. Once in the United States we realize that the physical dangers we have endured are only the preliminary stages to a life of exile. Slowly we begin to absorb the full impact of what has happened to us. A period of bereavement is followed by attempts to adjust to the new environment. Along with the loss of our culture and home comes the loss of the traditional patriarchal structures that flouted our lives in our own land. Exile in its disruptiveness resembles a rebirth. The pain of breaking out of our cultural cocoon brings with it the possibility of an expanded universe and a freer, more independent self. Reevaluation and reinvention of our lives leads to a new self that combines traits evolved in the old society and characteristics acquired in the new environment. Our lives are enriched by what we have known and surpassed. We are all "damaged," but we repair ourselves into larger, deeper, more humane personalities. Indeed, the similarities between our lives as women and as women in exile supersede every other experience we have encountered as members of different countries, classes, cultures, professions, and religions.

We appreciate the United States as a safe haven, a place which welcomes us and allows us to find ourselves. We appreciate the relative freedom of women in this society. We are, however, conscious that the country is hospitable for the young and the strong. We fear the loneliness and fragility of the old and the weak in this country. We regret that we have lost the closer ties and more committed interpersonal relationships with the extended family we enjoyed at home. Yet we know that for women, part of the price of having those close ties is loss of independence and freedom of action.

In the years since exile began, for some of us, conditions in our home countries have changed, allowing [us] to return. Those who returned home discovered the irreversible nature of the exile experience even when it became possible to return. They realized not only that their country had changed but that they themselves are no longer who they were before they left. They learned that once one looks at one's home from the outside, as a stranger, the past, whether in the self or in the land, cannot be recaptured.

We are aware that we have lost part of ourselves through the loss of our homeland. We find substitutes for our loss; for some work acts as a replacement, for others, language. We echo each other when we say the world is our home and repeat wistfully that it means we have no home. We talk of having gained identification with a more universal cause.

We have learned first hand that nothing is worth the suffering, death, and destruction brought about by ideologies that in their fervor uproot so much and destroy so many and then fade away, blow up, or self-destruct. We learned in looking back over our lives that nothing is worth the breach of the sanctity of an individual's body and spirit. The sharing of our narratives of exile made us conclude simply that we wish to seek a mildness of manner, a kindness of heart, and a softness of demeanor. When has a war, a revolution, an act of aggression brought something better for the people on whose behalf it was undertaken? we asked ourselves and each other. We have paid with the days of our lives for the knowledge that nothing good or beautiful can come from harshness and ugliness.

—SPEECH—

FAREWELL ADDRESS

JIMMY CARTER {JANUARY 14, 1981}

Jimmy Carter (b. 1924) wanted commitment to human rights to be the hallmark of his presidency. More often than not, however, his appeals to the Soviet Union and other nations to guarantee these basic, self-evident truths went unheard. He never gave up, though, and his active commitment to human rights continues to this day, and even won him the Nobel Peace Prize. As Carter left the White House in 1981, he made one last official presidential appeal for Americans to persevere in the struggle for human rights around the world.

Good evening. In a few days, I will lay down my official responsibilities in this office—to take up once more the only title in our democracy superior to that of president, the title of citizen.

Of Vice President Mondale, my Cabinet and the hundreds of others who have served with me during the last four years, I wish to say publicly what I have said in private: I thank them for the dedication and competence they have brought to the service of our country.

But I owe my deepest thanks to you, the American people, because you gave me this extraordinary opportunity to serve. We have faced great challenges together. We know that future problems will also be difficult, but I am now more convinced than ever that the United States—better than any other nation—can meet successfully whatever the future might bring.

These last four years have made me more certain than ever of the inner strength of our country—the unchanging value of our principles and ideals, the stability of our political system, the ingenuity and the decency of our people.

Tonight I would like first to say a few words about this most special office, the presidency of the United States.

This is at once the most powerful office in the world—and among the most severely constrained by law and custom. The president is given a broad responsibility to lead—but cannot do so without the support and consent of the people, expressed informally through the Congress and informally in many ways through a whole range of public and private institutions.

This is as it should be. Within our system of government every American has a right and duty to help shape the future course of the United States.

Thoughtful criticism and close scrutiny of all government officials by the press and the public are an important part of our democratic society. Now as in our past, only the understanding and involvement of the people through full and open debate can help to avoid serious mistakes and assure the continued dignity and safety of the nation.

Today we are asking our political system to do things of which the Founding Fathers never dreamed. The government they designed for a few hundred thousand people now serves a nation of almost 230 million people. Their small coastal republic now spans beyond a continent, and we now have the responsibility to help lead much of the world through difficult times to a secure and prosperous future.

Today, as people have become ever more doubtful of the ability of the government to deal with our problems, we are increasingly drawn to single-issue groups and special interest organizations to ensure that whatever else happens our own personal views and our own private interests are protected.

This is a disturbing factor in American political life. It tends to distort our purposes because the national interest is not always the sum of all our single or special interests. We are all Americans together—and we must not forget that the common good is our common interest and our individual responsibility.

Because of the fragmented pressures of special interests, it's very important that the office of the president be a strong one, and that its constitutional authority be preserved. The president is the only elected official charged with the primary responsibility of representing all the people. In the moments of decision, after the different and conflicting views have been aired, it is the president who then must speak to the nation and for the nation.

I understand after four years in office, as few others can, how formidable is the task the president-elect is about to undertake. To the very limits of conscience and conviction, I pledge to support him in that task. I wish him success, and Godspeed.

I know from experience that presidents have to face major issues that are controversial, broad in scope, and which do not arouse the natural support of a political majority.

For a few minutes now, I want to lay aside my role as leader of one nation, and speak to you as a fellow citizen of the world about three issues, three difficult issues: The threat of nuclear destruction, our stewardship of the physical resources of our planet, and the preeminence of the basic rights of human beings.

It's now been 35 years since the first atomic bomb fell on Hiroshima. The great majority of the world's people cannot remember a time when the nuclear shadow did not hang over the earth. Our minds have adjusted to it, as after a time our eyes adjust to the dark.

Yet the risk of a nuclear conflagration has not lessened. It has not happened yet, thank God, but that can give us little comfort—for it only has to happen once.

The danger is becoming greater. As the arsenals of the superpowers grow in size and sophistication and as other governments acquire these weapons, it may only be a matter of time before madness, desperation, greed or miscalculation lets loose this terrible force.

In an all-out nuclear war, more destructive power than in all of World War II would be unleashed every second during the long afternoon it would take for all the missiles and bombs to fall. A World War II every second— more people killed in the first few hours than all the wars of history put together. The survivors, if any, would live in despair amid the poisoned ruins of a civilization that had committed suicide.

National weakness—real or perceived—can tempt aggression and thus cause war. That's why the United States cannot neglect its military strength. We must and we will remain strong. But with equal determination, the United States and all countries must find ways to control and reduce the horrifying danger that is posed by the world's enormous stockpiles of nuclear arms.

This has been a concern of every American president since the moment we first saw what these weapons could do. Our leaders will require our understanding and our support as they grapple with this difficult but crucial challenge. There is no disagreement on the goals or the basic approach to controlling this enormous destructive force. The answer lies not just in the attitudes or actions of world leaders, but in the concern and demands of all of us as we continue our struggle to preserve the peace.

Nuclear weapons are an expression of one side of our human character. But there is another side. The same rocket technology that delivers nuclear warheads has also taken us peacefully into space. From that perspective, we see our Earth as it really is—a small and fragile and beautiful blue globe, the only home we have. We see no barriers of race or religion or country. We see the essential unity of our species and our planet; and with faith and common sense, that bright vision will ultimately prevail.

Another major challenge, therefore, is to protect the quality of this world within which we live. The shadows that fall across the future are cast not only by the kinds of weapons we have built, but by the kind of world we will either nourish or neglect.

There are real and growing dangers to our simple and most precious possessions: the air we breathe; the water we drink; and the land which sustains us. The rapid depletion of irreplaceable minerals, the erosion of topsoil, the destruction of beauty, the blight of pollution, the demands of increasing billions of people, all combine to create problems which are easy to observe and predict but difficult to resolve. If we do not act, the world of the year 2000 will be much less able to sustain life than it is now.

But there is no reason for despair. Acknowledging the physical realities of our planet does not mean a dismal future of endless sacrifice. In fact, acknowledging these realities is the first step in dealing with them. We can meet the resource problems of the world—water, food, minerals, farmlands, forests, overpopulation, pollution—if we tackle them with courage and foresight.

I have just been talking about forces of potential destruction that mankind has developed, and how we might control them. It is equally important that we remember the beneficial forces that we have evolved over the ages, and how to hold fast to them.

One of those constructive forces is enhancement of individual human freedoms through the strengthening of democracy, and the fight against deprivation, torture, terrorism and the persecution of people throughout the world. The struggle for human rights overrides all differences of color, nation or language.

Those who hunger for freedom, who thirst for human dignity, and who suffer for the sake of justice—they are the patriots of this cause.

I believe with all my heart that America must always stand for these basic human rights—at home and abroad. That is both our history and our destiny.

America did not invent human rights. In a very real sense, it is the other way round. Human rights invented America.

Ours was the first nation in the history of the world to be founded explicitly on such an idea. Our social and political progress has been based on one fundamental principle—the value and importance of the individual. The fundamental force that unites us is not kinship or place of origin or religious preference. The love of liberty is a common blood that flows in our American veins.

The battle for human rights—at home and abroad—is far from over. We should never be surprised nor discouraged because the impact of our efforts has had, and will always have, varied results. Rather, we should take pride that the ideals which gave birth to our nation still inspire the hopes of oppressed people around the world. We have no cause for self-righteousness or complacency. But we have every reason to persevere, both within our own country and beyond our borders.

If we are to serve as a beacon for human rights, we must continue to perfect here at home the rights and values which we espouse around the world: A decent education for our children, adequate medical care for all Americans, an end to discrimination against minorities and women, a job for all those able to work, and freedom from injustice and religious intolerance.

We live in a time of transition, an uneasy era which is likely to endure for the rest of this century. It will be a period of tensions both within nations and between nations—of competition for scarce resources, of social political and economic stresses and strains. During this period we may be tempted to abandon some of the time-honored principles and commitments which have been proven during the difficult times of past generations.

We must never yield to this temptation. Our American values are not luxuries but necessities—not the salt in our bread but the bread itself. Our common vision of a free and just society is our greatest source of cohesion at home and strength abroad—greater even than the bounty of our material blessings.

Remember these words:

"We hold these truths to be self-evident, that all men are created equal; that they are endowed by their Creator with certain inalienable rights; that among these are life, liberty and the pursuit of happiness."

This vision still grips the imagination of the world. But we know that democracy is always an unfinished creation. Each generation must renew its foundations. Each generation must rediscover the meaning of this hallowed vision in the light of its own modern challenges. For this generation, ours, life is nuclear survival; liberty is human rights; the pursuit of happiness is a planet whose resources are devoted to the physical and spiritual nourishment of its inhabitants.

During the next few days I will work hard to make sure that the transition from myself to the next president is a good one so that the American people are served well. And I will continue as I have the last 14 months to work hard and to pray for the lives and the well-being of the American hostages held in Iran. I can't predict yet what will happen, but I hope you will join me in my constant prayer for their freedom.

As I return home to the South where I was born and raised, I am looking forward to the opportunity to reflect and to further assess—I hope with accuracy—the circumstances of our times. I intend to give our new president my support, and I intend to work as a citizen, as I have worked in this office as president, for the values this nation was founded to secure.

Again, from the bottom of my heart, I want to express to you the gratitude I feel.

Thank you, fellow citizens, and farewell.

—ESSAY—

A GLIMPSE OF HOME

KATHRYN D. SULLIVAN {AUGUST 26, 2002}

Kathryn Sullivan (b. 1951) was a member of the first Space Shuttle astronaut class at NASA in 1978, and then the first American woman to carry out a space walk. Her 500-plus hours in space have given Sullivan many glimpses of our planet and much time to think about the importance of being responsible citizens, not just of our communities and countries, but of the earth.

I first saw the earth—the whole earth—from the shuttle *Challenger* in 1984. The view takes your breath away and fills you with childlike wonder. That's why every shuttle crew has to clean noseprints off their spacecraft's windows several times a day.

An incredibly beautiful tapestry of blue and white, tan, black and green seems to glide beneath you at an elegant, stately pace. But you're actually going so fast that the entire map of the world spins before your eyes with each 90-minute orbit. After just one or two laps, you feel, maybe for the first time, like a citizen of a planet.

All the colors and patterns you see—the visible evidence of the complex working of the natural systems that make our planet habitable—seem both vast and precise, powerful and yet somehow fragile.

You see volcanoes spewing smoke, hurricanes roiling the oceans and even fine tendrils of Saharan dust reaching across the Atlantic.

You also see the big, gray smudges of fields, paddies and pastures, and at night you marvel at the lights, like brilliant diamonds, that reveal a mosaic of cities, roads and coastlines—impressive signs of the hand of humanity. Scientists tell us that our hand is heavy, that we are wiping out other species at an unprecedented rate and probably transforming our climate.

Will the immense power of global systems withstand the impact of humanity? Or is it possible that our collective actions will change the nature of our planet enough to cripple its ability to support life?

I no longer believe that we can wait for all the scientific data needed to answer these questions conclusively. We must recognize immediately what it means to be citizens of this planet.

It means accepting our obligation to be stewards of the earth's life-giving capacities. As homeowners, we wouldn't neglect or damage our houses until they weren't fit to live in. Why would we do that with our planet?

—SONG—

TEACH YOUR CHILDREN

GRAHAM NASH {1970}

In March 1970, David Crosby, Stephen Stills, Graham Nash, and Neil Young released the album *Déjà Vu*. The gently inspirational song, "Teach Your Children," written by Nash (b.1942), went to the top of the charts. But two months later, when the Ohio National Guard shot and killed four students during an anti-war demonstration at Ohio's Kent State University, CSN&Y pulled "Teach Your Children" from the airwaves and put "Ohio" out in its place. "Ohio," the group's angry and immediate response to the Kent State tragedy, seemed to beg the question: How could Americans teach their children if their children were being gunned down?

> You who are on the road
> Must have a code that you can live by
> And so become yourself
> Because the past is just a good bye.
>
> Teach your children well,
> Their father's hell did slowly go by,
> And feed them on your dreams
> The one they picks, the one you'll know by.

Don't you ever ask them why, if they told you, you will cry,
So just look at them and sigh and know they love you.

And you, of tender years,
Can't know the fears that your elders grew by,
And so please help them with your youth,
They seek the truth before they can die.

Teach your parents well,
Their children's hell will slowly go by,
And feed them on your dreams
The one they picks, the one you'll know by.

Don't you ever ask them why, if they told you, you will cry,
So just look at them and sigh and know they love you.

LIBERTY

—SPEECH—

AIN'T I A WOMAN?

SOJOURNER TRUTH {1851}

Sojourner Truth (1797–1883) was born into slavery in Ulster County, New York, but escaped at 29, only months before the State of New York abolished slavery. In 1843, Truth changed her name from Isabella to Sojourner, reflecting her commitment to travel the nation preaching the gospel and fighting for women's rights, racial equality, and the emancipation of the slaves. Though illiterate, Truth was a commanding public speaker—deep-voiced and nearly six feet tall. In 1851, she delivered her most famous speech, "Ain't I a Woman," at the Women's Rights Convention in Akron, Ohio. Her remarks were in response to a male speaker who had been arguing that opposition to women's suffrage was grounded in the wish to shelter women from the harsh realities of political life. While no formal record of Sojourner Truth's speech exists, Frances Gage, an abolitionist and president of the Convention, recorded the words for posterity.

Well, children, where there is so much racket there must be something out of kilter. I think that 'twixt the Negroes of the South and the women at the North, all talking about rights, the white men will be in a fix pretty soon. But what's all this here talking about?

That man over there says that women need to be helped into carriages, and lifted over ditches, and to have the best place everywhere. Nobody ever helps me into carriages, or over mud-puddles, or gives me any best place! And ain't I a woman? Look at me! Look at my arm! I have ploughed and planted, and gathered into barns, and no man could head me! And ain't I a woman? I could work as much and eat as much as a man—when I could get it—and bear the lash as well! And ain't I a woman? I have borne thirteen children, and seen most all sold off to slavery, and when I cried out with my mother's grief, none but Jesus heard me! And ain't I a woman?

Then they talk about this thing in the head; what's this they call it? [*member of audience whispers, "Intellect"*] That's it, honey. What's that got to do with women's rights or Negroes' rights? If my cup won't hold but a pint, and yours holds a quart, wouldn't you be mean not to let me have my little half-measure full?

Then that little man in black there, he says women can't have as much rights as men, 'cause Christ wasn't a woman! Where did your Christ come from? Where did your Christ come from? From God and a woman! Man had nothing to do with Him.

If the first woman God ever made was strong enough to turn the world upside down all alone, these women together ought to be able to turn it back, and get it right side up again! And now they is asking to do it, the men better let them.

Obliged to you for hearing me, and now old Sojourner ain't got nothing more to say.

—ESSAY—

DEMOCRACY IN AMERICA
ALEXIS DE TOCQUEVILLE {1840}

Every year, a fresh batch of college students reads Alexis de Tocqueville's *Democracy in America* and is astonished to find that his portrait of American institutions and the American character is as true today as it was in 1835. De Tocqueville (1805–1859) had been sent by the government of France to the United States to study (of all things) the American penitentiary system. But what caught his attention was not the American way of incarceration, but the American way of freedom. Fascinated by the status-free, equality-conscious American character, de Tocqueville abandoned his prison tour and spent his nine-month visit investigating how a passion for freedom influenced the minds, feelings, manners, preferences, and prejudices of ordinary citizens.

I should imperfectly fulfill the purpose of this book if, after having shown what ideas and feelings are suggested by the principle of equality, I did not point out, before I conclude, the general influence that these same ideas and feelings may exercise upon the government of human societies. To succeed in this object I shall frequently have to retrace my steps, but I trust the reader will not refuse to follow me through paths already known to him, which may lead to some new truth . . . .

The principle of equality, which makes men independent of each other, gives them a habit and a taste for following in their private actions no other guide than their own will. This complete independence, which they constantly enjoy in regard to their equals and in the intercourse of private life, tends to make them look upon all authority with a jealous eye and speedily suggests to them the notion and the love of political freedom. Men living at such times have a natural bias towards free institutions. Take any one of them at a venture and search if you can his most deep-seated instincts, and you will find that, of all governments, he will soonest conceive and most highly value that government whose head he has himself elected and whose administration he may control.

Of all the political effects produced by the equality of conditions, this love of independence is the first to strike the observing and to alarm the timid; nor can it be said that their alarm is wholly misplaced, for anarchy has a more formidable aspect in democratic countries than elsewhere. As the citizens have no direct influence on each other, as soon as the supreme power of the nation fails, which kept them all in their several stations, it would seem that disorder must instantly reach its utmost pitch and that, every man drawing aside in a different direction, the fabric of society must at once crumble away.

I am convinced, however, that anarchy is not the principal evil that democratic ages have to fear, but the least. For the principle of equality begets two tendencies: the one leads men straight to independence and may suddenly drive them into anarchy; the other conducts them by a longer, more secret, but more certain road to servitude. Nations readily discern the former tendency and are prepared to resist it; they are led away by the latter, without perceiving its drift; hence it is peculiarly important to point it out.

Personally, far from finding fault with equality because it inspires a spirit of independence, I praise it primarily for that very reason. I admire it because it lodges in the very depths of each man's mind and heart that indefinable feeling, the instinctive inclination for political independence, and thus prepares the remedy for the ill which it engenders. It is precisely for this reason that I cling to it.

—DECLARATION—

DECLARATION OF SENTIMENTS AND RESOLUTIONS
{1848}

Thirty-two years old, married, and the mother of three children, Elizabeth Cady Stanton (1815–1902) said being isolated in her house made her feel like a "caged lioness." She found a sympathetic audience among some Quaker abolitionist friends. Out of their conversation emerged the first Women's Rights Convention in the United States. The 420 delegates—40 of them men—met in the Wesleyan Chapel in Seneca Falls, New York, in July 1848. On July 19, they published this statement, the Declaration of Sentiments and Resolutions, modeled on the Declaration of Independence. Among the 100 signers were Stanton, Susan B. Anthony, Lucretia Mott, and Frederick Douglass. Although the Seneca Falls Declaration had relatively little impact at the time, it has remained a touchstone for women's rights advocates ever since.

When, in the course of human events, it becomes necessary for one portion of the family of man to assume among the people of the earth a position different from that which they have hitherto occupied, but one to which the laws of nature and of nature's God entitle them, a decent respect to the opinions of mankind requires that they should declare the causes that impel them to such a course.

We hold these truths to be self-evident: that all men and women are created equal; that they are endowed by their Creator with certain inalienable rights; that among these are life, liberty, and the pursuit of happiness; that to secure these rights governments are instituted, deriving their just powers from the consent of the governed. Whenever any form of government becomes destructive of these ends, it is the right of those who suffer from it to refuse allegiance to it, and to insist upon the institution of a new government, laying its foundation on such principles, and organizing its powers in such form, as to them shall seem most likely to effect their safety and happiness. Prudence, indeed, will dictate that governments long established should not be changed for light and transient causes; and accordingly all experience hath shown that mankind are more disposed to suffer, while evils are sufferable, than to right themselves by abolishing the forms to which they were accustomed. But when a long train of abuses and usurpations, pursuing invariably the same object evinces a design to reduce them under absolute despotism, it is their duty to throw off such government, and to provide new guards for their future security. Such has been the patient sufferance of the women under this government, and such is now the necessity which constrains them to demand the equal station to which they are entitled.

The history of mankind is a history of repeated injuries and usurpations on the part of man toward woman, having in direct object the establishment of an absolute tyranny over her. To prove this, let facts be submitted to a candid world.

He has never permitted her to exercise her inalienable right to the elective franchise.

He has compelled her to submit to laws, in the formation of which she had no voice.

He has withheld from her rights which are given to the most ignorant and degraded men—both natives and foreigners.

Having deprived her of this first right of a citizen, the elective franchise, thereby leaving her without representation in the halls of legislation, he has oppressed her on all sides.

He has made her, if married, in the eye of the law, civilly dead.

He has taken from her all right in property, even to the wages she earns.

He has made her, morally, an irresponsible being, as she can commit many crimes with impunity, provided they be done in the presence of her husband. In the covenant of marriage, she is compelled to promise obedience to her husband, he becoming, to all intents and purposes, her master—the law giving him power to deprive her of her liberty, and to administer chastisement.

He has so framed the laws of divorce, as to what shall be the proper causes, and in case of separation, to whom the guardianship of the children shall be given, as to be wholly regardless of the happiness of women—the law, in all cases, going upon a false supposition of the supremacy of man, and giving all power into his hands.

After depriving her of all rights as a married woman, if single, and the owner of property, he has taxed her to support a government which recognizes her only when her property can be made profitable to it. He has monopolized nearly all the profitable employments, and from those she is permitted to follow, she receives but a scanty renumeration. He closes against her all the avenues to wealth and distinction which he considers most honorable to himself. As a teacher of theology, medicine, or law, she is not known.

He has denied her the facilities for obtaining a thorough education, all colleges being closed against her.

He allows her in Church, as well as State, but a subordinate position, claiming Apostolic authority for her exclusion from the ministry, and, with some exceptions, from any public participation in the affairs of the Church.

He has created a false public sentiment by giving to the world a different code of morals for men and women, by which moral delinquencies which exclude women from society, are not only tolerated, but deemed of little account in man.

He has usurped the prerogative of Jehovah himself, claiming it as his right to assign for her a sphere of action, when that belongs to her conscience and to her God.

He has endeavored, in every way that he could, to destroy her confidence in her own powers, to lessen her self-respect, and to make her willing to lead a dependent and abject life.

Now, in view of this entire disfranchisement of one-half the people of this country, their social and religious degradation—in view of the unjust laws above mentioned, and because women do feel themselves aggrieved, oppressed, and fraudulently deprived of their most sacred rights, we insist that they have immediate admission to all the rights and privileges which belong to them as citizens of the United States.

In entering upon the great work before us, we anticipate no small amount of misconception, misrepresentation, and ridicule; but we shall use every instrumentality within our power to effect our object. We shall employ agents, circulate tracts, petition the State and National legislatures, and endeavor to enlist the pulpit and the press in our behalf. We hope this Convention will be followed by a series of Conventions embracing every part of the country.

RESOLUTIONS

WHEREAS, The great precept of nature is conceded to be, that "man shall pursue his own true and substantial happiness." Blackstone in his Commentaries remarks, that this law of Nature being coeval with mankind, and dictated by God himself, is of course superior in obligation to any other. It is binding over all the globe, in all countries and at all times; no human laws are of any validity if contrary to this, and such of them as are valid, derive all their force, and all their validity, and all their authority, mediately and imme-diately, from this original; therefore,

Resolved, That such laws as conflict, in any way, with the true and sub-stantial happiness of woman, are contrary to the great precept of nature and of no validity, for this is "superior in obligation to any other."

Resolved, That all laws which prevent woman from occupying such a station in society as her conscience shall dictate, or which place her in a position inferior to that of man, are contrary to the great precept of nature, and therefore of no force or authority.

Resolved, That woman is man's equal—was intended to be so by the Creator, and the highest good of the race demands that she should be recog-nized as such.

Resolved, That the women of this country ought to be enlightened in regard to the laws under which they live, that they may no longer publish their degradation by declaring themselves satisfied with their present position, nor their ignorance, by asserting that they have all the rights they want.

Resolved, That inasmuch as man, while claiming for himself intellectual superiority, does accord to woman moral superiority, it is pre-eminently his duty to encourage her to speak and teach, as she has an opportunity, in all religious assemblies.

Resolved, That the same amount of virtue, delicacy, and refinement of behavior that is required of woman in the social state, should also be required of man, and the same transgressions should be visited with equal severity on both man and woman.

Resolved, That the objection of indelicacy and impropriety, which is so often brought against woman when she addresses a public audience, comes with a very ill-grace from those who encourage, by their attendance, her appearance on the stage, in the concert, or in feats of the circus.

Resolved, That woman has too long rested satisfied in the circumscribed limits which corrupt customs and a perverted application of the Scriptures have marked out for her, and that it is time she should move in the enlarged sphere which her great Creator has assigned her.

Resolved, That it is the duty of the women of this country to secure to themselves their sacred right to the elective franchise.

Resolved, That the equality of human rights results necessarily from the fact of the identity of the race in capabilities and responsibilities.

Resolved, therefore, That, being invested by the Creator with the same capabilities, and the same consciousness of responsibility for their exercise, it is demonstrably the right and duty of woman, equally with man, to promote every righteous cause by every righteous means; and especially in regard to the great subjects of morals and religion, it is self-evidently her right to participate with her brother in teaching them, both in private and in public, by writing and by speaking, by any instrumentalities proper to be used, and in any assemblies proper to be held; and this being a self-evident truth growing out of the divinely implanted principles of human nature, any custom or authority adverse to it, whether modern or wearing the hoary sanction of antiquity, is to be regarded as a self-evident falsehood, and at war with mankind.

—SPEECH—

COURTROOM SPEECH ON WOMEN'S RIGHT TO VOTE

Susan B. Anthony {1873}

When suffragist Susan B. Anthony (1820–1906) cast an "illegal" ballot in the presidential election of 1872, she was arrested, tried, and found guilty of a federal crime—voting without the right to vote. Before the judge pronounced his sentence, he asked Anthony a routine legal question. Anthony's reply, the following speech, made her famous. She was then fined $100, which she refused to pay.

Judge Hunt: (*ordering the defendant to stand up*) Has the prisoner anything to say why sentence shall not be pronounced?

Miss Anthony: Yes, Your Honor, I have many things to say; for in your ordered verdict of guilty, you have trampled under foot every vital principle of our government. My natural rights, my civil rights, my political rights, my judicial rights, are all alike ignored. Robbed of the fundamental privilege of citizenship, I am degraded from the status of a citizen to that of a subject; and not only myself individually, but all of my sex, are, by Your Honor's verdict, doomed to political subjection under this, so-called, form of government.

Judge Hunt: The Court cannot listen to a rehearsal of arguments the prisoner's counsel has already consumed three hours in presenting.

Miss Anthony: May it please Your Honor, I am not arguing the question, but simply stating the reasons why sentence cannot, in justice, be pronounced against me. Your denial of my citizen's right to vote, is the denial of my right of consent as one of the governed, the denial of my right of representation as one of the taxed, the denial of my right to a trial by a jury of my peers as an offender against law, therefore, the denial of my sacred rights to life, liberty, property and—

Judge Hunt: The Court cannot allow the prisoner to go on.

Miss Anthony: But Your Honor will not deny me this one and only poor privilege of protest against this high-handed outrage upon my citizen's rights. May it please the Court to remember that since the day of my arrest last November, this is the first time that either myself or any person of my disfranchised class has been allowed a word of defense before judge or jury—

Judge Hunt: The prisoner must sit down—the Court cannot allow it.

Miss Anthony: All of my prosecutors, from the 8th ward corner-grocery politician, who entered the complaint, to the United States Marshal, Commissioner, District Attorney, District Judge, Your Honor on the bench, not one is my peer, but each and all are my political sovereigns; and had Your Honor submitted my case to the jury, as was clearly your duty, even then I should have had just cause of protest, for not one of those men was my peer; but, native or foreign born, white or black, rich or poor, educated or ignorant, awake or asleep, sober or drunk, each and every man of them was my political superior; hence, in no sense, my peer. Even, under such circumstances, a commoner of England, tried before a jury of Lords, would have far less cause to complain than should I, a woman, tried before a jury of men. Even my counsel, the Hon. Henry R. Selden, who has argued my cause so ably, so earnestly, so unanswerably before Your Honor, is my political sovereign. Precisely as no disfranchised person is entitled to sit upon a jury, and no woman is entitled to the franchise, so, none but a regularly admitted lawyer is allowed to practice in the courts, and no woman can gain admission to the bar—hence, jury, judge, counsel, must all be of the superior class.

Judge Hunt: The Court must insist—the prisoner has been tried according to the established forms of law.

Miss Anthony: Yes, Your Honor, but by forms of law all made by men, interpreted by men, administered by men, in favor of men, and against women; and hence, Your Honor's ordered verdict of guilty; against a United States citizen for the exercise of "that citizen's right to vote," simply because that citizen was a woman and not a man. But, yesterday, the same man made forms of law, declared it a crime punishable with $1,000 fine and six months imprisonment, for you, or me, or you of us, to give a cup of cold water, a crust of bread, or a night's shelter to a panting fugitive as he was tracking his way to Canada. And every man or woman in whose veins coursed a drop of human sympathy violated that wicked law, reckless of consequences, and was justified in so doing. As then, the slaves who got their freedom must take it over, or under, or through the unjust forms of law, precisely so, now, must women, to get their right to a voice in this government, take it; and I have taken mine, and mean to take it at every possible opportunity.

Judge Hunt: The Court orders the prisoner to sit down. It will not allow another word.

Miss Anthony: When I was brought before Your Honor for trial, I hoped for a broad and liberal interpretation of the Constitution and its recent amendments, that should declare all United States citizens under its protecting [ae]gis—that should declare equality of rights the national guarantee to all persons born or naturalized in the United States. But failing to get this justice—failing, even, to get a trial by a jury not of my peers—I ask not leniency at your hands—but rather the full rigors of the law:

Judge Hunt: The Court must insist—

(Here the prisoner sat down.)

Judge Hunt: The prisoner will stand up.

(Here Miss Anthony arose again.)

The sentence of the Court is that you pay a fine of $100 and the costs of the prosecution.

Miss Anthony: May it please Your Honor, I shall never pay a dollar of your unjust penalty. All the stock in trade I possess is a $10,000 debt, incurred by publishing my paper—*The Revolution*—four years ago, the sole object of which was to educate all women to do precisely as I have done, rebel against your manmade, unjust, unconstitutional forms of law, that tax, fine, imprison and hang women, while they deny them the right of representation in the government; and I shall work on with might and main to pay every dollar of that honest debt, but not a penny shall go to this unjust claim. And I shall earnestly and persistently continue to urge all women to the practical recognition of the old revolutionary maxim, that "Resistance to tyranny is obedience to God."

Judge Hunt: Madam, the Court will not order you committed until the fine is paid.

136

—LETTER—

LETTER TO ELIZABETH CADY STANTON

SUSAN B. ANTHONY {OCTOBER 1902}

After devoting most of her life to fighting for women's suffrage, the 82-year-old Anthony wrote a letter to Elizabeth Cady Stanton, promising to celebrate the latter's 87th birthday with her, and reflecting on the fact that the two friends would not live to see their dream come true. Anthony's letter is sad, but never bitter: Like all people who change the world, she believed that people's desires for freedom and justice were strong enough to triumph in the end. She was right; a generation later, American women won the right to vote.

My Dear Ms. Stanton:

I shall indeed be happy to spend with you November 12, the day on which you round out your four-score and seven, over four years ahead of me, but in age as in all else I follow you closely. It is fifty-one years since first we met and we have been busy through every one of them, stirring up the world to recognize the rights of women. The older we grow the more keenly we feel the humiliation of disenfranchisement and the more vividly we realize its disadvantages in every department of life and most of all in the labor market.

We little dreamed when we began this contest, optimistic with the hope and buoyancy of youth, that half a century later we would be compelled to leave the finish of the battle to another generation of women. But our hearts are filled with joy to know that they enter upon this task equipped with a college education, with business experience, with the fully admitted right to speak in public—all of which were denied to women fifty years ago. They have practically but one point to gain—the suffrage; we had all. These strong, courageous, capable young women will take our place and complete our work. There is an army of them where we were but a handful. Ancient prejudice has become so softened, public sentiment so liberalized and women have so thoroughly demonstrated their ability as to leave no doubt that they will carry our cause to victory.

And we, dear, old friend, shall move on to the next sphere of existence—higher and larger, we cannot fail to believe, and one where women will not be placed in an inferior position but will be welcomed on a plane of perfect intellectual and spiritual equality.

Ever lovingly yours,
Susan B. Anthony

— SPEECH —

SPEECH BEFORE CONGRESS ON WOMEN'S SUFFRAGE

CARRIE CHAPMAN CATT {1917}

Carrie Chapman Catt (1859–1947) did not mind standing out in a crowd. She was the only woman in her graduating class at the Iowa Agricultural College and Model Farm in Ames (now Iowa State University). As a young widow in San Francisco, she supported herself as the city's first female newspaper reporter. Her work for the National American Woman Suffrage Association (NAWSA) so impressed Susan B. Anthony that Anthony asked Catt to address Congress on the necessity of recognizing women's right to vote. In 1916, when it appeared that the suffrage movement was stalled, Catt's "Winning Plan" called for NAWSA to campaign simultaneously for voting rights on the state and federal levels, and accept partial suffrage in those states that were most resistant to the idea. The strategy worked. The Senate and the House voted to support a women's suffrage amendment to the Constitution, and even President Woodrow Wilson confessed that he had been converted to the cause.

Woman suffrage is inevitable. Suffragists knew it before November 4, 1917; opponents afterward. Three distinct causes made it inevitable.

First, the history of our country. Ours is a nation born of revolution, of rebellion against a system of government so securely entrenched in the customs and traditions of human society that in 1776 it seemed impregnable. From the beginning of things, nations had been ruled by kings and for kings, while the people served and paid the cost. The American Revolutionists boldly proclaimed the heresies: "Taxation without representation is tyranny." "Governments derive their just powers from the consent of the governed." The colonists won, and the nation which was established as a result of their victory has held unfailingly that these two fundamental principles of democratic government are not only the spiritual source of our national existence but have been our chief historic pride and at all times the sheet anchor of our liberties.

Eighty years after the Revolution, Abraham Lincoln welded those two maxims into a new one: "Ours is a government of the people, by the people, and for the people." Fifty years more passed and the president of the United States, Woodrow Wilson, in a mighty crisis of the nation, proclaimed to the world: "We are fighting for the things which we have always carried nearest to our hearts: for democracy, for the right of those who submit to authority to have a voice in their own government."

All the way between these immortal aphorisms political leaders have declared unabated faith in their truth. Not one American has arisen to question their logic in the 141 years of our national existence. However stupidly our country may have evaded the logical application at times, it has never swerved from its devotion to the theory of democracy as expressed by those two axioms. . . .

With such a history behind it, how can our nation escape the logic it has never failed to follow, when its last unenfranchised class calls for the vote? Behold our Uncle Sam floating the banner with one hand, "Taxation without representation is tyranny," and with the other seizing the billions of dollars paid in taxes by women to whom he refuses "representation." Behold him again, welcoming the boys of twenty-one and the newly made immigrant citizen to "a voice in their own government" while he denies that fundamental right of democracy to thousands of women public school teachers from whom many of these men learn all they know of citizenship and patriotism, to women college presidents, to women who preach in our pulpits, interpret law in our courts, preside over our hospitals, write books and magazines, and serve in every uplifting moral and social enterprise. Is there a single man who can justify such inequality of treatment, such outrageous discrimination? Not one. . . .

S econd, the suffrage for women already established in the United States makes women suffrage for the nation inevitable. When Elihu Root, as president of the American Society of International Law, at the eleventh annual meeting in Washington, April 26, 1917, said, "The world cannot be half democratic and half autocratic. It must be all democratic or all Prussian. There can be no compromise," he voiced a general truth. Precisely the same intuition has already taught the blindest and most hostile foe of woman suffrage that our nation cannot long continue a condition under which government in half its territory rests upon the consent of half of the people and in the other half upon the consent of all the people; a condition which grants representation to the taxed in half of its territory and denies it in the other half; a condition which permits women in some states to share in the election of the president, senators, and representatives and denies them that privilege in others. It is too obvious to require demonstration that woman suffrage, now covering half our territory, will eventually be ordained in all the nation. No one will deny it. The only question left is when and how will it be completely established.

Third, the leadership of the United States in world democracy compels the enfranchisement of its own women. The maxims of the Declaration were once called "fundamental principles of government." They are now called "American principles" or even "Americanisms." They have become the slogans of every movement toward political liberty the world around, of every effort to widen the suffrage for men or women in any land. Not a people, race, or class striving for freedom is there anywhere in the world that has not made our axioms the chief weapon of the struggle. More, all men and women the world around, with farsighted vision into the verities of things, know that the world tragedy of our day is not now being waged over the assassination of an archduke, nor commercial competition, nor national ambitions, nor the freedom of the seas. It is a death grapple between the forces which deny and those which uphold the truths of the Declaration of Independence. . . .

Do you realize that in no other country in the world with democratic tendencies is suffrage so completely denied as in a considerable number of our own states? There are thirteen black states where no suffrage for women exists, and fourteen others where suffrage for women is more limited than in many foreign countries.

Do you realize that when you ask women to take their cause to state referendum you compel them to do this: that you drive women of education, refinement, achievement, to beg men who cannot read for their political freedom?

Do you realize that such anomalies as a college president asking her janitor to give her a vote are overstraining the patience and driving women to desperation?

Do you realize that women in increasing numbers indignantly resent the long delay in their enfranchisement?

Your party platforms have pledged women suffrage. Then why not be honest, frank friends of our cause, adopt it in reality as your own, make it a party program, and "fight with us"? As a party measure—a measure of all parties—why not put the amendment through Congress and the legislatures? We shall all be better friends, we shall have a happier nation, we women will be free to support loyally the party of our choice, and we shall be far prouder of our history.

"There is one thing mightier than kings and armies"—aye, than Congresses and political parties—"the power of an idea when its time has come to move." The time for woman suffrage has come. The woman's hour has struck. If parties prefer to postpone action longer and thus do battle with this idea, they challenge the inevitable. The idea will not perish; the party which opposes it may. Every delay, every trick, every political dishonesty from now on will antagonize the women of the land more and more, and when the party or parties which have so delayed woman suffrage finally let it come, their sincerity will be doubted and their appeal to the new voters will be met with suspicion. This is the psychology of the situation. Can you afford the risk? Think it over.

We know you will meet opposition. There are a few "women haters" left, a few "old males of the tribe," as Vance Thompson calls them, whose duty they believe it to be to keep women in the places they have carefully picked out for them. Treitschke, made world famous by war literature, said some years ago, "Germany, which knows all about Germany and France, knows far better what is good for Alsace-Lorraine than that miserable people can possibly know." A few American Treitschkes we have know better than women what is good for them. There are women, too, with "slave souls" and "clinging vines" for backbones. There are female dolls and male dandies. But the world does not wait for such as these, nor does Liberty pause to heed the plaint of men and women with a grouch. She does not wait for those who have a special interest to serve, nor a selfish reason for depriving other people of freedom. Holding her torch aloft, Liberty is pointing the way onward and upward and saying to America, "Come."

To you and the supporters of our cause in Senate and House, and the number is large, the suffragists of the nation express their grateful thanks. This address is not meant for you. We are more truly appreciative of all you have done than any words can express. We ask you to make a last, hard fight for the amendment during the present session. Since last we asked a vote on this amendment, your position has been fortified by the addition to suffrage territory of Great Britain, Canada, and New York.

Some of you have been too indifferent to give more than casual attention to this question. It is worthy of your immediate consideration. A question big enough to engage the attention of our allies in wartime is too big a question for you to neglect.

Some of you have grown old in party service. Are you willing that those who take your places by and by shall blame you for having failed to keep pace with the world and thus having lost for them a party advantage? Is there any real gain for you, for your party, for your nation by delay? Do you want to drive the progressive men and women out of your party?

Some of you hold to the doctrine of states' rights as applying to woman suffrage. Adherence to that theory will keep the United States far behind all other democratic nations upon this question. A theory which prevents a nation from keeping up with the trend of world progress cannot be justified.

Gentlemen, we hereby petition you, our only designated representatives, to redress our grievances by the immediate passage of the Federal Suffrage Amendment and to use your influence to secure its ratification in your own state, in order that the women of our nation may be endowed with political freedom before the next presidential election, and that our nation may resume its world leadership in democracy.

Woman suffrage is coming—you know it. Will you, Honorable Senators and Members of the House of Representatives, help or hinder it?

—POEM—

STILL I RISE

MAYA ANGELOU {1978}

One of America's great renaissance individuals—poet, historian, author, actress, playwright, civil-rights activist, producer, and director—Maya Angelou (b. 1928) began life in St. Louis, Missouri, as Marguerite Johnson. At the age of eight, abuse at the hands of her mother's boyfriend plunged her into four years of silence. Later, while working as a madam and a dancer at the Purple Onion Cabaret, she combined her first husband's last name, Angelos, and her childhood nickname, Maya, and eventually emerged as the author of *I Know Why the Caged Bird Sings*, the first bestseller by an African-American woman. In the 1960s, at the request of Dr. Martin Luther King Jr., she became the northern coordinator for the Southern Christian Leadership Conference. In 1993, when President Clinton chose her to deliver a poem at his inaugural, she was only the second poet ever to do so. "Still I Rise," a poem written in 1978, is marked by the power, passion, faith, and persistence that marks so much of her work—and life.

You may write me down in history
With your bitter, twisted lies,
You may trod me in the very dirt
But still, like dust, I'll rise.

Does my sassiness upset you?
Why are you beset with gloom?
'Cause I walk like I've got oil wells
Pumping in my living room.

Just like moons and like suns,
With the certainty of tides,
Just like hopes springing high,
Still I'll rise.

Did you want to see me broken?
Bowed head and lowered eyes?
Shoulders falling down like teardrops,
Weakened by my soulful cries.

Does my haughtiness offend you?
Don't you take it awful hard
'Cause I laugh like I've got gold mines
Diggin' in my own back yard.

You may shoot me with your words,
You may cut me with your eyes,
You may kill me with your hatefulness,
But still, like air, I'll rise.

Does my sexiness upset you?
Does it come as a surprise
That I dance like I've got diamonds
At the meeting of my thighs?

Out of the huts of history's shame
I rise
Up from a past that's rooted in pain
I rise
I'm a black ocean, leaping and wide,
Welling and swelling I bear in the tide.

Leaving behind nights of terror and fear
I rise
Into a daybreak that's wondrously clear
I rise
Bringing the gifts that my ancestors gave,
I am the dream and the hope of the slave.
I rise
I rise
I rise.

—LETTER—

LETTER TO HIS FORMER MASTER, CAPTAIN THOMAS AULD

FREDERICK DOUGLASS {SEPTEMBER 8, 1848}

For audacious correspondence, it's hard to beat Frederick Douglass' (1818–1895} letter to his former master. First Douglass rubs salt in Auld's wound by reminding him that he is writing on the tenth anniversary of his successful escape to the North; then Douglass recounts his achievements in his new life: marriage, family, a celebrated career as an orator, and an anti-slavery activist. Finally, Douglass accuses Auld of heartlessness for turning out his 80-year-old grandmother "like an old horse to die in the woods," and demands that he send the ailing woman to live with him in Rochester,

New York. In fact, Auld had not abandoned Douglass' grandmother, but was having her cared for in his own house. When Douglass learned of this a year later, he wrote to Auld again, this time to apologize.

SIR:

The long and intimate, though by no means friendly, relation which unhappily subsisted between you and myself, leads me to hope that you will easily account for the great liberty which I now take in addressing you in this open and public manner. The same fact may possibly remove any disagreeable surprise which you may experience on again finding your name coupled with mine, in any other way than in an advertisement, accurately describing my person, and offering a large sum for my arrest. In thus dragging you again before the public, I am aware that I shall subject myself to no inconsiderable amount of censure. I shall probably be charged with an unwarrantable, if not a wanton and reckless disregard of the rights and properties of private life. There are those north as well as south who entertain a much higher respect for rights which are merely conventional, than they do for rights which are personal and essential. Not a few there are in our country, who, while they have no scruples against robbing the laborer of the hard earned results of his patient industry, will be shocked by the extremely indelicate manner of bringing your name before the public. Believing this to be the case, and wishing to meet every reasonable or plausible objection to my conduct, I will frankly state the ground upon which I justify myself in this instance, as well as on former occasions when I have thought proper to mention your name in public. All will agree that a man guilty of theft, robbery, or murder, has forfeited the right to concealment and private life; that the community have a right to subject such persons to the most complete exposure. However much they may desire retirement, and aim to conceal themselves and their movements from the popular gaze, the public have a right to ferret them out, and bring their conduct before the proper tribunals of the country for investigation. Sir, you will undoubtedly make the proper application of these generally admitted principles, and will easily see the light in which you are regarded by me; I will not therefore manifest ill temper, by calling you hard names. I know you to be a man of some intelligence, and can readily determine the precise estimate which I entertain of your character. I may therefore indulge in language which may seem to others indirect and ambiguous, and yet be quite well understood by yourself.

I have selected this day on which to address you, because it is the anniversary of my emancipation; and knowing no better way, I am led to this as the best mode of celebrating that truly important event. Just ten years ago this beautiful September morning, yon bright sun beheld me a slave—a poor degraded chattel—trembling at the sound of your voice, lamenting that I was a man, and wishing myself a brute. The hopes which I had treasured up for weeks of a safe and successful escape from your grasp, were powerfully confronted at this last hour by dark clouds of doubt and fear, making my person shake and my bosom to heave with the heavy contest between hope and fear. I have no words to describe to you the deep agony of soul which I experienced on that never-to-be-forgotten morning— for I left by daylight. I was making a leap in the dark. The probabilities, so far as I could by reason determine them, were stoutly against the undertaking. The preliminaries and precautions I had adopted previously, all worked badly. I was like one going to war without weapons—ten chances of defeat to one of victory. One in whom I had confided, and one who had promised me assistance, appalled by fear at the trial hour, deserted me, thus leaving the responsibility of success or failure solely with myself. You, sir, can never know my feelings. As I look back to them, I can scarcely realize that I have passed through a scene so trying. Trying, however, as they were, and gloomy as was the prospect, thanks be to the Most High, who is ever the God of the oppressed, at the moment which was to

147

determine my whole earthly career, His grace was sufficient; my mind was made up. I embraced the golden opportunity, took the morning tide at the flood, and a free man, young, active, and strong is the result.

I have often thought I should like to explain to you the grounds upon which I have justified myself in running away from you. I am almost ashamed to do so now, for by this time you may have discovered them yourself. I will, however, glance at them. When yet but a child about six years old, I imbibed the determination to run away. The very first mental effort that I now remember on my part, was an attempt to solve the mystery—why am I a slave? and with this question my youthful mind was troubled for many days, pressing upon me more heavily at times than others. When I saw the slave-driver whip a slave-woman, cut the blood out of her neck, and heard her piteous cries, I went away into the corner of the fence, wept and pondered over the mystery. I had, through some medium, I know not what, got some idea of God, the Creator of all mankind, the black and the white, and that he had made the blacks to serve the whites as slaves. How he could do this and be *good*, I could not tell. I was not satisfied with this theory, which made God responsible for slavery, for it pained me greatly, and I have wept over it long and often. At one time, your first wife, Mrs. Lucretia, heard me singing and saw me shedding tears, and asked of me the matter, but I was afraid to tell her. I was puzzled with this question, till one night while sitting in the kitchen, I heard some of the old slaves talking of their parents having been stolen from Africa by white men, and were sold here as slaves. The whole mystery was solved at once. Very soon after this, my Aunt Jinny and Uncle Noah ran away, and the great noise made about it by your father-in-law, made me for the first time acquainted with the fact, that there were free states as well as slave states. From that time, I resolved that I would some day run away. The morality of the act I dispose of as follows: I am myself; you are yourself; we are two distinct persons, equal persons. What you are, I am. You are a man, and so am I. God created both, and made us separate beings. I am not by nature bond to you, or you to me. Nature does not make your existence depend upon me, or mine to depend upon yours. I cannot walk upon your legs, or you upon mine. I cannot breathe for you, or you for me; I must breathe for myself, and you for yourself. We are distinct persons, and are each equally provided with faculties necessary to our individual existence. In leaving you, I took nothing but what belonged to me, and in no way lessened your means for obtaining an *honest* living. Your faculties remained yours, and mine became useful to their rightful owner. I therefore see no wrong in any part of the transaction. It is true, I went off secretly; but that was more your fault than mine. Had I let you into the secret, you would have defeated the enterprise entirely; but for this, I should have been really glad to have made you acquainted with my intentions to leave.

You may perhaps want to know how I like my present condition. I am free to say, I greatly prefer it to that which I occupied in Maryland. I am, however, by no means prejudiced against the state as such. Its geography, climate, fertility, and products, are such as to make it a very desirable abode for any man; and but for the existence of slavery there, it is not impossible that I might again take up my abode in that state. It is not that I love Maryland less, but freedom more. You will be surprised to learn that people at the north labor under the strange delusion that if the slaves were emancipated at the south, they would flock to the north. So far from this being the case, in that event, you would see many old and familiar faces back again to the south. The fact is, there are few here who would not return to the south in the event of emancipation. We want to live in the land of our birth, and to lay our bones by the side of our fathers; and nothing short of an intense love of personal freedom keeps us from the south. For the sake of this most of us would live on a crust of bread and a cup of cold water.

Since I left you, I have had a rich experience. I have occupied stations which I never dreamed of when a slave. Three out of the ten years since I left you, I spent as a common laborer on the wharves of New Bedford, Massachusetts. It was there I earned my first free dollar. It was mine. I could spend it as I pleased. I could buy hams or herring with it, without asking any odds of anybody. That was a precious dollar to me. You remember when I used to make seven or eight, or even nine dollars a week in Baltimore, you would take every cent of it from me every Saturday night, saying that I belonged to you, and my earnings also. I never liked this conduct on your part—to say the best, I thought it a little mean. I would not have served you so. But let that pass. I was a little awkward about counting money in New England fashion when I first landed in New Bedford. I came near betraying myself several times. I caught myself saying phip, for fourpence; and at one time a man actually charged me with being a runaway, whereupon I was silly enough to become one by running away from him, for I was greatly afraid he might adopt measures to get me again into slavery, a condition I then dreaded more than death.

I soon learned, however, to count money, as well as to make it, and got on swimmingly. I married soon after leaving you; in fact, I was engaged to be married before I left you; and instead of finding my companion a burden, she was truly a helpmate. She went to live at service, and I to work on the wharf, and though we toiled hard the first winter, we never lived more happily. After remaining in New Bedford for three years, I met with William Lloyd Garrison, a person of whom you have *possibly* heard, as he is pretty generally known among slaveholders. He put it into my head that I might make myself serviceable to the cause of the slave, by devoting a portion of my time to telling my own sorrows, and those of other slaves, which had come under my observation. This was the commencement of a higher state of existence than any to which I had ever aspired. I was thrown into society the most pure, enlightened, and benevolent, that the country affords. Among these I have never forgotten you, but have invariably made you the topic of conversation—thus giving you all the notoriety I could do. I need not tell you that the opinion formed of you in these circles is far from being favorable. They have little respect for your honesty, and less for your religion.

But I was going on to relate to you something of my interesting experience. I had not long enjoyed the excellent society to which I have referred, before the light of its excellence exerted a beneficial influence on my mind and heart. Much of my early dislike of white persons was removed, and their manners, habits, and customs, so entirely unlike what I had been used to in the kitchen-quarters on the plantations of the south, fairly charmed me, and gave me a strong disrelish for the coarse and degrading customs of my former condition. I therefore made an effort so to improve my mind and deportment, as to be somewhat fitted to the station to which I seemed almost providentially called. The transition from degradation to respectability was indeed great, and to get from one to the other without carrying some marks of one's former condition, is truly a difficult matter. I would not have you think that I am now entirely clear of all plantation peculiarities, but my friends here, while they entertained the strongest dislike of them, regard me with that charity to which my past life somewhat entitles me, so that my condition in this respect is exceedingly pleasant. So far as my domestic affairs are concerned, I can boast of as comfortable a dwelling as your own. I have an industrious and neat companion, and four dear children—the oldest a girl of nine years, and three fine boys, the oldest eight, the next six, and the youngest four years old. The three oldest are now going regularly to school—two can read and write, and the other can spell, with tolerable correctness, words of two syllables. Dear fellows! they are all in comfortable beds, and are sound asleep, perfectly secure under my own roof. There are no slaveholders here to rend my heart by snatching them from my arms, or blast a mother's dearest hopes by tearing them from her bosom. These dear children are ours—not to work up into rice, sugar, and tobacco, but to watch over, regard, and protect, and to rear them to the paths of wisdom and virtue, and, as far as we can, to make them useful to the world and to themselves. Oh! Sir, a slaveholder never appears to me so completely an agent of hell, as when I think of and look upon my dear children. It is then that my feelings rise above my control. I meant to have said more with respect to my own prosperity and happiness, but thoughts and feelings which this recital has quickened, unfits me to proceed further in that direction. The grim horrors of slavery rise in all their ghastly terror before me; the wails of millions pierce my heart and chill my blood. I remember the chain, the gag, the bloody whip; the death-like gloom overshadowing the broken spirit of the fettered bondman; the appalling liability of his being torn away from wife and children, and sold like a beast in the market. Say not that this is a picture of fancy. You well know that I wear stripes on my back, inflicted by your direction; and that you, while we were brothers in the same church, caused this right hand, with which I am now penning this letter, to be closely tied to my left, and my person dragged at the pistol's mouth, fifteen miles, from the Bay side to Easton, to be sold like a beast in the market, for the alleged crime of intending to escape from your possession. All this, and more, you remember, and know to be perfectly true, not only of yourself, but of nearly all of the slaveholders around you.

At this moment, you are probably the guilty holder of at least three of my own dear sisters, and my only brother, in bondage. These you regard as your property. They are recorded on your ledger, or perhaps have been sold to human flesh-mongers, with a view to filling your own ever-hungry purse. Sir, I desire to know how and where these dear sisters are. Have you sold them? or are they still in your possession? What has become of them? Are they living or dead? And my dear old grandmother, whom you turned out like an old horse to die in the woods—is she still alive? Write and let me know all about them. If my grandmother be still alive, she is of no service to you, for by this time she must be nearly eighty years old—too old to be cared for by one to whom she has ceased to be of service; send her to me at Rochester, or bring her to Philadelphia, and it shall be the crowning happiness of my life to take care of her in her old age. Oh! she was to me a mother and a father, so far as hard toil for my comfort could make her such. Send me my grandmother! that I may watch over and take care of her in her old age. And my sisters—let me know all about them. I would write to them, and learn all I want to know of them, without disturbing you in any way, but that, through your unrighteous conduct, they have been entirely deprived of the power to read and write. You have kept them in utter ignorance, and have therefore robbed them of the sweet enjoyments of writing or receiving letters from absent friends and relatives. Your wickedness and cruelty, committed in this respect on your fellow-creatures, are greater than all the stripes you have laid upon my back or theirs. It is an outrage upon the soul, a war upon the immortal spirit, and one for which you must give account at the bar of our common Father and Creator.

The responsibility which you have assumed in this regard is truly awful, and how you could stagger under it these many years is marvelous. Your mind must have become darkened, your heart hardened, your conscience seared and petrified, or you would have long since thrown off' the accursed load, and sought relief at the hands of a sin-forgiving God. How, let me ask, would you look upon me, were I, some dark night, in company with a band of hardened villains, to enter the precincts of your elegant dwelling, and seize the person of your own lovely daughter, Amanda, and carry her off from your family, friends, and all the loved ones of her youth—make her my slave—compel her to work, and I take her wages—place her name on my

ledger as property—disregard her personal rights—fetter the
powers of her immortal soul by denying her the right and privilege of learning to read and write—feed her coarsely—clothe
her scantily, and whip her on the naked back occasionally;
more, and still more horrible, leave her unprotected—a
degraded victim to the brutal lust of fiendish overseers, who
would pollute, blight, and blast her fair soul—rob her of all
dignity—destroy her virtue, and annihilate in her person all
the graces that adorn the character of virtuous womanhood? I
ask, how would you regard me, if such were my conduct? Oh!
the vocabulary of the damned would not afford a word sufficiently infernal to express your idea of my God-provoking
wickedness. Yet, sir, your treatment of my beloved sisters is in
all essential points precisely like the case I have now supposed. Damning as would be such a deed on my part, it would
be no more so than that which you have committed against me
and my sisters.

I will now bring this letter to a close; you shall hear from
me again unless you let me hear from you. I intend to make use
of you as a weapon with which to assail the system of slavery—
as a means of concentrating public attention on the system,
and deepening the horror of trafficking in the souls and bodies of men. I shall make use of you as a means of exposing the
character of the American church and clergy—and as a means
of bringing this guilty nation, with yourself, to repentance. In
doing this, I entertain no malice toward you personally. There
is no roof under which you would be more safe than mine, and
there is nothing in my house which you might need for your
comfort, which I would not readily grant. Indeed, I should
esteem it a privilege to set you an example as to how mankind
ought to treat each other.

I am your fellow-man, but not your slave.

Frederick Douglass

154

—SONG—

DOWN BY THE RIVERSIDE

Traditional Negro Spiritual {1865}

With their African rhythms and Christian themes, spirituals straddle two worlds. The biblical text that inspired "Down by the Riverside" comes from the book of the prophet Isaiah: "They shall beat their swords into plowshares, and their spears into pruning hooks: Nation shall not lift up sword against nation, neither shall they learn war any more." The song was first popular during the American Civil War, then had a renaissance during the Vietnam War, when it became an anthem of the anti-war movement. "Down by the Riverside," once rarely heard outside black churches, was suddenly being sung by millions of white middle-class college students.

> Gonna lay down my sword and shield;
> Down by the riverside
> Down by the riverside
> Down by the riverside
> Gonna lay down my sword and shield
> Down by the riverside
> Ain't gonna study war no more.
>
> I ain't gonna study war no more,
> I ain't gonna study war no more,
> Study war no more.
> I ain't gonna study war no more,
> I ain't gonna study war no more,
> Gonna study war no more.

Gonna stick my sword in the golden sand;
Down by the riverside
Down by the riverside
Down by the riverside
Gonna stick my sword in the golden sand
Down by the riverside
Gonna study war no more.

Gonna put on my long white robe;
Down by the riverside
Down by the riverside
Down by the riverside
Gonna put on my long white robe;
Down by the riverside

Gonna study war no more.
Gonna put on my starry crown;
Down by the riverside

Down by the riverside
Down by the riverside
Gonna put on my starry crown;
Down by the riverside
Gonna study war no more.

Gonna put on my golden shoes;
Down by the riverside
Down by the riverside
Down by the riverside
Gonna put on my golden shoes
Down by the riverside
Gonna study war no more.

Gonna talk with the Prince of Peace;
Down by the riverside

Down by the riverside
Down by the riverside
Gonna talk with the Prince of Peace
Down by the riverside
Gonna study war no more.

Gonna shake hands around the world;
Down by the riverside
Down by the riverside
Down by the riverside
Gonna shake hands around the world
Down by the riverside
Gonna study war no more.

—DECLARATION—

THE EMANCIPATION PROCLAMATION
ABRAHAM LINCOLN {JANUARY 1, 1863}

Two hundred and forty-four years after the first twenty African slaves were auctioned at Jamestown, Virginia, Abraham Lincoln signed an executive order declaring that all the slaves held throughout the Confederacy "are, and henceforward ever shall be, free." It was a watershed. True, emancipation did not apply to any part of the South occupied by Union troops, or to the border states of Maryland, West Virginia, Kentucky, Tennessee, and Missouri, where a volatile pro-slavery segment of the population might have reacted to the liberation of their slaves by joining the Confederacy. Nonetheless, for all its imperfections, the Emancipation Proclamation carried tremendous psychological and moral weight. It declared plainly that the Civil War was now being fought as much to free millions of men, women, and children from bondage as to reunite the shattered Union.

Whereas on the twenty-second day of September, A.D. 1862, a proclamation was issued by the President of the United States, containing, among other things, the following, to wit:

"That on the first day of January, A.D. 1863, all persons held as slaves within any State or designated part of a State the people whereof shall then be in rebellion against the United States, shall be then, thenceforward, and forever free; and the executive government of the United States, including the military and naval authority thereof, will recognize and maintain the freedom of such persons and will do no act or acts to repress such persons, or any of them, in any efforts they may make for their actual freedom.

"That the Executive will on the first day of January aforesaid, by proclamation, designate the States and parts of States, if any, in which the people thereof, respectively, shall then be in rebellion against the United States; and the fact that any State or the people thereof shall on that day be, in good faith, represented in the Congress of the United States by members chosen thereto at elections wherein a majority of the qualified voters of such States shall have participated shall, in the absence of strong countervailing testimony, be deemed conclusive evidence that such State and the people thereof are not then in rebellion against the United States."

Now, therefore, I, Abraham Lincoln, President of the United States, by virtue of the power in me vested as Commander-In-Chief of the Army and Navy of the United States in time of actual armed rebellion against the authority and government of the United States, and as a fit and necessary war measure for supressing said rebellion, do, on this first day of January, A.D. 1863, and in accordance with my purpose so to do, publicly proclaimed for the full period of one hundred days from the first day above mentioned, order and designate as the States and parts of States wherein the people thereof, respectively, are this day in rebellion against the United States the following, to wit:

Arkansas, Texas, Louisiana (except the parishes of St. Bernard, Palquemines, Jefferson, St. John, St. Charles, St. James, Ascension, Assumption, Terrebonne, Lafourche, St. Mary, St. Martin, and Orleans, including the City of New Orleans), Mississippi, Alabama, Florida, Georgia, South Carolina, North Carolina, and Virginia (except the forty-eight counties designated as West Virginia, and also the counties of Berkeley, Accomac,

Northhampton, Elizabeth City, York, Princess Anne, and Norfolk, including the cities of Norfolk and Portsmouth), and which excepted parts, are for the present, left precisely as if this proclamation were not issued.

And by virtue of the power and for the purpose aforesaid, I do order and declare that all persons held as slaves within said designated States and parts of States are, and henceforward shall be, free; and that the Executive government of the United States, including the military and naval authorities thereof, will recognize and maintain the freedom of said persons.

And I hereby enjoin upon the people so declared to be free to abstain from all violence, unless in necessary self-defence; and I recommend to them that, in all cases when allowed, they labor faithfully for reasonable wages.

And I further declare and make known that such persons of suitable condition will be received into the armed service of the United States to garrison forts, positions, stations, and other places, and to man vessels of all sorts in said service.

And upon this act, sincerely believed to be an act of justice, warranted by the Constitution upon military necessity, I invoke the considerate judgment of mankind and the gracious favor of Almighty God.

—SPEECH—
ADDRESS TO THE NIAGARA CONFERENCE
W.E.B. DU BOIS {AUGUST 16, 1906}

At the same time as the U.S. Supreme Court in *Plessy v. Ferguson* was upholding segregation as the law of the land, W.E.B. Du Bois (1868–1963) founded the Niagara Movement, a group of young black intellectual activists who demanded that the federal government enforce their Constitutional right to vote and abolish racial segregation. Du Bois was a steadfast defender of equality, and a life-long firebrand who viewed Booker T. Washington's "go slow" approach to equality as accommodationist. Although he was among the original founders of the National Association for the Advancement of

Colored People (NAACP), he denounced it in 1948 when he thought it had become too cautious. In 1961, he joined the Communist Party; a year later, he emigrated to Africa, where he renounced his U.S. citizenship. Du Bois died in Accra, Ghana, on the eve of Dr. Martin Luther King Jr.'s 1963 Washington march.

The men of the Niagara Movement coming from the toil of the year's hard work and, pausing a moment from the earning of their daily bread, turn toward the nation and again ask, in the name of ten million the privilege of a hearing. In the past year the work of the Negro-hater has flourished in the land. Step-by-step the defenders of the rights of American citizens have retreated. The work of stealing the black man's ballot has progressed and the fifty and more representatives of stolen votes still sit in the nation's capital. Discrimination in travel and public accommodation has so spread that some of our weaker brethren are actually afraid to thunder against color discrimination as such and are simply whispering for ordinary decencies.

Against this the Niagara Movement eternally protests. We will not be satisfied to take one jot or tittle less than our full manhood rights. We claim for ourselves every single right that belongs to a freeborn American—political, civil, and social—and until we get these rights we will never cease to protest and assail the ears of America. The battle we wage is not for ourselves alone but for all true Americans. It is a fight for ideals, lest this, our common fatherland, false to its founding, become in truth, the land of the thief and the home of the slave, a byword and a hissing among the nations for its sounding pretensions and pitiful accomplishments.

Never before in the modern age has a great and civilized folk threatened to adopt so cowardly a creed in the treatment of its fellow citizens born and bred on its soil. Stripped of verbiage and subterfuge and in its naked nastiness, the new American creed says: "Fear to let black men even try to rise lest they become the equals of the white." And this is the land that professes to follow Jesus Christ. The blasphemy of such a course is only matched by its cowardice.

In detail, our demands are clear and unequivocal. First, we would vote. With the right to vote goes everything: freedom, manhood, the honor of your wives, the chastity of your daughters, the right to work, and the chance to rise, and let no man listen to those who deny this. We want full manhood suffrage, and we want it now, henceforth and forever!

Second, we want discrimination in public accommodation to cease. Separation in railway and street cars, based simply on race and color, is un-American, undemocratic, and silly.

Third, we claim the right of freemen to walk, talk, and be with them that wish to be with us. No man has a right to choose another man's friends, and to attempt to do so is an impudent interference with the most fundamental human privilege.

Fourth, we want the laws enforced against rich as well as poor; against capitalist as well as laborer; against white as well as black. We are not more lawless than the white race. We are more often arrested, convicted, and mobbed. We want justice even for criminals and outlaws. We want the Constitution of the country enforced. We want Congress to take charge of Congressional elections. We want the Fourteenth Amendment carried out to the letter and every state disfranchised in Congress which attempts to disfranchise its rightful voters. We want the Fifteenth Amendment enforced and no state allowed to base its franchise simply on color. . . .

Fifth, we want our children educated. The school system in the country districts of the South is a disgrace, and in few towns and cities are the Negro schools what they ought to be. We want the national government to step in and wipe out illiteracy in the South. Either the United States will destroy ignorance or ignorance will destroy the United States.

And when we call for education we mean real education. We believe in work—we ourselves are workers—but work is not necessarily education. Education is the development of power and ideal. We want our children trained as intelligent human beings should be, and we will fight for all time against any proposal to educate black boys and girls simply as servants and underlings, or simply for the use of other people. They have a right to know, to think, to aspire.

These are some of the chief things which we want. How shall we get them? By voting where we may vote; by persistent, unceasing agitation; by hammering at the truth; by sacrifice and work.

We do not believe in violence, neither in the despised violence of the raid nor the lauded violence of the soldier, nor the barbarous of the mob, but we do believe in John Brown, in that incarnate spirit of justice, that hatred of a lie, that willingness to sacrifice money, reputation, and life itself on the altar of right. And here on the scene of John Brown's martyrdom, we reconsecrate ourselves, our honor, our property to the final emancipation of the race which John Brown died to make free.

Our enemies, triumphant for the present, are fighting the stars in their courses. Justice and humanity must prevail. We live to tell these dark brothers of ours—scattered in counsel, wavering, and weak—that no bribe of money or notoriety, no promise of wealth or fame, is worth the surrender of a people's manhood or the loss of a man's self-respect. We refuse to surrender the leadership of this race to cowards and trucklers. We are men; we will be treated as men. On this rock we have planted our banners. We will never give up, though the trump of doom finds us still fighting.

And we shall win! The past promised it. The present foretells it. Thank God for John Brown. Thank God for Garrison and Douglass, Sumner and Phillips, Nat Turner and Robert Gould Shaw, and all the hallowed dead who died for freedom! Thank God for all those today, few though their voices be, who have not forgotten the divine brotherhood of all men, white and black, rich and poor, fortunate and unfortunate.

We appeal to the young men and women of this nation, to those whose nostrils are not yet befouled by greed and snobbery and racial narrowness: Stand up for the right, prove yourselves worthy of your heritage and, whether born North or South, dare to treat men as men. Cannot the nation that has absorbed ten million foreigners into its political life without catastrophe absorb ten million Negro Americans into that same political life at less cost than their unjust and illegal exclusion will involve?

Courage, brothers! The battle for humanity is not lost or losing. All across the skies sit signs of promise! The slave is rising in his might, the yellow millions are tasting liberty, the black Africans are writhing toward the light, and everywhere the laborer, with ballot in his hand, is voting open the gates of opportunity and peace. The morning breaks over blood-stained hills. We must not falter, we may not shrink. Above are the everlasting stars.

—RULING—

BROWN V. BOARD OF EDUCATION

U.S. SUPREME COURT {MAY 17, 1954}

Since 1849, African-American parents had contested segregated public schools, a policy made official by the U.S. Supreme Court's 1896 "separate but equal" decision in *Plessy v. Ferguson*. In Kansas alone, between 1881 and 1949, the courts heard 11 cases that challenged the existence of separate schools for white and black children. After McKinley Burnett, president of the Topeka chapter of the NAACP, had spent two years in vain lobbying public education officials to abolish school segregation, the NAACP recruited 13 parents in 1951, including the Brown family, to file a class-action suit. The case went all the way to the Supreme Court, where it was argued by Thurgood Marshall. On May 17, 1954, the justices ruled unanimously that racial segregation in public schools was unconstitutional.

MR. CHIEF JUSTICE WARREN delivered the opinion of the Court.

These cases come to us from the States of Kansas, South Carolina, Virginia, and Delaware. They are premised on different facts and different local conditions, but a common legal question justifies their consideration together in this consolidated opinion.

In each of the cases, minors of the Negro race, through their legal representatives, seek the aid of the courts in obtaining admission to the public schools of their community on a nonsegregated basis. In each instance, they had been denied admission to schools attended by white children under laws requiring or permitting segregation according to race. This segregation was alleged to deprive the plaintiffs of the equal protection of the laws under the Fourteenth Amendment. In each of the cases other than the Delaware case, a three-judge federal district court denied relief to the plaintiffs on the so-called "separate but equal" doctrine announced by this Court in *Plessy v. Ferguson,* 163 U.S. 537. Under that doctrine, equality of treatment is accorded when the races are provided substantially equal facilities, even though these facilities be separate. In the Delaware case, the Supreme Court of Delaware adhered to that doctrine, but ordered that the plaintiffs be admitted to the white schools because of their superiority to the Negro schools.

The plaintiffs contend that segregated public schools are not "equal" and cannot be made "equal," and that hence they are deprived of the equal protection of the laws. Because of the obvious importance of the question presented, the Court took jurisdiction. Argument was heard in the 1952 Term, and reargument was heard this Term on certain questions propounded by the Court.

Reargument was largely devoted to the circumstances surrounding the adoption of the Fourteenth Amendment in 1868. It covered exhaustively consideration of the Amendment in Congress, ratification by the states, then existing practices in racial segregation, and the views of proponents and opponents of the Amendment. This discussion and our own investigation convince us that, although these sources cast some light, it is not enough to resolve the problem with which we are faced. At best, they are inconclusive. The most avid proponents of the post-War Amendments undoubtedly intended them to remove all legal distinctions among "all persons born or naturalized in the United States." Their opponents, just as certainly, were antagonistic to both the letter and the spirit of the Amendments and wished them to have the most limited effect. What others in Congress and the state legislatures had in mind cannot be determined with any degree of certainty.

An additional reason for the inconclusive nature of the Amendment's history, with respect to segregated schools, is the status of public education at that time. In the South, the movement toward free common schools, supported by general taxation, had not yet taken hold. Education of white children was largely in the hands of private groups. Education of Negroes was almost nonexistent, and practically all of the race were illiterate. In fact, any education of Negroes was forbidden by law in some states. Today, in contrast, many Negroes have achieved outstanding success in the arts and sciences as well as in the business and professional world. It is true that public school education at the time of the Amendment had advanced further in the North, but the effect of the Amendment on Northern States was generally ignored in the congressional debates. Even in the North, the conditions of public education did not approximate those existing today. The curriculum was usually rudimentary; ungraded schools were common in rural areas; the school term was but three months a year in many states; and compulsory school attendance was virtually unknown. As a consequence, it is not surprising that there should be so little in the history of the Fourteenth Amendment relating to its intended effect on public education.

In the first cases in this Court construing the Fourteenth Amendment, decided shortly after its adoption, the Court interpreted it as proscribing all state-imposed discriminations against the Negro race. The doctrine of "separate but equal" did not make its appearance in this Court until 1896 in the case of *Plessy v. Ferguson,* supra, involving not education but transportation. American courts have since labored with the doctrine for over half a century. In this Court, there have been six cases involving the "separate but equal" doctrine in the field of public education. In *Cumming v. County Board of Education,* 175 U.S. 528, and *Gong Lum v. Rice,* 275 U.S. 78, the validity of the doctrine itself was not challenged. In more recent cases, all on the graduate school level, inequality was found in that specific benefits enjoyed by white students were denied to Negro students of the same educational qualifications. *Missouri ex rel. Gaines v. Canada,* 305 U.S. 337; *Sipuel v. Oklahoma,* 332 U.S. 631; *Sweatt v. Painter,* 339 U.S. 629; *McLaurin v. Oklahoma State Regents,* 339 U.S. 637. In none of these cases was it necessary to re-examine the doctrine to grant relief to the Negro plaintiff. And in *Sweatt v. Painter,* supra, the Court expressly reserved decision on the question whether *Plessy v. Ferguson* should be held inapplicable to public education.

In the instant cases, that question is directly presented. Here, unlike *Sweatt v. Painter,* there are findings below that the Negro and white schools involved have been equalized, or are being equalized, with respect to buildings, curricula, qualifications and salaries of teachers, and other "tangible" factors. Our decision, therefore, cannot turn on merely a comparison of these tangible factors in the Negro and white schools involved in each of the cases. We must look instead to the effect of segregation itself on public education.

In approaching this problem, we cannot turn the clock back to 1868 when the Amendment was adopted, or even to 1896 when *Plessy v. Ferguson* was written. We must consider public education in the light of its full development and its present place in American life throughout the Nation. Only in this way can it be determined if segregation in public schools deprives these plaintiffs of the equal protection of the laws.

Today, education is perhaps the most important function of state and local governments. Compulsory school attendance laws and the great expenditures for education both demonstrate our recognition of the importance of education to our democratic society. It is required in the performance of our most basic public responsibilities, even service in the armed forces. It is the very foundation of good citizenship. Today it is a principal instrument in awakening the child to cultural values, in preparing him for later professional training, and in helping him to adjust normally to his environment. In these days, it is doubtful that any child may reasonably be expected to succeed in life if he is denied the opportunity of an education. Such an opportunity, where the state has undertaken to provide it, is a right which must be made available to all on equal terms.

We come then to the question presented: Does segregation of children in public schools solely on the basis of race, even though the physical facilities and other "tangible" factors may be equal, deprive the children of the minority group of equal educational opportunities? We believe that it does.

In *Sweatt v. Painter,* supra, in finding that a segregated law school for Negroes could not provide them equal educational opportunities, this Court relied in large part on "those qualities which are incapable of objective measurement but which make for greatness in a law school." In *McLaurin v. Oklahoma State Regents,* supra, the Court, in requiring that a Negro admitted to a white graduate school be treated like all other students, again resorted to intangible considerations: ". . . his ability to study, to engage in discussions and exchange views with other students, and, in general, to learn his profession." Such considerations apply with added force to children in grade and high schools. To separate them from others of similar age and qualifications solely because of their race generates a feeling of inferiority as to their status in the community that may affect their hearts and minds in a way unlikely ever to be undone. The effect of this separation on their educational opportunities was well stated by a finding in the Kansas case by a court which nevertheless felt compelled to rule against the Negro plaintiffs:

"Segregation of white and colored children in public schools has a detrimental effect upon the colored children. The impact is greater when it has the sanction of the law; for the policy of separating the races is usually interpreted as denoting the inferiority of the negro group. A sense of inferiority affects the motivation of a child to learn. Segregation with the sanction of law, therefore, has a tendency to [retard] the educational and mental development of negro children and to deprive them of some of the benefits they would receive in a racial[ly] integrated school system."

Whatever may have been the extent of psychological knowledge at the time of *Plessy v. Ferguson,* this finding is amply supported by modern authority. Any language in *Plessy v. Ferguson* contrary to this finding is rejected.

We conclude that in the field of public education the doctrine of "separate but equal" has no place. Separate educational facilities are inherently unequal. Therefore, we hold that the plaintiffs and others similarly situated for whom the actions have been brought are, by reason of the segregation complained of, deprived of the equal protection of the laws guaranteed by the Fourteenth Amendment. This disposition makes unnecessary any discussion whether such segregation also violates the Due Process Clause of the Fourteenth Amendment.

Because these are class actions, because of the wide applicability of this decision, and because of the great variety of local conditions, the formulation of decrees in these cases presents problems of considerable complexity. On reargument, the consideration of appropriate relief was necessarily subordinated to the primary question—the constitutionality of segregation in public education. We have now announced that such segregation is a denial of the equal protection of the laws. In order that we may have the full assistance of the parties in formulating decrees, the cases will be restored to the docket, and the parties are requested to present further argument on Questions 4 and 5 previously propounded by the Court for the reargument this Term. The Attorney General of the United States is again invited to participate. The Attorneys General of the states requiring or permitting segregation in public education will also be permitted to appear as amici curiae upon request to do so by September 15, 1954, and submission of briefs by October 1, 1954.

It is so ordered.

—LETTER—

MY DUNGEON SHOOK: LETTER TO MY NEPHEW ON THE 100TH ANNIVERSARY OF THE EMANCIPATION

JAMES BALDWIN {1963}

James Baldwin (1924–1987), the Harlem-born son of a lay preacher (and a preacher himself at age 14), was one of America's great racial consciences, writing with profound eloquence, insight, and intimacy about racism's destruction of both the oppressed and the oppressor. He was highbrow and down-home at the same time—"champagne and barbecue," as friend Ossie Davis once put it. A protégé of novelist Richard Wright, Baldwin went to live in Europe for nine years in the 1950s in order to tell his own story, and returned to tell America's during the fiery years of the Civil Rights Movement. His novels, memoirs, essays, and plays were usually meant to shock, but Baldwin's belief in art and humanity usually prevailed over his exasperation with hate and materialism. However, following the assassinations of three of his friends—civil rights activist Medgar Evers, Martin Luther King Jr., and Malcolm X—he returned in despair to France, where he remained for much of the rest of his life.

Dear James:

I have begun this letter five times and torn it up five times. I keep seeing your face, which is also the face of your father and

168

my brother. Like him, you are tough, dark, vulnerable, moody—with a very definite tendency to sound truculent because you want no one to think you are soft. You may be like your grandfather in this, I don't know, but certainly both you and your father resemble him very much physically. Well, he is dead, he never saw you, and he had a terrible life; he was defeated long before he died because, at the bottom of his heart, he really believed what white people said about him. This is one of the reasons that he became so holy. I am sure that your father has told you something about all that. Neither you nor your father exhibit any tendency towards holiness: you really *are* of another era, part of what happened when the Negro left the land and came into what the late E. Franklin Frazier called "the cities of destruction." You can only be destroyed by believing that you really are what the white world calls a *nigger*. I tell you this because I love you, and please don't you ever forget it.

I have known both of you all your lives, have carried your Daddy in my arms and on my shoulders, kissed and spanked him and watched him learn to walk. I don't know if you've known anybody from that far back; if you've loved anybody that long, first as an infant, then as a child, then as a man, you gain a strange perspective on time and human pain and effort. Other people cannot see what I see whenever I look into your father's face, for behind your father's face as it is today are all those other faces which were his. Let him laugh and I see a cellar your father does not remember and a house he does not remember and I hear in his present laughter his laughter as a child. Let him curse and I remember him falling down the cellar steps, and howling, and I remember, with pain, his tears, which my hand or your grandmother's so easily wiped away. But no one's hand can wipe away those tears he sheds invisibly today, which one hears in his laughter and in his speech and in his songs. I know what the world has done to my brother and how narrowly he has survived it. And I know,

169

which is much worse, and this is the crime of which I accuse my country and my countrymen, and for which neither I nor time nor history will ever forgive them, that they have destroyed and are destroying hundreds of thousands of lives and do not know it and do not want to know it. One can be, indeed one must strive to become, tough and philosophical concerning destruction and death, for this is what most of mankind has been best at since we have heard of man. (But remember: *most* of mankind is not *all* of mankind.) But it is not permissible that the authors of devastation should also be innocent. It is the innocence which constitutes the crime.

Now, my dear namesake, these innocent and well-meaning people, your countrymen, have caused you to be born under conditions not very far removed from those described for us by Charles Dickens in the London of more than a hundred years ago. (I hear the chorus of the innocents screaming, "No! This is not true! How *bitter* you are!"—but I am writing this letter to *you*, to try to tell you something about how to handle *them*, for most of them do not yet really know that you exist. I *know* the conditions under which you were born, for I was there. Your countrymen were *not* there, and haven't made it yet. Your grandmother was also there, and no one has ever accused her of being bitter. I suggest that the innocents check with her. She isn't hard to find. Your countrymen don't know that *she* exists, either, though she has been working for them all their lives.)

Well, you were born, here you came, something like fifteen years ago; and though your father and mother and grand- mother, looking about the streets through which they were carrying you, staring at the walls into which they brought you, had every reason to be heavyhearted, yet they were not. For here you were, Big James, named for me—you were a big baby, I was not—here you were: to be loved. To be loved, baby, hard, at once, and forever, to strengthen you against the loveless world. Remember that: I know how black it looks today, for you. It looked bad that day, too, yes, we were trembling. We have not stopped trembling yet, but if we had not loved each other none of us would have survived. And now you must survive because we love you, and for the sake of your children and your children's children.

This innocent country set you down in a ghetto in which, in fact, it intended that you should perish. Let me spell out precisely what I mean by that, for the heart of the matter is here, and the root of my dispute with my country. You were born where you were born and faced the future that you faced because you were black and *for no other reason*. The limits of your ambition were, thus, expected to be set forever. You were born into a society which spelled out with brutal clarity, and in as many ways as possible, that you were a worthless human being. You were not expected to aspire to excellence: you were expected to make peace with mediocrity. Wherever you have turned, James, in your short time on this earth, you have been told where you could go and what you could do (and *how* you could do it) and where you could live and whom you could marry. I know your countrymen do not agree with me about this, and I hear them saying, "You exaggerate." They do not know Harlem, and I do. So do you. Take no one's word for anything, including mine—but trust your experience. Know whence you came. If you know whence you came, there is really no limit to where you can go. The details and symbols of your life have been deliberately constructed to make you believe what white people say about you. Please try to remember that what they believe, as well as what they do and cause you to endure, does not testify to your inferiority but to their inhumanity and fear. Please try to be clear, dear James, through the storm which rages about your youthful head today, about the reality which lies behind the words *acceptance* and *integration*. There is no reason for you to try to become like white people and there is no basis whatever for their impertinent assumption that *they* must accept you. The really terrible thing, old buddy, is that *you* must accept *them*. And I mean that very seriously. You must accept them and accept them with love. For these innocent people have no other hope. They are, in effect, still trapped in a history which they do not understand; and until they understand it, they cannot be released from it. They have had to believe for many years, and for innumerable reasons, that black men are inferior to white men. Many of them, indeed, know better, but, as you will discover, people find it very difficult to act on what they know. To act is to be committed, and to be committed is to be in danger. In this case, the danger, in the minds of most white Americans, is the loss of their identity. Try to imagine how you would feel if you woke up one morning to find the sun shining and all the stars aflame. You would be frightened because it is out of the order of nature. Any upheaval in the universe is terrifying because it so profoundly attacks one's sense of one's own reality. Well, the black man has functioned in the white man's world as a fixed star, as an immovable pillar: and as he moves out of his place, heaven and earth are shaken to their foundations. You, don't be afraid. I said that it was intended that you should perish in the ghetto, perish by never being allowed to go behind the white man's definitions, by never being allowed to spell your proper name. You have, and many of us have, defeated this intention; and, by a terrible law, a terrible paradox, those innocents who believed that your imprisonment made them safe are losing their grasp of reality. But these men are your brothers—your lost, younger brothers. And if the word *integration* means anything, this is what it means: that we, with love, shall force our brothers to see themselves as they are, to cease fleeing from reality and begin to change it. For this is your home, my friend, do not be driven from it; great men have done great things here, and will again, and we can make America what America must become. It will be hard, James, but you come from sturdy, peasant stock, men who picked cotton and dammed rivers and built railroads, and, in the teeth of the most terrifying odds, achieved an unassailable and monumental dignity. You come from a long line of great poets, some of the greatest poets since Homer. One of them said, *The very time I thought I was lost/My dungeon shook and my chains fell off.*

You know, and I know, that the country is celebrating one hundred years of freedom one hundred years too soon. We cannot be free until they are free. God bless you, James, and Godspeed.

Your uncle,
James

— S O N G —

SHED A LITTLE LIGHT

JAMES TAYLOR {1991}

Though singer-songwriter James Taylor's (b. 1948) work is usually more personal than political, he doesn't hesitate to embrace the world when something moves him. "Line 'Em Up" was a satirical response to President Nixon's resignation, and "Slap Leather" voiced his opposition to the Gulf War. Taylor's 1991 song, "Shed a Little Light" was inspired by *Eyes on the Prize,* the PBS series about the Civil Rights Movement.

Let us turn our thoughts today
To Martin Luther King
And recognize that there are ties between us
All men and women
Living on the Earth
Ties of hope and love
Sister and brotherhood
That we are bound together
In our desire to see the world become

A place in which our children
Can grow free and strong
We are bound together
By the task that stands before us
And the road that lies ahead
We are bound and we are bound

There is a feeling like the clenching of a fist
There is a hunger in the center of the chest
There is a passage through the darkness and the mist
And though the body sleeps the heart will never rest

(Chorus)

Shed a little light, oh Lord
So that we can see
Just a little light, oh Lord
Wanna stand it on up
Stand it on up, oh Lord
Wanna walk it on down
Shed a little light, oh Lord

Can't get no light from the dollar bill
Don't give me no light from a TV screen
When I open my eyes
I wanna drink my fill
From the well on the hill
Do you know what I mean?

(Chorus)

There is a feeling like the clenching of a fist
There is a hunger in the center of the chest
There is a passage through the darkness and the mist
And though the body sleeps the heart will never rest

Oh, Let us turn our thoughts today
To Martin Luther King
And recognize that there are ties between us
All men and women
Living on the Earth
Ties of hope and love
Sister and brotherhood

— S P E E C H —

REFLECTIONS ON THE BICENTENNIAL OF THE UNITED STATES CONSTITUTION

THURGOOD MARSHALL {MAY 6, 1987}

Thurgood Marshall (1908–1993) quietly changed the face of America. A staunch believer that integration—which would allow individuals to rise or fall on their merits—was the sole path to equal rights, he rose to become the legal director of the NAACP and, in 1967, the first black justice on the U. S. Supreme Court, where he served on the bench for 24 years. Marshall's idealism and passion for civil rights never wavered; it was he who developed and executed a successful strategy to end school segregation, which culminated in the Supreme Court's landmark *Brown v. Board of Education* decision in 1954. He gave this speech to the Annual Seminar of the San Francisco Patent and Trademark Law Association in Maui, Hawaii.

The year 1987 marks the 200th anniversary of the United States Constitution. A Commission has been established to coordinate the celebration. The official meetings, essay contests, and festivities have begun.

The planned commemoration will span three years, and I am told 1987 is "dedicated to the memory of the Founders and the document they drafted in Philadelphia." We are to "recall the achievements of our Founders and the knowledge and experience that inspired them, the nature of the government they established, its origins, its character, and its ends, and the rights and privileges of citizenship, as well as its attendant responsibilities."

Like many anniversary celebrations, the plan for 1987 takes particular events and holds them up as the source of all the very best that has followed. Patriotic feelings will surely swell, prompting proud proclamations of the wisdom, foresight, and sense of justice shared by the framers and reflected in a written document now yellowed with age. This is unfortunate—not the patriotism itself, but the tendency for the celebration to oversimplify, and overlook the many other events that have been instrumental to our achievements as a nation. The focus of this celebration invites a complacent belief that the vision of those who debated and compromised in Philadelphia yielded the "more perfect Union" it is said we now enjoy.

I cannot accept this invitation, for I do not believe that the meaning of the Constitution was forever "fixed" at the Philadelphia Convention. Nor do I find the wisdom, foresight, and sense of justice exhibited by the Framers particularly profound. To the contrary, the government they devised was defective from the start, requiring several amendments, a civil war, and momentous social transformation to attain the system of constitutional government, and its respect for the individual freedoms and human rights, that we hold as fundamental today. When contemporary Americans cite "The Constitution," they invoke a concept that is vastly different from what the Framers barely began to construct two centuries ago.

For a sense of the evolving nature of the Constitution we need look no further than the first three words of the document's preamble: "We the People." When the Founding Fathers used this phrase in 1787, they did not have in mind the majority of America's citizens. "We the People" included, in the words of the Framers, "the whole Number of free Persons." On a matter so basic as the right to vote, for example, Negro slaves were excluded, although they were counted for representational purposes—at three-fifths each. Women did not gain the right to vote for over a hundred and thirty years.

These omissions were intentional. The record of the Framers' debates on the slave question is especially clear: the Southern states acceded to the demands of the New England states for giving Congress broad power to regu-

176

late commerce, in exchange for the right to continue the slave trade. The economic interests of the regions coalesced: New Englanders engaged in the "carrying trade" would profit from transporting slaves from Africa as well as goods produced in America by slave labor. The perpetuation of slavery ensured the primary source of wealth in the Southern states.

Despite this clear understanding of the role slavery would play in the new republic, use of the words "slaves" and "slavery" was carefully avoided in the original document. Political representation in the lower House of Congress was to be based on the population of "free Persons" in each state, plus three-fifths of all "other Persons." Moral principles against slavery, for those who had them, were compromised, with no explanation of the conflicting principles for which the American Revolutionary War had ostensibly been fought: the self-evident truths "that all men are created equal, that they are endowed by their Creator with certain unalienable Rights, that among these are Life, Liberty and the pursuit of Happiness."

It was not the first such compromise. Even these ringing phrases from the Declaration of Independence are filled with irony, for an early draft of what became that declaration assailed the King of England for suppressing legislative attempts to end the slave trade and for encouraging slave rebellions. The final draft adopted in 1776 did not contain this criticism. And so again at the Constitutional Convention eloquent objections to the institution of slavery went unheeded, and its opponents eventually consented to a document which laid a foundation for the tragic events that were to follow.

Pennsylvania's Gouverneur Morris provides an example. He opposed slavery and the counting of slaves in determining the basis for representation in Congress. At the Convention he objected:

> that the inhabitant of Georgia [or] South Carolina who goes to the coast of Africa, and in defiance of the most sacred laws of humanity tears away his fellow creatures from their dearest connections and damns them to the most cruel bondages, shall have more votes in a Government instituted for protection of the rights of mankind, than the Citizen of Pennsylvania or New Jersey who views with a laudable horror, so nefarious a practice.

And yet Gouverneur Morris eventually accepted the three-fifths accommodation. In fact, he wrote the final draft of the Constitution, the very document the bicentennial will commemorate.

As a result of compromise, the right of the Southern states to continue importing slaves was extended, officially, at least until 1808. We know that it actually lasted a good deal longer, as the Framers possessed no monopoly on the ability to trade moral principles for self-interest. But they nevertheless set an unfortunate example. Slaves could be imported, if the commercial interests of the North were protected. To make the compromise even more palatable, customs duties would be imposed at up to ten dollars per slave as a means of raising public revenues.

No doubt it will be said, when the unpleasant truth of the history of slavery in America is mentioned during this bicentennial year, that the Constitution was a product of its times, and embodied a compromise which, under other circumstances, would not have been made. But the effects of the Framers' compromise have remained for generations. They arose from the contradiction between guaranteeing liberty and justice to all, and denying both to Negroes.

The original intent of the phrase, "We the People," was far too clear for any ameliorating construction. Writing for the Supreme Court in 1857, Chief Justice Taney penned the following passage in the *Dred Scott* case, on the issue of whether, in the eyes of the Framers, slaves were "constituent members of the sovereignty," and were to be included among "We the People":

> We think they are not, and that they are not included, and
> were not intended to be included. . . .
> They had for more than a century before been regarded as
> beings of an inferior order, and altogether unfit to associ-
> ate with the white race . . .; and so far inferior, that they had
> no rights which the white man was bound to respect; and
> that the negro might justly and lawfully be reduced to slav-
> ery for his benefit. . . .
> . . . [A]ccordingly, a negro of the African race was regarded
> . . . as an article of property, and held, and bought and sold
> as such. . . . [N]o one seems to have doubted the correct-
> ness of the prevailing opinion of the time.

And so, nearly seven decades after the Constitutional Convention, the Supreme Court reaffirmed the prevailing opinion of the Framers regarding the rights of Negroes in America. It took a bloody civil war before the thirteenth amendment could be adopted to abolish slavery, though not the consequences slavery would have for future Americans.

While the Union survived the Civil War, the Constitution did not. In its place arose a new, more promising basis for justice and equality, the fourteenth amendment, ensuring protection of the life, liberty, and property of *all* persons against deprivations without due process, and guaranteeing equal protection of the laws. And yet almost another century would pass before any significant recognition was obtained of the rights of black Americans to share equally even in such basic opportunities as education, housing, and employment, and to have their votes counted, and counted equally. In the meantime, blacks joined America's military to fight its wars and invested untold hours working in its factories and on its farms, contributing to the development of this country's magnificent wealth and waiting to share in its prosperity.

What is striking is the role legal principles have played throughout America's history in determining the condition of Negroes. They were enslaved by law, emancipated by law, disenfranchised and segregated by law; and, finally, they have begun to win equality by law. Along the way, new constitutional principles have emerged to meet the challenges of a changing society. The progress has been dramatic, and it will continue.

The men who gathered in Philadelphia in 1787 could not have envisioned these changes. They could not have imagined, nor would they have accepted, that the document they were drafting would one day be construed by a Supreme Court to which had been appointed a woman and the descendent of an African slave. "We the People" no longer enslave, but the credit does not belong to the Framers. It belongs to those who refused to acquiesce in outdated notions of "liberty," "justice," and "equality," and who strived to better them.

And so we must be careful, when focusing on the events which took place in Philadelphia two centuries ago, that we not overlook the momentous events which followed, and thereby lose our proper sense of perspective. Otherwise, the odds are that for many Americans the bicentennial celebration will be little more than a blind pilgrimage to the shrine of the original document now stored in a vault in the National Archives. If we seek, instead, a sensitive understanding of the Constitution's inherent defects, and its promising evolution through 200 years of history, the celebration of the "Miracle at Philadelphia" will, in my view, be a far more meaningful and humbling experience. We will see that the true miracle was not the birth of the Constitution, but its life, a life nurtured through two turbulent centuries of our own making, and a life embodying much good fortune that was not.

Thus, in this bicentennial year, we may not all participate in the festivities with flag-waving fervor. Some may more quietly commemorate the suffering, struggle, and sacrifice that has triumphed over much of what was wrong with the original document, and observe the anniversary with hopes not realized and promises not fulfilled. I plan to celebrate the bicentennial of the Constitution as a living document, including the Bill of Rights and the other amendments protecting individual freedoms and human rights.

—SPEECH—

SPEECH FROM THE PULPIT
WILLIAM JEFFERSON CLINTON
{NOVEMBER 13, 1993}

On November, 13, 1993, President William Jefferson Clinton (b. 1946) took the pulpit at The Church of God in Christ Mason Temple in South Memphis, Tennessee, and listened as a solo saxophonist performed "Amazing Grace." Clinton then proceeded to deliver a speech to a packed audience of ministers at the site of the Reverend Martin Luther King Jr.'s last address ("I've Been to the Mountaintop") before his assassination in 1968. Clinton wondered aloud how King would feel about racial and civil rights progress in the United States twenty-five years after his death.

I am glad to be here. You have touched my heart, and you brought tears to my eyes and joy to my spirit.

You know, in the last ten months, I've been called a lot of things, but nobody's called me a Bishop yet.

When I was about nine years old, my beloved and now departed grandmother—who was a very wise woman—looked at me and she said, "You know, I believe you could be a preacher if you were just a little better boy." The proverb says, "A happy heart doeth good like medicine, but a broken spirit dryeth the bone." This is a happy place, and I am happy to be here.

I thank you for your spirit.

By the grace of God and your help, last year, I was elected President of this great country. I never dreamed that I would ever have a chance to come to this hallowed place where Martin Luther King gave his last sermon. I ask you to think today about the purpose for which I ran and the purpose for which so many of you worked to put me in this great office. I have worked hard to keep faith with our common efforts—to restore the economy, to reverse the politics of helping only those at the top of our totem pole and not the hard-working middle class or the poor, to bring our people together across racial and regional and political lines, to make a strength out of our diversity instead of letting it tear us apart, to reward work and family and community, and try to move us forward into the 21st century.

I have tried to keep faith. Thirteen percent of all my presidential appointments are African Americans and there are five African Americans in the Cabinet of the United States—two-and-a-half times as many as have ever served in the history of this great land.

I have sought to advance the right to vote with the Motor-Voter Bill supported so strongly by all the churches in our country. And next week, it will be my great honor to sign the Restoration of Religious Freedoms Act—a bill supported widely by people across all religions and political philosophies, to put back the real meaning of the Constitution, to give you and every other American the freedom to do what is most important in your life—to worship God as your spirit leads you.

I say to you, my fellow Americans, we have made a good beginning. Inflation is down. Interest rates are down. The deficit is down. Investment is up. Millions of Americans, including—I bet—some people in this room, have refinanced their homes or their business loans just in the last year. And in the last ten months, this economy has produced more jobs in the private sector than in the previous four years.

We have passed a law, called the Family Leave Law, which says you can't be fired if you take a little time off when a baby is born or a parent is sick. We know that most Americans have to work, but you ought not to have to give up being a good parent just to take a job. If you can't succeed as a worker and a parent, this can't make it.

We have radically reformed the college loan program, as I've promised, to lower the costs of college loans and broaden the availability of it—and make the repayment terms easier. And we have passed the National Service Law that will give—three years from now—100,000 young Americans the chance to serve their communities at home to repair the frayed bonds of community, to build up the needs of people at the grassroots, and, at the same time, earn some money to pay for a college education. It is a wonderful idea.

On April the 15th, when people pay their taxes, somewhere between 15 and 18 million working families on modest incomes, families with children and incomes of under $23,000, will get a tax cut, not a tax increase, in the most important effort to ensure that we reward work and family in the last 20 years. Fifty million American parents and their children will be advantaged by putting the tax code back on the side of working American parents for a change. Under the leadership of the First Lady, we have produced a comprehensive plan to guarantee health care security to all Americans. How can we expect the American people to work and to live with all of the changes in a global economy, where the average 18-year-old will change work seven times in a lifetime, unless we can simply say, "We have joined the ranks of all the other advanced countries in the world. You can have decent health care that's always there, that can never be taken away." It is time we did that—long past time. I ask you to help us achieve that.

But we have so much more to do. You and I know that most people are still working harder for the same or lower wages, that many people are afraid that their job will go away. We have to provide the education and training our people need—not just for our children, but for our adults, too. If we cannot close this country up to the forces of change sweeping throughout the world, we have to at least guarantee people the security of being employable. They have to be able to get a new job, if they're going to have to get a new job. We don't do that today—and we must, and we intend to proceed until that is done. We have to guarantee that there will be some investment in those areas of our country—in the inner cities and in the destitute rural areas in the Mississippi Delta of my home state and this state and Louisiana and Mississippi and other places like it throughout America. It's all very well to train people, but if they don't have a job, they can be trained for nothing. We must get investment into those places where the people are dying for work.

And finally, let me say, we must find people who will buy what we have to produce. We are the most productive people on earth. That makes us proud.

But what that means is that, every year, one person can produce more in the same amount of time. Now, if fewer and fewer people can produce more and more things—and yet you want to create more jobs and raise people's incomes—you have to have more customers for what it is you're making. And that is why I have worked so hard to sell more American products around the world, why I have asked that we be able to sell billions of dollars of computers we used not to sell to foreign countries and foreign interests to put our people to work. Why, next week, I am going all the way to Washington State to meet with the President of China and the Prime Minister of Japan and the heads of 13 other Asian countries—the fastest growing part of the world—to say, "We want to be your partners. We will buy your goods, but we want you to buy ours, too—if you please."

That is why—that is why I have worked so hard for this North American Trade Agreement that Congressman Ford endorsed today, and Congressman Jefferson endorsed, and Congressman Cooper, and Congressman Clement—because we know that Americans can compete and win only if people will buy what it is we have to sell. There are 90 million people in Mexico. Seventy cents of every dollar they spend on foreign goods, they spend on American goods. People worry, fairly, about people shutting down plants in America and going—not just to Mexico, but to any place where the labor is cheap. It has happened. What I want to say to you, my fellow Americans, is that nothing in this agreement makes that more likely. That has happened already.

It may happen again. What we need to do is to keep the jobs here by finding customers there. That's what this agreement does. It gives us a chance to create opportunities for people.

I would never—there are people—I have friends in this audience, people who are ministers from my state, fathers and sons, people I have looked out all over this vast crowd, and I see people I've known for years. They know, I've spent my whole life working to create jobs. I would never, knowingly, do anything that would take a job away from the American people. This agreement will make more jobs.

But, I guess what I really want to say to you today, my fellow Americans, is that we can do all of this and still fail unless we meet the great crisis of the spirit that is gripping America today. When I leave you, Congressman Ford and I are going to a Baptist Church near here to a town meeting he's having on health care and violence. I tell you, unless we do something about crime and violence and drugs that is ravaging the community, we will not be able to repair this country.

If Martin Luther King—who said, "Like Moses, I am on the mountain top and I can see the Promised Land, but I'm not going to be able to get there with you. But we will get there."—If he were to reappear by my side today and give us a report card on the last 25 years, what would he say? "You did a good job," he would say, "voting and electing people who formerly were not electable because of the color of their skin." You have more political power—and that is good. "You did a good job," he would say, "letting people who have the ability to do so, live wherever they want to live, go wherever they want to go in this great country."

"You did a good job," he would say, "elevating people of color into the ranks of the United States Armed Forces to the very top or into the very top of our government. You did a very good job," he would say. He would say, "You did a good job creating a black middle class of people who really are doing well, and the middle class is growing more among African Americans than among non-African Americans. You did a good job. You did a good job in opening opportunity." But he would say, "I did not live and die to see the American family destroyed. I did not live and die to see 13-year-old boys get automatic weapons and gun down 9-year-olds just for the kick of it. I did not live and die to see young people destroy their own lives with drugs and then build fortunes destroying the lives of others. That is not what I came here to do. I fought for freedom," he would say, "but not for the freedom of people to kill each other with reckless abandonment, not for the freedom of children to have children and the fathers of the children to walk away from them and abandon them, as if they don't amount to anything. I fought for people to have the right to work, but not to have whole communities and people abandoned. This is not what I lived and died for." My fellow Americans, he would say, "I fought to stop white people from being so filled with hate that they would wreak violence on black people. I did not fight for the right of black people to murder other black people with reckless abandonment."

The other day, the Mayor of Baltimore, a dear friend of mine, told me a story of visiting the family of a young man who had been killed—18 years old—on Halloween. He always went out with little-bitty kids so they could trick-or-treat safely. And across the street from where they were walking on Halloween, a 14-year-old boy gave a 13-year-old boy a gun and dared him to shoot the 18-year-old boy—and he shot him dead. And the Mayor had to visit the family.

In Washington, DC, where I live—your nation's capital, the symbol of freedom throughout the world—look how that freedom is being exercised. The other night, a man came along the street and grabbed a one-year-old child and put the child in his car. The child may have been the child of the man. And two people were after him and they chased him in the car and they just kept shooting with reckless abandonment—knowing that baby was in the car. And they shot the man dead, and a bullet went through his body into the baby's body and blew the little booty off the child's foot.

The other day on the front page of our paper, the nation's capital—"Are We Talking About World Peace or World Conflict?" You know, a big article on the front page of the Washington Post about an 11-year-old child planning her funeral. "These are the hymns I want sung. This is the dress I want to wear. I know I'm not going to live very long." That is not the freedom—the freedom to die before you're a teenager is not what Martin Luther King lived and died for.

More than 37,000 people die from gunshot wounds in this country every year. Gunfire is the leading cause of death in young men. And now that we've all gotten so cool that everybody can get a semiautomatic weapon, a person shot now is three times more likely to die than 15 years ago, because they're likely to have three bullets in them—160,000 children stay home from school every day because they are scared they will be hurt in their school. The other day, I was in California at a town meeting, and a handsome young man stood up and said, "Mr. President, my brother and I, we don't belong to gangs. We don't have guns. We don't do drugs. We want to go to school. We want to be professionals. We want to work hard. We want to do well. We want to have families. And we changed our school, because the school we were in was so dangerous. So, when we showed up to the new school to register, my brother and I were standing in line, and somebody ran in the school and started shooting a gun, and my brother was shot down standing right in front of me at the safer school." The freedom to do that kind of thing is not what Martin Luther King lived and died for. Not what people gathered in this hallowed church for the night before he was assassinated in April of 1968. If you had told anybody who was here in that church on that night that we would abuse our freedom in that way, they would have found it hard to believe. And I tell you, it is our moral duty to turn it around.

And now, I think, finally, we have a chance. Finally, I think, we have a chance. We have a pastor here from New Haven, Connecticut. I was in his church, with Reverend Jackson, when I was running for President, on a snowy day in Connecticut, to mourn the deaths of children who had been killed in that city. And afterward, we walked down the street for more than a mile in the snow. Then, the American people were not ready. People would say, "Oh, this is a terrible thing, but what can we do about it?" Now, when we read that foreign visitors come to our shores and are killed at random in our fine state of Florida, when we see our children planning their funerals, when the American people are finally coming to grips with the accumulated waste of crime and violence and the breakdown of family and community and the increase in drugs and the decrease in jobs, I think, finally, we may be ready to do something about it.

And there is something for each of us to do. There are changes we can make from the outside in—that's the job of the President and the Congress and the governors and the mayors and the social service agencies. And then, there are some changes we're going to have to make from the inside out, or the others won't matter. That's what that magnificent song was about, isn't it?

Sometimes, there are no answers from the outside in. Sometimes, all of the answers have to come from the values and the stirrings and the voices that speak to us from within.

So, we are beginning. We are trying to pass a bill to make our people safer, to put another 100,000 police officers on the streets, to provide boot camps instead of prisons for young people who could still be rescued—to provide more safety in our schools, to restrict the availability of these awful assault weapons, to pass the Brady Bill and at least require people to have their criminal background checked before they get a gun, and to say, if you're not old enough to vote and you're not old enough to go to war, you ought not to own a handgun and you ought not to use one unless you're on a target range.

We want to pass a health care bill that will make drug treatment available for everyone. And we also have to do it—we have to have drug treatment and education available to everyone, and especially those who are in prison, who are coming out.

We have a drug czar now in Lee Brown, who was the police chief of Atlanta, of Houston, of New York, who understands these things. And, when the Congress comes back next year, we will be moving forward on that. We need this crime bill now. We ought to give it to the American people for Christmas. And we need to move forward on all these other fronts. But I say to you, my fellow Americans, we need some other things as well. I do not believe we can repair the basic fabric of society until people who are willing to work have work.

Work organizes life. It gives structure and discipline to life. It gives meaning and self-esteem to people who are parents. It gives a role model to children.

The famous African-American sociologist, William Julius Wilson, has written a stunning book, called *The Truly Disadvantaged,* in which he chronicles in breathtaking terms how the inner cities of our country have crumbled as work has disappeared. And we must find a way, through public and private sources, to enhance the attractiveness of the American people who live there to get investment there. We cannot—I submit to you—repair the American community and restore the American family until we provide the structure, the values, the discipline, and the reward that work gives.

I read a wonderful speech the other day, given at Howard University, in a lecture series funded by Bill and Camille Cosby, in which the speaker said, "I grew up in Anacostia years ago. Even then it was all black and it was a very poor neighborhood. But, you know, when I was a child in Anacostia—a 100 percent African-American neighborhood, a very poor neighborhood—we had a crime rate that was lower than the average of the crime rate of our city. Why? Because we had coherent families. We had coherent communities. The people who filled the church on Sunday lived in the same place they went to church. The guy that owned the drugstore lived down the street. The person that owned the grocery store lived in our community. We were whole." And I say to you, we have to make our people whole again. This church has stood for that. Why do you think you have 5 million members in this country?

Because people know you are filled with the spirit of God to do the right thing in this life by them.

So, I say to you, we have to make a partnership—all the government agencies, all the business folks. But where there are no families, where there is no order, where there is no hope, where we are reducing the size of armed services because we have won the Cold War, who will be there to give structure, discipline, and love to these children? You must do that and we must help you. The Scripture says, "You are the salt of the earth and the light of the world," that, "If your light shines before men, they will give glory to the Father in Heaven." That is what we must do. How would we explain it to Martin Luther King if he showed up today and said, "Yes, we won the Cold War. Yes, the biggest threat that all of us grew up under—Communism and nuclear war—Communism is gone; nuclear war receding. Yes, we developed all of these miraculous technologies. Yes, we all got a VCR in our home. It's interesting. Yes, we get 50 channels on the cable. Yes, without regard to race, if you work hard, play by the rules, you get into a service academy or a good college, you'll do just great." How would we explain to him all these kids getting killed and killing each other? How would we justify the things that we permit that no other country in the world would permit? How could we explain that we gave people the freedom to succeed and we created conditions in which millions abuse that freedom to destroy the things that make life worth living and life itself? We cannot.

And so, I say to you today, my fellow Americans, you gave me this job, and we're making progress on the things you hired me to do. But unless we deal with the ravages of crime and drugs and violence, and unless we recognize that it's due to the breakdown of the family, the community, and the disappearance of jobs, and unless we say, "Some of this cannot be done by government because we have to reach deep inside to the values, the spirit, the soul, and the truth of human nature," none of the other things we seek to do will ever take us where we need to go.

So, in this pulpit, on this day, let me ask all of you in your heart to say, "We will honor the life and the work of Martin Luther King. We will honor the meaning of our church. We will somehow, by God's grace, we will turn this around. We will give these children a future. We will take away their guns and give them books. We will take away their despair and give them hope. We will rebuild the families and the neighborhoods and the communities. We won't make all the work that has gone on here benefit just a few. We will do it together by the grace of God." Thank you.

— SCREENPLAY —

MR. SMITH GOES TO WASHINGTON

SIDNEY BUCHMAN {1939}

An idealistic and naive young man, Jefferson Smith (James Stewart), is chosen to replace a recently deceased U.S. Senator precisely because crooked business and political interests in his state are counting on his obliviousness to their venality and greed. His beautiful assistant (Jean Arthur) indulges the young man's idealism, then opens his eyes to harsh political realities. Instead of growing cynical, the young man attacks graft and corruption on the Senate floor by filibustering, eloquently defending democracy and quoting from the Declaration of Independence to win the day.

The life of screenwriter Sidney Buchman (1902–1975) did not have a Hollywood ending. After writing *Mr. Smith Goes to Washington*, Buchman went on to become a Hollywood producer, but the House Un-American Activities Committee put a halt to his career in 1951. Called to testify, Buchman admitted being a former member of the Communist Party, but refused to provide other names—and was blacklisted.

JEFFERSON SMITH

. . . Now, you're not gonna have a country that can make these kind of rules work, if you haven't got men that have learned to tell human rights from a punch in the nose. (*The Senate applauds*) It's a funny thing about men, you know. They all start life being boys. I wouldn't be a bit surprised if some of these Senators were boys once. And that's why it seemed like a pretty good idea for me to get boys out of crowded cities and stuffy basements for a couple of months out of the year. And build their bodies and minds for a man-sized job, because those boys are gonna be behind these desks some of these days. And it seemed like a pretty good idea, getting boys from all over the country, boys of all nationalities and ways of living. Getting them together. Let them find out what makes different people tick the way they do. Because I wouldn't give you two cents for all your fancy rules if, behind them, they didn't have a little bit of plain, ordinary, everyday kindness and a—a little lookin' out for the other fella, too . . . That's pretty important, all that. It's just the blood and bone and sinew of this democracy that some great men handed down to the human race, that's all. But of course, if you've got to build a dam where that boys camp ought to be, to get some graft to pay off some political army or something, well that's a different thing. Oh no! If you think I'm going back there and tell those boys in my state and say: 'Look. Now fellas. Forget about it. Forget all this stuff I've been tellin' you about this land you live in is a lot of hooey. This isn't your country. It belongs to a lot of James Taylors.' Oh no! Not me! And anybody here that thinks I'm gonna do that, they've got another thing comin'. (*He whistles loudly with his fingers in his mouth, startling Senators who are dozing or reading other materials*) That's all right. I just wanted to find out if you still had faces. I'm sorry gentlemen. I—I know I'm being disrespectful to this honorable body, I know that. I—A guy like me should never be allowed to get in here in the first place. I know that! And I hate to stand here and try your patience like this, but EITHER I'M DEAD RIGHT OR I'M CRAZY.

. . . Just get up off the ground. That's all I ask. Get up there with that lady, that's up on top of this Capitol Dome. That lady that stands for Liberty. Take a look at this country through her eyes if you really want to see somethin'. And you won't just see scenery. You'll see the whole parade of what man's carved out for himself after centuries of fighting. And fighting for something better than just jungle law. Fighting so as he can stand on his own two feet free and decent, like he was created—no matter what his race, color, or creed. That's what you'd see. There's no place out there for graft or greed or lies! Or compromise with human liberties! And if that's what the grown-ups have done with this world that was given to them, then we'd better get those boys camps started fast and see what the kids can do. And it's not too late. Because this country is bigger than the Taylors or you or me or anything else. Great principles don't get lost once they come to light. They're right here. You just have to see them again.

. . . I guess this is just another lost cause, Mr. Paine. All you people don't know about the lost causes. Mr. Paine does. He said once they were the only causes worth fighting for. And he fought for them once, for the only reason that any man ever fights for them. Because of just one plain simple rule: "Love thy neighbor." And in this world today, full of hatred, a man who knows that one rule has a great trust. You know that rule, Mr. Paine. And I loved you for it, just as my father did. And you know that you fight for the lost causes harder than for any others. Yes, you even die for them. Like a man we both knew, Mr. Paine.

. . . You think I'm licked. You all think I'm licked. Well, I'm not licked, and I'm gonna stay right here and fight for this lost cause even if this room gets filled with lies like these, and the Taylors and all their armies come marching into this place. Somebody'll listen to me. Some . . .

Smith faints, staggers and falls to the floor.

—SPEECH—

SPECIAL MESSAGE TO THE CONGRESS: THE AMERICAN PROMISE

Lyndon B. Johnson {March 15, 1965}

Lyndon B. Johnson (1908–1973) had always put civil rights high on his agenda, so it surprised few that he used the presidency to pass two of the most important pieces of civil rights legislation—the 1964 Civil Rights Act and in January 1965, the Voting Rights Act. This bill called for the federal government to intervene if local counties discriminated against blacks registering to vote. When the bill stalled in Congress, Martin Luther King Jr. led a series of marches in Alabama. The first, in Selma, erupted in violence, and images of police brutality against protesters stunned much of the nation. Johnson, taking advantage of the outrage, delivered this speech to Congress. He signed the act into law five months later.

Mr. Speaker, Mr. President, members of the Congress: I speak tonight for the dignity of man and the destiny of democracy.

I urge every member of both parties, Americans of all religions and of all colors, from every section of this country, to join me in that cause.

At times history and fate meet at a single time in a single place to shape a turning point in man's unending search for freedom. So it was at Lexington and Concord. So it was a century ago at Appomattox. So it was last week in Selma, Alabama.

There, long-suffering men and women peacefully protested the denial of their rights as Americans. Many were brutally assaulted. One good man, a man of God, was killed.

There is no cause for pride in what has happened in Selma. There is no cause for self-satisfaction in the long denial of equal rights of millions of Americans. But there is cause for hope and for faith in our democracy in what is happening here tonight.

For the cries of pain and the hymns and protests of oppressed people have summoned into convocation all the majesty of this great Government— the Government of the greatest nation on earth.

Our mission is at once the oldest and the most basic of this country: to right wrong, to do justice, to serve man.

In our time we have come to live with moments of great crisis. Our lives have been marked with debate about great issues; issues of war and peace, issues of prosperity and depression. But rarely in any time does an issue lay bare the secret heart of America itself. Rarely are we met with a challenge, not to our growth or abundance, our welfare or our security, but rather to the values and the purposes and the meaning of our beloved nation.

The issue of equal rights for American Negroes is such an issue. And should we defeat every enemy, should we double our wealth and conquer the stars, and still be unequal to this issue, then we will have failed as a people and as a nation.

For with a country as with a person, "What is a man profited, if he shall gain the whole world, and lose his own soul?"

There is no Negro problem. There is no Southern problem. There is no Northern problem. There is only an American problem. And we are met here

193

tonight as Americans—not as Democrats or Republicans—we are met here as Americans to solve that problem.

This was the first nation in the history of the world to be founded with a purpose. The great phrases of that purpose still sound in every American heart, North and South: "All men are created equal"—"Government by consent of the governed"—"Give me liberty or give me death." Well, those are not just clever words, or those are not just empty theories. In their name Americans have fought and died for two centuries, and tonight around the world they stand there as guardians of our liberty, risking their lives.

Those words are a promise to every citizen that he shall share in the dignity of man. This dignity cannot be found in a man's possessions; it cannot be found in his power, or in his position. It really rests on his right to be treated as a man equal in opportunity to all others. It says that he shall share in freedom, he shall choose his leaders, educate his children, and provide for his family according to his ability and his merits as a human being.

To apply any other test—to deny a man his hopes because of his color or race, his religion or the place of his birth—is not only to do injustice, it is to deny America and to dishonor the dead who gave their lives for American freedom.

THE RIGHT TO VOTE

Our fathers believed that if this noble view of the rights of man was to flourish, it must be rooted in democracy. The most basic right of all was the right to choose your own leaders. The history of this country, in large measure, is the history of the expansion of that right to all of our people.

Many of the issues of civil rights are very complex and most difficult. But about this there can and should be no argument. Every American citizen must have an equal right to vote. There is no reason which can excuse the denial of that right. There is no duty which weighs more heavily on us than the duty we have to ensure that right.

Yet the harsh fact is that in many places in this country men and women are kept from voting simply because they are Negroes.

Every device of which human ingenuity is capable has been used to deny this right. The Negro citizen may go to register only to be told that the day is wrong, or the hour is late, or the official in charge is absent. And if he persists, and if he manages to present himself to the registrar, he may be disqualified because he did not spell out his middle name or because he abbreviated a word on the application.

And if he manages to fill out an application he is given a test. The registrar is the sole judge of whether he passes this test. He may be asked to recite the entire Constitution, or explain the most complex provisions of State law. And even a college degree cannot be used to prove that he can read and write.

For the fact is that the only way to pass these barriers is to show a white skin.

Experience has clearly shown that the existing process of law cannot overcome systematic and ingenious discrimination. No law that we now have on the books—and I have helped to put three of them there—can ensure the right to vote when local officials are determined to deny it.

In such a case our duty must be clear to all of us. The Constitution says that no person shall be kept from voting because of his race or his color. We have all sworn an oath before God to support and to defend that Constitution. We must now act in obedience to that oath.

GUARANTEEING THE RIGHT TO VOTE

Wednesday I will send to Congress a law designed to eliminate illegal barriers to the right to vote.

The broad principles of that bill will be in the hands of the Democratic and Republican leaders tomorrow. After they have reviewed it, it will come here formally as a bill. I am grateful for this opportunity to come here tonight at the invitation of the leadership to reason with my friends, to give them my views, and to visit with my former colleagues.

I have had prepared a more comprehensive analysis of the legislation which I had intended to transmit to the clerk tomorrow but which I will submit to the clerks tonight. But I want to really discuss with you now briefly the main proposals of this legislation.

This bill will strike down restrictions to voting in all elections—Federal, State, and local—which have been used to deny Negroes the right to vote.

This bill will establish a simple, uniform standard which cannot be used, however ingenious the effort, to flout our Constitution.

It will provide for citizens to be registered by officials of the United States Government if the State officials refuse to register them.

It will eliminate tedious, unnecessary lawsuits which delay the right to vote.

Finally, this legislation will ensure that properly registered individuals are not prohibited from voting.

I will welcome the suggestions from all of the members of Congress— I have no doubt that I will get some—on ways and means to strengthen this law and to make it effective. But experience has plainly shown that this is the only path to carry out the command of the Constitution.

To those who seek to avoid action by their National Government in their own communities; who want to and who seek to maintain purely local control over elections, the answer is simple:

Open your polling places to all your people.

Allow men and women to register and vote whatever the color of their skin.

Extend the rights of citizenship to every citizen of this land.

THE NEED FOR ACTION

There is no constitutional issue here. The command of the Constitution is plain.

There is no moral issue. It is wrong—deadly wrong—to deny any of your fellow Americans the right to vote in this country.

There is no issue of States' rights or national rights. There is only the struggle for human rights.

I have not the slightest doubt what will be your answer.

The last time a President sent a civil rights bill to the Congress it contained a provision to protect voting rights in Federal elections. That civil rights bill was passed after eight long months of debate. And when that bill came to my desk from the Congress for my signature, the heart of the voting provision had been eliminated.

This time, on this issue, there must be no delay, no hesitation and no compromise with our purpose.

We cannot, we must not, refuse to protect the right of every American to vote in every election that he may desire to participate in. And we ought not and we cannot and we must not wait another eight months before we get a bill. We have already waited a hundred years and more, and the time for waiting is gone.

So I ask you to join me in working long hours—nights and weekends, if necessary—to pass this bill. And I don't make that request lightly. For from the window where I sit with the problems of our country I recognize that outside this chamber is the outraged conscience of a nation, the grave concern of many nations, and the harsh judgment of history on our acts.

WE SHALL OVERCOME

But even if we pass this bill, the battle will not be over. What happened in Selma is part of a far larger movement which reaches into every section and State of America. It is the effort of American Negroes to secure for themselves the full blessings of American life.

Their cause must be our cause too. Because it is not just Negroes, but really it is all of us, who must overcome the crippling legacy of bigotry and injustice.

And we shall overcome.

As a man whose roots go deeply into Southern soil, I know how agonizing racial feelings are. I know how difficult it is to reshape the attitudes and the structure of our society.

But a century has passed, more than a hundred years, since the Negro was freed. And he is not fully free tonight.

It was more than a hundred years ago that Abraham Lincoln, a great President of another party, signed the Emancipation Proclamation, but emancipation is a proclamation and not a fact.

A century has passed, more than a hundred years, since equality was promised. And yet the Negro is not equal.

A century has passed since the day of promise. And the promise is unkept.

The time of justice has now come. I tell you that I believe sincerely that no force can hold it back. It is right in the eyes of man and God that it should come. And when it does, I think that day will brighten the lives of every American.

For Negroes are not the only victims. How many white children have gone uneducated, how many white families have lived in stark poverty, how many white lives have been scarred by fear, because we have wasted our energy and our substance to maintain the barriers of hatred and terror?

So I say to all of you here, and to all in the Nation tonight, that those who appeal to you to hold on to the past do so at the cost of denying you your future.

This great, rich, restless country can offer opportunity and education and hope to all: black and white, North and South, sharecropper and city dweller. These are the enemies: poverty, ignorance, disease. They are the enemies and not our fellow man, not our neighbor. And these enemies too—poverty, disease, and ignorance—we shall overcome.

AN AMERICAN PROBLEM

Now let none of us in any sections look with prideful righteousness on the troubles in another section, or on the problems of our neighbors. There is really no part of America where the promise of equality has been fully kept. In Buffalo as well as in Birmingham, in Philadelphia as well as in Selma, Americans are struggling for the fruits of freedom.

This is one nation. What happens in Selma or in Cincinnati is a matter of legitimate concern to every American. But let each of us look within our own hearts and our own communities, and let each of us put our shoulder to the wheel to root out injustice wherever it exists.

As we meet here in this peaceful, historic chamber tonight, men from the South, some of whom were at Iwo Jima, men from the North who have carried Old Glory to far corners of the world and brought it back without a stain on it, men from the East and from the West, are all fighting together without regard to religion, or color, or region, in Vietnam. Men from every region fought for us across the world 20 years ago.

And in these common dangers and these common sacrifices the South made its contribution of honor and gallantry no less than any other region of the great Republic—and in some instances, a great many of them, more.

And I have not the slightest doubt that good men from everywhere in this country, from the Great Lakes to the Gulf of Mexico, from the Golden Gate to the harbors along the Atlantic, will rally together now in this cause to vindicate the freedom of all Americans. For all of us owe this duty; and I believe that all of us will respond to it.

Your President makes that request of every American.

PROGRESS THROUGH
THE DEMOCRATIC PROCESS

The real hero of this struggle is the American Negro. His actions and protests, his courage to risk safety and even to risk his life, have awakened the conscience of this Nation. His demonstrations have been designed to call attention to injustice, designed to provoke change, designed to stir reform.

He has called upon us to make good the promise of America. And who among us can say that we would have made the same progress were it not for his persistent bravery, and his faith in American democracy.

For at the real heart of the battle for equality is a deep-seated belief in the democratic process. Equality depends not on the force of arms or tear gas but upon the force of moral right; not on recourse to violence but on respect for law and order.

There have been many pressures upon your President and there will be others as the days come and go. But I pledge to you tonight that we intend to fight this battle where it should be fought: in the courts, and in the Congress, and in the hearts of men.

We must preserve the right of free speech and the right of free assembly. But the right of free speech does not carry with it, as has been said, the right to holler fire in a crowded theater. We must preserve the right to free assembly, but free assembly does not carry with it the right to block public thoroughfares to traffic.

We do have a right to protest, and a right to march under conditions that do not infringe the constitutional rights of our neighbors. And I intend to protect all those rights as long as I am permitted to serve in this office.

We will guard against violence, knowing it strikes from our hands the very weapons which we seek—progress, obedience to law, and belief in American values.

In Selma as elsewhere we seek and pray for peace. We seek order. We seek unity. But we will not accept the peace of stifled rights, or the order imposed by fear, or the unity that stifles protest. For peace cannot be purchased at the cost of liberty.

In Selma tonight, as in every—and we had a good day there—as in every city, we are working for just and peaceful settlement. We must all remember that after this speech I am making tonight, after the police and the FBI and the marshals have all gone, and after you have promptly passed this bill, the people of Selma and the other cities of the nation must still live and work together. And when the attention of the nation has gone elsewhere they must try to heal the wounds and to build a new community.

This cannot be easily done on a battleground of violence, as the history of the South itself shows. It is in recognition of this that men of both races have shown such an outstandingly impressive responsibility in recent days—last Tuesday, again today.

RIGHTS MUST BE OPPORTUNITIES

The bill that I am presenting to you will be known as a civil rights bill. But, in a larger sense, most of the program I am recommending is a civil rights program. Its object is to open the city of hope to all people of all races.

Because all Americans just must have the right to vote. And we are going to give them that right.

All Americans must have the privileges of citizenship regardless of race. And they are going to have those privileges of citizenship regardless of race.

But I would like to caution you and remind you that to exercise these privileges takes much more than just legal right. It requires a trained mind and a healthy body. It requires a decent home, and the chance to find a job, and the opportunity to escape from the clutches of poverty.

Of course, people cannot contribute to the nation if they are never taught to read or write, if their bodies are stunted from hunger, if their sickness goes untended, if their life is spent in hopeless poverty just drawing a welfare check.

So we want to open the gates to opportunity. But we are also going to give all our people, black and white, the help that they need to walk through those gates.

THE PURPOSE OF THIS GOVERNMENT

My first job after college was as a teacher in Cotulla, Texas, in a small Mexican-American school. Few of them could speak English, and I couldn't speak much Spanish. My students were poor and they often came to class without breakfast, hungry. They knew even in their youth the pain of prejudice. They never seemed to know why people disliked them. But they knew it was so, because I saw it in their eyes. I often walked home late in the afternoon, after the classes were finished, wishing there was more that I could do. But all I knew was to teach them the little that I knew, hoping that it might help them against the hardships that lay ahead.

Somehow you never forget what poverty and hatred can do when you see its scars on the hopeful face of a young child.

I never thought then, in 1928, that I would be standing here in 1965. It never even occurred to me in my fondest dreams that I might have the chance to help the sons and daughters of those students and to help people like them all over this country.

But now I do have that chance—and I'll let you in on a secret—I mean to use it. And I hope that you will use it with me.

This is the richest and most powerful country which ever occupied the globe. The might of past empires is little compared to ours. But I do not want to be the President who built empires, or sought grandeur, or extended dominion.

I want to be the President who educated young children to the wonders of their world. I want to be the President who helped to feed the hungry and to prepare them to be taxpayers instead of tax eaters.

I want to be the President who helped the poor to find their own way and who protected the right of every citizen to vote in every election.

I want to be the President who helped to end hatred among his fellow men and who promoted love among the people of all races and all regions and all parties.

I want to be the President who helped to end war among the brothers of this earth.

And so at the request of your beloved Speaker and the Senator from Montana; the majority leader, the Senator from Illinois; the minority leader,

Mr. McCulloch, and other Members of both parties, I came here tonight—not as President Roosevelt came down one time in person to veto a bonus bill, not as President Truman came down one time to urge the passage of a railroad bill—but I came down here to ask you to share this task with me and to share it with the people that we both work for. I want this to be the Congress, Republicans and Democrats alike, which did all these things for all these people.

Beyond this great chamber, out yonder in fifty States, are the people that we serve. Who can tell what deep and unspoken hopes are in their hearts tonight as they sit there and listen? We all can guess, from our own lives, how difficult they often find their own pursuit of happiness, how many problems each little family has. They look most of all to themselves for their futures. But I think that they also look to each of us.

Above the pyramid on the great seal of the United States it says—in Latin—"God has favored our undertaking."

God will not favor everything that we do. It is rather our duty to divine His will. But I cannot help believing that He truly understands, and that He really favors the undertaking that we begin here tonight.

———•·•———

—LETTER—
LETTER TO THEODORE ROOSEVELT
MOTHER JONES {1903}

Mother Jones (1830–1930), the turn-of-the-century labor activist/crusader, used creative strategies to attract sympathy for workers' causes. Noticing in 1903 that the Liberty Bell was drawing great crowds as it toured the country, Jones decided to organize a similar freedom tour with some of the striking Pennsylvania child-laborers—uneducated, malnourished, often maimed by machinery—who had become her latest cause. She brought the kids to Trenton, Princeton, New York City, and finally to Oyster Bay, Long Island, where she hoped to introduce them to President Theodore Roosevelt and ask him to sponsor federal laws protecting child-laborers. When the president refused to meet with the children, Jones wrote him this letter. Roosevelt later claimed that he had no power to act on the federal level and Jones campaigned against him in the next election. Though Jones lost that battle, Pennsylvania soon passed anti-child-labor laws.

Your Excellency:

Twice before I have written to you requesting an audience that I might lay my mission before you and have your advice on a matter which bears upon the welfare of the whole nation. I speak of the emancipation from mills and factories of the hundreds of thousands of young children who are yielding up their lives for the commercial supremacy of the nation. Failing to receive a reply to either of the two letters, I yesterday went to Oyster Bay, taking with me three of these children that they might plead with you personally.

Secretary Barnes informed us that before we might hope for an interview, we must first lay the whole matter before you in a letter. He assured me of its delivery to you personally, and also that it would receive your attention.

I have espoused the cause of the laboring class in general and of suffering children in particular. For what affects the child must ultimately affect the adult. It was for them that our march of principle was begun. We sought to bring the attention of the public upon these little ones, so that ultimately sentiment would be aroused and the children freed from the workshops and sent to school. I know of no question to-day that demands great attention from those who have at heart the perpetuation of the Republic.

The child of to-day is the man or woman of to-morrow, the citizen and the mother of still future citizens. I ask Mr. President, what kind of citizen will be the child who toils twelve hours a day, in an unsanitary atmosphere, stunted mentally and physically, and surrounded with immoral influences? Denied education, he cannot assume the true duties of citizenship, and enfeebled physically and mentally, he falls a ready victim to the perverting influences which the present economic conditions have created.

I grant you, Mr. President, that there are State laws which should regulate these matters, but results have proven that they are inadequate. In my little band are three boys, the oldest 11 years old, who have worked in mills a year or more without interferences from the authorities. All efforts to bring about reform have failed.

I have been moved to this crusade, Mr. President, because of actual experiences in the mills. I have seen little children without the first rudiments of education and no prospect of acquiring any. I have seen other children with hands, fingers and other parts of their tiny bodies mutilated because of their childish ignorance of machinery. I feel that no nation can truly be great while such conditions exist without attempted remedy.

It is to be hoped that our crusade will stir up a general sentiment in behalf of enslaved childhood, and secure enforcement of present laws.

But that is not sufficient.

As this is not alone the question of the separate States, but of the whole Republic, we come to you as the chief representative of the nation.

I believe that the Federal laws should be passed governing this evil and including a penalty for violation. Surely, Mr. President, if this is practicable—and I believe that you will agree that it is—you can advise me of the necessary steps to pursue.

I have with me three boys who have walked a hundred miles serving as living proof of what I say. You can see and talk with them, Mr. President, if you are interested. If you decide to see these children, I will bring them before you at any time you may set. Secretary Barnes has assured me of an early reply, and this should be sent care of the Ashland Hotel, New York City.

Very respectfully yours,
Mother Jones

—LETTER—

LETTER TO E.L. BARR JR.
CESAR E. CHAVEZ {GOOD FRIDAY, 1969}

Cesar E. Chavez (1927–1993), whose family's land was lost during the Great Depression, spent years working in the fields and vineyards of Arizona and California. Appalled by the working conditions, Chavez organized other migrant workers, first into the National Farm Workers Association and then into the United Farm Workers (UFW). In 1969, when E.L. Barr Jr., president of the California Grape and Tree Fruit League, accused Cesar Chavez's UFW of planning to resort to violence, Chavez responded with a letter. Chavez, who embraced Ghandian principles and practices, had recently completed a thirty-day fast to discourage strikers from using violence. The nonviolent strike was successful—the union received a contract the following year, but the struggle was far from over.

Good Friday, 1969
E.L. Barr Jr., President
California Grape and Tree Fruit League
717 Market St.
San Francisco, California

Dear Mr. Barr,

I am sad to hear about your accusations in the press that our union movement and table grape boycott have been successful because we have used violence and terror tactics. If what you say is true, I have been a failure and should withdraw from the struggle; but you are left with the awesome moral responsibility, before God and Man, to come forward with whatever information you have so that corrective action can begin at once. If for any reason you fail to come forth to substantiate your charges, then you must be held responsible for committing violence against us, albeit of the tongue. I am convinced that you as a human being did not mean what you said but rather acted hastily under pressure from the public relations firm that has been hired to try to counteract the tremendous moral force of our movement. How many times we ourselves have felt the need to lash out in anger and bitterness.

Today on Good Friday, 1969, we remember the life and the sacrifice of Martin Luther King Jr., who gave himself totally to the nonviolent struggle for peace and justice. In his *Letter from a Birmingham Jail* Dr. King describes better than I could our hopes for the strike and boycott: "Injustice must be exposed, with all the tensions its exposure creates, to the light of human conscience and the air of national opinion before it can be cured." For our part I admit that we have seized upon every tactic and strategy consistent with the morality of our cause to expose that injustice and thus to heighten the sensitivity of the American conscience so that farmworkers will have, without bloodshed, their own union and the dignity of bargaining with their agribusiness employers. By lying about the nature of our movement, Mr. Barr, you are working against nonviolent social change. Unwittingly perhaps, you may unleash the other force which our union by discipline and deed, censure and education has sought to avoid, that panacean shortcut: that senseless violence which honors no color, class, or neighborhood.

You must understand—I must make you understand—that our membership and the hopes and aspirations of the hundreds and thousands of the poor and dispossessed that have been raised on our account are, above all, human beings, no better and no worse than any other cross-section of human society; we are not saints because we are poor; but by the same measure neither are we immoral. We are men and women who have suffered and endured much, and not only because of our abject poverty but because we have been kept poor. The colors of our skins, the languages of our cultural and native origins, the lack of our formal education, the exclusion from the democratic process, the numbers of our men slain in recent wars—through all these burdens generation after generation have sought to demoralize us, to break our human spirit. But God knows that we are not beasts of burden, agricultural implements or rented slaves; we are men. And mark this well Mr. Barr, we are men locked in a death struggle against man's inhumanity to man in the industry that you represent. And this struggle itself gives meaning to our life and ennobles our dying.

As your industry has experienced, our strikers here in Delano and those who represent us throughout the world are well trained for this struggle. They have been under the gun, they have been kicked and beaten and herded by dogs, they have been cursed and ridiculed, they have been stripped and chained and jailed, they have been sprayed with the poisons used in the vineyards; but they have been taught not to lie down and die nor flee in shame, but to resist with every ounce of human endurance and spirit. To resist not with retaliation in kind but to overcome with love and compassion, with ingenuity and creativity, with hard work and longer hours, with stamina and patient tenacity, with truth and public appeal, with friends and allies, with mobility and discipline, with politics and law, and with prayer and fasting. They were not trained in a month or even a year; after all, this new harvest season will mark our fourth full year of strike and even now we continue to plan and prepare for the years to come. Time accomplishes for the poor what money does for the rich.

This is not to pretend that we have everywhere been successful enough or that we have not made mistakes. And while we do not belittle or underestimate our adversaries—for they are the rich and the powerful and they possess the land—we are not afraid nor do we cringe from the confrontation. We welcome it! We have planned for it. We know that our cause is just, that history is a story of social revolution, and that the poor shall inherit the land.

Once again, I appeal to you as the representative of your industry and as a man. I ask you to recognize and bargain with our union before the economic pressure of the boycott and strike takes an irrevocable toil; but if not, I ask you to at least sit down with us to discuss the safeguards necessary to keep our historic struggle free of violence. I make this appeal because as one of the leaders of our nonviolent movement, I know and accept my responsibility for preventing, if possible, the destruction of human life and property. For these reasons, and knowing Gandhi's admonition that fasting is the last resort in place of the sword, during a most critical time in our movement last February 1968 I undertook a 25-day fast. I repeat to you the principle enunciated to the membership at the start of the fast: if to build our union required the deliberate taking of life, either the life of a grower or his child, or the life of a farmworker or his child, then I choose not to see the union built.

Mr. Barr, let me be painfully honest with you. You must understand these things. We advocate militant nonviolence as our means for social revolution and to achieve justice for our people, but we are not blind or deaf to the desperate and moody winds of human frustration, impatience and rage that blow among us. Gandhi himself admitted that if his only choice were cowardice or violence, he would choose violence. Men are not angels, and time and tide wait for no man. Precisely because of these powerful human emotions, we have tried to involve masses of people in their own struggle. Participation and self-determination remain the best experience of freedom, and free men instinctively prefer democratic change and even protect the rights guaranteed to seek it. Only the enslaved in despair have need for violent overthrow.

This letter does not express all that I have in my heart, Mr. Barr. But if it says nothing else it says that we do not hate you or rejoice to see your industry destroyed; we hate the agribusiness system that seeks to keep us enslaved and we shall overcome and change it not by retaliation or bloodshed but by a determined nonviolent struggle carried on by those masses of farm workers who intend to be free and human.

Sincerely yours,
Cesar E. Chavez
United Farm Workers Organizing Committee
A.F.L-C.I.O
Delano, California

—LETTER—

LETTER TO BASEBALL COMMISSIONER BOWIE KUHN

CURT FLOOD {DECEMBER 24, 1969}

The lifetime batting average of Curt Flood (1938–1997) was .293, but he was 0–1 in his only at-bat before the U.S. Supreme Court in 1972. When, after a long career with the St. Louis Cardinals, Flood was traded to the Philadelphia Phillies in 1969, he took the first swing at Major League Baseball's long-standing Reserve Clause, which bound players to their teams in perpetuity. Flood accused Major League Baseball of violating anti-trust laws and forcing players into "involuntary servitude," a violation of the Thirteenth Amendment of the U.S. Constitution. Although he struck out with his Supreme Court challenge, Flood opened the door for ballplayers' rights, and there was no turning back. Arbitrator Peter Seitz ruled that the Reserve Clause was not binding, ushering in the era of free agency.

December 24, 1969

Mr. Bowie K. Kuhn
Commissioner of Baseball
680 Fifth Avenue
New York, New York 10019

Dear Mr. Kuhn,

After twelve years in the major leagues, I do not feel I am a piece of property to be bought and sold irrespective of my wishes. I believe that any system which produces that result violates my basic rights as a citizen and is inconsistent with the laws of the United States and of the sovereign States.

It is my desire to play baseball in 1970, and I am capable of playing. I have received a contract offer from the Philadelphia club, but I believe I have the right to consider offers from other clubs before making any decisions. I, therefore, request that you make known to all major league clubs my feelings in this matter, and advise them of my availability for the 1970 season.

Curt Flood

—SONG—

THE REVOLUTION WILL NOT BE TELEVISED
GIL SCOTT-HERON {1974}

After his father, a professional soccer player from Jamaica, and his mother, a librarian, divorced early in his life, the multitalented poet and musician Gil Scott-Heron (b. 1949) moved to Tennessee to live with his grandmother, who instilled in him both literary and musical ambitions. He was one of three children picked to integrate a nearby elementary school. To escape the resulting racial abuse, he moved to New York to live with his mother and wrote his first volume of poetry at the age of 13, then published his first novel at 19. He came under the influence of the poetry of Langston Hughes and LeRoi Jones before legendary jazz producer Bob Thiele suggested he record his polemical poems, launching him on an eclectic musical career that continues to this day. In "The Revolution Will Not Be Televised," as in so much of his work, the seminal Scott-Heron shows himself to be a harbinger of both hip-hop and rap.

> You will not be able to stay home, brother.
> You will not be able to plug in, turn on and cop out.
> You will not be able to lose yourself on skag and skip,
> Skip out for beer during commercials,
> Because the revolution will not be televised.
> The revolution will not be televised.

The revolution will not be brought to you by Xerox
In 4 parts without commercial interruption.
The revolution will not show you pictures of Nixon
Blowing a bugle and leading a charge by John
Mitchell, General Abrams and Spiro Agnew to eat
Hog maws confiscated from a Harlem sanctuary.

The revolution will not be televised.

The revolution will not be brought to you by the
Schaefer Award Theatre and will not star Natalie
Wood and Steve McQueen or Bullwinkle and Julia.
The revolution will not give your mouth sex appeal.
The revolution will not get rid of the nubs.
The revolution will not make you look five pounds
Thinner, because

The revolution will not be televised, Brother.

There will be no pictures of you and Willie Mays
Pushing that cart down the block on the dead run,
Or trying to slide that color television into a stolen ambulance.
NBC will not predict the winner at 8:32
or the count from 29 districts.

The revolution will not be televised.

There will be no pictures of pigs shooting down
Brothers in the instant replay.
There will be no pictures of Whitney Young being
Run out of Harlem on a rail with a brand new process.
There will be no slow motion or still life of Roy
Wilkens strolling through Watts in a red, black and
Green liberation jumpsuit that he had been saving
For just the right occasion.

Green Acres, The Beverly Hillbillies, and Hooterville
Junction will no longer be so damned relevant, and
Women will not care if Dick finally gets down with
Jane on Search for Tomorrow because Black people
will be in the street looking for a brighter day.

The revolution will not be televised.

There will be no highlights on the eleven o'clock
News and no pictures of hairy armed women
Liberationists and Jackie Onassis blowing her nose.
The theme song will not be written by Jim Webb,
Francis Scott Key, nor sung by Glen Campbell, Tom
Jones, Johnny Cash, Englebert Humperdink, or the Rare Earth.

The revolution will not be televised.

The revolution will not be right back after a message
About a white tornado, white lightning, or white people.
You will not have to worry about a dive in your
Bedroom, a tiger in your tank, or the giant in your toilet bowl.
The revolution will not go better with Coke.
The revolution will not fight the germs that cause bad breath.
The revolution will put you in the driver's seat.

The revolution will not be televised, will not be televised,
Will not be televised.
The revolution will be no re-run brothers;
The revolution will be live.

—LETTER—
LETTER TO CHARLES MCCARTHY
KURT VONNEGUT {NOVEMBER 16, 1973}

The novel that made Kurt Vonnegut's (b. 1922) literary reputation was *Slaughterhouse-Five* (1969). Its blend of black comedy, science fiction, and biting satire has won it an army of fans, but many enemies as well. Every year there are school boards around the country that debate whether *Slaughterhouse-Five* should be part of the curriculum. In 1973, the school board of Drake, North Dakota, took a more extreme stand: It confiscated copies of the book and burned them.

*M*y novel Slaughterhouse-Five *was actually burned in a furnace by a school janitor in Drake, North Dakota, on instructions from the school committee there, and the school board made public statements about the unwholesomeness of the book. Even by the standards of Queen Victoria, the only offensive line in the entire novel is this: "Get out of the road, you dumb m(____)." This is spoken by an American antitank gunner to an unarmed American chaplain's assistant during the Battle of the Bulge in Europe in December 1944, the largest single defeat of American arms (the confederacy excluded) in history. The chaplain's assistant had attracted enemy fire.*

So on November 16, 1973, I wrote as follows to Charles McCarthy of Drake, North Dakota:

Dear Mr. McCarthy:

I am writing to you in your capacity as chairman of the Drake School Board. I am among those American writers whose books have been destroyed in the now famous furnace of your school.

Certain members of your community have suggested that my work is evil. This is extraordinarily insulting to me. The news from Drake indicated to me that books and writers are very unreal to you people. I am writing this letter to let you know how real I am.

214

I want you to know, too, that my publisher and I have done absolutely nothing to exploit the disgusting news from Drake. We are not clapping each other on the back, crowing about all the books we sell because of the news. We have declined to go on television, have written no fiery letters to editorial pages, have granted no lengthy interviews. We are angered and sickened and saddened. And no copies of this letter have been sent to anybody else. You now hold the only copy in your hands. It is a strictly private letter from me to the people of Drake, who have done so much to damage my reputation in the eyes of their children and then in the eyes of the world. Do you have the courage and ordinary decency to show this letter to the people, or will it, too, be consigned to the fires of your furnace?

I gather from what I read in the papers and hear on television that you imagine me, and some other writers, too, as being sort of ratlike people who enjoy making money from poisoning the minds of young people. I am in fact a large, strong person, fifty-one years old, who did a lot of farm work as a boy, who is good with tools. I have raised six children, three of my own and three adopted. They have all turned out well. Two of them are farmers. I am a combat infantry veteran from World War II, and hold a Purple Heart. I have earned whatever I own by hard work. I have never been arrested or sued for anything. I am so trusted with young people and by young people that I have served on the faculties of the University of Iowa, Harvard, and the City College of New York. Every year I receive at least a dozen invitations to be commencement speaker at colleges and high schools. My books are probably more widely used in schools than those of any other living American fiction writer.

If you were to bother to read my books, to behave as educated persons would, you would learn that they are not sexy, and do not argue in favor of wildness of any kind. They beg that people be kinder and more responsible than they often are. It is true that some of the characters speak coarsely. That is because people speak coarsely in real life. Especially soldiers and hardworking men speak coarsely, and even our most sheltered children know that. And we know, too, that those words really don't damage children much. They didn't damage us when we were young. It was evil deeds and lying that hurt us.

After I have said all this, I am sure you are still ready to respond, in effect, "Yes, yes—but it still remains our right and our responsibility to decide what books our children are going to be made to read in our community." This is surely so. But it is also true that if you exercise that right and fulfill that responsibility in an ignorant, harsh, un-American manner, then people are entitled to call you bad citizens and fools. Even our own children are entitled to call you that.

I read in the newspaper that your community is mystified by the outcry from all over the country about what you have done. Well, you have discovered that Drake is a part of American civilization, and your fellow Americans can't stand it that you have behaved in such an uncivilized way. Perhaps you will learn from this that books are sacred to free men for very good reasons, and that wars have been fought against nations which hate books and burn them. If you are an American, you must allow all ideas to circulate freely in your community, not merely your own.

If you and your board are now determined to show that you in fact have wisdom and maturity when you exercise your powers over the education of your young, then you should acknowledge that it was a rotten lesson you taught young people in a free society when you denounced and then burned books—books you haven't even read. You should also resolve to expose your children to all sorts of opinions and information, in order that they will be better equipped to make decisions and survive.

Again: you have insulted me, and I am a good citizen, and I am very real.

Kurt Vonnegut

*T*hat was seven years ago. There has so far been no reply. At this moment, as I write in New York City, Slaughterhouse-Five has been banned from school libraries not fifty miles from here (on Long Island). A legal battle begun several years ago rages on. The school board in question has found lawyers eager to attack the First Amendment tooth and nail. There is never a shortage anywhere of lawyers eager to attack the First Amendment, as though it were nothing more than a clause in a lease from a crooked slumlord.

— P O E M —
CENSORS
D.H. LAWRENCE {1929}

If anybody knew firsthand about censors, it was D.H. Lawrence (1885–1930). The "naughty" passages were excised from his first novel, *The White Peacock*. The British government banned *The Rainbow* as obscene. No publisher would touch *Women in Love*. And although an Italian publisher released *Lady Chatterley's Lover* intact in 1928, no unexpurgated edition of the novel was available in the United States until 1960.

> Censors are dead men
> set up to judge between life and death.
> For no live, sunny man would be a censor,
> he'd just laugh.
> But censors, being dead men,
> have a stern eye on life.
> —That thing's alive! It's dangerous. Make away
>   with it!—
> And when the execution is performed
> you hear the stertorous, self-righteous heavy
>   breathing of the dead men,
> the censors, breathing with relief.

— SPEECH —

SPIRIT OF LIBERTY

JUDGE LEARNED HAND {MAY 1944}

Judge Learned Hand (1872–1961) of the U.S. Second Circuit Court of Appeals is arguably the greatest United States judge never to sit on the highest court. He had "drifted" into Harvard Law School—leaving behind his first love, philosophy—and was appointed to the federal bench in 1909 after a stint on Wall Street. He delivered a speech in New York City's Central Park during "I Am an American Day" to rally the homefront in 1944. Hand was well-equipped to speak on the subject of liberty, for he had decided a landmark First Amendment case in 1917, *Masses Publishing Co. v. Patten*. When the postmaster tried to stop mailings of the irreverent journal *The Masses*, Hand ruled that dissident speech was protected as long as it aimed at persuading rather than inciting immediate action.

We have gathered here to affirm a faith, a faith in a common purpose, a common conviction, a common devotion. Some of us have chosen America as the land of our adoption; the rest have come from those who did the same. For this reason we have some right to consider ourselves a picked group, a group of those who had the courage to break from the past and brave the dangers and the loneliness of a strange land. What was the object that nerved us, or those who went before us, to this choice? We sought liberty— freedom from oppression, freedom from want, freedom to be ourselves. This we then sought; this we now believe that we are by way of winning. What do we mean when we say that first of all we seek liberty? I often wonder whether we do not rest our hopes too much upon constitutions, upon laws, and upon courts. These are false hopes; believe me, these are false hopes. Liberty lies in the hearts of men and women; when it dies there, no constitution, no law, no court can save it; no constitution, no law, no court can even do much to help it. And what is this liberty which must lie in the hearts of men and women? It is not the ruthless, unbridled will; it is not the freedom to do as one likes. That is the denial of liberty, and leads straight to its overthrow. A society in which men recognize no check upon their freedom soon becomes a society where freedom is the possession of only a savage few—as we have learned to our sorrow.

What, then, is the spirit of liberty? I cannot define it; I can only tell you my own faith. The spirit of liberty is the spirit which is not too sure that it is right; the spirit of liberty is the spirit which seeks to understand the minds of other men and women; the spirit of liberty is the spirit which weighs their interests alongside its own without bias; the spirit of liberty remembers that not even a sparrow falls to earth unheeded; the spirit of liberty is the spirit of him who, near two thousand years ago, taught mankind that lesson it has never learned, but has never quite forgotten—that there may be a kingdom where the least shall be heard and considered side by side with the greatest. And now in that spirit, that spirit of an America that has never been, and which may never be—nay, which never will be except as the conscience and courage of Americans create it—yet in that spirit of that America which lies hidden in some form in the aspirations of us all; in that spirit of that America for which our young men are at this moment fighting and dying; in that spirit of liberty and of America so prosperous, and safe, and contented, we shall have failed to grasp its meaning, and shall have been truant to its promise, except as we strive to make it a signal, a beacon, a standard, to which the best hopes of mankind will ever turn? In confidence that you share that belief, I now ask you to raise your hands and repeat with me this pledge:

"I pledge allegiance to the flag of the United States of America, and to the Republic for which it stands—one nation, indivisible, with liberty and justice for all."

—POEM—
I AM AN AMERICAN
STEVE CONNELL {2003}

The California poet Steve Connell (b. 1975) uses Da Poetry Lounge in Los Angeles as his home base, but his poems are resonating around the country, thanks to appearances on Black Entertainment Television and Russell Simmons' *Def Poetry Jam* on HBO. According to *The Los Angeles Times,* Connell is one of the "rock stars of an emerging spoken word scene that merges poetry, hip-hop culture, and theatre in a polished production package." He helped found the collective The Underground Poets Railroad. And in the spirit of the original Underground Railroad that provided a passage to freedom for slaves, Connell's poems give a new kind of freedom to both the spoken word and the meaning of democracy.

I am an American.

I have the right to remain silent.
I wish to refuse that right—
and if you refuse that right
everything you say can and will be used
against you.
Well, I am a poet also . . .
so that is what I want.
I am of the opinion
that words are not mine until
I am accountable to them.
I am of the opinion that words are the greatest power
Man can have,
and if I don't have words that are mine then I am powerless.
I will not be powerless
And I will not be silent.
I have that right
I am an American.

I am an American.
I have the right to say whatever I want,
And I am a poet
So I can say that shit well.
And you have been warned.

In the mouths of poets
Words are like actions:
They define you.

And if your words don't define you,
Then why are you talking?
If you're not trying to go forward
Then why are you walking?
You should sit down and shut up
And you have that right
But I'm a poet and an American
And my pencil sparks light
With each word that I write;
And I will stand here and fight
To the dawns early light;
As the bombs burst in air
I will stand right there
And I will speak my fucking mind.
I have that right.

I am an American

I, truthfully, am the truth
You never fully told.
And still don't tell,
but I tell the truth of who you are,
because I am who you are—
I am an American . . .
And I tell the truth.

I am old women in department stores
Built atop the consecrated bones
Of Crazy Horse.
I sign credit card receipts like treaties I don't intend to honor.
A legacy of a debt that can never be repayed.
I am restitution
For the sweet dreams that can't come
to the children who die
because . . .
Hush—little baby, don't say a word
and you can't say a word . . .
because we built Sears atop your grave
so you can't talk about the blankets soaked with smallpox
that the government gave.
I am the dead Iroquois babies swaddled in smallpox
Who watch the chickens come home.
I, Malcolm X, I—
"I am not here to condemn America
I am here to tell the truth
And if the truth condemns America,
she stands condemned."
I am the so many bones, of the so many black men and women,
That fell to ocean bottoms like tracks of the underwater railroad
That led the wrong way to freedom.
I am all the blank walls standing tall
A middle passage memorial
To the names we do not know.
I am Japanese-American families
Standing in US internment camps
concentrating on blank walls,
remembering Harriet Tubman,
And slow dancing with the ghosts of Cherokees
imprisoned in Alcatraz
before they admitted Alcatraz was a prison
and they called it a reservation.

I am all the people imprisoned by the lies we don't admit to
I am all the people trapped inside the history that never happened
I am the skeletons in the closet of people who died waiting for their
    truth to come out.
I am the truth coming out
I am America.

And if you say I am wrong,
That we are not our history,
If there is nothing but our present
Then we must re-examine our scriptures with an eye for
    historical context
And look at our constitution with a mind to reaffirm.
For we are not created equal until we say so,
And no commandments are contractually binding,
And all rights are alienable again.
And freedom isn't certain
But this is—
I am an American
And I pledge allegiance to no flag
And our States are not United.
And to the republic for which it stands
One nation under God
I say to you this:
There can be no one nation under God,
Unless that nation is the world.
For God made
the world
and man made
nations,
And if God were to honor man-made nations
He would do so under this condition . . .
That he honor them all equally,
The way he made them.
So to pledge to one

Is to pledge against others
And to pledge against others
Is to pledge against God
And I'm not ready to go to war with God.
And despite the fact that I think war is wrong . . .
I am an American.

And I pledge to no flag
but to the people . . .
who made it,
who wave it,
who salute it,
who burn it,
who hide behind it,
I pledge to you.
I pledge to see you clearly
And love you dearly
like people,
Like mortals,
Like flawed individuals
Who bring your flaws to my America
And sometimes make mistakes.
And when you do I will tell you,
And if you do not hear me
I will not get silent
But the opposite:
I will make noise.
You are wrong to go to war
You are wrong to ignore the homeless,
and exploit the poor.
You are wrong to put money
above life on this earth.
You are wrong to judge people
by how much they are worth.
You are wrong to think

you are entirely free,
If you want me to be silent because you don't agree.
I am an American
And I will not be silent.

I will not be silent because you will be
Or because you want me to be
Or because you think it wrong to disagree with my country.
You should read the Bill of Rights and understand . . .
This poem was my country's idea.
I am an American
And I will not be silent
I will not be silent
I will not be silent
And you should use these words against me.

———•◆•———

THE PURSUIT OF HAPPINESS

—ESSAY—

SELF-RELIANCE

RALPH WALDO EMERSON {1841}

Born into a family of non-conformist Puritan clergymen, and solitary by nature, Ralph Waldo Emerson (1803–1882) resigned from the ministry at the age of 29 and became a public lecturer. But his blend of German Transcendentalism, Eastern philosophy, and Yankee contrarianism found its immortal expression in essays such as "Self-Reliance" (1841), which often feel as though they were written in a state of ecstatic inspiration. Emerson believed that America had become a shallow, materialistic society infatuated with European manners and culture. He urged his readers to look within and discover their own natural genius—and the nature of God. "Self-Reliance" is Emerson's declaration of independence for the American soul. His credo— "Insist on yourself"—continues to strike a chord for mindful Americans; in the last few decades alone, it has reappeared as the injunctions "Do your own thing," "Follow your bliss," and "Just do it."

To believe your own thought, to believe that what is true for you in your private heart is true for all men,—that is genius. Speak your latent conviction, and it shall be the universal sense; for the inmost in due time becomes the outmost, and our first thought is rendered back to us by the trumpets of the Last Judgment. Familiar as the voice of the mind is to each, the highest merit we ascribe to Moses, Plato, and Milton is, that they set at naught books and traditions, and spoke not what men but what they thought. A man should learn to detect and watch that gleam of light which flashes across his mind from within, more than the lustre of the firmament of bards and sages. Yet he dismisses without notice his thought, because it is his. In every work of genius we recognize our own rejected thoughts: they come back to us with a certain alienated majesty. Great works of art have no more affecting lesson for us than this. They teach us to abide by our spontaneous impression with good-humored inflexibility then most when the whole cry of voices is on the other side. Else, to-morrow a stranger will say with masterly good sense precisely what we have thought and felt all the time, and we shall be forced to take with shame our own opinion from another.

There is a time in every man's education when he arrives at the conviction that envy is ignorance; that imitation is suicide; that he must take himself for better, for worse, as his portion; that though the wide universe is full of good, no kernel of nourishing corn can come to him but through his toil bestowed on that plot of ground which is given to him to till. The power which resides in him is new in nature, and none but he knows what that is which he can do, nor does he know until he has tried. Not for nothing one face, one character, one fact, makes much impression on him, and another none. This sculpture in the memory is not without preestablished harmony. The eye was placed where one ray should fall, that it might testify of that particular ray. We but half express ourselves, and are ashamed of that divine idea which each of us represents. It may be safely trusted as proportionate and of good issues, so it be faithfully imparted, but God will not have his work made manifest by cowards. A man is relieved and gay when he has put his heart into his work and done his best; but what he has said or done otherwise, shall give him no peace. It is a deliverance which does not deliver. In the attempt his genius deserts him; no muse befriends; no invention, no hope.

Trust thyself: every heart vibrates to that iron string. Accept the place the divine providence has found for you, the society of your contemporaries, the connection of events. Great men have always done so, and confided themselves childlike to the genius of their age, betraying their perception that the absolutely trustworthy was seated at their heart, working through their hands, predominating in all their being. And we are now men, and must accept in the highest mind the same transcendent destiny; and not minors and invalids in a protected corner, not cowards fleeing before a revolution, but guides, redeemers, and benefactors, obeying the Almighty effort, and advancing on Chaos and the Dark. . . .

Virtues are, in the popular estimate, rather the exception than the rule. There is the man *and* his virtues. Men do what is called a good action, as some piece of courage or charity, much as they would pay a fine in expiation of daily non-appearance on parade. Their works are done as an apology or extenuation of their living in the world,—as invalids and the insane pay a high board. Their virtues are penances. I do not wish to expiate, but to live. My life is for itself and not for a spectacle. I much prefer that it should be of a lower strain, so it be genuine and equal, than that it should be glittering and unsteady. I wish it to be sound and sweet, and not to need diet and bleeding. I ask primary evidence that you are a man, and refuse this appeal from the man to his actions. I know that for myself it makes no difference whether I do or forbear those actions which are reckoned excellent. I cannot consent to pay for a privilege where I have intrinsic right. Few and mean as my gifts may be, I actually am, and do not need for my own assurance or the assurance of my fellows any secondary testimony.

What I must do is all that concerns me, not what the people think. This rule, equally arduous in actual and in intellectual life, may serve for the whole distinction between greatness and meanness. It is the harder, because you will always find those who think they know what is your duty better than you know it. It is easy in the world to live after the world's opinion; it is easy in solitude to live after our own; but the great man is he who in the midst of the crowd keeps with perfect sweetness the independence of solitude. . . .

For nonconformity the world whips you with its displeasure. And therefore a man must know how to estimate a sour face. The by-standers look askance on him in the public street or in the friend's parlour. If this aversation had its origin in contempt and resistance like his own, he might well go home with a sad countenance; but the sour faces of the multitude, like their sweet faces, have no deep cause, but are put on and off as the wind blows and a newspaper directs. Yet is the discontent of the multitude more formidable than that of the senate and the college. It is easy enough for a firm man who knows the world to brook the rage of the cultivated classes. Their rage is decorous and prudent, for they are timid as being very vulnerable themselves. But when to their feminine rage the indignation of the people is added, when the ignorant and the poor are aroused, when the unintelligent brute force that lies at the bottom of society is made to growl and mow, it needs the habit of magnanimity and religion to treat it godlike as a trifle of no concernment.

The other terror that scares us from self-trust is our consistency; a reverence for our past act or word, because the eyes of others have no other data for computing our orbit than our past acts, and we are loath to disappoint them.

But why should you keep your head over your shoulder? Why drag about this corpse of your memory, lest you contradict somewhat you have stated in this or that public place? Suppose you should contradict yourself; what then? It seems to be a rule of wisdom never to rely on your memory alone, scarcely even in acts of pure memory, but to bring the past for judgment into the thousand-eyed present, and live ever in a new day. In your metaphysics you have denied personality to the Deity: yet when the devout motions of the soul come, yield to them heart and life, though they should clothe God with shape and color. Leave your theory, as Joseph his coat in the hand of the harlot, and flee.

A foolish consistency is the hobgoblin of little minds, adored by little statesmen and philosophers and divines. With consistency a great soul has simply nothing to do. He may as well concern himself with his shadow on the wall. Speak what you think now in hard words, and to-morrow speak what to-morrow thinks in hard words again, though it contradict every thing you said to-day.—'Ah, so you shall be sure to be misunderstood.'—Is it so bad, then, to be misunderstood? Pythagoras was misunderstood, and Socrates, and Jesus, and Luther, and Copernicus, and Galileo, and Newton, and every pure and wise spirit that ever took flesh. To be great is to be misunderstood.

I suppose no man can violate his nature. All the sallies of his will are rounded in by the law of his being, as the inequalities of Andes and Himmalaya are insignificant in the curve of the sphere. Nor does it matter how you gauge and try him. A character is like an acrostic or Alexandrian stanza;—read it forward, backward, or across, it still spells the same thing. In this pleasing, contrite wood-life which God allows me, let me record day by day my honest thought without prospect or retrospect, and, I cannot doubt, it will be found symmetrical, though I mean it not, and see it not. My book should smell of pines and resound with the hum of insects. The swallow over my window should interweave that thread or straw he carries in his bill into my web also. We pass for what we are. Character teaches above our wills. Men imagine that they communicate their virtue or vice only by overt actions, and do not see that virtue or vice emit a breath every moment.

There will be an agreement in whatever variety of actions, so they be each honest and natural in their hour. For of one will, the actions will be harmonious, however unlike they seem. These varieties are lost sight of at a little distance, at a little height of thought. One tendency unites them all. The voyage of the best ship is a zigzag line of a hundred tacks. See the line from a sufficient distance, and it straightens itself to the average tendency. Your genuine action will explain itself, and will explain your other genuine actions. Your conformity explains nothing. . . .

And now at last the highest truth on this subject remains unsaid; probably cannot be said; for all that we say is the far-off remembering of the intuition. That thought, by what I can now nearest approach to say it, is this. When good is near you, when you have life in yourself, it is not by any known or accustomed way; you shall not discern the foot-prints of any other; you shall not see the face of man; you shall not hear any name;—the way, the thought, the good, shall be wholly strange and new. It shall exclude example and experience. You take the way from man, not to man. All persons that ever existed are its forgotten ministers. Fear and hope are alike beneath it. There is somewhat low even in hope. In the hour of vision, there is nothing that can be called gratitude, nor properly joy. The soul raised over passion beholds identity and eternal causation, perceives the self-existence of Truth and Right, and calms itself with knowing that all things go well. Vast spaces of nature, the Atlantic Ocean, the South Sea,—long intervals of time, years, centuries,—are of no account. This which I think and feel underlay every former state of life and circumstances, as it does underlie my present, and what is called life, and what is called death. . . .

So use all that is called Fortune. Most men gamble with her, and gain all, and lose all, as her wheel rolls. But do thou leave as unlawful these winnings, and deal with Cause and Effect, the chancellors of God. In the Will work and acquire, and thou hast chained the wheel of Chance, and shalt sit hereafter out of fear from her rotations. A political victory, a rise of rents, the recovery of your sick, or the return of your absent friend, or some other favorable event, raises your spirits, and you think good days are preparing for you. Do not believe it. Nothing can bring you peace but yourself. Nothing can bring you peace but the triumph of principles.

—POEM—

THE ROAD NOT TAKEN

ROBERT FROST {1920}

In "The Road Not Taken," published in 1920, Robert Frost meditates at a fork in the road on free will, fate, and the choices that inevitably must be made by individuals—and, at times, entire nations.

Two roads diverged in a yellow wood,
And sorry I could not travel both
And be one traveler, long I stood
And looked down one as far as I could
To where it bent in the undergrowth;

Then took the other, as just as fair,
And having perhaps the better claim
Because it was grassy and wanted wear;
Though as for that, the passing there
Had worn them really about the same,

And both that morning equally lay
In leaves no step had trodden black.
Oh, I marked the first for another day!
Yet knowing how way leads on to way
I doubted if I should ever come back.

I shall be telling this with a sigh
Somewhere ages and ages hence:
Two roads diverged in a wood, and I,
I took the one less traveled by,
And that has made all the difference.

—ESSAY—

COURAGE

HARRIET MCBRYDE JOHNSON {APRIL 2001}

Harriet McBryde Johnson (b. 1957) has lived most of her life in Charleston, South Carolina, where her solo law practice specializes in Social Security Disability, the Americans with Disabilities Act, and other disability issues. She has been involved locally and nationally with the disability rights movement for more than 20 years. As a child, she attended special-education classes until the age of 13, when she was invited to leave because she was campaigning to get the teacher fired.

It's a frequent irritation in my life. I'm out on the street, in a shop, or in line for a movie. Someone comes up to me and says, "I really admire your courage."

It's awkward, to say the least. Usually I look for a quick getaway. But sometimes I am moved to question, "Just what do you know about me that makes you think I have courage?"

The answer is usually vague. You're a fighter. You have a positive outlook. You haven't given up. When I press for specifics, things often get strange. Like when this woman called me a "fighter," and then offered as specific proof, "Well—you know, I've seen you at concerts for years."

In fact, I think I know what's going on. These people have to be reacting to my appearance. How do I look? This is radio so I'll tell you. Petite, white, female, rolling in a power wheelchair. I have one of those neuromuscular diseases that are paraded around every Labor Day on the Jerry Lewis Telethon. I've had it since birth. At age 43, my spine is spectacularly twisted. After so many years of muscle wasting, I'm thinner than a supermodel.

For some people, I represent scary things. Disability, deformity, difference, death. Not knowing anything about my life, they expect people like me to be afraid to show ourselves in public; they expect us to languish in despair or retreat into impossible dreams of a cure. Maybe they expect us to just curl up and die.

If we don't do what's expected, they figure, we must have lots of courage. Courage to carry on about.

My experience is far from unique. From the wheelchair athlete to the person in the iron lung, people with conspicuous disabilities are subject to intrusion from courage-mongers. The mere fact that we have a disease or survived an accident is enough to provoke this kind of attention. The phenomenon is regularly analyzed in the disability press. In the disability rights movement, the very word "courage" provokes moans, groans, and out-and-out fury.

Yes, we've tried to set the public straight. We make it clear that we enjoy life. I did tell that woman that it doesn't take courage to go to a concert—at least, not if you like music. When people marvel, as they often do, that it takes courage for me to practice law and do local politics, I explain that some things—listening, talking, reading, writing—come easy to me, and it's natural for me to do what I do. I say I'm entirely comfortable in my body, the only body I've ever lived in.

But, more often than not, all this is taken for bravado, further proof of amazing courage. Some people don't believe the plain truth when we run over their feet with it.

Sometimes I'm told, "If I were like you, I couldn't handle it." I respond, sometimes nicely, sometimes not, "You'd handle it. People do. It's only sensible."

But they can't accept our truth. They've been brainwashed by the cure industry and by the stereotypes of millennia. They're programmed to see extraordinary courage in our most ordinary doings. It's all about their fears and low expectations, not our realities.

Perhaps what's most irksome about this projected, false courage is that it makes the real thing invisible. Through disability rights work, I've come to know people with real courage. People who accept challenges I can only imagine. People who put their bodies on the line and do civil disobedience, looking to jailers for the help they need to get washed, to use the toilet, and to turn over at night. People who demand freedom when teams of professionals and their own families insist that they're better off in institutions. And people who embrace labels like "cripple" and "mad" and the parts of themselves that are most scorned by the larger world.

To use another word that causes groans among disability rights people, the real courage these people show is, truly, inspirational. It has inspired me.

Now, I've never been arrested, and have certainly never stared down the barrel of a gun or dashed into a burning building. I have no desire for life-and-death heroism. But from time to time I do need inspiration—to go out on a limb, to try something new, to accept a task someone else has reasonably declined, to risk looking foolish for a higher purpose. Witnessing real courage has given me that inspiration.

The false idea of courage harbored by those well-meaning people on the street separates people with disabilities from the larger society. It declares our very presence astonishing, our everyday lives frightening. In contrast, we all, disabled or not, share a capacity for real courage—seeing beyond self-interest, and risking things we value for a greater good.

— LETTER —

LETTER TO HIS SON

WILLIAM CARLOS WILLIAMS {MARCH 13, 1935}

Long before he took his place as one of America's most influential poets, William Carlos Williams (1883–1963) studied medicine and rose to become head pediatrician at the General Hospital in Paterson, New Jersey. In his poetry, including his five-volume epic poem named after that working-class city, Williams, much like Walt Whitman before him, strove to capture the essence of ordinary American speech and life. In a letter to his college-age son, he captures the essence of what it means to be a father.

Dearest Bill:

This I can say for certain, you seem not far different from what I was myself at your age. I don't mind saying I went through hell, what with worrying about my immortal soul and my hellish itch to screw almost any female I could get my hands on—which I never did. I can tell you it is almost as vivid today as it was then when I hear you speak of it. Everything seems upside down and one's self the very muck under one's foot.

It comes from many things, my dear boy, but mostly from the inevitable maladjustment consequent upon growing up in a more or less civilized environment. Any bum on the street, any crook who is his own master at the expense of the law is happier than the man who is trying to mould himself to a society which revolts his entire manhood. We do not want to fit into anything, we want to be free, potent, self-reliant—and that society cannot and will not permit. Nor would we be really satisfied if we found ourselves antisocial in our success. That is the situation of the great fortunes, the Morgans, the Vanderbilts, as well as the Al Capones of the world. They are "free" but at a terrific cost.

But more immediately, your difficulties arise from a lack of balance in your daily life, a lack of balance which has to be understood and withstood—for it cannot be avoided for the present. I refer to the fact that your intellectual life, for the moment, has eclipsed the physical life, the animal life, the normal he-man life, which every man needs and craves. If you were an athlete, a powerful body, one who could be a hero on the field or the diamond, a *Big* Hero, many of your mental tortures would be lulled to sleep. But you cannot be that—so what? You'll have to wait and take it by a different course.

And after all, the athletes haven't it as easy as it seems. They may be soothed during the difficult years but they've got to face the music some day, and that some day may be too late. They can't always be physical figures, and when the real test comes later, they often fold up and disappear completely.

You, dear Bill, have a magnificent opportunity to enjoy life ahead of you. You have sensibility (even if it drives you nuts at times), which will be the source of keen pleasures later and the source of useful accomplishments too. You've got a brain, as you have been told *ad nauseam*. But these are the very things which are tormenting you, the very things which are your most valued possessions and which will be your joy tomorrow. Sure you are sentimental, sure you admire a man like Wordsworth and his "Tintern Abbey." It is natural, it is the correct reaction of your age in life. It is also a criticism of Wordsworth as you will see later. All I can say about that is, wait! Not wait cynically, idly, but wait while looking, believing, getting fooled, changing from day to day. Wait with the only kind of faith I have ever recognized, the faith that says I wanna know! I wanna see! I think I will understand when I do know and see. Meanwhile I'm not making any final judgments. Wait it out. Don't worry too much. You've got time. You're all right. You're reacting to life in the only way an intelligent, sensitive young man in a college can. In another year you'll enter another sphere of existence, the practical one. The knowledge, abstract now, which seems unrelated to sense to you (at times) will get a different color.

Sooner or later we all of us knock our heads against the ceiling of the world. It's like breaking a record: the last fifth of a second, which marks the difference between a good runner and a world beater is the hardest part of the whole proceeding. I mean that you, Bill, will be one of the minds of the world tomorrow. You will be the one, you and your generation, who will have to push knowledge of all sorts that inch ahead, which will make life tolerable in your day. Knowledge is limited, very limited, and it is only because you are in the preliminary stages of knowing that you think men, certain men, know so much more than you do. They may know a little more, but not the great amount that you imagine. For this reason, wait! Believe in yourself and your generation. Take it with a smile. That's what they mean when they speak of humor. It doesn't mean a guffaw or a grin. It means steadiness of nerves that is willing to bide its time, certain that with time a human adjustment can and will be made. It is the most that any man has ever been able to do.

Jumping to practical things: Have the Ford put in condition up there if you think the local mechanics can be trusted. Send me the bill. . . .

Mother and I both send love. Don't let *anything* get your goat and don't think you have to duck anything in life. There is a way out for every man who has the intellectual fortitude to go on in the face of difficulties.

Yours,
Dad

— ESSAY —

ADVICE, LIKE YOUTH, PROBABLY JUST WASTED ON THE YOUNG

MARY SCHMICH {JUNE 1, 1997}

When long-time *Chicago Tribune* columnist Mary Schmich (b. 1954) sat down to write her June 1, 1997 column, she could not have foreseen that it would soon be the stuff that urban legends are made of. Her arch, pithy words of wisdom became a hit in cyberspace, soon turning up as a commencement address that Kurt Vonnegut had given at the Massachusetts Institute of Technology. Vonnegut corrected the error, but not before millions of people had read Schmich's misattributed advice for living a good life. E-mail has made the column, which also became a book and a hit song, one of the country's most widely read documents, even more widely read than the comic strip "Brenda Starr," which Schmich has written since 1985.

Inside every adult lurks a graduation speaker dying to get out, some world-weary pundit eager to pontificate on life to young people who'd rather be Rollerblading. Most of us, alas, will never be invited to sow our words of wisdom among an audience of caps and gowns, but there's no reason we can't entertain ourselves by composing a Guide to Life for Graduates.

I encourage anyone over 26 to try this and thank you for indulging my attempt.

239

Ladies and gentlemen of the class of '97:

Wear sunscreen.

If I could offer you only one tip for the future, sunscreen would be it. The long-term benefits of sunscreen have been proved by scientists, whereas the rest of my advice has no basis more reliable than my own meandering experience. I will dispense this advice now.

Enjoy the power and beauty of your youth. Oh, never mind. You will not understand the power and beauty of your youth until they've faded. But trust me, in 20 years, you'll look back at photos of yourself and recall in a way you can't grasp now how much possibility lay before you and how fabulous you really looked. You are not as fat as you imagine.

Don't worry about the future. Or worry, but know that worrying is as effective as trying to solve an algebra equation by chewing bubble gum. The real troubles in your life are apt to be things that never crossed your worried mind, the kind that blindside you at 4 p.m. on some idle Tuesday.

Do one thing every day that scares you.

Sing.

Don't be reckless with other people's hearts. Don't put up with people who are reckless with yours.

Floss.

Don't waste your time on jealousy. Sometimes you're ahead, sometimes you're behind. The race is long and, in the end, it's only with yourself.

Remember compliments you receive. Forget the insults. If you succeed in doing this, tell me how.

Keep your old love letters. Throw away your old bank statements.

Stretch.

Don't feel guilty if you don't know what you want to do with your life. The most interesting people I know didn't know at 22 what they wanted to do with their lives. Some of the most interesting 40-year-olds I know still don't.

Get plenty of calcium. Be kind to your knees. You'll miss them when they're gone. Maybe you'll marry, maybe you won't. Maybe you'll have children, maybe you won't. Maybe you'll divorce at 40, maybe you'll dance the funky chicken on your 75th wedding anniversary. Whatever you do, don't congratulate yourself too much, or berate yourself either. Your choices are half chance. So are everybody else's.

Enjoy your body. Use it every way you can. Don't be afraid of it or of what other people think of it. It's the greatest instrument you'll ever own.

Dance, even if you have nowhere to do it but your living room.

Read the directions, even if you don't follow them.

Do not read beauty magazines. They will only make you feel ugly.

Get to know your parents. You never know when they'll be gone for good. Be nice to your siblings. They're your best link to your past and the people most likely to stick with you in the future.

Understand that friends come and go, but with a precious few you should hold on. Work hard to bridge the gaps in geography and lifestyle, because the older you get, the more you need the people who knew you when you were young.

Live in New York City once, but leave before it makes you hard. Live in Northern California once, but leave before it makes you soft. Travel.

Accept certain inalienable truths: Prices will rise. Politicians will philander. You, too, will get old. And when you do, you'll fantasize that when you were young, prices were reasonable, politicians were noble and children respected their elders.

Respect your elders.

Don't expect anyone else to support you. Maybe you have a trust fund. Maybe you'll have a wealthy spouse. But you never know when either one might run out.

Don't mess too much with your hair or by the time you're 40 it will look 85.

Be careful whose advice you buy, but be patient with those who supply it. Advice is a form of nostalgia. Dispensing it is a way of fishing the past from the disposal, wiping it off, painting over the ugly parts and recycling it for more than it's worth.

But trust me on the sunscreen.

———•◦•———

— POEM —

POEM OF REMEMBRANCES FOR A GIRL OR A BOY OF THESE STATES

WALT WHITMAN {1856}

Whitman's *Leaves of Grass* was a poem-in-progress, periodically revised and expanded to accommodate the poet's ecstatic, garrulous, sweeping view of American life. In this excerpt of a poem from the second edition of *Leaves of Grass,* Whitman invokes the Declaration of Independence to bolster his historically precocious vision of liberated women.

You just maturing youth! You male or female!

Remember the organic compact of These States!

Remember the pledge of the Old Thirteen thence-
    forward to the rights, life, liberty, equality, of man!
Remember what was promulged by the founders,
    ratified by The States, signed in black and
    white by the Commissioners, read by Washington at the head of
      the army!
Remember the purposes of the founders!—Remember Washington!
Remember the copious humanity streaming from
    every direction toward America!
Remember the hospitality that belongs to nations
    and men!—(Cursed be nation, woman, man,
    without hospitality!)
Remember, government is to subserve individuals!
Not any, not the President, is to have one jot more
    than you or me,
Not any habitant of America is to have one jot less
    than you or me.

Anticipate when the thirty or fifty millions are to
    become the hundred, or two hundred, or five
    hundred millions, of equal freemen and free-
    women, amicably joined.

Recall ages—One age is but a part—ages are
    but a part,
Recall the angers, bickerings, delusions,
    superstitions of the idea of caste,
Recall the bloody cruelties and crimes.

Anticipate the best women!
I say an unnumbered new race of hardy and
    well-defined women are to spread through all
    These States,
I say a girl fit for These States must be free,
    capable, dauntless, just the same as a boy.

Anticipate your own life—retract with merciless
    power,
Shirk nothing—retract in time—Do you see those
    errors, diseases, weaknesses, lies, thefts?
Do you see that lost character?—Do you see
    decay, consumption, rum-drinking, dropsy,
    fever, mortal cancer or inflammation?
Do you see death, and the approach of death?

Think of the soul!
I swear to you that body of yours gives proportions
    to your soul somehow to live in other spheres,
I do not know how, but I know it is so.
Think of loving and being loved!
I swear to you, whoever you are, you can interfuse
    yourself with such things that everybody that
    sees you shall look longingly upon you!

Think of the past!
I warn you that in a little while others will find
    their past in you and your times.

The race is never separated—nor man nor woman escapes,
All is inextricable—things, spirits, nature, nations,
    you too—from precedents you come.

Recall the ever-welcome defiers!
    (The mothers precede them;)

Recall the sages, poets, saviours, inventors,
    lawgivers, of the earth,
Recall Christ, brother of rejected persons—
    brother of slaves, felons, idiots, and of insane
    and diseased persons.

Think of the time when you was not yet born!
Think of times you stood at the side of the dying!
Think of the time when your own body will be dying!

Think of spiritual results!
Sure as the earth swims through the heavens,
    does every one of its objects pass into
    spiritual results!

Think of manhood, and you to be a man!
Do you count manhood, and the sweet of manhood,
    nothing?

Think of womanhood, and you to be a woman!
The creation is womanhood,
Have I not said that womanhood involves all?
Have I not told how the universe has nothing
    better than the best womanhood?

—LETTER—

LETTER TO WALT WHITMAN

MARK TWAIN {MAY 24, 1889}

Although cynical by nature, Mark Twain (1835–1910) was infatuated with technological progress—he was the first professional author to turn out a book on a typewriter. He was 54 when he wrote this optimistic letter to Walt Whitman on the poet's 70th birthday. However, for Twain, the next decade would be filled with sorrow, frustration, and uncertainty. The same man who once dreamed of making a fortune in land speculation and instead made a name and fortune with books such as *Tom Sawyer* and *Huckleberry Finn*, had to deal with business failures, bankruptcy, the sudden death of his favorite daughter, and the fear that his best writing days were behind him.

May 24, 1889

To Walt Whitman:

You have lived just the seventy years which are the greatest in the world's history and richest in benefit and advancement to its peoples. These seventy years have done more to widen the interval between man and the other animals than was accomplished by any of the five centuries which preceded them.

What great births you have witnessed! The steam press, the steamship, the steelship, the railroad, the perfect cotton gin, the telegraph, the phonograph, photogravure, the electrotype, the gaslight, the electric light, the sewing machine and the amazing infinitely varied and innumerable products of coal tar, those latest and strangest marvels of a marvelous age. And you have seen even greater births than these; for you have seen the application of anesthesia to surgery-practice, whereby the ancient dominion of pain, which began with the first created life, came to an end on this earth forever, you have seen the slave set free, you have seen monarchy banished from France and reduced in England to a machine which makes an imposing show of diligence and attention to business, but isn't connected with the works. Yes you have indeed seen much—but tarry for a while, for the greatest is yet to come. Wait thirty years, and *then* look out over the earth! You shall see marvels upon marvels added to those whose nativity you have witnessed; and conspicuous above them you shall see their formidable Result—man at almost his full stature at last!—and still growing, visibly growing while you look. Wait till you see that great figure appear, and catch the far glint of the sun upon his banner; then you may depart satisfied, as knowing you have seen him for whom the earth was made, and that he will proclaim that human wheat is more than human tears, and proceed to organize human values on that basis.

Mark Twain

— S P E E C H —

COMMENCEMENT ADDRESS AT JAMES MADISON UNIVERSITY

WILLIAM SAFIRE {MAY 5, 2001}

William Safire (b. 1929)—journalist, speechwriter, historian, novelist, lexicographer—worked on Dwight Eisenhower's 1952 presidential campaign, and later became a senior speechwriter in the Nixon White House, from which he escaped in time to write a history of Nixon's pre-Watergate administration. As a lexicographer, he is the author of *Safire's New Political Dictionary*, a half-million-word study of the words that have inspired and inflamed the electorate. *Lend Me Your Ears*, his anthology of the world's greatest speeches, has become a classic. Thirty years ago, he began writing a twice-weekly column for *The New York Times*, opining from the point of view of a libertarian conservative. He is a winner of the Pulitzer Prize for distinguished commentary, and is now a member of the Pulitzer Board.

Before I begin this commencement address, I have something to say. That is, I join with you and all lovers of liberty to salute James Madison on his quattromillennial year. There are those who'll respond, "Madison's what?" We all know this is the year we celebrate his 250th birthday. You had quite a week here about that very subject. But what's with the word: *quattromillennial*? The word was coined at my request. Last month at the James Madison Building of the Library of Congress, a dinner was held to salute the contributions made to our nation by the man you all know here as the Father of the Constitution. A famous jurist whispered to me, "You're a wordsmith. What do you call two centennials and a half?" I did what all professional lexicographers are trained to do: I turned to the Librarian of Congress, Jim Billington, and said, "Yeah, a hundred and fifty is sesquicentennial. What's the word for 250?" On the spot, he coined the word *quattromillennial*. And it was particularly apt for this reason: Americans have been thinking on past national birthdays of bicentennials and other multiples of a hundred years. But with Madison at 250, we should start taking the long view—a quarter of a thousand years.

That's because the experiment that Madison helped conduct in Philadelphia in the 18th century is working better than any of the worried men working secretly through that hot summer had a right to expect. They produced what Ben Franklin called "A republic, if you can keep it"—and we kept it. There's now reason to believe that if any nation exists in the distant future, this university's class of 3001 will be celebrating James Madison's millennium.

These long-range thoughts are brought to mind by another ceremony that took place in Washington last month. The National Archives will soon be undergoing renovation and putting some of its treasures on the road to other libraries around the country. They range from a copy of the Emancipation Proclamation to letters from the Founding Fathers, including Madison, down to an application during World War II from John Wayne to become an American spy. Because one of the least valuable items in the

247

traveling collection is a speech that I wrote a generation ago, I was asked by the National Archivist to give its background. And, briefly, here it is.

It was back in '69. We were just about to launch Apollo 11, our reach to put men on the moon. I had prepared a speech for President Nixon hailing this event, welcoming the men back. Then one of the astronauts said to me quietly, "In case of disaster, do you have another speech?" I said, "What do you mean?" And he said, "Well, what do you say to the widows?" Then it hit me—that these men were, indeed, not just off on a great adventure, but were taking their lives in their hands. At a crucial moment, when the lunar module was on the moon, the crisis would come when the men tried to get back up off the moon into the command module. And, if they didn't, they would just be forced to—to use the euphemism—"close down communication" and starve to death on the moon. Well, of course, that did not happen. The standby speech was never given. And, 30 years later, somebody digging around in the Archives, probably looking for some more scandals, came up with that speech. Tim Russert on NBC—with the three astronauts there, Neil Armstrong and [Michael] Collins and Buzz Aldrin—read that speech to them, about how proud America was of its lost heroes on the moon. And there was a lump in the throat. One of the astronauts said to me afterwards, "It's a good idea never to count your chickens, never to assume success." That little speech is now part of the National Archives. Frankly, I had forgotten it, because I never even kept a copy. The lesson there, besides never taking success for granted, is: Whatever you do in life, keep a souvenir.

The third thing I want to say before my address also touches on your university's namesake. An auction was held in Bethesda, Maryland, three days ago. It included letters from presidents Washington, Madison and Jackson. Knowing I was coming here today, I read Madison's letter. It was to Benjamin Franklin's grandson in 1818 in reply to a letter trying to sell a subscription to a new journal the young man was starting. Madison did not subscribe, noting with disapproval the licentiousness of the press, but wished the young man well and said he would be pleased to accept the newspaper for nothing. Thanks to his First Amendment and the freedom of expression that it enshrines, I can tell you today—James Madison was cheap. His letter, by the way, sold at auction for $4,000, which would delight him.

You're now wondering: When do we get the commencement address? When do we start with the heavy dose of advice that we don't need and will quickly forget? I will, as the occasion demands, impart some warm words of wisdom today that you can wrap around you to take out into the cold, cruel world. ("Cold, cruel world" is a metaphor we use on hot days.) Over the years, in politics and in journalism, I've collected these words of wisdom—not my own advice, and not the usual proverbs that guided our grandfathers. But "views you can use"—sage new sayings and fresh adages that will help you claw your way up what Prime Minister Benjamin Disraeli called "the greasy pole of success." I should warn you—this dozen is offbeat. Some of the sayings are not grounded in middle-class morality. A few even border on cynicism. But they distill some of the off-the-record practical wisdom of our great leaders.

One is attributed to Simon Cameron, Lincoln's first secretary of war. It was: "You scratch my back and I'll scratch yours." Psychologists express this today in terms of interpersonal dynamics—something to do with mutual respect. It is sometimes derogated as "the art of the deal," or even prosecuted as a venial quid pro quo. But in a legal, practical sense: Two-way backscratching will get you far.

A second underground proverb is attributed to Claude Swanson, FDR's Secretary of the Navy, on when it is wise to abandon ship. The proverb goes: "When the water reaches the upper level, follow the rats." This somewhat lugubrious metaphor attacks the notion of excessive, prolonged loyalty, such as that practiced by the boy who stood on the burning deck when all the rest had very wisely fled. The same idea has been more recently set forth in a country song, sung by poker players: "You gotta know when to hold 'em and when to fold 'em." I'm the last one to knock steadfastness, but as John Kennedy said, "Sometimes party loyalty asks too much." Don't follow the leader over the cliff.

A more courageous bit of advice was the motto of President Harry Truman, in the teeth of constant criticism: "If you can't stand the heat, get out of the kitchen." In our time, this has been adopted wholeheartedly by many in the women's movement. Toward the end of his elected term, however, Truman was discouraged, and offered this advice to those unwilling to endure the loneliness of power. Truman said, "If you want a friend in Washington, buy a dog." To that I would add, "Do not pour your heart out to just anyone. Choose a journalist you trust."

Woodrow Wilson, who was president of Princeton before becoming president of the United States, is the source of this political saying about how to handle yourself when engaged in a contest with a fool. He said, "Never murder a man who is committing suicide." A modern journalist version of this is: "Kick 'em when they're up." The faculty here will appreciate the story of Wilson, who when asked why he left academic life to campaign for the White House, replied, "I wanted to get out of politics."

John F. Kennedy and the whole Kennedy clan had this motto to answer those who too often turned the other cheek: "Forgive—but never forget." A related political adage is: "Revenge is sweetest when tasted cold," and is often expressed, "Don't get mad, get even." In recent years, the Clinton political consultant, James Carville, refined that to: "Don't get mad. Don't get even. Get elected, and then get even."

The sixth in this collection of unconventional guidance needed to get on in real life is a saying back in the '30s of the labor leader Walter Reuther about how to tell a Communist. This is an important notion to grasp for all of us who are too convoluted in our thinking to deal with the obvious, and it goes: "If it walks like a duck and quacks like a duck, then it just may be a duck."

A great economist, Walter Heller, speaking about what he thought was the need for wage and price controls, offered this quotation that he attributed to the gangster, Al Capone. Capone said, "You can get a lot more done with a kind word and a gun than with a kind word alone." I wrote the speech for Richard Nixon that imposed wage and price controls, which turned out to be a policy disaster. Some of the guys broke into the Watergate; I froze wages and prices. Where was the greater sin?

As a *New York Times* columnist, I won my Pulitzer for driving a top budget official, who was in financial trouble, out of Washington. He's now my good friend, and he is the author of the wise words so often quoted today to restrain the zealots of unnecessary reform. Bert Lance's adage was: "If it ain't broke, don't fix it."

Here is offbeat advice for the disillusioned dot-com investors in the bleachers. First, I'll have to explain that in olden times, there were mechanical tickers that spewed out tape on which were imprinted stock prices, and during campaigns and parades hailing returning heroes, this tickertape was thrown out of Wall Street windows like confetti. All right, you've got the old metaphor. Now to the adage of Fiorella La Guardia, mayor of New York: "Tickertape ain't spaghetti." Maybe I should have pointed out that spaghetti is now called pasta. I suppose that adage's language is thoroughly outdated, but the thought is worth preserving. In politics and in life, praise is not nourishment. Tickertape ain't spaghetti.

Let me take a chance at another outdated metaphor: If you hope to make diplomacy your dodge, remember this advice from Winston Churchill. Before World War II, he was asked by the British ambassador in Rome whether to raise an issue with Count Ciano, the foreign minister, or with the dictator himself, Benito Mussolini. Said Churchill: "Never hold discussions with the monkey when the organ grinder is in the room."

More philosophical and fatalistic, perhaps, and less practical, is this bit of Middle Eastern wisdom, so old as not to have a source. It goes: "The dogs may bark, but the caravan moves on." It's a nice reminder to those of us in the media who think that the power of the press can be as great as the power of unimpressed people. It's not the critic who counts; it's the doer who makes the caravan move on.

Finally, the 12th proverb, from Abraham Lincoln. This is not one of those high-minded quotations from his magnificent and mysterious inaugural addresses. It's more in the nature of his reply to a man who came to the White House and saw the president, brush in hand, shining his shoes. "Mr. President," said the astonished visitor, "Do you black your own boots?" And Lincoln glowered back at him, and replied, "Whose boots do you think I black?" But that's not the proverb I have in mind, which has to do with the futility of arguing against great shifts in public opinion. It's one that can't be found in Lincoln's speeches, but some scholars attribute this folk wisdom to him. I've always committed it to memory and I don't have to read it today: "If you have an elephant on a string, and the elephant starts to run, better let him run."

Think about that elephant, my graduated friends, as you choose your battles in life. Think also about the foolishness of fixing the unbroken and think about what to do when the water reaches the upper level. Think about how to address your message to the producer grinding at the organ and not the salesman with the cup. And consider whether you want to bark at the caravan or be a part of it.

And if long commencement speeches from Dutch-uncle orators irritate you, don't get mad. Don't even get even. Do as I did, get elected a media biggie and then get even. And so happy graduation day, graduates, and happy quattromillennial Jimmy Madison, wherever you are.

—ESSAY—

THE MYTH OF SISYPHUS

ALBERT CAMUS {1955}

French existentialist writer and Nobel Prize winner Albert Camus (1913–1960) spent his impoverished childhood in North Africa. He escaped through academics—philosophy, mainly—and soccer, a game from which he would claim he had learned his entire sense of ethics. After stints in the auto parts and shipping businesses, he found a home in journalism and the theater. During World War II, he became one of the leading writers and editors of the French Resistance and went on to write, among other classics, the novels *The Stranger* and *The Plague*. He himself was dogged by misfortune, including a string of failed marriages, a long bout with tuberculosis, and feuds with colleagues, including long-time friend Jean-Paul Sartre. In a tragic irony, he was killed in an automobile accident, the manner of death he most dreaded. In this title essay from *The Myth of Sisyphus*, Camus meditates on the possibility of happiness.

The gods had condemned Sisyphus to ceaselessly rolling a rock to the top of a mountain, whence the stone would fall back of its own weight.

They had thought with some reason that there is no more dreadful punishment than futile and hopeless labor.

If one believes Homer, Sisyphus was the wisest and most prudent of mortals. According to another tradition, however, he was disposed to practice the profession of highwayman. I see no contradiction in this. Opinions differ as to the reasons why he became the futile laborer of the underworld. To begin with, he is accused of a certain levity in regard to the gods. He stole their secrets. Ægina, the daughter of Æsopus, was carried off by Jupiter. The father was shocked by that disappearance and complained to Sisyphus. He, who knew of the abduction, offered to tell about it on condition that Æsopus would give water to the citadel of Corinth. To the celestial thunderbolts he preferred the benediction of water. He was punished for this in the underworld. Homer tells us also that Sisyphus had put Death in chains. Pluto could not endure the sight of his deserted, silent empire. He dispatched the god of war, who liberated Death from the hands of her conqueror.

It is said that Sisyphus, being near to death, rashly wanted to test his wife's love. He ordered her to cast his unburied body into the middle of the public square. Sisyphus woke up in the underworld. And there, annoyed by an obedience so contrary to human love, he obtained from Pluto permission to return to earth in order to chastise his wife. But when he had seen again the face of this world, enjoyed water and sun, warm stones and the sea, he no longer wanted to go back to the infernal darkness. Recalls, signs of anger, warnings were of no avail. Many years more he lived facing the curve of the gulf, the sparkling sea, and the smiles of earth. A decree of the gods was necessary. Mercury came and seized the impudent man by the collar and, snatching him from his joys, led him forcibly back to the underworld, where his rock was ready for him.

You have already grasped that Sisyphus is the absurd hero. He *is*, as much through his passions as through his torture. His scorn of the gods, his hatred of death, and his passion for life won him that unspeakable penalty in which the whole being is exerted toward accomplishing nothing. This is the price that must be paid for the passions of this earth. Nothing is told us about Sisyphus in the underworld. Myths are made for the imagination to breathe life into them. As for this myth, one sees merely the whole effort of a body straining to raise the huge stone, to roll it, and push it up a slope a hundred times over; one sees the face screwed up, the cheek tight against the stone, the shoulder bracing the clay-covered mass, the foot wedging it, the fresh start with arms outstretched, the wholly human security of two earth-clotted hands. At the very end of his long effort measured by skyless space and time without depth, the purpose is achieved. Then Sisyphus watches the stone rush down in a few moments toward that lower world whence he will have to push it up again toward the summit. He goes back down to the plain.

It is during that return, that pause, that Sisyphus interests me. A face that toils so close to stones is already stone itself! I see that man going back down with a heavy yet measured step toward the torment of which he will never know the end. That hour like a breathing-space which returns as surely as his suffering, that is the hour of consciousness. At each of those moments when he leaves the heights and gradually sinks toward the lairs of the gods, he is superior to his fate. He is stronger than his rock.

If this myth is tragic, that is because its hero is conscious. Where would his torture be, indeed, if at every step the hope of succeeding upheld him? The workman of today works everyday in his life at the same tasks, and his fate is no less absurd. But it is tragic only at the rare moments when it becomes conscious. Sisyphus, proletarian of the gods, powerless and rebellious, knows the whole extent of his wretched condition: it is what he thinks of during his descent. The lucidity that was to constitute his torture at the same time crowns his victory. There is no fate that cannot be surmounted by scorn.

If the descent is thus sometimes performed in sorrow, it can also take place in joy. This word is not too much. Again I fancy Sisyphus returning toward his rock, and the sorrow was in the beginning. When the images of earth cling too tightly to memory, when the call of happiness becomes too insistent, it happens that melancholy rises in man's heart: this is the rock's victory, this is the rock itself. The boundless grief is too heavy to bear. These are our nights of Gethsemane. But crushing truths perish from being acknowledged. Thus, Œdipus at the outset obeys fate without knowing it. But from the moment he knows, his tragedy begins. Yet at the same moment, blind and desperate, he realizes that the only bond linking him to the world is the cool hand of a girl. Then a tremendous remark rings out: "Despite so many ordeals, my advanced age and the nobility of my soul make me conclude that all is well."

Sophocles' Œdipus, like Dostoevsky's Kirilov, thus gives the recipe for the absurd victory. Ancient wisdom confirms modern heroism.

One does not discover the absurd without being tempted to write a manual of happiness. "What!—by such narrow ways—?" There is but one world, however. Happiness and the absurd are two sons of the same earth. They are inseparable. It would be a mistake to say that happiness necessarily springs from the absurd discovery. It happens as well that the feeling of the absurd springs from happiness. "I conclude that all is well," says Œdipus, and that remark is sacred. It echoes in the wild and limited universe of man. It teaches that all is not, has not been, exhausted. It drives out of this world a god who had come into it with dissatisfaction and a preference for futile suffering. It makes of fate a human matter, which must be settled among men.

All Sisyphus' silent joy is contained therein. His fate belongs to him. His rock is a thing. Likewise, the absurd man, when he contemplates his torment, silences all the idols. In the universe suddenly restored to its silence, the myriad wondering little voices of the earth rise up. Unconscious, secret calls, invitations from all the faces, they are the necessary reverse and price of victory. There is no sun without shadow, and it is essential to know the night. The absurd man says yes and his efforts will henceforth be unceasing. If there is a personal fate, there is no higher destiny, or at least there is, but one which he concludes is inevitable and despicable. For the rest, he knows himself to be the master of his days. At that subtle moment when man glances backward over his life, Sisyphus returning toward his rock, in that slight pivoting he contemplates that series of unrelated actions which become his fate, created by him, combined under his memory's eye and soon sealed by his death. Thus, convinced of the wholly human origin of all that is human, a blind man eager to see who knows that the night has no end, he is still on the go. The rock is still rolling.

I leave Sisyphus at the foot of the mountain! One always finds one's burden again. But Sisyphus teaches the higher fidelity that negates the gods and raises rocks. He too concludes that all is well. This universe henceforth without a master seems to him neither sterile nor futile. Each atom of that stone, each mineral flake of that night-filled mountain, in itself forms a world. The struggle itself toward the heights is enough to fill a man's heart. One must imagine Sisyphus happy.

—BROADCAST—

I BELIEVE

JOHN D. ROCKEFELLER JR. {JULY 8, 1941}

His father was famous for creating Standard Oil and becoming the world's wealthiest man, but John Jr. (1874–1960), his only son, was better known for philanthropy and public service. In 1941, John Jr. broadcast a speech— a personal statement of principles—on behalf of the United Service Organizations for National Defense. To honor his legacy, it was engraved in 1962 near the ice-skating rink at Rockefeller Center in New York City.

Some of these things have been relegated to bygone days; some are regarded as long since outgrown. Nevertheless, I believe they are every one of them fundamental and eternal. They are the principles on which my wife and I have tried to bring up our family. They are the principles in which my father believed and by which he governed his life. They are the principles, many of them, which I learned at my mother's knee.

They point the way to usefulness and happiness in life, to courage and peace in death. If they mean to you what they mean to me, they may perhaps be helpful also to our sons for their guidance and inspiration.

Let me state them:

I believe in the supreme worth of the individual and his right to life, liberty, and the pursuit of happiness.

I believe that every right implies a responsibility; every opportunity, an obligation; every possession, a duty.

I believe that the law was made for man and not man for the law; that government is the servant of the people and not their master.

I believe in the dignity of labor, whether with head or hand; that the world owes no man a living but that it owes every man an opportunity to make a living.

I believe that thrift is essential to well-ordered living and that economy is a prime requisite of a sound financial structure, whether in government, business, or in personal affairs.

I believe that truth and justice are fundamental to an enduring social order.

I believe in the sacredness of a promise, that a man's word should be as good as his bond, that character—not wealth or power or position—is of supreme worth.

I believe that the rendering of useful service is the common duty of mankind and that only in the purifying fire of sacrifice is the dross of selfishness consumed and the greatness of the human soul set free.

I believe in an all-wise and all-loving God, named by whatever name, and that the individual's highest fulfillment, greatest happiness, and widest usefulness are to be found living in harmony with his will.

I believe that love is the greatest thing in the world; that it alone can overcome hate; that right can and will triumph over might.

These are the principles, however formulated, for which all good men and women throughout the world, irrespective of race or creed, education, social position, or occupation, are standing, and for which many of them are suffering and dying.

These are the principles upon which a new world recognizing the brotherhood of man and the fatherhood of God can be established. . . .

—SONG—

SOMETHING FOR NOTHING

NEIL PEART AND GEDDY LEE {1976}

Well-read drummer Neil Peart (b. 1952) joined the Canadian rock band
Rush in 1974 and brought with him an aggressive virtuoso percussive
style and thought-provoking lyrics about human nature and society, many
of them influenced by such writers as Ayn Rand, William Faulkner, and
Ernest Hemingway. With bassist/vocalist Geddy Lee (b. 1953) he wrote
"Something for Nothing."

Waiting for the winds of change
To sweep the clouds away
Waiting for the rainbow's end
To cast its gold your way
Countless ways
You pass the days

Waiting for someone to call
And turn your world around
Looking for an answer
To the question you have found
Looking for
An open door

You don't get something for nothing
You don't get freedom for free
You won't get wise
With the sleep still in your eyes
No matter what your dreams might be

What you own is your own kingdom
What you do is your own glory

What you love is your own power
What you live is your own story
In your head is the answer
Let it guide you along
Let your heart be the anchor
And the beat of your own song

You don't get something for nothing
You don't get freedom for free
You won't get wise
With the sleep still in your eyes
No matter what your dreams might be

— SPEECH —

A LEFT-HANDED COMMENCEMENT ADDRESS AT MILLS COLLEGE

URSULA K. LE GUIN {1983}

Like her mother, Ursula K. Le Guin (b. 1929) writes children's books. Unlike her mother, she did not stop there. The prolific Le Guin has written novels, short stories, and poetry, but is best known for her science fiction. In her commencement address to the all-women Mills College in California, Le Guin likens women to aliens in their own land. Although some of her rhetoric is dated, some of her advice is timeless: "I hope you live without the need to dominate," she says, "and without the need to be dominated."

I want to thank the Mills College Class of '83 for offering me a rare chance: to speak aloud in public in the language of women.

I know there are men graduating, and I don't mean to exclude them, far from it. There is a Greek tragedy where the Greek says to the foreigner,

259

"If you don't understand Greek, please signify by nodding." Anyhow, commencements are usually operated under the unspoken agreement that everybody graduating is either male or ought to be. That's why we are all wearing these twelfth-century dresses that look so great on men and make women look either like a mushroom or a pregnant stork. Intellectual tradition is male. Public speaking is done in the public tongue, the national or tribal language; and the language of our tribe is the men's language. Of course women learn it. We're not dumb. If you can tell Margaret Thatcher from Ronald Reagan, or Indira Gandhi from General Somoza, by anything they say, tell me how. This is a man's world, so it talks a man's language. The words are all words of power. You've come a long way, baby, but no way is long enough. You can't even get there by selling yourself out: because there is theirs, not yours.

Maybe we've had enough words of power and talk about the battle of life. Maybe we need some words of weakness. Instead of saying now that I hope you will all go forth from this ivory tower of college into the Real World and forge a triumphant career or at least help your husband to and keep our country strong and be a success in everything—instead of talking about power, what if I talked like a woman right here in public? It won't sound right. It's going to sound terrible. What if I said what I hope for you is first, if—only if—you want kids, I hope you have them. Not hordes of them. A couple, enough. I hope they're beautiful. I hope you and they have enough to eat, and a place to be warm and clean in, and friends, and work you like doing. Well, is that what you went to college for? Is that all? What about success?

Success is somebody else's failure. Success is the American Dream we can keep dreaming because most people in most places, including thirty million of ourselves, live wide awake in the terrible reality of poverty. No, I do not wish you success. I don't even want to talk about it. I want to talk about failure.

Because you are human beings you are going to meet failure. You are going to meet disappointment, injustice, betrayal, and irreparable loss. You will find you're weak where you thought yourself strong. You'll work for possessions and then find they possess you. You will find yourself—as I know you already have—in dark places, alone, and afraid.

What I hope for you, for all my sisters and daughters, brothers and sons, is that you will be able to live there, in the dark place. To live in the place that our rationalizing culture of success denies, calling it a place of exile, uninhabitable, foreign.

Well, we're already foreigners. Women as women are largely excluded from, alien to, the self-declared male norms of this society, where human beings are called Man, the only respectable god is male, the the only direction is up. So that's their country; let's explore our own. I'm not talking about sex; that's a whole other universe, where every man and woman is on their own. I'm talking about society, the so-called man's world of institutionalized competition, aggression, violence, authority, and power. If we want to live as women, some separatism is forced upon us: Mills College is a wise embodiment of that separatism. The war-games world wasn't made by us or for us; we can't even breathe the air there without masks. And if you put the mask on you'll have a hard time getting it off. So how about going on doing things our own way, as to some extent you did here at Mills? Not *for* men and the male power hierarchy—that's their game. Not *against* men, either—that's still playing by their rules. But *with* any men who are with us: that's our game. Why should a free woman with a college education either fight Machoman or serve him? Why should she live her life on his terms?

Machoman is afraid of our terms, which are not all rational, positive, competitive, etc. And so he has taught us to despise and deny them. In our society, women have lived, and have been despised for living, the whole side of life that includes and takes responsibility for helplessness, weakness, and illness, for the irrational and the irreparable, for all that is obscure, passive, uncontrolled, animal, unclean—the valley of the shadow, the deep, the depths of life. All that the Warrior denies and refuses is left to us and the men who share it with us and therefore, like us, can't play doctor, only nurse, can't be warriors, only civilians, can't be chiefs, only indians. Well, so that is our country. The night side of our country. If there is a day side to it, high sierras, prairies of bright grass, we only know pioneers' tales about it, we haven't got there yet. We're never going to get there by imitating Machoman. We are only going to get there by going our own way, by living there, by living through the night in our own country.

So what I hope for you is that you live there not as prisoners, ashamed of being women, consenting captives of a psychopathic social system, but as natives. That you will be at home there, keep house there, be your own mistress, with a room of your own. That you will do your work there, whatever you're good at, art or science or tech or running a company or sweeping under the beds, and when they tell you that it's second-class work because a woman is doing it, I hope you tell them to go to hell and while they're going to give you equal pay for equal time. I hope you live without the need to dominate, and without the need to be dominated. I hope you are never victims, but I hope you have no power over other people. And when you fail, and are defeated, and in pain, and in the dark, then I hope you will remember that darkness is your country, where you live, where no wars are fought and no wars are won, but where the future is. Our roots are in the dark; the earth is our country. Why did we look up for blessing—instead of around, and down? What hope we have lies there. Not in the sky full of orbiting spy-eyes and weaponry, but in the earth we have looked down upon. Not from above, but from below. Not in the light that blinds, but in the dark that nourishes, where human beings grow human souls.

—SONG—

AMERICA THE BEAUTIFUL
KATHERINE LEE BATES {1893}

In 1893, Katherine Lee Bates (1859–1929) stood atop Pikes Peak in Colorado. Inspired by the glorious scenery spread out before her, she wrote a poem. Samuel A. Ward, a composer, set the words to music, and today "America the Beautiful" is one of the best-known and best-loved American anthems. More than twenty years after she wrote the poem, Bates was asked why "America the Beautiful" had proven to be so popular. "Clearly," she replied, "Americans are at heart idealists, with a fundamental faith in human brotherhood."

O beautiful for spacious skies,
    For amber waves of grain,
For purple mountain majesties
    Above the fruited plain!
America! America!
    God shed His grace on thee
And crown thy good with brotherhood
    From sea to shining sea!

O beautiful for pilgrim feet,
    Whose stern, impassioned stress
A thoroughfare for freedom beat
    Across the wilderness!
America! America!
    God mend thine every flaw,
Confirm their soul in self-control,
    Thy liberty in law!

O beautiful for heroes proved
    In liberating strife,
Who more than self their country loved,
    And mercy more than life!
America! America!
    May God thy gold refine,
Till all success be nobleness
    And every gain divine!

O beautiful for patriot dream
    That sees beyond the years
Thine alabaster cities gleam
    Undimmed by human tears!
America! America!
    God shed His grace on thee,
And crown thy good with brotherhood
    From sea to shining sea!

—SPEECH—

I HAVE A DREAM

MARTIN LUTHER KING JR. {AUGUST 28, 1963}

The "I Have a Dream" speech, which King delivered from the steps of the Lincoln Memorial in Washington, D.C., on August 28, 1963, as part of a massive March on Washington for Jobs and Freedom, is one of the greatest addresses of all time. Oddly, it almost wasn't delivered at all. King departed from a somber prepared speech and resorted to rousing language—including the "I have a dream" litany—that he had used before on audiences in cities around the American South. After the march, attended by upward of a quarter of a million people, King and other civil rights leaders met with President John F. Kennedy Jr., who promised his support. Kennedy was assassinated three months later, but not before he had helped pave the way for President Lyndon Johnson's Civil Rights Act of 1964.

I am happy to join with you today in what will go down in history as the greatest demonstration for freedom in the history of our nation.

Five score years ago, a great American, in whose symbolic shadow we stand today, signed the Emancipation Proclamation. This momentous decree came as a great beacon light of hope to millions of Negro slaves who had been seared in the flames of withering injustice. It came as a joyous daybreak to end the long night of their captivity.

But one hundred years later, the Negro still is not free. One hundred years later, the life of the Negro is still sadly crippled by the manacles of segregation and the chains of discrimination. One hundred years later, the Negro lives on a lonely island of poverty in the midst of a vast ocean of material prosperity. One hundred years later the Negro is still languished in the corners of American society and finds himself an exile in his own land. So we have come here today to dramatize an appalling condition.

In a sense we've come to our nation's capital to cash a check. When the architects of our republic wrote the magnificent words of the Constitution and the Declaration of Independence, they were signing a promissory note to which every American was to fall heir. This note was a promise that all men would be guaranteed the unalienable rights of life, liberty, and the pursuit of happiness.

It is obvious today that America has defaulted on this promissory note insofar as her citizens of color are concerned. Instead of honoring this sacred obligation, America has given the Negro people a bad check, a check which has come back marked "insufficient funds." But we refuse to believe that the bank of justice is bankrupt. We refuse to believe that there are insufficient funds in the great vaults of opportunity of this nation. And so we have come to cash this check—a check that will give us upon demand the riches of freedom and the security of justice. We have also come to this hallowed spot to remind America of the fierce urgency of *now*. This is no time to engage in the luxury of cooling off or to take the tranquilizing drug of gradualism. *Now* is the time to make real the promises of democracy. *Now* is the time to rise from the dark and desolate valley of segregation to the sunlit path of racial justice. *Now* is the time to open the doors of opportunity to all of God's children. *Now* is the time to lift our nation from the quicksands of racial injustice to the solid rock of brotherhood.

It would be fatal for the nation to overlook the urgency of the moment. This sweltering summer of the Negro's legitimate discontent will not pass until there is an invigorating autumn of freedom and equality. Nineteen sixty-three is not an end, but a beginning. And those who hope that the Negro needed to blow off steam and will now be content will have a rude awakening if the nation returns to business as usual. There will be neither rest nor tranquility in America until the Negro is granted his citizenship rights. The whirlwinds of revolt will continue to shake the foundations of our nation until the bright day of justice emerges.

But there is something that I must say to my people, who stand on the warm threshold which leads into the palace of justice. In the process of gaining our rightful place, we must not be guilty of wrongful deeds. Let us not seek to satisfy our thirst for freedom by drinking from the cup of bitterness and hatred. We must forever conduct our struggle on the high plane of dignity and discipline. We must not allow our creative protest to degenerate into physical violence. Again and again, we must rise to the majestic heights of meeting physical force with soul force. The marvelous new militancy which has engulfed the Negro community must not lead us to a distrust of all white people, for many of our white brothers, as evidenced by their presence here today, have come to realize that their destiny is tied up with our destiny and their freedom is inextricably bound to our freedom. We cannot walk alone.

And as we walk, we must make the pledge that we shall always march ahead. We cannot turn back. There are those who are asking the devotees of civil rights, "When will you be satisfied?" We can never be satisfied as long as the Negro is the victim of the unspeakable horrors of police brutality. We can never be satisfied as long as our bodies, heavy with the fatigue of travel, cannot gain lodging in the motels of the highways and the hotels of the cities. We cannot be satisfied as long as the Negro's basic mobility is from a smaller ghetto to a larger one. We cannot be satisfied as long as a Negro in Mississippi cannot vote and a Negro in New York believes he has nothing for which to vote. No, no, we are not satisfied and we will not be satisfied until justice rolls down like waters and righteousness like a mighty stream.

I am not unmindful that some of you have come here out of great trials and tribulations. Some of you have come fresh from narrow jail cells. Some of you have come from areas where your quest for freedom left you battered by the storms of persecution and staggered by the winds of police brutality. You have been the veterans of creative suffering. Continue to work with the faith that unearned suffering is redemptive. Go back to Mississippi, go back to Alabama, go back to South Carolina, go back to Georgia, go back to Louisiana, go back to the slums and ghettos of our northern cities, knowing that somehow this situation can and will be changed. Let us not wallow in the valley of despair.

I say to you today, my friends, that in spite of the difficulties and frustrations of the moment I still have a dream. It is a dream deeply rooted in the American dream.

I have a dream that one day this nation will rise up and live out the true meaning of its creed: "We hold these truths to be self-evident, that all men are created equal."

I have a dream that one day on the red hills of Georgia, the sons of former slaves and the sons of former slave owners will be able to sit down together at the table of brotherhood.

I have a dream that one day even the state of Mississippi, a desert state sweltering the heat of injustice and oppression, will be transformed into an oasis of freedom and justice.

I have a dream that my four little children will one day live in a nation where they will not be judged by the color of their skin but by the content of their character.

I have a dream today.

I have a dream that one day down in Alabama, whose governor's lips are presently dripping with the words of interposition and nullification, will be transformed into a situation where little black boys and black girls will be able to join hands with little white boys and white girls and walk together as sisters and brothers.

I have a dream today.

I have a dream that one day every valley shall be exalted and every hill and mountain shall be made low; the rough places will be made plain, and the crooked places will be made straight, and the glory of the Lord shall be revealed, and all flesh shall see it together.

This is our hope. This is the faith with which I return to the South. With this faith we will be able to hew out of the mountain of despair a stone of hope. With this faith we will be able to transform the jangling discords of our nation into a beautiful symphony of brotherhood. With this faith we will be able to work together, to pray together, to struggle together, to go to jail together, to stand up for freedom together, knowing that we will be free one day.

This will be the day when all of God's children will be able to sing with new meaning: "My country, 'tis of thee, Sweet land of liberty, of thee I sing. Land where my fathers died! Land of the Pilgrims' pride! From every mountainside, let freedom ring!"

And if America is to be a great nation, this must become true. So let freedom ring from the prodigious hilltops of New Hampshire. Let freedom ring from the mighty mountains of New York. Let freedom ring from the heightening Alleghenies of Pennsylvania!

Let freedom ring from the snowcapped Rockies of Colorado!

Let freedom ring from the curvaceous slopes of California!

But not only that; Let freedom ring from Stone Mountain of Georgia!

Let freedom ring from Lookout Mountain of Tennessee!

Let freedom ring from every hill and molehill of Mississippi!

From every mountainside, let freedom ring!

When we let freedom ring, when we let it ring from every village and every hamlet, from every state and every city, we will be able to speed up that day when all of God's children, black men and white men, Jews and Gentiles, Protestants and Catholics, will be able to join hands and sing in the words of the old Negro spiritual: "Free at last! Free at last! Thank God Almighty, we are free at last!"

OUR LIVES, OUR FORTUNES, OUR SACRED HONOR

—ESSAY—

PAY ATTENTION, KIDS

ROBERT J. SAMUELSON {AUGUST 23, 2000}

Robert J. Samuelson (b. 1945) has been a columnist for *The Washington Post* since 1977 and is a contributing editor for *Newsweek*. He is a four-time winner of the National Headliner Award for a consistently outstanding column and is a recipient of the John Hancock Award for best business and financial columnist. He is the author of the 1995 book, *The Good Life and Its Discontents: The American Dream in the Age of Entitlement, 1945–1995.*

Dear Kids,

I know you don't read my columns, and that's okay. At 10, 13 and 15, you're a little young for my serious stuff. You'd find most of it boring. But I want you to read this one. Here it is— no TV until you read it. It's about the election.

I notice you're not paying much attention. This has got to change. You don't have to read every speech or listen to every interview. You don't even have to decide whether you like George Bush or Al Gore better. But you've got to follow, in a general way, what's happening. Why?

This question is harder than it seems. I know you have more interesting things to do. There's MTV, ESPN, *Sports Illustrated,* PlayStation and the Internet. Soccer and hockey seasons are around the corner. Once school begins, homework will rear its ugly head, and your mother and I—cruel as we are—won't let you forget it. Somehow you'll still have to find time for the election.

You're not alone in your lack of interest. Many young voters find the campaign dull and have ignored it, according to public opinion polls. There's a theory that today's young are so selfish and self-centered that they've lost interest in government and elections. I don't buy the theory. Times have simply changed.

When I grew up in the 1950s and 1960s, it was hard not to pay attention. The old Soviet Union had nuclear weapons and might have blown us up. In the 1960s, the civil rights movement—the struggle to end legal discrimination against black Americans—and the war in Vietnam generated mass marches and violent protests. We watched the president and government, because decisions made in Washington could dramatically affect millions of people.

The same was true of my parents' generation. They lived through the Great Depression of the 1930s (when unemployment was huge) and World War II (when 405,000 Americans died). All during these decades, politics was in the air. Elections seemed to matter more.

It's different now. You've grown up in a period of peace and great prosperity. There are no big threats from abroad or massive crises at home. The president has become, at least for the time being, less important. Your main introduction to the White House was Bill Clinton's sex scandal and impeachment; the president looked more like a character from "reality TV" than a national leader.

All this may explain your low interest. But it's not a good excuse. You've got to care more about the election, because it goes to the heart of who we are as a nation. The greatness of the United States is not McDonald's or Microsoft. It's our basic beliefs about how we should govern ourselves—including elections. Through the Declaration of Independence and the Constitution, we gave the modern world two wonderful ideas: liberty and democracy.

Liberty means that government can't control your life. We respect the individual. Government can't tell you what to do, think or say. It can't tell you what religion to practice—or whether to practice any religion. It can't take your property without cause—and without a law. Our second idea (democracy)

271

insists that government springs from the people. We don't have kings, queens or dictators or rule by one political party. The people decide who holds government's powers and what those powers will be.

Until recently, most countries didn't practice either liberty or democracy. Many still don't (China, for instance). Elections are one way that we argue about our basic ideas. How big and powerful can government become before it interferes with our freedom? Who should run government?

Elections are not always pretty or inspiring. Political campaigns often seem part circus and part swindle. Promises are made that can't be kept. Political candidates—including candidates for president—sometimes say things about their opponents, either directly or in their TV ads, that are mean, ugly or untrue.

Likewise, our democracy has always had shortcomings. In the beginning, only men with property—farms, homes, shops—could vote. Before the Civil War, most black Americans obviously couldn't vote; even for much of the 20th century, many in the South were barred from the ballot box by physical intimidation or discriminatory voting laws. Women didn't win the right to vote until the 19th Amendment to the Constitution in 1920.

But on the whole, our system has worked well. Except for the Civil War, people generally agree to disagree in a peaceful way. Power is transferred peacefully from one leader—and party—to another. Throughout history, not many other countries have managed to do this consistently.

As a result, we have maintained a fair amount of freedom and social order. It is this blessed combination that forms the foundation for much of what is good about America: its concern for every individual's dignity and potential; its creativity; its economic vitality (including Microsoft and McDonald's); and its general optimism.

The United States is a very special place. It will stop being special if we take it for granted. Every generation must renew its commitment to our basic beliefs. That's why you must follow the election news on TV and in newspapers. You need to begin asking questions about the candidates, the issues and the campaign. You may get different answers from Mom and me. Mom is smart, but Dad is correct. (Just kidding. That's what elections are about—disagreement.)

And also remember: If you don't ask enough questions, I'll take your CD players away.

Love,
Dad

—POEM—

AMERICA

HENRY DUMAS {CIRCA 1960}

Henry Dumas (1934–1968), born in Sweet Home, Arkansas, was considered one of the best, and certainly most prolific, young writers of his era. He participated in the Civil Rights, Black Power, and Black Arts movements of the 1960s, and in a tragic case of mistaken identity, he was killed by a New York Transit Authority policeman on the 125th Street subway station in Manhattan. He left behind numerous books of poetry and prose, including *Poetry for My People* (published posthumously in 1970), from which "America" is taken.

If an eagle be imprisoned
on the back of a coin,
and the coin be tossed
into the sky,
the coin will spin
the coin will flutter,
but the eagle will never fly.

— SPEECH —

GREAT SOCIETY

LYNDON B. JOHNSON {1964}

Like George W. Bush, Lyndon B. Johnson was a folksy Texan embroiled in U.S. military intervention far from home. Johnson was elected to the presidency by the greatest popular majority in American history, and centered his domestic agenda around social programs to benefit the poor. Johnson's speechwriter, Richard N. Goodwin, who first worked for the Kennedy administration as a speechwriter and Latin America consultant, introduced the expression "Great Society."

I have come today from the turmoil of your capital to the tranquility of your campus to speak about the future of your country.

The purpose of protecting the life of our nation and preserving the liberty of our citizens is to pursue the happiness of our people. Our success in that pursuit is the test of our success as a nation. For a century we labored to settle and to subdue a continent. For half a century we called upon unbounded invention and untiring industry to create an order of plenty for all of our people. The challenge of the next half-century is whether we have the wisdom to use that wealth to enrich and elevate our national life, and to advance the quality of our American civilization. Your imagination, your initiative, and your indignation will determine whether we build a society where progress is the servant of our needs, or a society where old values and new visions are buried under unbridled growth. For in your time we have the opportunity to move not only toward the rich society and the powerful society, but upward to the Great Society.

The Great Society rests on abundance and liberty for all. It demands an end to poverty and racial injustice, to which we are totally committed in our time. But that is just the beginning. The Great Society is a place where every child can find knowledge to enrich his mind and to enlarge his talents. It is a place where leisure is a welcome chance to build and reflect, not a feared cause of boredom and restlessness. It is a place where the city of man serves not only the needs of the body and the demands of commerce but the desire for beauty and the hunger for community. It is a place where man can renew contact with nature. It is a place which honors creation for its own sake and for what it adds to the understanding of the race. It is a place where men are more concerned with the quality of their goals than the quantity of their goods.

But most of all, the Great Society is not a safe harbor, a resting place, a final objective, a finished work. It is a challenge constantly renewed, beckoning us toward a destiny where the meaning of our lives matches the marvelous products of our labor.

So I want to talk to you today about three places where we begin to build the Great Society: in our cities, in our countryside, and in our classrooms. Many of you will live to see the day, perhaps 50 years from now, when there will be 400 million Americans—four-fifths of them in urban areas. In the remainder of this century urban population will double, city land will double, and we will have to build homes, highways, and facilities equal to all those built since this country was first settled. So in the next 40 years we must rebuild the entire urban United States.

Aristotle said, "Men come together in cities in order to live, but they remain together in order to live the good life." It is harder and harder to live the good life in American cities today. The catalog of ills is long: There is the decay of the centers and the despoiling of the suburbs. There is not enough housing for our people or transportation for our traffic. Open land is vanishing and old landmarks are violated. Worst of all, expansion is eroding the precious and time-honored values of community with neighbors and communion with nature. The loss of these values breeds loneliness and boredom and indifference.

Our society will never be great until our cities are great. Today the frontier of imagination and innovation is inside those cities and not beyond their borders. New experiments are already going on. It will be the task of your generation to make the American city a place where future generations will come, not only to live but to live the good life. . . .

A second place where we begin to build the Great Society is in our countryside. We have always prided ourselves on being not only America the strong and America the free, but America the beautiful. Today that beauty is in danger. The water we drink, the food we eat, the very air that we breathe, are threatened with pollution. Our parks are overcrowded, our seashores overburdened. Green fields and dense forests are disappearing. A few years ago we were greatly concerned about the "ugly American." Today we must act to prevent an ugly America. For once the battle is lost, once our natural splendor is destroyed, it can never be recaptured. And once man can no longer walk with beauty or wonder at nature, his spirit will wither and his sustenance be wasted.

A third place to build the Great Society is in the classrooms of America. There your children's lives will be shaped. Our society will not be great until every young mind is set free to scan the farthest reaches of thought and imagination. We are still far from that goal.

Today, 8 million adult Americans, more than the entire population of Michigan, have not finished 5 years of school. Nearly 20 million have not finished 8 years of school. Nearly 54 million—more than one quarter of all America—have not even finished high school. Each year more than 100,000 high school graduates, with proved ability, do not enter college because they cannot afford it. And if we cannot educate today's youth, what will we do in 1970 when elementary school enrollment will be 5 million greater than 1960? And high school enrollment will rise by 5 million. College enrollment will increase by more than 3 million.

In many places, classrooms are overcrowded and curricula are outdated. Most of our qualified teachers are underpaid, and many of our paid teachers are unqualified. So we must give every child a place to sit and a teacher to learn from. Poverty must not be a bar to learning, and learning must offer an escape from poverty.

But more classrooms and more teachers are not enough. We must seek an educational system which grows in excellence as it grows in size. This means better training for our teachers. It means preparing youth to enjoy their hours of leisure as well as their hours of labor. It means exploring new techniques of teaching, to find new ways to stimulate the love of learning and the capacity for creation.

These are three of the central issues of the Great Society. While our Government has many programs directed at those issues, I do not pretend that we have the full answer to those problems. But I do promise this: We are going to assemble the best thought and the broadest knowledge from all over the world to find those answers for America. I intend to establish working groups to prepare a series of White House conferences and meetings on the cities, on natural beauty, on the quality of education, and on other emerging challenges. And from these meetings and from this inspiration and from these studies we will begin to set our course toward the Great Society.

The solution to these problems does not rest on a massive program in Washington, nor can it rely solely on the strained resources of local authority. They require us to create new concepts of cooperation, a creative federalism, between the national capital and the leaders of local communities.

Woodrow Wilson once wrote: "Every man sent out from his university should be a man of his nation as well as a man of his time." Within your lifetime, powerful forces, already loosed, will take us toward a way of life beyond the realm of our experience, almost beyond the bounds of our imagination. For better or for worse, your generation has been appointed by history to deal with those problems and to lead America toward a new age. You have the chance never before afforded to any people in any age. You can help build a society where the demands of morality and the needs of the spirit can be realized in the life of the nation.

So, will you join in the battle to give every citizen the full equality which God enjoins and the law requires, whatever his belief, or race, or the color of his skin? Will you join in the battle to give every citizen an escape from the crushing weight of poverty? Will you join in the battle to make it possible for all nations to live in enduring peace as neighbors and not as mortal enemies? Will you join in the battle to build the Great Society, to prove that our material progress is only the foundation on which we will build a richer life of mind and spirit?

There are those timid souls who say this battle cannot be won, that we are condemned to a soulless wealth. I do not agree. We have the power to shape the civilization that we want. But we need your will, your labor, your hearts if we are to build that kind of society. Those who came to this land sought to build more than just a new country. They sought a new world. So

I have come here today . . . to say that you can make their vision our reality. So let us from this moment begin our work so that in the future men will look back and say: "It was then, after a long and weary way, that man turned the exploits of his genius to the full enrichment of his life."

—SONG—

TALKIN' BOUT A REVOLUTION

TRACY CHAPMAN {1988}

In an era of Reaganomics and soulless pop, one young, black, working-class musical prodigy from Cleveland made headlines by singing about revolution. Tracy Chapman (b. 1964) had a surprise hit, "Fast Car," about the effects of poverty, which she knew intimately, but it was at a 1988 concert to free Nelson Mandela that Chapman, then 24, made a stronger statement. She was called to the stage as a result of a last minute cancellation, and responded by singing "Talkin' Bout a Revolution," which she had written in high school and now was being broadcast around the world.

> Don't you know
> They're talkin' bout a revolution
> It sounds like a whisper
> Don't you know
> They're talkin' bout a revolution
> It sounds like a whisper
>
> While they're standing in the welfare lines
> Crying at the doorsteps of those armies of salvation
> Wasting time in the unemployment lines
> Sitting around waiting for a promotion

Poor people gonna rise up
And get their share
Poor people gonna rise up
And take what's theirs

Don't you know
You better run, run, run . . .
Oh I said you better
Run, run, run . . .

Finally the tables are starting to turn
Talkin' bout a revolution

—ESSAY—

WHAT AMERICA MEANS TO ME

PEARL S. BUCK {1944}

Pearl S. Buck (1892–1973), the daughter of two Presbyterian missionaries, spent most of the first forty years of her life in China, where she witnessed great political unrest, and also gathered material for her 1932 Pulitzer Prize–winning, best-selling second novel, *The Good Earth*. Six years later, she became the first American woman to win the Nobel Prize in Literature. By this time, she had been back in the United States for almost a decade, devoting herself and her writing to women's rights and civil rights, particularly for the Chinese. During World War II, Buck became a leading figure in the movement to abolish the Chinese Exclusion Act of 1882, which was eventually repealed by President Franklin Roosevelt on December 17, 1943.

One of the things in my life which brings me comfort, these days, is that my mail, for example, is crowded with letters from people I do not know and will probably never know, people from all over America. What do they write to me for? Why, simply to tell me that they like or don't like something I have said or written. They divide fairly evenly between approval and disapproval, but the point is not whether they approve. The point is that they take it as their right to tell me straight what they think. And they have that right, just as I have the right to speak or write in the first place. We all have the right to speak as we think, and we have the right to denounce or uphold our leaders and each other.

It is the most glorious right in the world, for it means that the people in our country have freedom from fear, because we are a free people. We are not ruled by a foreign government, or by a political system which forbids the plain people to speak aloud. We govern ourselves through those whom we choose and we are not subject to them, but they to us.

We must never forget this. The only real danger to our country is from within, that we forget our own power to be what we want to be. Let no American today take refuge in resignation, in that state of willful helplessness which shrugs its shoulders and says, "What can *I* do?" We have the right and the power to make our country what we want it to be. We are the kind of people that democracy produces—free, independent in our thought and behavior, fearless, forthright, and kind. I have seen many peoples of the earth, and it is not only patriotism, I think, when I say that we possess these qualities to a greater degree than any other people. It is not boasting when I say this, for, like a child born with great gifts, we have these qualities not by any effort of ours, but bestowed upon us by our ancestors, by those brave men and women who came here from other lands because freedom was essential to them—the freedom to worship God as they willed, the freedom to work and keep themselves and their families from want, the freedom to believe and to speak as they believed, the freedom to live unafraid, and at peace, beneath the open sky.

We who are the children of these people who gathered here from over all the earth, from many nations and many races, to build a new country, which should be the land of the free, must today march on to fuller freedom. Our great strides have always been taken in the cause of freedom—freedom from empire first, freedom from slavery second, and now it must be the third and greatest freedom for which we fight—the freedom of all mankind. . . .

—ESSAY—

THE AMERICAN CAUSE

ARCHIBALD MACLEISH {1941}

When President Franklin Delano Roosevelt nominated poet Archibald MacLeish (1892–1982) to head the Library of Congress in 1939, opponents accused the poet of Communist leanings (the left sometimes accused him of being a Fascist, but in fact he was a liberal humanist). MacLeish won the nomination and went on to become one of the most active Librarians of Congress—he reorganized the Library's offices, established a series of poetry readings, commissioned murals to be painted in the Jefferson Reading Room based on Jefferson's ideas about freedom, and made sure that the rough draft of the Declaration of Independence was moved to Fort Knox for safekeeping during World War II. Throughout the war, MacLeish also directed propaganda campaigns for the Office of War Information, and wrote essays and speeches. In his 1941 book, *The American Cause*, published when the outcome of World War II and the fate of democracy were darkly in doubt, he worried that the definition of democracy was being sabotaged by our enemies, and threatened—much as Ralph Waldo Emerson had feared when he composed "Self-Reliance" exactly a hundred years before—by America's preoccupation with accumulating wealth.

The issue before the American people is not a political issue nor an issue to be decided by a public act. It is an issue between the American people and themselves: an issue which involves the vitality and the resources of the American soul.

These, I am well aware, are large and ornate words. They are words which a man would have used at the risk of his reputation for sincerity a dozen months ago. But they are the words which none of us can help but use today. History, not rhetoric, has put them in our mouths. History has shown us at late last that the issue which divides our time is far more than an issue between armed forces. History has shown us that it is an issue between worlds: an issue which depends more surely on our souls than on our weapons: an issue which no nation can avoid. Specifically and precisely, history has made plain to us a fact we had refused before to see—the fact that the enemy which attacks us attacks us not with planes alone or tanks alone or arms, but with violence of belief. And the issue which the people of this country face, the issue which lies between this people and itself, is the issue whether or not those who believe in democracy—those specifically who believe in democracy in the United States—can bring against the violence and fanatical obsession of that invading faith a stronger faith, a more resisting ardor of their own.

Before the Battle of France—a battle which may prove to have been more decisive in our own history than in the history of Europe— fascism had seemed to us a force of weapons driven onward by the fear of force behind. But in the Battle of France we learned, in the words of a manifesto issued by a group of the most distinguished scholars in this country, that the enemy "were stronger in arms because they were stronger in heart. It was their fanatical faith that gave them wings and fire. It was the singleness of their purpose that quickened the spearhead of their march." In France also we learned that the weakness of the democracies—the weakness at least of the democracy which there fell—was not, as we had wished to believe, a weakness only in arms, only in mechanical contrivances. We learned, in the words of the same manifesto, that the blindness of democratic diplomacy and the helplessness of democratic strategy "were the external symptoms of a decay of the men. . . . This they called appeasement. It implied that no conviction is worth fighting for and that the boundaries between good and evil had fallen. Military defeat was the embodiment of moral abdication."

It was the Battle of France which posed the issue we now face. Before that battle we had thought ourselves spectators of a war in Europe. After it, we knew the war was not in Europe but nearer—in the darker and more vulnerable countries of men's hearts. And after it we were not certain it was we who were spectators.

But the Battle of France did more than pose this issue. It weighted it— and weighted it against us. Before the Battle of France we had not understood—as a nation we had not understood—that the vitality of our democratic faith was put in issue. After the Battle of France we feared the issue was already lost. We saw then that the war was not, as we had wished to believe, a war between European powers which wanted conflicting things but a war between human beings who believed conflicting things. We saw that the differences of belief were differences as to the kind of society in which men should live. We saw that those who believed in the kind of society in which we also believe had been opposed not only by weapons, not only by machines, but by other men who believed, and believed fanatically, in the total destruction of that society. We saw that in the fighting which followed it had been those who believed fanatically in destruction who had been stronger and those who believed in the society in which we believe who had been less strong—less strong not only in their weapons but in their devotion to their cause. And we had wondered. We wondered whether the sickness of democracy in France would prove to be the sickness of democracy in every country. We wondered whether democracy, which had been unable to match conviction with conviction and certainty with certainty in France, would be able to match conviction with conviction elsewhere. We still are wondering. We are wondering whether democracy in the United States has other spiritual weapons than the doubts and misgivings which ten years of depression and twenty years of skepticism provided for the men of France to fight with.

It is of this fear I wish to speak. And to speak as candidly and earnestly as I am capable of speaking, it is a fear which exists—and which exists in the minds not of foolish or of frightened people, but of responsible men who love this country as well as any of its people love it. It is also an understandable fear, for events which all of us have witnessed make it understandable. It is not a fear therefore which scornful men can put aside, or which demagogues can shout down, or which the patriotic societies can suppress with resolutions. It is a fear of which we must take account. But it is nevertheless—or so at least it seems to me—a fear both needless and mistaken. For it rests upon a total misconception of the democratic cause. It rests, to be precise, upon the misconception of democracy which those who most despise democracy have done their best to propagate and broadcast through the world. It is the fear of those who, being democrats themselves, accept the definition of democracy their enemies have written.

The enemies of liberty are not saboteurs in material things alone. They are saboteurs also in the things of the mind. And it is in the things of the mind that their sabotage is most dangerous. To destroy a machine or a manufacturing plant is one thing. The loss is great but the plant or the machine is replaceable. To destroy the integrity of words and to destroy the credibility of the users of words is another: neither can be replaced. The enemies of liberty, here as in other countries, practice the destruction of the integrity of words and the destruction of the credibility of the users of words. Indeed, it is this practice which principally characterizes the enemies of freedom in our time. They are the first men—the first men in the five hundred years since Johannes Gutenberg, Zum Jungen, Knight of Mainz, invented the art of printing—the first men to use the printing press, deliberately and systematically, as an instrument of confusion and deceit. They are the first men in the five centuries of printing to turn the printing presses, like machine guns, on the people.

A nd nowhere have they used these Kulturwaffen to destroy a word more skillfully than with the word democracy—the word essential to our cause—the word which *is* our cause—the word we must defend whatever else we lose, or fail to fight for, or do not defend. What the enemies of liberty would have us take the word democracy to mean is not what Adams thought it meant, or Jefferson, or those who took it westward through the Shenandoah, or those who came to find it here by shipload after shipload through a hundred years. What the enemies of liberty would have us take the word to mean is something men and money and machines created in the nineteenth century and *called* democracy—a way of owning property, a scheme of doing business, an opportunity for comfort or for power or for certain forms of gain or entertainment.

It is this the enemies of liberty would have us take the word to mean. And it is with this meaning in our minds that they would have us make the choice before us—a choice, they say, between the new oncoming order of their fascist world and an old corrupted system full of fat and death—a choice between the new and iron cause for which a people can forget itself and sacrifice itself and go without and suffer and if need be die, and, on the other side, a world of goods and things and comforts and amusements with nothing to believe in but more goods, more things.

This was the choice which their confusions and their defamations and deceits presented to the citizens of France—and which the citizens of France, duped by confusions and deceits, accepted. It is the choice which many in this country, duped or themselves the dupers, would accept as well. The diplomat who tells us that democracy is dead in England, meaning by democracy a way of trading stocks, a chance to make ten millions in the market, accepts the choice the citizens of France accepted. The famous woman who assures us in a beautiful and cadenced prose that democracy is old in every country, and that the future like a wave will drown it down, accepts the same alternatives of terror and despair.

But the fears and desperations and defeat which these and others like them breed and scatter are unreal fears. The democracy of which this writer and this statesman speak is not democracy but a distorted lie which both, but for their different reasons, take for true. Democracy itself has never been and is not now and never can become a way of trade, a world of goods, a heap of products, whether those products are of gold or steel or corn or silk or what—not: whether the trade is large or small or free or planned or neither. And only a very foolish man—only a man who had no understanding of the word democracy, or what it had been once, or what it can be—would take the issue in these terms and let his enemies compel him to defend, not the dream of freedom in the mind, not the way of freedom toward the future, but things already made, systems established, ways of trading, heaps of goods piled up.

If democracy is what the fascists say it is—if democracy is nothing but the world of innumerable automobiles and the best telephone system on earth and a new gadget just around the corner and the radios driveling on in the hotel lobbies eighteen hours out of twenty-four and the simpering legs in the magazine advertisements and the simpering voices on the movie screen and the hundreds of thousands of miles of roadside billboards with the billboard faces and the ten millions of unemployed waiting for the next boom—if democracy is only this, then democracy cannot survive attack, for democracy is not a cause that men will fight for.

But the true issue is not this issue; democracy is not the world that men and money and machines built in the nineteenth century and called democracy. The real issue is an issue to be fought in the hard and stony passes of the human spirit—the strict Thermopylaes of time where even if a man is killed he cannot die. And democracy itself is neither things nor goods nor fatness and indifference and an empty heart, but winter on the Massachusetts Bay and cold at Trenton and the gunfire in Kentucky and the hungry ground. The real issue is an issue between the frenzy on the one side of a herded, whipped-up, crowd-begotten "cause," and on the other side the single man's belief in liberty of mind and spirit; his willingness to sacrifice his goods and comforts and his earnings for its sake.

The democratic faith which swept the world—the democratic faith which men believed in and men fought for, the faith which men believe in and will fight for still, is not a faith in things or goods or fortunes. John Milton knew the democratic faith that men will fight for. He spoke of it not once but often:

"And as for you, citizens, it is of no small concern, what manner of men ye are, whether to acquire, or to keep possession of your liberty. Unless your liberty be of that kind which can neither be gotten nor taken away by arms (and that alone is such which springing from piety, justice, temperance, in fine from real virtue, shall take deep and intimate root in your minds) you may be assured that there will not be wanting one, who, even without arms, will speedily deprive you of what it is your boast to have gained by force of arms. . . . For know (that you may not feel resentment, or be able to blame anybody but yourselves), that as to be free is precisely the same thing as to be pious, wise, just and temperate, careful of one's own, abstinent from what is another's, and thence fine, magnanimous and brave—so to be the opposite of these, is the same thing as to be a slave; and by the wonted judgment and as it were by the just retribution of God, it comes to pass, that the nation, which has been incapable of governing and ordering itself, and has delivered itself up to the slavery of its own lusts, is itself delivered over against its will to other masters—and whether it will or no is compelled to serve."

John Milton's democracy was a democracy in which men believed. It was a democracy for which a band of sober and unmilitary men fought as armies had not fought before them. It was a faith more powerful than any faith or cause which could be brought against it. It has been a faith more powerful than any other for three centuries of time and on two continents. It is still a faith more powerful than any other. All our history has made this plain. Whenever in the history of this nation we have given ourselves to the labor creating upon this continent a life in which every man might have the freedom of his mind, we have been confident and certain of our future and assured and asked no questions either of ourselves or anyone. Whenever we have given ourselves to other labors, we have lost the meaning of our lives and lost our certainty and questioned everyone and most of all ourselves.

Three generations back in the thirties and the forties of the last century when the four-hundred-foot side-wheelers with the crystal chandeliers and the mahogany bars and the eight course dinners and the filigree funnels with their sparks like crazy stars went hooting and slapping up the Ohio and the Hudson and the Mississippi, the Americans had no questions about democracy. They had a job to do. They had the toughest job a people ever undertook—the job of clearing and settling and tying together with ships and roads and rails and words and names the largest area lived on as a single social unit by any nation, at any time. They had the job of creating on an undiscovered continent a country where a hundred million men could live in freedom from the rest and from each other. They had the actual and present job of clearing on this continent the quarter sections where a man could build his freedom out of logs and nails.

And while they had that job to do they asked no questions. They knew what democracy was. They knew what they were too. They were the smartest, toughest, luckiest, leanest, all-around knowingest nation on God's green earth. Their way of living was the handsomest way of living human beings had ever hit on. Their institutions were the institutions history had been waiting for. If you had told them anyone else had a harder hold on the earth than they had, or anyone else believed in himself more than they believed in themselves, they would have laughed in your face. And gone on with their working.

Who they were, what they were, never bothered the Americans. Virginia gentlemen and Boston philosophers and Long Island poets and visiting British lecturers might write and talk and wonder about American manners and American origins and American politics and the American soul.

Americans didn't wonder. They knew all about them. They knew about origins. They had all the origins of Europe in their veins before the century was over—all the races a man ever heard of and a lot more beside. Races didn't bother the Americans. They were something a lot better than any race. They were a People. They were the first self-constituted, self-declared, self-created People in the history of the world. And their manners were their own business. And so were their politics. And so, but ten times so, were their souls.

Who an American was and what democracy was, was nothing to talk about. You could see for your self. An American was a man who had the luck to be born on this continent where the heat was hotter and the cold was colder and the sun was brighter and the nights were blacker and the distances were farther and the faces were nearer and the rain was more like rain and the mornings were more like mornings than anywhere else on earth—sooner and sweeter and lovelier over unused hills.

An American was a man who knew which way to take to reach tomorrow. An American was a man who could let himself in and let himself out and nobody asking him "please" not even the President. An American was a man who never asked anyone anything—who he was or where he came from or what he did—because it was answer enough to be a man. At least in America.

That was the way it used to be in this country. That was the way it was while the people of this country were clearing the quarter sections for a free man's field. That is the way it has been whenever we have remembered clearly and understood with reality what democracy is.

For democracy is never a thing done. Democracy is always something that a nation must be doing. The quarter sections which were freedom a hundred years ago are now not freedom. Freedom will be somewhere else. But the labor of creating freedom is the same. And the consequence.

What is necessary now is one thing and one thing only—that the issue of democracy be made precise and clear—that democracy become again democracy in action, not democracy accomplished and piled up in goods and gold.

Democracy in action is a cause for which the stones themselves will fight.

— POEM —

OPEN LETTER TO THE POET ARCHIBALD MACLEISH WHO HAS FORSAKEN HIS MASSACHUSETTS FARM TO MAKE PROPAGANDA FOR FREEDOM

CARL SANDBURG {1940}

The Illinois-born poet and author Carl Sandburg (1878–1967), who called Chicago the "city of big shoulders," was no physical slouch himself. Son of a blacksmith's helper, Sandburg quit school after the eighth grade to harvest ice, lay bricks, thresh wheat, and shine shoes. After a long stint as a hobo and a short one in the Spanish–American War, he went to college and started a writing career, out of which poured poetry, socialist pamphlets, newspaper coverage of the labor movement, a six-volume biography of Abraham Lincoln, children's stories, and more poems. His *Complete Poems* won him a second Pulitzer Prize in 1951.

> Thomas Jefferson had red hair and a violin
> and he loved life and people and music
> and books and writing and quiet thoughts—
> a lover of peace, decency, good order,
> summer corn ripening for the bins of winter,
> cows in green pastures, colts sucking at mares,
> apple trees waiting to laugh with pippins—
> Jefferson loved peace like a good farmer.
> And yet—for eight years he fought in a war—
> writing with his own hand the war announcement
> named The Declaration of Independence
> making The Fourth of July a sacred calendar date.
> And there was his friend and comrade

289

Ben Franklin, the printer, bookman, diplomat:
all Franklin asked was they let him alone
so he could do his work as lover of peace and work—
Franklin too made war for eight years—
the same Franklin who said two nations
would better throw dice than go to war—
he threw in with fighters for freedom—
for eight years he threw in all he had:
the books, the printshop, fun with electricity,
searches and researches in science pure and applied—
these had to wait while he joined himself
to eight long years of war for freedom, independence.

Now, of course, these two odd fellows
stand as only two among many:
the list runs long of these fellows,
lovers of a peace, decency, good order,
who throw in with all they've got
for the abstractions "freedom," "independence."
Strictly they were gentle men, not hunting trouble.
Strictly they wanted quiet, the good life, freedom.
They would rather have had the horses of instruction
those eight years they gave to the tigers of wrath.
The record runs they were both dreamers
at the same time they refused imitations of the real thing
at the same time they stood up and talked back
at the same time they met the speech of steel and cunning
with their own relentless steel and cunning.

—ESSAY—

LET THAT OLD-TIME FREEDOM RING OUT

JOHN BALZAR {JULY 4, 2001}

A correspondent for the *The Los Angeles Times* with a taste for adventure, and a Scripps–Howard Foundation Prize winner for human-interest writing, John Balzar (b. 1947) has worked on a riverboat in Alaska's Brooks Range Mountains and sailed across the Pacific. His book, *Yukon Alone*, published in 2000, is an account of the 1,023-mile Yukon Quest International Dog Sled Race. In an Independence Day editorial in 2001, Balzar reported on one of the most fantastic adventures of all: living in "a nation founded on the principle of self-governance that has always been skeptical of government."

We are two peoples looking in different directions: those who believe we're on the right track, and those who think we're not. We are a hundred peoples, fragmented by wealth, language, culture, ability, sensibility and opportunity. We are two peoples divided by commitment. Half of us vote, half do not. We are one people with red, white and blue bunting on our lampposts.

With our cook grills sizzling in the shade. With our eyes uplifted to fireworks blooming over dimpled water.

This Fourth of July falls on Wednesday, the most ambivalent day of the week. This is fitting. Travel across the United States. People worry that the country is going nowhere fast. But ask them about their lives. They thrive on ever-bigger ambitions for themselves.

Independence Day is a fanciful wisp of hope. Just like the nation whose birthday we celebrate. Independence Day marks a trail of bread crumbs from our past to our present, one as uncertain as the other. Independence Day is a flagpole we grasp once a year to try to steady ourselves.

We are an improbable nation of people and peoples. Calculating the odds 225 years ago, you couldn't have found a bookie in the world to dare a bet on the future of the United States. Nothing like it had ever survived. There was no model for a congregation of angry malcontents with a conceit that they could govern themselves. History, and common sense, told otherwise.

Yes, republics founded on individual sovereignty are commonplace now. For most of human experience, though, the idea suggested mob rule. The Greek city-states were an experiment to the contrary. And the Swiss pulled it off 800 years ago with their cantons. But there had never been anything to succeed on the scale of the 13 squabbling colonies of this New World.

We are people born of optimism but united by cynicism. A nation founded on the principle of self-governance that has always been skeptical of government. Today we have more democracy and more government than anyone in the beginning could have imagined. But no less cynicism. "A cynic," said that old cynic H.L. Mencken, "is a man who, when he smells flowers, looks around for a coffin."

We are people united by idealism too. The Declaration of Independence grants as self-evident that all men are created equal. When the last of the 56 delegates signed this declaration on July 4, 1776, they surely meant to assert only that the people in the colonies were equal to the people of mother England. For not then, and not now, was individual equality ever self-evident—as meaning that you and I and everyone else in the land stands on the same footing. Some of the white men who wrote and signed this declaration held dominion over slaves and others tolerated slavery.

But in the decades since, equality has come to mean just that—a nearly universal aspiration, never attained and maybe unattainable. But a right. And when denied, denounced as a wrong.

We are battle-scarred people. The Declaration of Independence was an act of war. On average, this country has gone to war every 20 years since. The nation sent me to war. My newspaper dispatched me to another. My father fought two wars. Our grandfathers fought in the war to end all wars. Their fathers fought Spain. And their fathers fought each other. Our last war was 10 years ago.

Today, we deploy our soldiers to be peacekeepers. We are ever-busier people, but without clear purpose. Our material gains are the envy of the world. Our material values are not. John Adams, a conservative among the founding fathers, expressed hope that America's Revolutionary War generation could create the security for a commercial class that would bring prosperity so that, finally, our citizens could pursue enlightenment. Instead, we pour our lives into our accumulations, following the wiggy exhortation of that other signer of the Declaration of Independence, Ben Franklin: "Time is money."

We are young people, and we are restless about what we've been bequeathed: a single-minded world of corporate growth. We are baby boomers and we ask—at least some of us ask: Is this the best we can do with our turn at leadership? We are the aging "greatest generation" and we've seen it all, but we've never seen anything like now.

We are people of faith, separated by faiths. We are charitable people and me-first people and predatory people—and there seems to be too many of some and not enough of another. We are down-to-earth people, but we scoop up those lottery tickets by the handful, just in case. We speak of forgiveness on Sunday; we vote for vengeance on Tuesday. We believe in nothing so dearly as freedom, except conformity. We are TV people and book people and golf-on-Sunday people and my-grandpa-gave-me-this-T-shirt people.

In celebration of it all, in spite of it all, we are millions of people with our arms locked around a shared dream: the American Dream.

"I love America because it is a confused, chaotic mess," philosopher Edward Abbey said, "and I hope we can keep it this way for at least another thousand years. . . . Who gave us permission to live this way? Nobody did. We did."

— ESSAY —

WHY I REFUSED THE NATIONAL MEDAL FOR THE ARTS

ADRIENNE RICH {AUGUST 3, 1997}

In 1997, poet Adrienne Rich (b. 1929), the author of nearly twenty volumes of poetry, was chosen to be one of twelve recipients of the National Medal for the Arts at the White House. She declined in a letter to Jane Alexander, then head of the National Endowment for the Arts, saying that "the very meaning of art, as I understand it, is incompatible with the cynical politics of this administration." A month later, she expanded on her beliefs about the role of art in a free society.

The invitation from the White House came by telephone on July 3, just before the national holiday, a time of public contention about the relationship of government to the arts. After several years' erosion of arts funding and hostile propaganda from the religious right and the Republican Congress, the House vote to end the National Endowment for the Arts was looming. That vote would break as news on July 10; my refusal of the National Medal for the Arts would run as a sidebar story in *The New York Times* and the *San Francisco Chronicle*.

In fact, I was unaware of the timing. My "no" came directly out of my work as a poet and essayist and citizen drawn to the interfold of personal and public experience. I had recently been thinking and writing about the growing fragmentation of the social compact, of whatever it was this country had ever meant when it called itself a democracy: the shredding of the vision of government of the people, by the people, for the people. "We the people—still an excellent phrase," said the prize-winning playwright Lorraine Hansberry in 1962, well aware who had been excluded, yet believing the phrase might someday come to embrace us all. And I had for years been feeling both personal and public grief, fear, hunger and the need to render this, my time, in the language of my art.

Whatever was "newsworthy" about my refusal was not about a single individual—not myself, not President Clinton. Nor was it about a single political party. Both major parties have displayed a crude affinity for the interests of corporate power while deserting the majority of the people, especially the most vulnerable. Like so many others, I've watched the dismantling of our public education, the steep rise in our incarceration rates, the demonization of our young black men, the accusations against our teenage mothers, the selling of health care—public and private—to the highest bidders, the export of subsistence-level jobs in the United States to even lower-wage countries, the use of below-minimum-wage prison labor to break strikes and raise profits, the scapegoating of immigrants, the denial of dignity and minimal security to our working and poor people. At the same time, we've witnessed the acquisition of publishing houses, once risk-taking conduits of creativity, by conglomerates driven single-mindedly to fast profits, the acquisition of major communications and media by those same interests, the sacrifice of the arts and public libraries in stripped-down school and civic budgets and, most recently, the evisceration of the National Endowment for the Arts. Piece by piece the democratic process has been losing ground to the accumulation of private wealth.

There is no political leadership in the White House or the Congress that has spoken to and for the people who, in a very real sense, have felt abandoned by their government.

Hansberry spoke her words about government during the Cuban missile crisis, at a public meeting in New York to abolish the House Un-American Activities Committee. She also said in that speech, "My government is wrong." She did not say, I abhor all government. She claimed her government as a citizen, African American and female, and she challenged it. (I listened to her words again, on an old vinyl recording, this past Fourth of July.)

In a similar spirit, many of us today might wish to hold government accountable, challenge the agendas of private power and wealth that have displaced historical tendencies toward genuinely representative government in the United States. We might still wish to claim our government, to say, This belongs to us—we, the people, as we are now.

We would have to start asking questions that have been defined as non-questions—or as naive, childish questions. In the recent official White House focus on race, it goes consistently unsaid that the all-embracing enterprise of our early history was the slave trade, which left nothing, no single life, untouched and was, along with the genocide of the native population and the seizure of their lands, the foundation of our national prosperity and power. Promote dialogues on race? Apologize for slavery? We would need to perform an autopsy on capitalism itself.

Marxism has been declared dead. Yet the questions Marx raised are still alive and pulsing, however the language and the labels have been co-opted and abused. What is social wealth? How do the conditions of human labor infiltrate other social relationships? What would it require for people to live and work together in conditions of radical equality? How much inequality will we tolerate in the world's richest and most powerful nation? Why and how have these and similar questions become discredited in public discourse?

And what about art? Mistrusted, adored, pietized, condemned, dismissed as entertainment, auctioned at Sotheby's, purchased by investment-seeking celebrities, it dies into the "art object" of a thousand museum basements. It's also reborn hourly in prisons, women's shelters, small-town garages, community college workshops, halfway houses—wherever someone picks up a pencil, a wood-burning tool, a copy of "The Tempest," a tag-sale camera, a whittling knife, a stick of charcoal, a pawnshop horn, a video of "Citizen Kane," whatever lets you know again that this deeply instinctual yet self-conscious expressive language, this regenerative process, could help you save your life. "If there were no poetry on any day in the world," the poet Muriel Rukeyser wrote, "poetry would be invented that day. For there would be an intolerable hunger." In an essay on the Caribbean poet Aimé Césaire, Clayton Eshleman names this hunger as "the desire, the need, for a more profound and ensouled world." There is a continuing dynamic between art repressed and art reborn, between the relentless marketing of the superficial and the "spectral and vivid reality that employs all means" (Rukeyser again) to reach through armoring, resistances, resignation, to recall us to desire.

Art is both tough and fragile. It speaks of what we long to hear and what we dread to find. Its source and native impulse, the imagination, may be shackled in early life, yet may find release in conditions offering little else to the spirit. For a recent document on this, look at Phyllis Kornfeld's "Cellblock Visions: Prison Art in America," notable for the variety and emotional depth of the artworks reproduced, the words of the inmate artists and for Kornfeld's unsentimental and lucid text. Having taught art to inmates for 14 years in 18 institutions (including maximum security units), she sees recent incarceration policy overall as rapidly devolving from rehabilitation to dehumanization, including the dismantling of prison arts programs.

Art can never be totally legislated by any system, even those that reward obedience and send dissident artists to hard labor and death; nor can it, in our specifically compromised system, be really free. It may push up through cracked macadam, by the merest means, but it needs breathing space, cultivation, protection to fulfill itself. Just as people do. New artists, young or old, need education in their art, the tools of their craft, chances to study examples from the past and meet practitioners in the present, get the criticism and encouragement of mentors, learn that they are not alone. As the social compact withers, fewer and fewer people will be told, yes, you can do this, this also belongs to you. Like government, art needs the participation of the many in order not to become the property of a powerful and narrowly self-interested minority.

Art is our human birthright, our most powerful means of access to our own and another's experience and imaginative life. In continually rediscovering and recovering the humanity of human beings, art is crucial to the democratic vision. A government tending further and further away from the search for democracy will see less and less "use" in encouraging artists, will see art as obscenity or hoax.

In 1987, the late Justice William Brennan spoke of "formal reason severed from the insights of passion" as a major threat to due-process principles. "Due process asks whether government has treated someone fairly, whether individual dignity has been honored, whether the worth of an individual has been acknowledged. Officials cannot always silence these questions by pointing to rational action taken according to standard rules. They must plumb their conduct more deeply, seeking answers in the more complex equations of human nature and experience."

It is precisely where fear and hatred of art join the pull toward quantification and abstraction, where the human face is mechanically deleted, that human dignity disappears from the social equation. Because it is to those "complex equations of human nature and experience" that art addresses itself.

In a society tyrannized by the accumulation of wealth as Eastern Europe was tyrannized by its own false gods of concentrated power, recognized artists have, perhaps, a new opportunity to work out our connectedness, as artists, with other people who are beleaguered, suffering, disenfranchised—precariously employed workers, trashed elders, throwaway youth, the "unsuccessful" and the art they too are nonetheless making and seeking.

I wish I didn't feel the necessity to say here that none of this is about imposing ideology or style or content on artists; it is about the inseparability of art from acute social crisis in this century and the one now coming up.

We have a short-lived model in our history for the place of art in relation to government. During the Depression of the 1930s, under New Deal legislation, thousands of creative and performing artists were paid modest stipends to work in the Federal Writers Project, the Federal Theatre Project, the Federal Art Project. Their creativity, in the form of novels, murals, plays, performances, public monuments, the providing of music and theater to new audiences, seeded the art and the consciousness of succeeding decades. By 1939, this funding was discontinued.

Federal funding for the arts, like the philanthropy of private arts patrons, can be given and taken away. In the long run, art needs to grow organically out of a social compost nourishing to everyone, a literate citizenry, a free, universal, public education complex with art as an integral element, a society without throwaway people, honoring both human individuality and the search for a decent, sustainable common life. In such conditions, art would still be a voice of hunger, desire, discontent, passion, reminding us that the democratic project is never-ending.

For that to happen, what else would have to change? I hope the discussion will continue.

—POEM—
THE CONGRESSIONAL LIBRARY
AMY LOWELL {1922}

Amy Lowell (1874–1925) grew up in a prominent Massachusetts family and struck out on her own to became a well-known Imagist poet. She owed part of her fame to her striking, studied appearance: She often dressed in a starched shirt, suit, and tie, and smoked cigars. While many of her poems were erotic in nature, "The Congressional Library" was inspired by her visit to the Library, where she found that the "confusion and brilliance of the whole, from floor to roof, are, I think, very typical of America." The poem was published to rousing silence, but the Congressional Library later high-lighted the poem as part of its bicentennial celebration.

> The earth is a colored thing.
> See the red clays, and the umbers and salt greys of
>   the mountains;
> See the clustered and wandering greens of plains
>   and hillsides,
> The leaf-greens, bush-greens, water-plant and
>   snow-greens
> Of gardens and forests.
> See the reds of flowers—hibiscus, poppy,
>   geranium;
> The rose-red of little flowers—may-flowers,
>   primroses;
> The harlequin shades of sweet-peas, orchids,
>   pansies;
> The madders, saffrons, chromes, of still waters,
> The silver and star-blues, the wine-blues of seas
>   and oceans.

Observe the stars at nighttime, name the color of
    them;
Count and recount the hues of clouds at sunset and
    at dawn.
And the colors of the races of men—
What are they?
And what are we?
We, the people without a race,
Without a language;
Of all races, and of none;
Of all tongues, and one imposed;
Of all traditions and all pasts,
With no tradition and no past.
A patchwork and an altar-piece,
Vague as sea-mist,
Myriad as forest-trees,
Living into a present,
Building a future.
Our color is the vari-colored world.
No colors clash,
All clash and change,
And, in changing, new colors come and go and
    dominate and remain,
And no one shall say which remain,
Since those that have vanished return,
And those no man has seen take the light and are.

Where else in all America are we so symbolized
As in this hall?
White columns polished like glass,
A dome and a dome,
A balcony and a balcony,
Stairs and the balustrades to them,
Yellow marble and red slabs of it,
All mounting, spearing, flying into color.

Color round the dome and up to it,
Color curving, kite-flying, to the second dome,
Light, dropping, pitching down upon the color,
Arrow-falling upon the glass-bright pillars,
Mingled colors spinning into a shape of white pillars,
Fusing, cooling, into balanced shafts of shrill and
    interthronging light.
This is America,
This vast, confused beauty,
This staring, restless speed of loveliness,
Mighty, overwhelming, crude, of all forms,
Making grandeur out of profusion,
Afraid of no incongruities,
Sublime in its audacity,
Bizarre breaker of moulds,
Laughing with strength,
Charging down on the past,
Glorious and conquering,
Destroyer, builder,
Invincible pith and marrow of the world,
An old world remaking,
Whirling into the no-world of all-colored light.
But behind the vari-colored hall?
The entrails, the belly,
The blood-run veins, the heart and viscera,
What of these?
Only at night do they speak,
Only at night do the voices rouse themselves and speak.
There are words in the veins of this creature,
There are still notes singing in its breast:
Silent voices, whispering what it shall speak,
Frozen music beating upon its pulses.
These are the voices of the furious dead who
    never die,
Furious with love, and life, unquenchable,

Dictating their creeds across the vapors of time.
This is the music of the Trumpeters of the Almighty
Weeping for a lost estate,
Sounding to a new birth which is tomorrow.
Hark! This hurricane of music has no end,
The speech of these voices has neither end nor
    beginning;
They are inter-riven as the colors of the sky
Over the graveyards of ten thousand generations.
When we are as Nineveh, our white columns
    thrown and scattered,
Our dome of colors striped with the crawling of
    insects,
Spotted with the thrust of damp clay—
Our words, our music, who will build a dome to
    hive them?
In whose belly shall we come to life?
A new life,
Beyond submergence and destruction,
The implacable life of silent words,
Of tumultuous stillness of never-ceasing music,
Lost to being that so it may triumph
And become the blood and heat and urge
Of that hidden distance which forever whips and
    harries the static present
Of mankind.

— SPEECH —

DEMOCRATIC NATIONAL CONVENTION KEYNOTE ADDRESS: WHO THEN WILL SPEAK FOR THE COMMON GOOD?

BARBARA JORDAN {JULY 12, 1976}

Barbara Jordan (1936–1996) lived a life of firsts: She was the first African-American woman to serve in the Texas Senate—and the first African American elected to that body since 1883. In 1972, she became the first African-American woman from the South to be elected to the U. S. Congress, where, as a member of the House Judiciary Committee, she played a pivotal role investigating the Nixon administration's involvement in the Watergate cover-up. Her considerable oratory skills helped win her an invitation to present the keynote address to the 1976 Democratic National Convention, the first African American to do so. Jordan, as a rule, did not mince words. "What the people want is simple," she once said in a Harvard commencement address. "They want an America as good as its promise."

One hundred and forty-four years ago, members of the Democratic Party first met in convention to select a Presidential candidate. Since that time, Democrats have continued to convene once every four years and draft a party platform and nominate a Presidential candidate. And our meeting this week is a continuation of that tradition.

But there is something different about tonight. There is something special about tonight. What is different? What is Special? I, Barbara Jordan, am a keynote speaker.

A lot of years passed since 1832, and during that time it would have been most unusual for any national political party to ask that a Barbara Jordan deliver a keynote address . . . but tonight here I am. And I feel that notwithstanding the past that my presence here is one additional bit of evidence that the American Dream need not forever be deferred.

Now that I have this grand distinction, what in the world am I supposed to say?

I could easily spend this time praising the accomplishments of this party and attacking the Republicans but I don't choose to do that.

I could list the many problems which Americans have. I could list the problems which cause people to feel cynical, angry, frustrated: problems which include lack of integrity in government; the feeling that the individual no longer counts; the reality of material and spiritual poverty; the feeling that the grand American experiment is failing or has failed. I could recite these problems and then I could sit down and offer no solutions. But I don't choose to do that either.

The citizens of America expect more. They deserve and they want more than a recital of problems.

We are a people in a quandary about the present. We are a people in search of our future. We are a people in search of a national community.

We are a people trying not only to solve the problems of the present: unemployment, inflation . . . but we are attempting on a larger scale to fulfill the promise of America. We are attempting to fulfill our national purpose; to create and sustain a society in which all of us are equal.

Throughout our history, when people have looked for new ways to solve their problems, and to uphold the principles of this nation, many times they have turned to political parties. They have often turned to the Democratic Party.

What is it, what is it about the Democratic Party that makes it the instrument that people use when they search for ways to shape their future? Well, I believe the answer to that question lies in our concept of governing. Our concept of governing is derived from our view of people. It is a concept deeply rooted in a set of beliefs firmly etched in the national conscience, of all of us.

Now what are these beliefs?

First, we believe in equality for all and privileges for none. This is a belief that each American regardless of background has equal standing in the public forum, all of us. Because we believe this idea so firmly, we are inclusive rather than an exclusive party. Let everybody come.

I think it no accident that most of those emigrating to America in the 19th century identified with the Democratic Party. We are a heterogeneous party made up of Americans of diverse backgrounds.

We believe that the people are the source of all governmental power; that the authority of the people is to be extended, not restricted. This can be accomplished only by providing each citizen with every opportunity to participate in the management of the government. They must have that.

We believe that the government which represents the authority of all the people, not just one interest group, but all the people, has an obligation to actively underscore, actively seek to remove those obstacles which would block individual achievement . . . obstacles emanating from race, sex, economic condition. The government must seek to remove them.

We are a party of innovation. We do not reject our traditions, but we are willing to adapt to changing circumstances, when change we must. We are willing to suffer the discomfort of change in order to achieve a better future.

We have a positive vision of the future founded on the belief that the gap between the promise and reality of America can one day be finally closed. We believe that.

This, my friends, is the bedrock of our concept of governing. This is a part of the reason why Americans have turned to the Democratic Party. These are the foundations upon which a national community can be built.

Let's all understand that these guiding principles cannot be discarded for short-term political gains. They represent what this country is all about. They are indigenous to the American idea. And these are principles which are not negotiable.

In other times, I could stand here and give this kind of exposition on the beliefs of the Democratic Party and that would be enough. But today that is not enough. People want more. That is not sufficient reason for the majority of the people of this country to vote Democratic. We have made mistakes. In our haste to do all things for all people, we did not foresee the full consequences of our actions. And when the people raised their voices, we didn't hear. But our deafness was only a temporary condition, and not an irreversible condition.

Even as I stand here and admit that we have made mistakes, I still believe that as the people of America sit in judgment on each party, they will recognize that our mistakes were mistakes of the heart. They'll recognize that.

And now we must look to the future. Let us heed the voice of the people and recognize their common sense. If we do not, we not only blaspheme our political heritage, we ignore the common ties that bind all Americans.

Many fear the future. Many are distrustful of their leaders, and believe that their voices are never heard. Many seek only to satisfy their private work wants. To satisfy private interests.

But this is the great danger America faces. That we will cease to be one nation and become instead a collection of interest groups: city against suburb, region against region, individual against individual. Each seeking to satisfy private wants.

If that happens, who then will speak for America?

Who then will speak for the common good?

This is the question which must be answered in 1976.

Are we to be one people bound together by common spirit sharing in a common endeavor or will we become a divided nation?

For all of its uncertainty, we cannot flee the future. We must not become the new puritans and reject our society. We must address and master the future together. It can be done if we restore the belief that we share a sense of national community, that we share a common national endeavor. It can be done.

There is no executive order; there is no law that can require the American people to form a national community. This we must do as individuals and if we do it as individuals, there is no President of the United States who can veto that decision.

As a first step, We must restore our belief in ourselves. We are a generous people, so why can't we be generous with each other? We need to take to heart the words spoken by Thomas Jefferson:

"Let us restore to social intercourse the harmony and that affection without which liberty and even life are but dreary things.

A nation is formed by the willingness of each of us to share in the responsibility for upholding the common good.

A government is invigorated when each of us is willing to participate in shaping the future of this nation."

In this election year, we must define the common good and begin again to shape a common good and begin again to shape a common future. Let each person do his or her part. If one citizen is unwilling to participate, all of us are going to suffer. For the American idea, though it is shared by all of us, is realized in each one of us.

And now, what are those of us who are elected public officials supposed to do? We call ourselves public servants but I'll tell you this: we as public servants must set an example for the rest of the nation. It is hypocritical for the public official to admonish and exhort the people to uphold the common good. More is required of public officials than slogans and handshakes and press releases. More is required. We must hold ourselves strictly accountable. We must provide the people with a vision of the future.

If we promise as public officials, we must deliver. If we as public officials propose, we must produce. If we say to the American people it is time for you to be sacrificial; sacrifice. If the public official says that, we (public officials) must be the first to give. We must be. And again, if we make mistakes, we must be willing to admit them. We have to do that. What we have to do is strike a balance between the idea, the belief, that government ought to do nothing. Strike a balance.

Let there be no illusions about the difficulty of forming this kind of a national community. It's tough, difficult, not easy. But a spirit of harmony will survive in America only if each of us remembers that we share a common destiny.

I have confidence that we can form this kind of national community.

I have confidence that the Democratic Party can lead the way. I have confidence. We cannot improve on the system of government handed down to us by the founders of the Republic, there is no way to improve upon that. But what we can do is to find new ways to implement that system and realize our destiny.

Now, I began this speech by commenting to you on the uniqueness of a Barbara Jordan making the keynote address. Well, I am going to close my speech by quoting a Republican president and I ask you that as you listen to these words of Abraham Lincoln, relate them to the concept of national community in which every last one of us participates:

307

"As I would not be a slave, so I would not be a master. This expresses my idea of Democracy. Whatever differs from this, to the extent of the difference is no Democracy."

—SPEECH—

COMMENCEMENT ADDRESS AT NORTHERN ARIZONA UNIVERSITY

WILMA MANKILLER {DECEMBER 18, 1992}

From 1985 to 1995, Wilma Mankiller (b. 1945) was the Principal Chief—the first woman ever to hold this position—of the 139,000 members of the Cherokee Nation. She is a well-known national advocate for civil rights and community development and the recipient of numerous awards for her public service.

Iran into someone at the hotel this morning who asked me about how to address me on my credit card. It has "Wilma Mankiller, Principal Chief," and that is interesting because I think some people still have a little trouble identifying with a female principal chief. It reminded me of the first time I had to address this issue. I went to a very prestigious Eastern college to do a panel on Indian economic development, and this young man picked me up at the airport to take me to the university. He asked me, "Since principal chief is a male term, how should I address you?" I just ignored him and looked out the window of the car, and then he asked me if he should address me as "chieftainess." I continued to look out the window, and then he thought he would get silly and cute. He asked me if he should address me as "Chiefette." I finally told him to address me as Ms. Chief—mischief. So we went out to the university, and this young man had the fortune or misfortune, I am not sure, to be one of the people who got to ask the panel questions. His question to me was about my last name.

Mankiller is my maiden name, and way back in Cherokee history, Mankiller was like the "keeper of the village"—like the equivalent of a general or someone who watched over a village—and this one fellow liked the title so much he kept it as his name; but that's not what I told this young man. I told him it was a nickname and I had earned it. So somewhere back East there is a young man who is wondering what I did to earn my last name.

I am not going to give the standard advice about going out into the world, because many of you have already been out in the world and worked and been very involved in your communities. What I would like to do is encourage you in whatever you pursue or wherever you go from here to get involved. What I have seen, I think, in the United States, not just in my community or tribal community or rural community but in the United States in general, is a trend for all of us to think that somebody else is going to solve our problems for us.

It was interesting during this last year watching the presidential election and being aware of all these daunting sets of problems we face in this country—economy, education, health care, problems in the inner city; and everybody expecting somebody else to solve them. In the presidential election, no matter who was chosen for a candidate, people were counting on this one man to be able to articulate a clear vision for the future and then take care of all of the problems for the country. Do not think this is going to happen. Even in my own community I have heard people talk about the environment, housing, hopelessness, or any of the problems that we have; "Well, they're going to solve that problem." I see that also in American society it is always, "They're going to solve that problem." I don't know who "they" are. I always tell our own people that I don't know who they are referring to. To me the only people who are going to solve our problems are ourselves—people like you and me. We have got to personally take charge and solve our problems. I do not think that a great prophet is going to come along and save this country or save us and deal with all of these problems in a vacuum. We all have to take part in that. So I would encourage you to get involved; you will be immensely rewarded by getting into public service or by doing small things around your community and trying to help others.

The other advice I have to give you is, do not live your life safely. I would take risks and not do things just because everybody else does them. In my generation someone who had a big impact on me was Robert Kennedy, who in one speech said, "Some people see things the way they are and ask why, and others dream things that never were and ask why not?" I think that is where I hope many of you will be—people that question why things are and why we have to do them the way we have always done them. I hope you will take some risks, exert some real leadership on issues, and, if you will, dance along the edge of the roof as you continue your life here.

Finally, I just want to make a couple of comments about where I see our country going in general. I just came back from the Economic Summit in Little Rock, Arkansas, which was an intense two-day session focusing specifically on how to stimulate the economy, both short term and long term. I was encouraged by the number and diversity of people there—Republicans and Democrats. People from every sector of the business community and every sector of society talking collectively about how to get the country moving again.

I think one of the things we have to do as a nation, besides addressing specific issues like the economy, health care, education, inner cities, and that sort of thing, is we have to examine the extent to which we continue to have stereotypes about one another. I think it is very difficult for us to collectively and symbolically join hands and begin to move forward in solving this country's problems if we continue to have these stereotypes about one another. There still exist in this country many negative stereotypes about black people, Latin people, and Asian people. God knows there are terrible stereotypes about Native Americans; these have to be overcome before we can move forward.

Sometimes I sit down with a diverse group of people in Oklahoma to work on some problem that we all have in common; it is almost like sitting down with people who have some kind of veil over their face or something. We all look at each other through this veil that causes us to see each other through these stereotypes. I think we need to lift back the veil and deal with each other on a more human level in order to continue to progress.

The minority population in this country is dramatically increasing, and that is a fact. If we continue to have this increase in minority population, we need to find ways of dealing with each other and working with each other in much better ways, because it affects everybody. I do not think that we can say that what happens in Detroit does not somehow affect all America, because it does. I would urge all of you who are here today, both graduates and families, to examine the extent to which we hold those stereotypes about one another. And finally, I would hope my being here and spending just a couple of minutes today would help you to eliminate any stereotypes you might have about what a chief looks like.

— SPEECH —

SPEECH ON SENATE FLOOR: DECLARATION OF CONSCIENCE

MARGARET CHASE SMITH {JUNE 1, 1950}

On June 1, 1950, Senator Margaret Chase Smith (1897–1995) of Maine became the first member of the U.S. Senate to denounce the tactics of intimidation and character assassination employed by her colleague and fellow Republican, Senator Joseph McCarthy of Wisconsin, in his campaign to purge the government and the nation of Communists. Smith reminded the Senate—and the nation—that the fundamental American right to freedom of expression includes the right to hold unpopular beliefs. But what really shook up her audience was her declaration that a Republican Fascist—and she clearly meant McCarthy—was just as dangerous to liberty as any subversive American Communist.

I would like to speak briefly and simply about a serious national condition. It is a national feeling of fear and frustration that could result in national suicide and the end of everything that we Americans hold dear. It is a condition that comes from the lack of effective leadership in either the Legislative Branch or the Executive Branch of our Government.

That leadership is so lacking that serious and responsible proposals are being made that national advisory commissions be appointed to provide such critically needed leadership.

I speak as briefly as possible because too much harm has already been done with irresponsible words of bitterness and selfish political opportunism. I speak as simply as possible because the issue is too great to be obscured by eloquence. I speak simply and briefly in the hope that my words will be taken to heart.

I speak as a Republican. I speak as a woman. I speak as a United States Senator. I speak as an American.

The United States Senate has long enjoyed worldwide respect as the greatest deliberative body in the world. But recently that deliberative character has too often been debased to the level of a forum of hate and character assassination sheltered by the shield of congressional immunity.

It is ironical that we Senators can, in debate in the Senate directly or indirectly, by any form of words, impute any American who is not a Senator any conduct or motive unworthy or unbecoming an American—and without that non-Senator American having any legal redress against us—yet if we say the same thing in the Senate about our colleagues we can be stopped on the grounds of being out of order.

It is strange that we can verbally attack anyone else without restraint and with full protection and yet we hold ourselves above the same type of criticism here on the Senate Floor. Surely the United States Senate is big enough to take self-criticism and self-appraisal. Surely we should be able to take the same kind of character attacks that we "dish out" to outsiders.

I think that it is high time for the United States Senate and its members to do some soul-searching—for us to weigh our consciences—on the manner in which we are performing our duty to the people of America—on the manner in which we are using or abusing our individual powers and privileges.

I think that it is high time that we remembered that we have sworn to uphold and defend the Constitution. I think that it is high time that we remembered that the Constitution, as amended, speaks not only of the freedom of speech but also of trial by jury instead of trial by accusation.

Whether it be a criminal prosecution in court or a character prosecution in the Senate, there is little practical distinction when the life of a person has been ruined.

Those of us who shout the loudest about Americanism in making character assassinations are all too frequently those who, by our own words and acts, ignore some of the basic principles of Americanism:

The right to criticize;

The right to hold unpopular beliefs;

The right to protest;

The right of independent thought.

The exercise of these rights should not cost one single American citizen his reputation or his right to a livelihood nor should he be in danger of losing his reputation or livelihood merely because he happens to know someone who holds unpopular beliefs. Who of us doesn't? Otherwise none of us could call our souls our own. Otherwise thought control would have set in.

The American people are sick and tired of being afraid to speak their minds lest they be politically smeared as "Communists" or "Fascists" by their opponents. Freedom of speech is not what it used to be in America. It has been so abused by some that it is not exercised by others.

The American people are sick and tired of seeing innocent people smeared and guilty people whitewashed. But there have been enough proved cases such as the Amerasia case, the Hiss case, the Coplon case, the Gold case, to cause nationwide distrust and suspicion that there may be something to the unproved, sensational accusations.

As a Republican, I say to my colleagues on this side of the aisle that the Republican Party faces a challenge today that is not unlike the challenge that it faced back in Lincoln's day. The Republican Party so successfully met that challenge that it emerged from the Civil War as the champion of a united nation—in addition to being a Party that unrelentingly fought loose spending and loose programs.

Today our country is being psychologically divided by the confusion and the suspicions that are bred in the United States Senate to spread like cancerous tentacles of "know nothing, suspect everything" attitudes. Today we have a Democratic Administration that has developed a mania for loose spending and loose programs. History is repeating itself and the Republican Party again has the opportunity to emerge as the champion of unity and prudence.

The record of the present Democratic Administration has provided us with sufficient campaign issues without the necessity of resorting to political smears. America is rapidly losing its position as leader of the world simply because the Democratic Administration has pitifully failed to provide effective leadership.

The Democratic Administration has completely confused the American people by its daily contradictory grave warnings and optimistic assurances—that show the people that our Democratic Administration has no idea of where it is going.

The Democratic Administration has greatly lost the confidence of the American people by its complacency to the threat of communism here at home and the leak of vital secrets to Russia through key officials of the Democratic Administration. There are enough proved cases to make this point without diluting our criticism with unproved charges.

Surely these are sufficient reasons to make it clear to the American people that it is time for a change and that a Republican victory is necessary to the security of this country. Surely it is clear that this nation will continue to suffer as long as it is governed by the present ineffective Democratic Administration.

Yet to displace it with a Republican regime embracing a philosophy that lacks political integrity or intellectual honesty would prove equally disastrous to this nation. The nation sorely needs a Republican victory. But I don't want to see the Republican Party ride to political victory on the Four Horsemen of Calumny—Fear, Ignorance, Bigotry, and Smear.

I doubt if the Republican Party could—simply because I don't believe the American people will uphold any political party that puts political exploitation above national interest. Surely we Republicans aren't that desperate for victory.

I don't want to see the Republican Party win that way. While it might be a fleeting victory for the Republican Party, it would be a more lasting defeat for the American people. Surely it would ultimately be suicide for the Republican Party and the two-party system that has protected our American liberties from the dictatorship of a one-party system.

As members of the Minority Party, we do not have the primary authority to formulate the policy of our Government. But we do have the responsibility of rendering constructive criticism, of clarifying issues, of allaying fears by acting as responsible citizens.

As a woman, I wonder how the mothers, wives, sisters, and daughters feel about the way in which members of their families have been politically mangled in Senate debate—and I use the word "debate" advisedly.

As a United States Senator, I am not proud of the way in which the Senate has been made a publicity platform for irresponsible sensationalism. I am not proud of the reckless abandon in which unproved charges have been hurled from this side of the aisle. I am not proud of the obviously staged, undignified countercharges that have been attempted in retaliation from the other side of the aisle.

I don't like the way the Senate has been made a rendezvous for vilification, for selfish political gain at the sacrifice of individual reputations and national unity. I am not proud of the way we smear outsiders from the Floor of the Senate and hide behind the cloak of Congressional immunity and still place ourselves beyond criticism on the Floor of the Senate.

As an American, I am shocked at the way Republicans and Democrats alike are playing directly into the Communist design of "confuse, divide, and conquer." As an American, I don't want a Democratic Administration "whitewash" or "cover-up" any more than I want a Republican smear or witch hunt.

As an American, I condemn a Republican "Fascist" just as much as I condemn a Democrat "Communist." I condemn a Democrat "Fascist" just as much as I condemn a Republican "Communist." They are equally dangerous to you and me and to our country. As an American, I want to see our nation recapture the strength and unity it once had when we fought the enemy instead of ourselves.

It is with these thoughts that I have drafted what I call a "Declaration of Conscience." I am gratified that Senator Tobey, Senator Aiken, Senator Morse, Senator Ives, Senator Thye, and Senator Hendrickson have concurred in that declaration and have authorized me to announce their concurrence.

—SPEECH—

COMMENCEMENT ADDRESS AT THE COLLEGE OF SANTA FE

TOM BROKAW {MAY 15, 1999}

Tom Brokaw (b. 1940) joined NBC News in 1966 as a reporter in Los Angeles and has been the anchor of *NBC Nightly News* since 1983. To his many accomplishments and honors as a broadcast journalist, Brokaw has added articles and essays, and three books, including the best-selling *The Greatest Generation,* an account of the generation that survived the Depression and World War II to build post-war American prosperity. He himself was raised working class in South Dakota, where he studied political science at the University of South Dakota before landing a $100-a-week job at an Omaha television station.

One hundred years ago, another class of '99 was anticipating a new century, rich with the possibility of new technologies—electricity, the automobile, the first tentative steps toward flight. The men who controlled the railroads and steel and oil were amassing great fortunes and making America the new industrial and financial capital of the world. . . .

As it turns out, all of that exciting and empowering new technology was in its seminal stages, primitive, really, compared to what was to come—the splitting of the atom, jet travel and the space age, the mapping of the body's molecular structure, the expansive new universe of cyber-technology.

God, the possibilities for advancing the human condition and expanding the cosmos of intellectual understanding! In fact, giant steps were taken, great leaps well beyond what the most prescient member of the class of 1899 could have anticipated.

The twentieth century—what a triumph. And what an ugly scar on the face of history.

Two world wars with millions of casualties, holocausts in the heart of Western civilization, in Southeast Asia and in Africa killing millions more. An ideology designed to empower the masses became one of the most ruthless instruments of oppression. Rival nations pointed at each other terrible weapons capable of destroying life on Earth as we know it.

In the closing days of this momentous time, in the American culture, maniacal homicide committed by schoolboys shocked the nation into a dialogue of ill-defined blame—while in Europe the most powerful political military alliance on the globe made a clumsy attempt to neutralize a murderous tyrant and in the execution of that attempt, set off a refugee crisis of historic proportions.

The short lesson: technology is not enough, not even when it comes with a generous package of stock options, sabbaticals, and leased time on a private plane.

The long lesson? It is not enough to wire the world if you short-circuit the soul. It is not enough to probe the hostile environments of distant galaxies if we fail to resolve the climate of mindless violence, ethnic and racial hate here in the bosom of Mother Earth. It is not enough to identify the gene that predetermines the prospect of Alzheimer's disease if we go through the prime of life with a closed mind.

I am incapable of helping you advance your knowledge in the matters that brought you to this institution. Frankly, I still don't understand how the picture gets from where I work to your television set. I call it a miracle and leave it at that.

So I am all the more in awe of your capacity to change the gears on all the machinery of the world, broadly speaking. But I have learned something of the political and social possibilities—and failings—of mankind in my thirty-seven years as a journalist.

First, for all of its shocking and brutal stretches of oppression and extermination, the most powerful idea of the twentieth century is freedom. There is so much more political and individual freedom at the end of the twentieth century than at the beginning, and that is a tribute to the enduring and inherent instinct for self-determination, even in the darkest shadows of tyrannical control.

If we fail to first recognize then deal with these societal cancers in our system we will have squandered a priceless legacy left to us by what I have come

317

to call the Greatest Generation. Some of them are here today, although they would not have you know it for they are characteristically modest. They prefer to let their lives and sacrifices speak for them.

They are the men and women who came of age in the Great Depression, when economic despair was on the land like a plague. There were great bands of migrant workers, drifting across the American landscape, looking for enough of a wage to get through the next day. In families youngsters quit school to go to work—not to buy a car for themselves or a new video game. They quit to earn enough to help their family get through another week.

Then, just as the economic gloom was beginning to lift, World War. Two powerful and ruthless regimes, one east, the other west, were determined to choke off the idea of political freedom, political and ethnic pluralism—and to impose their twisted ideology on vast areas of the globe with brutal military might.

Here, the young men and women who had just been tested by the Great Depression were to be tested again—in the battlefields thousands of miles across the Atlantic or thousands of miles across the Pacific. In bitter European cold and the suffocating heat of the jungle. In the air and on the seas, they fought—often hand to hand—for more than three years, day in and day out. More than twelve million in uniform, millions more at home on the assembly lines, converting the American economy into a war machine overnight. Women went to work where only men had prevailed—in the cabs of trucks, in research labs, in shipbuilding yards.

It was a tense, dangerous, and vibrant time. The world was at stake—and at a time in their lives when their days should have been filled with the rewards of starting careers and families, their nights filled with love and innocent adventure, this generation was fighting for survival—theirs and the world's. They prevailed through extraordinary acts of courage and heroism by ordinary people from the farms and the small towns, from the pavement of big cities, from the bucolic and privileged surroundings of great universities.

They saved the world. Nothing less.

Then, they came rushing home to go to college in record numbers; married in record numbers; gave us new art and breakthroughs in science and industry; and expanded political freedoms and, always, a sense of the possible. They rebuilt their enemies and drew the line against a new form of oppression rising like a dark cloud out of Moscow.

They weren't perfect: they were slow to recognize the equal place of women—and racial minorities, especially black and Asian Americans. But those women and black and Asian Americans were part of the tensile strength of this generation, for they never gave up.

They all recognized that for all of the genius of the American political system and the framework of laws, beginning with the Constitution, the enduring strength of this immigrant nation has been its common ground, wide enough and strong enough to accommodate all races and beliefs.

Now great fault lines run through that common ground. We have allowed it to be so fractured we are in danger of becoming less than the sum of our parts. We have become the culture of cheap confrontation rather than resolution.

We have political leaders too eager to divide for their selfish aims rather than unify for the common good. And, yes, we have a mass media much too inclined to exploit these instincts. The quick hit has become a suitable substitute for thoughtful dialogue in both the political and journalistic arena.

In the business arena, we celebrate the astonishing good fortune of those at the top without raising enough questions about the economic opportunity of those at the bottom.

I wonder, is this what the Greatest Generation made all those sacrifices for? Did we win the war—then—and the Cold War later to lose our way?

Francis Fukuyama, the provocative student of social and historical trends, has given voice to the concerns of many, most recently in a long article in the *Atlantic Monthly*. He concludes that in this post-industrial information age, the old conceit that social order has come from a centralized, rational, bureaucratic hierarchy is outdated. Instead, he argues that in the twenty-first century, societies and corporations will decentralize and devolve power and rely on people to be self-organizing, using the new tools of this age.

Social order norms have been disrupted by new technologies before. The shift from rural agrarian to urban industrial economies representing only the most recent example—the impact of freeways and jet travel—in establishing new living patterns.

So now, in this new age of spellbinding possibilities for communication, information retrieval, marketing, and proselytizing, we are undergoing another major shift in the norms of how society is organized for everyday life, work, and play.

It is wildly exciting to be on the frontier of such an empowering era. But no piece of software, no server or search engine will offer you the irreplaceable rewards of a loving personal relationship, the strength and comfort of a real community of shared values and common dreams, the moral underpinning of a life lived well, whatever the financial scorecard. Nor will this new technology by itself make you more racially tolerant—more sensitive to the plight of the disenfranchised—more courageous to take a firm stand for what you know is right.

These are mere tools in your hands. Your hands are an extension not only of your mind, but also of your heart and soul.

Taken altogether they're a powerful combination.

Use them well.

Take care of your Mother, Mother Earth.

Become color-blind.

Hate hate.

Fight violence.

And take care of each other.

You have a whole new century to shape. I envy you, but I want to stand aside now because you have work to do.

—POEM—

I WILL LIVE AND SURVIVE

IRINA RATUSHINSKAYA {1987}

In 1982, poet Irina Ratushinskaya (b. 1954) was charged with anti-Soviet agitation and sentenced to seven years in a labor camp. While in prison, she wrote her poems on bars of soap; once she had them memorized, she washed the words away. In 1987, after her release from prison, Ratushinskaya emigrated to the United States, where she continues to write poetry.

I will live and survive and be asked;
How they slammed my head against a trestle,
How I had to freeze at night,
How my hair started to turn grey . . .
I will smile. And will crack some joke
And brush away the encroaching shadow.
And I will render homage to the dry September
That became my second birth.
And I'll be asked: "Doesn't it hurt you to remember?"
Not being deceived by my outward flippancy.
But the former names will detonate in my memory—
Magnificent as old canon.
And I will tell of the best people in all the earth,
The most tender, but also the most invincible,
How they said farewell, how they went to be tortured,
How they waited for letters from their loved ones,
And I'll be asked: what helped us to live
When there were neither letters nor any bad news—only walls,
And the cold of the cell, and the blather of official lies,
And the sickening promises made in exchange for betrayal.
And I will tell of the first beauty

I saw in captivity.
A frost-covered window! No doors, nor walls,
Nor cell-bars, nor the long-endured pain—
Only a blue radiance on a tiny pane of glass
A cast pattern—none more beautiful could be dreamt!
The more clearly you looked, the more powerfully dawned
Those brigand forests, campfires, and birds!
And how many times there was bitter cold weather
And how many windows sparkled after that one—
But never was repeated,
That upheaval of rainbow ice!
And anyway, what good would it be to me now,
And what would be the pretext for that festival?
Such a gift can only be received once,
And once is probably enough.

—SPEECH—

AMERICA'S CHALLENGE: REVITALIZING OUR NATIONAL COMMUNITY

BILL BRADLEY {FEBRUARY 9, 1995}

While still an All-American basketball player at Princeton University in the 1960s, Bill Bradley (b. 1943) was the subject of a book by John McPhee, *A Sense of Where You Are*. Whether on the basketball court for Princeton, and later for the New York Knicks, or on the floor of the U. S. Senate, Bradley has always been a team player with great peripheral vision. It's hardly surprising that in his 1995 speech at the National Press Club in Washington, D.C., he stressed the importance of "a true civil society in which citizens interact on a regular basis to grapple with common problems."

Today I will suggest that any prescription for America must understand the advantages and limits of both the market and government, but more importantly, how neither is equipped to solve America's central problems: the deterioration of our civil society and the need to revitalize our democratic process.

Civil society is the place where Americans make their home, sustain their marriages, raise their families, hang out with their friends, meet their neighbors, educate their children, worship their god. It is the churches, schools, fraternities, community centers, labor unions, synagogues, sports leagues, PTAs, libraries and barber shops. It is where opinions are expressed and refined, where views are exchanged and agreements made, where a sense of common purpose and consensus are forged. It lies apart from the realms of the market and the government, and possesses a different ethic. The market is governed by the logic of economic self-interest, while government is the domain of laws with all their coercive authority. Civil society, on the other hand, is the sphere of our most basic humanity—the personal, everyday realm that is governed by values such as responsibility, trust, fraternity, solidarity and love. In a democratic civil society such as ours we also put a special premium on social equality—the conviction that men and women should be measured by the quality of their character and not the color of their skin, the shape of their eyes, the size of their bank account, the religion of their family, or the happenstance of their gender.

What both Democrats and Republicans fail to see is that the government and the market are not enough to make a civilization. There must also be a healthy, robust civic sector—a space in which the bonds of community can flourish. Government and the market are similar to two legs on a three-legged stool. Without the third leg of civil society, the stool is not stable and cannot provide support for a vital America.

. . . Public policy, as these suggestions illustrate, can help facilitate the revitalization of democracy and civil society, but it cannot create civil society. We can insist that fathers support their children financially, but fathers have to see the importance of spending time with their children. We can figure out ways, such as parental leave, to provide parents with more time with their children, but parents have to use that time to raise their children. We can create community schools, but communities have to use them. We can provide mothers and fathers with the tools they need to influence the storytelling of the mass media, but they ultimately must exercise that control. We can take special interests out of elections, but only people can vote. We can provide opportunities for more deliberative citizenship at both the national and the local level, but citizens have to seize those opportunities and take individual responsibility.

We also have to give the distinctive moral language of civil society a more permanent place in our public conversation. The language of the marketplace says, "Get as much as you can for yourself." The language of government says, "Legislate for others what is good for them." But the language of community, family and citizenship at its core is about receiving undeserved gifts. What this nation needs to promote is the spirit of giving something freely, without measuring it out precisely or demanding something in return.

At a minimum, the language of mutual obligation has to be given equal time with the language of rights that dominates our culture. Rights talk properly supports an individual's status and dignity within a community. It has done much to protect the less powerful in our society and should not be abandoned. The problem comes in the adversarial dynamic that rights talk sets up in which people assert themselves through confrontation, championing one right to the exclusion of another. Instead of working together to improve our collective situation, we fight with each other over who has superior rights. Americans are too often given to speaking of America as a country in which you have the right to do whatever you want. On reflection, most of us will admit that no country could long survive that lived by such a principle. And this talk is deeply at odds with the best interests of civil society.

Forrest Gump and Rush Limbaugh are the surprise stars of the first half of the '90s because they poke fun at hypocrisy and the inadequacy of what we have today. But they are not builders. The builders are those in localities across America who are constructing bridges of cooperation and dialogue in face-to-face meetings with their supporters and their adversaries. Alarmed at the decline of civil society, they know how to understand the legitimate point of view of those with whom they disagree. Here in Washington, action too often surrounds only competition for power. With the media's help, words are used to polarize and destroy people. In cities across America where citizens are working together, words are tools to build bridges between people. . . . In these places there are more barn-raisers than there are barn-burners. Connecting their idealism with national policy offers us our greatest hope and our biggest challenge.

Above all, we need to understand that a true civil society in which citizens interact on a regular basis to grapple with common problems will not occur because of the arrival of a hero. Rebuilding civil society requires people talking and listening to each other, not blindly following a hero.

. . . If the problem is a deteriorating civic culture, then a charismatic leader, be he the president or a general, is not the answer. He or she might make us feel better momentarily but then we are only spectators thrilled by the performance, how have we progressed collectively? A character in Bertolt Brecht's *Galileo* says, "Pity the nation that has no heroes," to which Galileo responds, "Pity the nation that needs them." All of us have to go out in the public square and all of us have to assume our citizenship responsibilities. For me that means trying to tell the truth as I see it to both parties and to the American people without regard for consequences. In a vibrant civil society, real leadership at the top is made possible by the understanding and evolution of leaders of awareness at the bottom and in the middle, that is, citizens engaged in a deliberative discussion about our common future. . . . That's a discussion that I want to be a part of. The more open our public dialogue, the larger the number of Americans who join our deliberation, the greater chance we have to build a better country and a better world.

—SPEECH—

COMMENCEMENT ADDRESS AT VASSAR COLLEGE

TONY KUSHNER {MAY 26, 2001}

The son of classical musicians who encouraged his interest in the theater from an early age, Tony Kushner (b. 1956) grew up in Lake Charles, Louisiana, where his family moved after inheriting a lumber business. After college in New York, he founded a theater group and began writing and producing plays that address issues of political involvement and moral responsibility. He burst onto the theatrical and cultural stage in the early 1990s with his sweeping, controversial, seven-hour, two-part epic *Angels in America: A Gay Fantasia on National Themes*. The play, which weaves together the stories of one man dying of AIDS, another coming to terms with his sexuality, and a third—the controversial lawyer Roy Cohn—denying his homosexuality all the way to his deathbed, earned Kushner a Pulitzer Prize, two Tony Awards, and a host of other honors.

I am here to organize. I am here to be political. I am here to be a citizen in a pluralist democracy. I am here to be effective, to have agency, to make a claim on power, to spread it around, to rearrange it, to democratize it, to legislate it into justice. Why you? Because the world will end if you don't act. You are the citizen of a flawed but actual democracy. Citizens are not actually capable of not acting, it is not given to a citizen that she doesn't act; this is the price you pay for being a citizen of a democracy, your life is married to the political beyond the possibility of divorcement. You are always an agent. When you don't act, you act. When you don't vote, you vote. When you accept the loony logic of some of the left that there is no political value in supporting the lesser of two evils, you open the door to greater evil. That's what happens when you despair, you open the door to evil, and evil is always happy to enter, sit down, abolish the Clean Air Act and the Kyoto Accords and refuse to participate in the World Court or the ban on landmines. Evil is happy refusing funds to American clinics overseas that counsel abortion and evil is happy drilling for oil in Alaska; evil is happy pinching pennies while 40 million people worldwide suffer and perish from AIDS; and evil will sit there, carefully chewing pretzels and fondly flipping through the scrapbook reminiscing about the 131 people he executed when he was governor, while his wife reads Dostoevsky in the corner. Evil has a brother in Florida and a whole bunch of relatives; evil settles in and it's the devil of a time getting him to vacate. Look at the White House. Look at France, look at Italy, Austria, the Netherlands. Look at Israel. See what despair and inaction on the part of citizens produces. Act! Organize. It's boring, but do it. The world ends if you don't.

—POEM—

TO THE PATRIOTS AND THE ACTIVIST POETS

ARIANA WAYNES {1999}

Ariana Waynes (b. 1979) is a National Poetry Slam Champion and a member of the 1999, 2000, and 2001 San Francisco National Poetry Slam teams. Her work has been published in, among other places, the anthology *Poetry Slam: The Competitive Art of Performance Poetry* and *The New York Times*.

i sit in the audience
reeling from the words of the soft-spoken revolutionaries
wondering if i should hate my country
as i am strangled by my stars and stripes
mexican, armenian, cuban, puerto rican, yugoslavian, bosnian
children cry for inclusion

would you have me forget
that the blessed first amendment of these united
states that i can raise my voice to shake the world
or at least the termite-infested foundation
of this atrocious, ferocious
land that i love
but have never been exactly proud of

would you have me forget
that when i come upon the box
check if you are black-but-not-hispanic,
would you have me forget
that i am African
and Cuban
and native american
and irish
and jamaican
and chinese

would you have me forget
that i am all of these
that i am none of these
that i am more than the sum of the census bureau's statistics
or the stereotypes held against me
that i am the product of my everything
that my ancestors butchered
my ancestors who enslaved
my ancestors who raped
my ancestors who drove
my ancestors out of their land

would you have me forget
that i am not my ancestors
and i'm proud to be an american
where at least i know i'm free—

that is, if i don't exercise my freedom
too loudly or act too naturally me
that is as long as i don't offend
my country men,
don't color outside the lines of
'good girl.'

would you have me forget
that there are millions literally dying to be included in that
we the people
who hold those truths to be self-evident
that all (straight) men upper-middle class, conservative, and christian
will be treated equal—
would that make my friends non-people?

oh, beautiful, for bright blue eyes
for amber golden hair
as long as you're a barbie doll,
they'll have to treat you fair
please pick up your apple pie at the door
and leave quietly, b'bye—

would you have me forget
those children who say "amerika" softly at night
like a prayer before nightmares—
and the monolingual anglosaxon men
in their tailored business suits
shaking their heads and reading their text
"you have to go through the right channels
i'm *sorry—NEXT!*"

oh, say can you see
by the white fluorescent right—
the king of clubs is painting the roses white—
and deporting immigrant children

in the middle of the night
because they cannot write in english.

god bless America
that racist, sexist, classist, ageist, ableist, heightist, imageist,
heterosexist, capitalist community
which i call home, which,
would you have me forget,
is nevertheless one of the few on earth
in which I can speak my mind
and pray or not pray
to what ever god or goddess i choose or choose to refuse
without being mutilated or murdered for it—

would you have me forget
that in a large country in southeast asia
the lips of my labia
would have been sewn together
with a white-hot needle when i was twelve
would you have me forget
that in a mid-sized nation in central africa
i would be the property of my husband,
lord and master

would you have me forget
that in a modern industrialized nation in western europe,
i would have to flee the country
to have an abortion
or a divorce
would you have me forget
that i could be shot
as a matter of course
for raising my voice
there

and i pray to a god that i gave up with santa claus
to thank her

for birthing me here
where the sidewalks, at least, are paved with potholes of potential
and where else would you rather be?

i sit, here, in the audience,
reeling from the weight of my internal contradictions
and hysterical afflictions of patriotic asphyxiation
for loving a broken nation
that it's up to us to fix—
power of the people, remember?
at least it doesn't take a military coup
ask not what your country can do for you
cuz i'm tired through and through of waiting
of hating my home
i still love my country
i guess it's like my mama says—
i yell because i care.

—SPEECH—

CLOSING ARGUMENT IN THE HENRY SWEET TRIAL

CLARENCE DARROW {MAY 19, 1926}

Most people associate Clarence Darrow (1857–1938) with his defense of Darwinian evolution during the Scopes trial of 1925, but his sweetest victory came the following year, during a racially charged Detroit murder trial. African American Henry Sweet had shot at a lynch mob surrounding his brother's home. A white man was killed, and the all-white jury surely would have convicted Sweet of murder had it not been for Darrow's brilliant defense. In a seven-hour closing statement, Darrow condemned America's racist legacy and challenged the members of the jury to look past their own prejudices in order to embrace the principles of liberty and humanity. When the jury announced its verdict—not guilty—tears welled up in Darrow's eyes.

We come now to lay this man's case in the hands of a jury of our peers. The first defense and the last defense is the protection of home and life as provided by our law. We are willing to leave it here.

I feel, as I look at you, that we will be treated fairly and decently, even understandingly and kindly. You know what this case is. You know why it is. You know that if white men had been fighting their way against colored men, nobody would ever have dreamed of a prosecution. And you know that from the beginning of this case to the end, up to the time you write your verdict, the prosecution is based on race prejudice and nothing else.

Gentlemen, I feel deeply on this subject; I cannot help it. Let us take a little glance at the history of the Negro race. It only needs a minute. It seems to me that the story would melt hearts of stone. I was born in America. I could have left it if I had wanted to go away. Some other men, reading about this land of freedom that we brag about on the Fourth of July, came voluntarily to America. These men, the defendants, are here because they could not help it. Their ancestors were captured in the jungles and on the plains of Africa, captured as you capture wild beasts, torn from their homes and their kindred; loaded into slave ships, packed like sardines in a box, half of them dying on the ocean passage; some jumping into the sea in their frenzy, when they had a chance to choose death in place of slavery. They were captured and brought here. They could not help it. They were bought and sold as slaves, to work without pay, because they were black. They were subject to all of this for generations, until finally they were given their liberty, so far as the law goes—and that is only a little way, because, after all, every human being's life in this world is inevitably mixed with every other life and, no matter what laws we pass, no matter what precautions we take, unless the people we meet are kindly and decent and humane and liberty-loving, then there is no liberty. Freedom comes from human beings, rather than from laws and institutions.

Now, that is their history. These people are the children of slavery. If the race that we belong to owes anything to any human being, or to any power in the universe, they owe it to these black men. Above all other men, they owe an obligation and a duty to these black men that can never be repaid. I never see one of them that I do not feel I ought to pay part of the debt of my race—and if you gentlemen feel as you should feel in this case, your emotions will be like mine.

Gentlemen, you are called into this case by chance. It took us a week to find you, a week of culling out prejudice and hatred. Probably we did not cull it all out at that; but we took the best and the fairest that we could find. It is up to you.

Your verdict means something in this case. It means something more than the fate of this boy. It is not often that a case is submitted to twelve men where the decision may mean a milestone in the history of the human race. But this case does. And I hope and I trust that you have a feeling of responsibility that will make you take it and do your duty as citizens of a great nation, and as members of the human family, which is better still. . . .

L et me say just a parting word for Henry Sweet, who has well-nigh been forgotten. I am serious, but it seems almost like a reflection upon this jury to talk as if I doubted your verdict. What has this boy done? This one boy now that I am culling out from all of the rest, and whose fate is in your hands—can you tell me what he has done? Can I believe myself? Am I standing in a court of justice where twelve men on their oaths are asked to take away the liberty of a boy twenty-one years of age, who has done nothing more than what Henry Sweet has done?

Gentlemen, you may think he shot too quick; you may think he erred in judgment; you may think that Dr. Sweet should not have gone there prepared to defend his home. But, what of this case of Henry Sweet? What has he done? I want to put it up to you, each one of you, individually. Dr. Sweet was his elder brother. He had helped Henry through school. He loved him. He had taken him into his home. Henry had lived with him and his wife; he had fondled his baby. The doctor had promised Henry the money to go through school. Henry was getting his education, to take his place in the world, gentlemen—and this is a hard job. With his brother's help, he has worked his way through college up to the last year. The doctor had bought a home. He feared danger. He moved in with his wife and he asked this boy to go with him. And this boy went to defend his brother, and his brother's wife, and his child, and his home.

Do you think more of him or less of him for that? I never saw twelve men in my life—and I have looked at a good many faces of a good many juries—I never saw twelve men in my life that, if you could get them to understand a human case, were not true and right.

Should this boy have gone along and helped his brother? Or, should he have stayed away? What would you have done? And yet, gentlemen, here is a boy, and the president of his college came all the way from Ohio to tell you what he thinks of him. His teachers have come here, from Ohio, to tell you what they think of him. The Methodist bishop has come here to tell you what he thinks of him.

So, gentlemen, I am justified in saying that this boy is as kindly, as well disposed, as decent a man as one of you twelve. Do you think he ought to be taken out of his school and sent to the penitentiary? All right, gentlemen, if you think so, do it. It is your job, not mine. If you think so, do it. But if you do, gentlemen, if you should ever look into the face of your own boy, or your own brother, or look into your own heart, you will regret it in sackcloth and ashes. You know, if he committed any offense, it was being loyal and true to his brother whom he loved. I know where you will send him, and it will not be to a penitentiary.

Now, gentlemen, just one more word, and I am through with this case. I do not live in Detroit. But I have no feeling against this city. In fact, I shall always have the kindest remembrance of it, especially if this case results as I think and feel it will. I am the last one to come here to stir up race hatred, or any other hatred. I do not believe in the law of hate. I may not be true to my ideals always, but I believe in the law of love, and I believe you can do nothing with hatred. I would like to see a time when man loves his fellow man and forgets his color or his creed. We will never be civilized until that time comes.

I know the Negro race has a long road to go. I believe that the life of the Negro race has been a life of tragedy, of injustice, of oppression. The law has made him equal, but man has not. And, after all, the last analysis is: What has man done?—and not what has the law done? I know there is a long road ahead of him before he can take the place which I believe he should take. I know that before him there is sorrow, tribulation, and death among the blacks, and perhaps the whites. I am sorry. I would do what I could to avert it. I would advise patience; I would advise tolerance; I would advise understanding; I would advise all those things which are necessary for men who live together.

Gentlemen, what do you think of your duty in this case? I have watched day after day these black, tense faces that have crowded this court. These black faces that now are looking to you twelve whites, feeling that the hopes and fears of a race are in your keeping.

This case is about to end, gentlemen. To them, it is life. Not one of their color sits on this jury. Their fate is in the hands of twelve whites. Their eyes are fixed on you, their hearts go out to you, and their hopes hang on your verdict.

This is all I ask you, on behalf of this defendant, on behalf of these help-less ones who turn to you, and more than that—on behalf of this great state, and this great city, which must face this problem and face it fairly—I ask you, in the name of progress and of the human race, to return a verdict of not guilty in this case.

—SCREENPLAY—

THE AMERICAN PRESIDENT

Aaron Sorkin {1995}

———◦•◦———

Aaron Sorkin (b. 1961) grew up in Scarsdale, New York, and first hoped to become an actor. His award-winning 1989 Broadway play *A Few Good Men* (later a movie) changed all that. He is best known as the creator and writer of the television drama, *West Wing*. In his script for *The American President*, a romantic-comedy film, Andrew Shepherd, widowed president (Michael Douglas) falls in love with lobbyist Sydney Ellen Wade (Annette Benning) and takes political heat for his personal passion. The movie's high point is Douglas's angry speech at a presidential press conference.

CUT TO:

INT. THE PRESS BRIEFING ROOM—EARLY MORNING

ROBIN is on her last drops of energy and patience.

REPORTER #4

Robin, will the president ever respond to Senator Rumson's question about being a member of the American Civil Liberties Union?

But instead of hands going up, the PRESS CORPS suddenly stands. ROBIN turns to see SHEPHERD stride in and step up to the podium.

SHEPHERD

Yes, he will. 'Morning.

ROBIN

Good morning, Mr. President.

SHEPHERD takes the podium. There's a palpable BUZZ in the room as video operators adjust their equipment, etc. People start to stand.

SHEPHERD

That's all right, you can keep your seats. For the last couple of months, Senator Rumson has suggested that being president of this country, was to a certain extent, about character . . .

ANGLE—ROBIN who's picked up the receiver from a wall phone and punches in four numbers. She turns in to the wall to shield her conversation from the rest of the room.

ROBIN

(into phone)

Lewis . . . call A.J. and come on down here . . . I don't know, but something's happening.

SHEPHERD

... and although I have not been willing to engage in his attacks on me, I've been here three years and three days, and I can tell you without hesitation: Being President of this country is entirely about character.

LEWIS enters with A.J.

SHEPHERD

For the record: Yes, I am a card-carrying member of the A.C.L.U. But the more important question is why aren't you, Bob? This is an organization whose sole purpose is to defend the Bill of Rights, so it naturally begs the questions.

Why would a senator, his party's most powerful spokesman and a candidate for president, choose to reject upholding the Constitution? If you can answer that question, then, folks, you're smarter than I am, because I didn't understand it until a couple of minutes ago. Everybody knows being American isn't easy. America is advanced citizenship.

You gotta want it bad, 'cause it's gonna put up a fight. It's gonna say, "You want free speech? Let's see you acknowledge a man whose words make your blood boil, who's standing center stage and advocating, at the top of his lungs, that which you would spend your lifetime opposing at the top of yours. You want to claim this land as the land of the free, then the symbol of your country can't be a flag; the symbol has to be one of its citizens exercising his right to burn that flag in protest." Show me that, defend that, celebrate that in your classrooms. Then you can stand up and sing about the land of the free. I've known Bob Rumson for years. I've been operating under the assumption that the reason Bob devotes so much time and energy to shouting at the rain was that he simply didn't get it. Well, I was wrong.

SHEPHERD
(continuing)

Bob's problem isn't that he doesn't get it. Bob's problem is that he can't sell it. Nobody has ever won an election by talking about what I was just talking about.

This is a country made up of people with hard jobs that they're terrified of losing. The roots of freedom are of little or no interest to them at the moment. We are a nation afraid to go out at night. We're a society that has assigned low priority to education and has looked the other way while our public schools have been decimated. We have serious problems to solve, and we need serious men to solve them. And whatever your particular problem is, I promise you, Bob Rumson is not the least bit interested in solving it. He is interested in two things and two things only: Making you afraid of it and telling you who's to blame for it. That, ladies and gentlemen, is how you win elections. You gather a group of middle-aged, middle-class, middle-income voters who remember with longing an easier time, and you talk to them about family and American values and personal character. Then you have an old photo of the President's girlfriend. You scream about patriotism and you tell them she's to blame for their lot in life, you go on television and you call her a whore. Sydney Ellen Wade has done nothing to you, Bob. She has done nothing but put herself through law school, prosecute criminals for five years, represent the interests of public school teachers for two years, and lobby for the safety of our natural resources.

You want a character debate? Fine, but you better stick with me, 'cause Sydney Ellen Wade is way out of your league. I've loved two women in my life. I lost one to cancer, and I lost the other 'cause I was so busy keeping my job that I forgot to do my job. Well, that ends right now.

Tomorrow morning the White House is sending a bill to Congress for its consideration. It's White House Resolution 455, an energy bill requiring a 20 percent reduction of the emission of fossil fuels over the next ten years. It is by far the most aggressive stride ever taken in the fight to reverse the effects of global warming. The other piece of legislation is the crime bill. As of today it no longer exists. I'm throwing it out. I'm throwing it out and writing a law that makes sense. You cannot address crime prevention without getting rid of assault weapons and handguns.

I consider them a threat to national security, and I will go door to door if I have to, but I'm gonna convince Americans that I'm right, and I'm gonna get the guns. We've got serious problems, and we need serious men, and if you want to talk about character, Bob, you'd better come at me with more than a burning flag and a member-ship card. If you want to talk about character and American values, fine. Just tell me where and when, and I'll show up. This is a time for serious men, Bob, and your fifteen minutes are up. My name's Andrew Shepherd, and I am the President.

SHEPHERD exits the press room, leaving a stunned room in his wake.

The MURMURS begin from the PRESS CORPS. They're talking among themselves, confirming that they just saw what they just saw. ROBIN steps to the podium.

ROBIN

Any questions?

———•—•——

—POEM—

I SING OF CHANGE

Niyi Osundare {1981}

Celebrated Nigerian dramatist, professor, and poet Niyi Osundare (b. 1947) sees poetry as inevitably political and the poet as a kind of town crier. During Nigeria's military dictatorship, which lasted from 1983 to 1999, Osundare was put under surveillance, his work censored, and informed on by his own students, but he still managed to write a weekly poetry column called "Songs of the Season." To evade arrest, Osundare used symbolism— a hyena would symbolize the dictator, an antelope the people—to communicate his ideas. The child of poor farmers, Osundare was raised with an oral tradition, and chants or sings his poetry to musical accompaniment. So when Osundare says "I sing of change"—the poem was written in 1981 during a brief period of Nigerian democracy—he means it both literally and figuratively.

I sing
of the beauty of Athens
without its slaves

Of a world free
of kings and queens
and other remnants
of an arbitrary past

Of earth
with no
sharp north
or deep south
without blind curtains
or iron walls

of the end
of warlords and armories
and prisons of hate and fear

Of deserts treeing
and fruiting
after the quickening rains

Of the sun
radiating ignorance
and stars informing
nights of unknowing

I sing of a world reshaped

—ESSAY—

KEEPERS OF DEMOCRACY

ELEANOR ROOSEVELT {JANUARY 1939}

Eleanor Roosevelt's (1884–1962) essay on moral courage capped a year in which she gave the nation and the world a vivid example of that virtue. In 1939, she had resigned from the Daughters of the American Revolution when they refused to let black contralto Marian Anderson perform in the DAR's Constitution Hall; she arranged for Anderson to perform at the Lincoln Memorial; she worked on behalf of the anti-Nazi underground in Europe; and she lobbied husband FDR (unsuccessfully) to push a bill through Congress that would have permitted 20,000 Jewish refugee children to emigrate from Europe to the United States. Many of the positions Eleanor Roosevelt adopted were controversial, yet a 1939 poll showed that she had the approval of 67 percent of the American public.

Recently a radio broadcast was given, based on a story written by H. G. Wells some years ago, called "War of the Worlds." For the purpose of dramatization it was placed in the United States with the names of regions and people who would naturally be involved if such a thing were to happen today. The basic idea was not changed; these invaders were supernatural beings from another planet who straddled the skyway and dealt in death rays, but it was dramatically done with many realistic touches.

I do not wish to enter into a discussion here as to whether the broadcasting company should do dramatizations of this type, nor do I wish to cast aspersions on people who may not have read the original book. But the results of this broadcast were the best illustration of the state of mind in which we as a nation find ourselves today. A sane people, living in an atmosphere of fearlessness, does not suddenly become hysterical at the threat of invasion, even from more credible sources, let alone by the Martians from another planet, but we have allowed ourselves to be fed on propaganda which has created a fear complex. For the past few years, nearly all of our organizations and many individuals have said something about the necessity for fighting dangerous and subversive elements in our midst.

If you are in the South someone tells you solemnly that all the members of the Committee of Industrial Organization are Communists, or that the Negroes are all Communists. This last statement derives from the fact that, being for the most part unskilled labor, Negroes are more apt to be organized by the Committee for Industrial Organization. In another part of the country someone tells you solemnly that the schools of the country are menaced because they are all under the influence of Jewish teachers and that the Jews, forsooth, are all Communists. And so it goes, until finally you realize that people have reached a point where anything which will save them from Communism is a godsend; and if Fascism or Nazism promises more security than our own democracy we may even turn to them.

It is all as bewildering as our growing hysterical over the invasion of the Martians! Somehow or other I have a feeling that our forefathers, who left their women and children in the wildernesses while they traveled weary miles to buy supplies, and who knew they were leaving them to meet Indians if need be, and to defend themselves as best they could, would expect us to meet present-day dangers with more courage than we seem to have. It is not only physical courage which we need, the kind of physical courage which in the face of danger can at least control the outward evidences of fear. It is moral courage as well, the courage which can make up its mind whether it thinks something is right or wrong, make a material or personal sacrifice if necessary, and take the consequences which may come.

I shall always remember someone, it may have been Theodore Roosevelt, saying in my hearing when I was young that when you were afraid to do a thing, that was the time to go and do it. Every time we shirk making up our minds or standing up for a cause in which we believe, we weaken our character and our ability to be fearless. There is a growing wave in this country of fear, and of intolerance which springs from fear. Sometimes it is a religious intolerance, sometimes it is a racial intolerance, but all intolerance grows from the same roots. I can best illustrate this fear by telling you that a short time ago someone told me in all seriousness that the American Youth Congress was a Communist organization and that the World Youth Congress was Communist controlled. This person really believed that the young people who were members of these organizations were attempting to overthrow by force the governments of the countries in which they belonged.

Undoubtedly, in the World Youth Congress there were young Communists, just as there are a group of young Communists and a group of young Socialists in the American Youth Congress, but this does not mean that either of these bodies is Communist controlled. It simply means that they conform to the pattern of society, which at all times has groups thinking over a wide range, from what we call extreme left to extreme right. The general movement of civilization, however, goes on in accordance with the thinking of the majority of the people, and that was exactly what happened in both the American Youth Congress and the World Youth Congress.

The resolutions finally passed by both bodies were rather sane and calm, perhaps a trifle idealistic and certainly very optimistic. There were amendments offered for discussion, and voted down, which many people might have considered radical; but since there is radical thinking among both young and old, it seems to me wiser to discuss and vote down an idea than to ignore it. By so doing we know in which direction the real trend of thought is growing. If we take the attitude that youth, even youth when it belongs to the Communist party, cannot be met on the basis of equal consideration and a willingness to listen, then we are again beginning to allow our fears of this particular group to overwhelm us and we are losing the opportunity to make our experience available and useful to the next generation.

I do not believe that oppression anywhere or injustice which is tolerated by the people of any country toward any group in that country is a healthy influence. I feel that unless we learn to live together as individuals and as groups, and to find ways of settling our difficulties without showing fear of each other and resorting to force, we cannot hope to see our democracy successful. It is an indisputable fact that democracy cannot survive where force and not law is the ultimate court of appeal. Every time we permit force to enter into a situation between employer and employee we have weakened the power of democracy and the confidence which a democratic people must have in their ability to make laws to meet the conditions under which they live, and, when necessary, to change those laws with due political process according to the will of the majority of the people.

When we permit religious prejudice to gain headway in our midst, when we allow one group of people to look down upon another, then we may for a short time bring hardship on some particular group of people, but the real hardship and the real wrong is done to democracy and to our nation as a whole. We are then breeding people who cannot live under a democratic form of government but must be controlled by force. We have but to look out into the world to see how easy it is to become stultified, to accept without protest wrongs done to others, and to shift the burden of decision and of responsibility for any action onto some vague thing called a government or some individual called a leader.

It is true today that democracies are in danger because there are forces opposed to their way of thinking abroad in the world; but more than democracies are at stake. When force becomes so necessary that practically all nations decide that they must engage in a race which will make them able to back up what they have to say with arms and will thus oblige the rest of the world to listen to them, then we face an ultimate Armageddon, unless at the same time an effort to find some other solution is never abandoned.

We in this country may look at it more calmly than the rest of the world, for we can pay for force over a longer period of time; and for a while at least our people will not suffer as much as some of the other nations of the world, but the building up of physical forces is an interminable race. Do you see where it will end unless some strong movement for an ultimate change is afoot?

Someone may say: "But we need only to go on until the men who at present have power in the world and who believe in force are gone." But when in the past has there been a time when such men did not exist? If our civilization is to survive and democracies are to live, then the people of the world as a whole must be stronger than such leaders. That is the way of democracy, that is the only way to a rule of law and order as opposed to a rule of force.

We can read the history of civilization, its ups and its downs as they have occurred under the rule of force. Underlying that history is the story of each individual's fears. It seems to me a challenge to women in this period of our civilization to foster democracy and to refuse to fall a prey to fear. Only our young people still seem to have some strength and hope, and apparently we are afraid to give them a helping hand.

Someone said to me the other day that, acknowledging all the weaknesses of human nature, one must still believe in the basic good of humanity or fall into cynicism and the philosophy of old Omar Khayyam. I do still believe that there is within most of us a basic desire to live uprightly and kindly with our neighbors, but I also feel that we are at present in the grip of a wave of fear which threatens to overcome us. I think we need a rude awakening, to make us exert all the strength we have to face facts as they are in our country and in the world, and to make us willing to sacrifice all that we have from the material standpoint in order that freedom and democracy may not perish from this earth.

—POEM—

GENERATIONS OF LOST ANGELS FOUND

BEAU SIA {2003}

Beau Sia (b. 1976), a Chinese-American poet raised in Oklahoma City, discovered the spoken word after seeing MTV's *Spoken Word Unplugged,* moved to New York City, and became active in the poetry slam community. He has been a member of six National Poetry Slam teams, two of which have won championships, and placed second in the 2001 National Poetry Slam individual competition. Sia has been featured in the award-winning film *Slam*, the documentary *Slam Nation*, and is the author of *A Night Without Armor II: The Revenge* and two spoken-word CDs, *Attack! Attack! Go* and *Dope and Wack*. He made his Broadway debut in *Russell Simmons' Def Poetry Jam on Broadway*. In the hip-hop poem "Generations of Lost Angels Found," "angel island" refers to Angel Island, California (the "Ellis Island of the West"), the immigration station that controlled the flow of Chinese into America until 1941.

These words are not
To be carved into your guilt

Or forgotten
In a museum.

They are not
Drawn birds released
Into the past,

Never to be seen again,
Once you
Go home to sleep.

These words are for years I've never seen.
These words are for years I've yet to be.
These words are for cities that never touch angel island,
These words are for people
I do not know,

I have come as poet
To show you that
It's good
We had to return
All of those American history books
In tenth grade.

They are of no use to us now.

I'd conjure howard zinn,
But
You'll just have to settle for me.

Not to re-write history,
Not to erase history,
Not to create a history

To make you feel bad about yourself,

But to ask that
We become involved with history.

That we release ourselves from judgements
Of good
And evil,

That our past does not bind us
To its time.

That it only helps us
To grow in ours.

We can do nothing for the seven layers of paint
Over heartache and lament.
We can do nothing
For those
Who have had to walk in the names of strangers.

We can do nothing
For the misplaced windows,
Miscounted doors,
and missed wives
In
Other places of the world.

It is 2003 and
Our culture is obsessed
With the moment,

That we often see the next moment
Before the one
We are in is over,

And we forget the last one
As easily
As the first line of this poem.

Because this is the place we are in now.

And I'm here to tell you
That it's not angel island.

That it's not the immigration station.

That it's not Chinese exclusion.

That it's not immigration.

That it's not American history.

We are here because
If we can share this moment in history,

Regardless of our incomes,

Our
Birth dates,
And
Our ever-imposed ethnic origin,

Then
Any moment in history,

Given the right sequence of events,
The right combination of relationships,
The exact wording of documents,

Could put us all together in the same place.

In the same country,
In the same city,
In the same room,

Writing poems together,

When our previous lives
Found us
Living separate ones.

We need to strip away the layers necessary
To learn how similar we are.

because
We have no control
Over where life takes us,

We have no control
Over the world in which we live,

We have no control over
What history will do to us,

And we must never forget
Where we might've come from,
What
We might've gone through,
And
Who we might've been
To the rest of the world,

Given the circumstances.

Because history is more
Than remembering the structures.

It's carrying the moments
And the people with you
On your journey through life,

To grow,
To give,
And to show
Your children
How far we've come
And how much further
They will have to take us.

A MEDITATION PRECEDING
THE DECLARATION OF INDEPENDENCE
BY 150 YEARS

DEVOTIONS UPON EMERGENT OCCASIONS, NUMBER XVII

JOHN DONNE {1624}

A moneyed libertine in his youth and an eloquent, prominent Anglican priest in his maturity, John Donne (1572–1631) is most famous for the surprisingly secular poetry and meditations—most of it published posthumously—that he left behind. "Devotions upon Emergent Occasions, Number XVII," his most famous meditation, was embedded in modern consciousness thanks to Ernest Hemingway's use of one of its phrases as the title of his novel *For Whom The Bell Tolls*. Inspired by the sound of a distant funeral bell, and written 150 years before the Declaration of Independence, it remains one of the world's most beautiful evocations of what it means to be human, and free.

> No man is an island, entire of itself;
> Every man is a piece of the continent, a part of the main.
> If a clod be washed away by the sea, Europe is the less,
> As well as if a promontory were,
> As well as if a manor of thy friends or of thine own were.
> Any man's death diminishes me, because I am involved
>   in mankind;
> And therefore never send to know for whom the bell tolls;
> It tolls for thee.

APPENDIX

THE CONSTITUTION OF
THE UNITED STATES OF AMERICA

We the People of the United States, in Order to form a more perfect Union, establish Justice, insure domestic Tranquility, provide for the common defense, promote the general Welfare, and secure the Blessings of Liberty to ourselves and our Posterity, do ordain and establish this Constitution for the United States of America.

ARTICLE I

SECTION 1

All legislative Powers herein granted shall be vested in a Congress of the United States, which shall consist of a Senate and House of Representatives.

SECTION 2

The House of Representatives shall be composed of Members chosen every second Year by the People of the several States, and the Electors in each State shall have the Qualifications requisite for Electors of the most numerous Branch of the State Legislature.

No Person shall be a Representative who shall not have attained to the Age of twenty five Years, and been seven Years a Citizen of the United States, and who shall not, when elected, be an Inhabitant of that State in which he shall be chosen.

Representatives and direct Taxes shall be apportioned among the several States which may be included within this Union, according to their respective Numbers, which shall be determined by adding to the whole Number of free Persons, including those bound to Service for a Term of Years, and excluding Indians not taxed, three fifths of all other Persons. The actual Enumeration shall be made within three Years after the first Meeting of the Congress of the United States, and within every subsequent Term of ten Years, in such Manner as they shall by Law direct. The Number of Representatives shall not exceed one for every thirty Thousand, but each

State shall have at Least one Representative; and until such enumeration shall be made, the State of New Hampshire shall be entitled to chuse three, Massachusetts eight, Rhode-Island and Providence Plantations one, Connecticut five, New-York six, New Jersey four, Pennsylvania eight, Delaware one, Maryland six, Virginia ten, North Carolina five, South Carolina five, and Georgia three.

When vacancies happen in the Representation from any State, the Executive Authority thereof shall issue Writs of Election to fill such Vacancies.

The House of Representatives shall chuse their Speaker and other Officers; and shall have the sole Power of Impeachment.

SECTION 3

The Senate of the United States shall be composed of two Senators from each State, chosen by the Legislature thereof for six Years; and each Senator shall have one Vote.

Immediately after they shall be assembled in Consequence of the first Election, they shall be divided as equally as may be into three Classes. The Seats of the Senators of the first Class shall be vacated at the Expiration of the second Year, of the second Class at the Expiration of the fourth Year, and of the third Class at the Expiration of the sixth Year, so that one third may be chosen every second Year; and if Vacancies happen by Resignation, or otherwise, during the Recess of the Legislature of any State, the Executive thereof may make temporary Appointments until the next Meeting of the Legislature, which shall then fill such Vacancies.

No Person shall be a Senator who shall not have attained to the Age of thirty Years, and been nine Years a Citizen of the United States, and who shall not, when elected, be an Inhabitant of that State for which he shall be chosen.

The Vice President of the United States shall be President of the Senate, but shall have no Vote, unless they be equally divided.

The Senate shall chuse their other Officers, and also a President pro tempore, in the Absence of the Vice President, or when he shall exercise the Office of President of the United States.

The Senate shall have the sole Power to try all Impeachments. When sitting for that Purpose, they shall be on Oath or Affirmation. When the President of the United States is tried, the Chief Justice shall preside: And no Person shall be convicted without the Concurrence of two thirds of the Members present.

Judgment in Cases of Impeachment shall not extend further than to removal from Office, and disqualification to hold and enjoy any Office of honor, Trust or Profit under the United States: but the Party convicted shall nevertheless be liable and subject to Indictment, Trial, Judgment and Punishment, according to Law.

SECTION 4

The Times, Places and Manner of holding Elections for Senators and Representatives, shall be prescribed in each State by the Legislature thereof; but the Congress may at any time by Law make or alter such Regulations, except as to the Places of chusing Senators.

The Congress shall assemble at least once in every Year, and such Meeting shall be on the first Monday in December, unless they shall by Law appoint a different Day.

SECTION 5

Each House shall be the Judge of the Elections, Returns and Qualifications of its own Members, and a Majority of each shall constitute a Quorum to do Business; but a smaller Number may adjourn from day to day, and may be authorized to compel the Attendance of absent Members, in such Manner, and under such Penalties as each House may provide.

Each House may determine the Rules of its Proceedings, punish its Members for disorderly Behaviour, and, with the Concurrence of two thirds, expel a Member.

Each House shall keep a Journal of its Proceedings, and from time to time publish the same, excepting such Parts as may in their Judgment require Secrecy; and the Yeas and Nays of the Members of either House on any question shall, at the Desire of one fifth of those Present, be entered on the Journal.

Neither House, during the Session of Congress, shall, without the Consent of the other, adjourn for more than three days, nor to any other Place than that in which the two Houses shall be sitting.

SECTION 6

The Senators and Representatives shall receive a Compensation for their Services, to be ascertained by Law, and paid out of the Treasury of the United States. They shall in all Cases, except Treason, Felony and Breach of the Peace, be privileged from Arrest during their Attendance at the Session of their respective Houses, and in going to and returning from the same; and for any Speech or Debate in either House, they shall not be questioned in any other Place.

No Senator or Representative shall, during the Time for which he was elected, be appointed to any civil Office under the Authority of the United States, which shall have been created, or the Emoluments whereof shall have been encreased during such time; and no Person holding any Office under the United States, shall be a Member of either House during his Continuance in Office.

SECTION 7

All Bills for raising Revenue shall originate in the House of Representatives; but the Senate may propose or concur with Amendments as on other Bills.

Every Bill which shall have passed the House of Representatives and the Senate, shall, before it become a Law, be presented to the President of the United States: If he approve he shall sign it, but if not he shall return it, with his Objections to that House in which it shall have originated, who shall enter the Objections at large on their Journal, and proceed to reconsider it. If after such Reconsideration two thirds of that House shall agree to pass the Bill, it shall be sent, together with the Objections, to the other House, by which it shall likewise be reconsidered, and if approved by two thirds of that House, it shall become a Law. But in all such Cases the Votes of both Houses shall be determined by yeas and Nays, and the Names of the Persons voting for and against the Bill shall be entered on the Journal of each House respectively. If any Bill shall not be returned by the President within ten Days (Sundays excepted) after it shall have been presented to him, the Same shall be a Law, in like Manner as if he had signed it, unless the Congress by their Adjournment prevent its Return, in which Case it shall not be a Law.

Every Order, Resolution, or Vote to which the Concurrence of the Senate and House of Representatives may be necessary (except on a question of Adjournment) shall be presented to the President of the United States; and before the Same shall take Effect, shall be approved by him, or being disapproved by him, shall be repassed by two thirds of the Senate and House of Representatives, according to the Rules and Limitations prescribed in the Case of a Bill.

SECTION 8

The Congress shall have Power To lay and collect Taxes, Duties, Imposts and Excises, to pay the Debts and provide for the common Defence and general Welfare of the United States; but all Duties, Imposts and Excises shall be uniform throughout the United States;

To borrow Money on the credit of the United States;

To regulate Commerce with foreign Nations, and among the several States, and with the Indian Tribes;

To establish an uniform Rule of Naturalization, and uniform Laws on the subject of Bankruptcies throughout the United States;

To coin Money, regulate the Value thereof, and of foreign Coin, and fix the Standard of Weights and Measures;

To provide for the Punishment of counterfeiting the Securities and current Coin of the United States;

To establish Post Offices and post Roads;

To promote the Progress of Science and useful Arts, by securing for limited Times to Authors and Inventors the exclusive Right to their respective Writings and Discoveries;

To constitute Tribunals inferior to the supreme Court;

To define and punish Piracies and Felonies committed on the high Seas, and Offences against the Law of Nations;

To declare War, grant Letters of Marque and Reprisal, and make Rules concerning Captures on Land and Water;

To raise and support Armies, but no Appropriation of Money to that Use shall be for a longer Term than two Years;

To provide and maintain a Navy;

To make Rules for the Government and Regulation of the land and
naval Forces;

To provide for calling forth the Militia to execute the Laws of the Union,
suppress Insurrections and repel Invasions;

To provide for organizing, arming, and disciplining, the Militia, and
for governing such Part of them as may be employed in the Service
of the United States, reserving to the States respectively, the
Appointment of the Officers, and the Authority of training the
Militia according to the discipline prescribed by Congress;

To exercise exclusive Legislation in all Cases whatsoever, over such
District (not exceeding ten Miles square) as may, by Cession of
particular States, and the Acceptance of Congress, become the Seat
of the Government of the United States, and to exercise like Authority
over all Places purchased by the Consent of the Legislature of the
State in which the Same shall be, for the Erection of Forts, Magazines,
Arsenals, dock-Yards, and other needful Buildings;—And

To make all Laws which shall be necessary and proper for carrying into
Execution the foregoing Powers, and all other Powers vested by this
Constitution in the Government of the United States, or in any
Department or Officer thereof.

SECTION 9

The Migration or Importation of such Persons as any of the States now existing shall think proper to admit, shall not be prohibited by the Congress prior
to the Year one thousand eight hundred and eight, but a Tax or duty may be
imposed on such Importation, not exceeding ten dollars for each Person.

The Privilege of the Writ of Habeas Corpus shall not be suspended, unless
when in Cases of Rebellion or Invasion the public Safety may require it.

No Bill of Attainder or ex post facto Law shall be passed.

No Capitation, or other direct, Tax shall be laid, unless in Proportion to
the Census or enumeration herein before directed to be taken.

No Tax or Duty shall be laid on Articles exported from any State.

No Preference shall be given by any Regulation of Commerce or Revenue
to the Ports of one State over those of another; nor shall Vessels

bound to, or from, one State, be obliged to enter, clear, or pay Duties in another.

No Money shall be drawn from the Treasury, but in Consequence of Appropriations made by Law; and a regular Statement and Account of the Receipts and Expenditures of all public Money shall be published from time to time.

No Title of Nobility shall be granted by the United States: And no Person holding any Office of Profit or Trust under them, shall, without the Consent of the Congress, accept of any present, Emolument, Office, or Title, of any kind whatever, from any King, Prince, or foreign State.

SECTION 10

No State shall enter into any Treaty, Alliance, or Confederation; grant Letters of Marque and Reprisal; coin Money; emit Bills of Credit; make any Thing but gold and silver Coin a Tender in Payment of Debts; pass any Bill of Attainder, ex post facto Law, or Law impairing the Obligation of Contracts, or grant any Title of Nobility.

No State shall, without the Consent of the Congress, lay any Imposts or Duties on Imports or Exports, except what may be absolutely necessary for executing it's inspection Laws: and the net Produce of all Duties and Imposts, laid by any State on Imports or Exports, shall be for the Use of the Treasury of the United States; and all such Laws shall be subject to the Revision and Controul of the Congress.

No State shall, without the Consent of Congress, lay any Duty of Tonnage, keep Troops, or Ships of War in time of Peace, enter into any Agreement or Compact with another State, or with a foreign Power, or engage in War, unless actually invaded, or in such imminent Danger as will not admit of delay.

ARTICLE II

SECTION 1

The executive Power shall be vested in a President of the United States of America. He shall hold his Office during the Term of four Years, and, together with the Vice President, chosen for the same Term, be elected, as follows:

Each State shall appoint, in such Manner as the Legislature thereof may direct, a Number of Electors, equal to the whole Number of Senators and Representatives to which the State may be entitled in the Congress: but no Senator or Representative, or Person holding an Office of Trust or Profit under the United States, shall be appointed an Elector.

The Electors shall meet in their respective States, and vote by Ballot for two Persons, of whom one at least shall not be an Inhabitant of the same State with themselves. And they shall make a List of all the Persons voted for, and of the Number of Votes for each; which List they shall sign and certify, and transmit sealed to the Seat of the Government of the United States, directed to the President of the Senate. The President of the Senate shall, in the Presence of the Senate and House of Representatives, open all the Certificates, and the Votes shall then be counted. The Person having the greatest Number of Votes shall be the President, if such Number be a Majority of the whole Number of Electors appointed; and if there be more than one who have such Majority, and have an equal Number of Votes, then the House of Representatives shall immediately chuse by Ballot one of them for President; and if no Person have a Majority, then from the five highest on the List the said House shall in like Manner chuse the President. But in chusing the President, the Votes shall be taken by States, the Representation from each State having one Vote; A quorum for this purpose shall consist of a Member or Members from two thirds of the States, and a Majority of all the States shall be necessary to a Choice. In every Case, after the Choice of the President, the Person having the greatest Number of Votes of the Electors shall be the Vice President. But if there should remain two or more who have equal Votes, the Senate shall chuse from them by Ballot the Vice President.

The Congress may determine the Time of chusing the Electors, and the Day on which they shall give their Votes; which Day shall be the same throughout the United States.

No Person except a natural born Citizen, or a Citizen of the United States, at the time of the Adoption of this Constitution, shall be eligible to the Office of President; neither shall any Person be eligible to that Office who shall not have attained to the Age of thirty five Years, and been fourteen Years a Resident within the United States.

In Case of the Removal of the President from Office, or of his Death, Resignation, or Inability to discharge the Powers and Duties of the said Office, the Same shall devolve on the Vice President, and the Congress may by Law provide for the Case of Removal, Death, Resignation or Inability, both of the President and Vice President, declaring what Officer shall then act as President, and such Officer shall act accordingly, until the Disability be removed, or a President shall be elected.

The President shall, at stated Times, receive for his Services, a Compensation, which shall neither be increased nor diminished during the Period for which he shall have been elected, and he shall not receive within that Period any other Emolument from the United States, or any of them.

Before he enter on the Execution of his Office, he shall take the following Oath or Affirmation:—"I do solemnly swear (or affirm) that I will faithfully execute the Office of President of the United States, and will to the best of my Ability, preserve, protect and defend the Constitution of the United States."

SECTION 2

The President shall be Commander in Chief of the Army and Navy of the United States, and of the Militia of the several States, when called into the actual Service of the United States; he may require the Opinion, in writing, of the principal Officer in each of the executive Departments, upon any Subject relating to the Duties of their respective Offices, and he shall have Power to grant Reprieves and Pardons for Offences against the United States, except in Cases of Impeachment.

He shall have Power, by and with the Advice and Consent of the Senate, to make Treaties, provided two thirds of the Senators present concur; and he shall nominate, and by and with the Advice and Consent of the Senate, shall appoint Ambassadors, other public Ministers and Consuls, Judges of the supreme Court, and all other Officers of the United States, whose Appointments are not herein otherwise provided for, and which shall be established by Law: but the Congress may by Law vest the Appointment of such inferior Officers, as they think proper, in the President alone, in the Courts of Law, or in the Heads of Departments.

The President shall have Power to fill up all Vacancies that may happen during the Recess of the Senate, by granting Commissions which shall expire at the End of their next Session.

SECTION 3

He shall from time to time give to the Congress Information of the State of the Union, and recommend to their Consideration such Measures as he shall judge necessary and expedient; he may, on extraordinary Occasions, convene both Houses, or either of them, and in Case of Disagreement between them, with Respect to the Time of Adjournment, he may adjourn them to such Time as he shall think proper; he shall receive Ambassadors and other public Ministers; he shall take Care that the Laws be faithfully executed, and shall Commission all the Officers of the United States.

SECTION 4

The President, Vice President and all civil Officers of the United States, shall be removed from Office on Impeachment for, and Conviction of, Treason, Bribery, or other high Crimes and Misdemeanors.

ARTICLE III

SECTION 1

The judicial Power of the United States shall be vested in one supreme Court, and in such inferior Courts as the Congress may from time to time ordain and establish. The Judges, both of the supreme and inferior Courts, shall hold their Offices during good Behaviour, and shall, at stated Times, receive for their Services a Compensation, which shall not be diminished during their Continuance in Office.

SECTION 2

The judicial Power shall extend to all Cases, in Law and Equity, arising under this Constitution, the Laws of the United States, and Treaties made, or which shall be made, under their Authority;—to all Cases affecting Ambassadors, other public Ministers and Consuls;—to all Cases of admiralty and maritime Jurisdiction;—to Controversies to which the United States shall be a Party;—to Controversies between two or more States;— between a State and Citizens of another State;—between Citizens of different States;—between Citizens of the same State claiming Lands under

Grants of different States, and between a State, or the Citizens thereof, and foreign States, Citizens or Subjects.

In all Cases affecting Ambassadors, other public Ministers and Consuls, and those in which a State shall be Party, the supreme Court shall have original Jurisdiction. In all the other Cases before mentioned, the supreme Court shall have appellate Jurisdiction, both as to Law and Fact, with such Exceptions, and under such Regulations as the Congress shall make.

The Trial of all Crimes, except in Cases of Impeachment, shall be by Jury; and such Trial shall be held in the State where the said Crimes shall have been committed; but when not committed within any State, the Trial shall be at such Place or Places as the Congress may by Law have directed.

SECTION 3

Treason against the United States, shall consist only in levying War against them, or in adhering to their Enemies, giving them Aid and Comfort. No Person shall be convicted of Treason unless on the Testimony of two Witnesses to the same overt Act, or on Confession in open Court.

The Congress shall have Power to declare the Punishment of Treason, but no Attainder of Treason shall work Corruption of Blood, or Forfeiture except during the Life of the Person attainted.

ARTICLE IV

SECTION 1

Full Faith and Credit shall be given in each State to the public Acts, Records, and judicial Proceedings of every other State. And the Congress may by general Laws prescribe the Manner in which such Acts, Records and Proceedings shall be proved, and the Effect thereof.

SECTION 2

The Citizens of each State shall be entitled to all Privileges and Immunities of Citizens in the several States.

A Person charged in any State with Treason, Felony, or other Crime, who shall flee from Justice, and be found in another State, shall on Demand of the executive Authority of the State from which he fled, be delivered up, to be removed to the State having Jurisdiction of the Crime.

No Person held to Service or Labour in one State, under the Laws thereof, escaping into another, shall, in Consequence of any Law or Regulation therein, be discharged from such Service or Labour, but shall be delivered up on Claim of the Party to whom such Service or Labour may be due.

SECTION 3

New States may be admitted by the Congress into this Union; but no new State shall be formed or erected within the Jurisdiction of any other State; nor any State be formed by the Junction of two or more States, or Parts of States, without the Consent of the Legislatures of the States concerned as well as of the Congress.

The Congress shall have Power to dispose of and make all needful Rules and Regulations respecting the Territory or other Property belonging to the United States; and nothing in this Constitution shall be so construed as to Prejudice any Claims of the United States, or of any particular State.

SECTION 4

The United States shall guarantee to every State in this Union a Republican Form of Government, and shall protect each of them against Invasion; and on Application of the Legislature, or of the Executive (when the Legislature cannot be convened), against domestic Violence.

ARTICLE V

The Congress, whenever two thirds of both Houses shall deem it necessary, shall propose Amendments to this Constitution, or, on the Application of the Legislatures of two thirds of the several States, shall call a Convention for proposing Amendments, which, in either Case, shall be valid to all Intents and Purposes, as Part of this Constitution, when ratified by the Legislatures of three fourths of the several States, or by Conventions in three fourths thereof, as the one or the other Mode of Ratification may be proposed by the Congress; Provided that no Amendment which may be made prior to the Year One thousand eight hundred and eight shall in any Manner affect the first and fourth Clauses in the Ninth Section of the first Article; and that no State, without its Consent, shall be deprived of its equal Suffrage in the Senate.

ARTICLE VI

All Debts contracted and Engagements entered into, before the Adoption of this Constitution, shall be as valid against the United States under this Constitution, as under the Confederation.

This Constitution, and the Laws of the United States which shall be made in Pursuance thereof; and all Treaties made, or which shall be made, under the Authority of the United States, shall be the supreme Law of the Land; and the Judges in every State shall be bound thereby, any Thing in the Constitution or Laws of any State to the Contrary notwithstanding.

The Senators and Representatives before mentioned, and the Members of the several State Legislatures, and all executive and judicial Officers, both of the United States and of the several States, shall be bound by Oath or Affirmation, to support this Constitution; but no religious Test shall ever be required as a Qualification to any Office or public Trust under the United States.

ARTICLE VII

The Ratification of the Conventions of nine States, shall be sufficient for the Establishment of this Constitution between the States so ratifying the Same.

Done in Convention by the Unanimous Consent of the States present the Seventeenth Day of September in the Year of our Lord one thousand seven hundred and Eighty seven and of the Independence of the United States of America the Twelfth In witness whereof We have hereunto sub-scribed our Names . . .

AMENDMENTS

Congress of the United States begun and held at the City of New-York, on Wednesday the fourth of March, one thousand seven hundred and eighty nine.

THE Conventions of a number of the States, having at the time of their adopting the Constitution, expressed a desire, in order to prevent misconstruction or abuse of its powers, that further declaratory and restrictive clauses should be added: And as extending the ground of public confidence in the Government, will best ensure the beneficent ends of its institution.

RESOLVED by the Senate and House of Representatives of the United States of America, in Congress assembled, two thirds of both Houses concurring, that the following Articles be proposed to the Legislatures of the several States, as amendments to the Constitution of the United States, all, or any of which Articles, when ratified by three fourths of the said Legislatures, to be valid to all intents and purposes, as part of the said Constitution; viz.

ARTICLES in addition to, and Amendment of the Constitution of the United States of America, proposed by Congress, and ratified by the Legislatures of the several States, pursuant to the fifth Article of the original Constitution.

AMENDMENT I

Congress shall make no law respecting an establishment of religion, or prohibiting the free exercise thereof; or abridging the freedom of speech, or of the press; or the right of the people peaceably to assemble, and to petition the Government for a redress of grievances.

AMENDMENT II

A well regulated Militia, being necessary to the security of a free State, the right of the people to keep and bear Arms, shall not be infringed.

AMENDMENT III

No Soldier shall, in time of peace be quartered in any house, without the consent of the Owner, nor in time of war, but in a manner to be prescribed by law.

AMENDMENT IV

The right of the people to be secure in their persons, houses, papers, and effects, against unreasonable searches and seizures, shall not be violated, and no Warrants shall issue, but upon probable cause, supported by Oath or affirmation, and particularly describing the place to be searched, and the persons or things to be seized.

AMENDMENT V

No person shall be held to answer for a capital, or otherwise infamous crime, unless on a presentment or indictment of a Grand Jury, except in cases arising in the land or naval forces, or in the Militia, when in actual service in time of War or public danger; nor shall any person be subject for the same offence to be twice put in jeopardy of life or limb; nor shall be compelled in any criminal case to be a witness against himself, nor be deprived of life, liberty, or property, without due process of law; nor shall private property be taken for public use, without just compensation.

AMENDMENT VI

In all criminal prosecutions, the accused shall enjoy the right to a speedy and public trial, by an impartial jury of the State and district wherein the crime shall have been committed, which district shall have been previously ascertained by law, and to be informed of the nature and cause of the accusation; to be confronted with the witnesses against him; to have compulsory process for obtaining witnesses in his favor, and to have the Assistance of Counsel for his defence.

AMENDMENT VII

In suits at common law, where the value in controversy shall exceed twenty dollars, the right of trial by jury shall be preserved, and no fact tried by a jury, shall be otherwise reexamined in any Court of the United States, than according to the rules of the common law.

AMENDMENT VIII

Excessive bail shall not be required, nor excessive fines imposed, nor cruel and unusual punishments inflicted.

AMENDMENT IX

The enumeration in the Constitution, of certain rights, shall not be construed to deny or disparage others retained by the people.

AMENDMENT X

The powers not delegated to the United States by the Constitution, nor prohibited by it to the States, are reserved to the States respectively, or to the people.

AMENDMENT XI

Passed by Congress March 4, 1794. Ratified February 7, 1795.

Note: Article III, section 2, of the Constitution was modified by the amendment 11.

The Judicial power of the United States shall not be construed to extend to any suit in law or equity, commenced or prosecuted against one of the United States by Citizens of another State, or by Citizens or Subjects of any Foreign State.

AMENDMENT XII

Passed by Congress December 9, 1803. Ratified June 15, 1804.

Note: A portion of Article II, section 1 of the Constitution was superseded by the 12th amendment.

The Electors shall meet in their respective states and vote by ballot for President and Vice-President, one of whom, at least, shall not be an inhabitant of the same state with themselves; they shall name in their ballots the person voted for as President, and in distinct ballots the person voted for as Vice-President, and they shall make distinct lists of all persons voted for as President, and of all persons voted for as Vice-President, and of the number of votes for each, which lists they shall sign and certify, and transmit sealed to the seat of the government of the United States, directed to the President of the Senate;—the President of the Senate shall, in the presence of the Senate and House of Representatives, open all the certificates and the votes shall then be counted;—The person having the greatest number of votes for President, shall be the President, if such number be a majority of the whole number of Electors appointed; and if no person have such majority, then from the persons having the highest numbers not exceeding three on the list of those voted for as President, the House of Representatives shall choose immediately, by ballot, the President. But in choosing the President, the votes shall be taken by states, the representation from each state having one vote; a quorum for this purpose shall consist of a member or members from two-thirds of the states, and a majority of all the states shall be necessary to a choice. [And if the House of Representatives shall not choose a President whenever the right of choice shall devolve upon them, before the fourth day of March next following, then the Vice-President shall act as President, as in case of the death or other constitutional disability of the President. —]* The person having the greatest number of votes as Vice-President, shall be the Vice-President, if such number be a majority of the whole number of Electors appointed, and if no person have a majority, then from the two highest numbers on the list, the Senate shall choose the Vice-President; a quorum for the purpose shall consist of two-thirds of the whole number of Senators, and a majority of the whole number shall be necessary to a choice. But no person constitutionally ineligible to the office of President shall be eligible to that of Vice-President of the United States.

*Superseded by section 3 of the 20th amendment.

AMENDMENT XIII
Passed by Congress January 31, 1865. Ratified December 6, 1865.

Note: A portion of Article IV, section 2, of the Constitution was superseded by the 13th amendment.

SECTION 1
Neither slavery nor involuntary servitude, except as a punishment for crime whereof the party shall have been duly convicted, shall exist within the United States, or any place subject to their jurisdiction.

SECTION 2

Congress shall have power to enforce this article by appropriate legislation.

AMENDMENT XIV

Passed by Congress June 13, 1866. Ratified July 9, 1868.

Note: Article I, section 2, of the Constitution was modified by section 2 of the 14th amendment.

SECTION 1

All persons born or naturalized in the United States, and subject to the jurisdiction thereof, are citizens of the United States and of the State wherein they reside. No State shall make or enforce any law which shall abridge the privileges or immunities of citizens of the United States; nor shall any State deprive any person of life, liberty, or property, without due process of law; nor deny to any person within its jurisdiction the equal protection of the laws.

SECTION 2

Representatives shall be apportioned among the several States according to their respective numbers, counting the whole number of persons in each State, excluding Indians not taxed. But when the right to vote at any election for the choice of electors for President and Vice-President of the United States, Representatives in Congress, the Executive and Judicial officers of a State, or the members of the Legislature thereof, is denied to any of the male inhabitants of such State, being twenty-one years of age,* and citizens of the United States, or in any way abridged, except for participation in rebellion, or other crime, the basis of representation therein shall be reduced in the proportion which the number of such male citizens shall bear to the whole number of male citizens twenty-one years of age in such State.

*Changed by section 1 of the 26th amendment.

SECTION 3

No person shall be a Senator or Representative in Congress, or elector of President and Vice-President, or hold any office, civil or military, under the

United States, or under any State, who, having previously taken an oath, as a member of Congress, or as an officer of the United States, or as a member of any State legislature, or as an executive or judicial officer of any State, to support the Constitution of the United States, shall have engaged in insurrection or rebellion against the same, or given aid or comfort to the enemies thereof. But Congress may by a vote of two-thirds of each House, remove such disability.

SECTION 4

The validity of the public debt of the United States, authorized by law, including debts incurred for payment of pensions and bounties for services in suppressing insurrection or rebellion, shall not be questioned. But neither the United States nor any State shall assume or pay any debt or obligation incurred in aid of insurrection or rebellion against the United States, or any claim for the loss or emancipation of any slave; but all such debts, obligations and claims shall be held illegal and void.

SECTION 5

The Congress shall have the power to enforce, by appropriate legislation, the provisions of this article.

AMENDMENT XV

Passed by Congress February 26, 1869. Ratified February 3, 1870.

SECTION 1

The right of citizens of the United States to vote shall not be denied or abridged by the United States or by any State on account of race, color, or previous condition of servitude.

SECTION 2

The Congress shall have the power to enforce this article by appropriate legislation.

AMENDMENT XVI

Passed by Congress July 2, 1909. Ratified February 3, 1913.

Note: Article I, section 9, of the Constitution was modified by the amendment 16.

The Congress shall have power to lay and collect taxes on incomes, from whatever source derived, without apportionment among the several States, and without regard to any census or enumeration.

AMENDMENT XVII

Passed by Congress May 13, 1912. Ratified April 8, 1913.

Note: Article I, section 3, of the Constitution was modified by the 17th amendment.

The Senate of the United States shall be composed of two Senators from each State, elected by the people thereof, for six years; and each Senator shall have one vote. The electors in each State shall have the qualifications requisite for electors of the most numerous branch of the State legislatures.

When vacancies happen in the representation of any State in the Senate, the executive authority of such State shall issue writs of election to fill such vacancies: *Provided,* That the legislature of any State may empower the executive thereof to make temporary appointments until the people fill the vacancies by election as the legislature may direct.

This amendment shall not be so construed as to affect the election or term of any Senator chosen before it becomes valid as part of the Constitution.

AMENDMENT XVIII

Passed by Congress December 18, 1917. Ratified January 16, 1919.
Repealed by amendment 21.

SECTION 1

After one year from the ratification of this article the manufacture, sale, or transportation of intoxicating liquors within, the importation thereof into, or the exportation thereof from the United States and all territory subject to the jurisdiction thereof for beverage purposes is hereby prohibited.

SECTION 2

The Congress and the several States shall have concurrent power to enforce this article by appropriate legislation.

SECTION 3

This article shall be inoperative unless it shall have been ratified as an amendment to the Constitution by the legislatures of the several States, as provided in the Constitution, within seven years from the date of the submission hereof to the States by the Congress.

AMENDMENT XIX

Passed by Congress June 4, 1919. Ratified August 18, 1920.

The right of citizens of the United States to vote shall not be denied or abridged by the United States or by any State on account of sex.

Congress shall have power to enforce this article by appropriate legislation.

AMENDMENT XX

Passed by Congress March 2, 1932. Ratified January 23, 1933.

Note: Article I, section 4, of the Constitution was modified by section 2 of this amendment. In addition, a portion of the 12th Amendment was superseded by section 3.

SECTION 1

The terms of the President and the Vice President shall end at noon on the 20th day of January, and the terms of Senators and Representatives at noon on the 3d day of January, of the years in which such terms would have ended if this article had not been ratified; and the terms of their successors shall then begin.

SECTION 2

The Congress shall assemble at least once in every year, and such meeting shall begin at noon on the 3d day of January, unless they shall by law appoint a different day.

SECTION 3

If, at the time fixed for the beginning of the term of the President, the President elect shall have died, the Vice President elect shall become President. If a President shall not have been chosen before the time fixed for the beginning of his term, or if the President elect shall have failed to qualify, then the Vice President elect shall act as President until a President shall have qualified; and the Congress may by law provide for the case wherein neither a President elect nor a Vice President shall have qualified, declaring who shall then act as President, or the manner in which one who is to act shall be selected, and such person shall act accordingly until a President or Vice President shall have qualified.

SECTION 4

The Congress may by law provide for the case of the death of any of the persons from whom the House of Representatives may choose a President whenever the right of choice shall have devolved upon them, and for the case of the death of any of the persons from whom the Senate may choose a Vice President whenever the right of choice shall have devolved upon them.

SECTION 5

Sections 1 and 2 shall take effect on the 15th day of October following the ratification of this article.

SECTION 6

This article shall be inoperative unless it shall have been ratified as an amendment to the Constitution by the legislatures of three-fourths of the several States within seven years from the date of its submission.

AMENDMENT XXI

Passed by Congress February 20, 1933. Ratified December 5, 1933.

SECTION 1

The eighteenth article of amendment to the Constitution of the United States is hereby repealed.

SECTION 2

The transportation or importation into any State, Territory, or Possession of the United States for delivery or use therein of intoxicating liquors, in violation of the laws thereof, is hereby prohibited.

SECTION 3

This article shall be inoperative unless it shall have been ratified as an amendment to the Constitution by conventions in the several States, as provided in the Constitution, within seven years from the date of the submission hereof to the States by the Congress.

AMENDMENT XXII

Passed by Congress March 21, 1947. Ratified February 27, 1951.

SECTION 1

No person shall be elected to the office of the President more than twice, and no person who has held the office of President, or acted as President, for more than two years of a term to which some other person was elected President shall be elected to the office of President more than once. But this Article shall not apply to any person holding the office of President when this Article was proposed by Congress, and shall not prevent any person who may be holding the office of President, or acting as President, during the term within which this Article becomes operative from holding the office of President or acting as President during the remainder of such term.

SECTION 2

This article shall be inoperative unless it shall have been ratified as an amendment to the Constitution by the legislatures of three-fourths of the several States within seven years from the date of its submission to the States by the Congress.

AMENDMENT XXIII

Passed by Congress June 16, 1960. Ratified March 29, 1961.

SECTION 1

The District constituting the seat of Government of the United States shall appoint in such manner as Congress may direct:

A number of electors of President and Vice President equal to the whole number of Senators and Representatives in Congress to which the District would be entitled if it were a State, but in no event more than the least populous State; they shall be in addition to those appointed by the States, but they shall be considered, for the purposes of the election of President and Vice President, to be electors appointed by a State; and they shall meet in the District and perform such duties as provided by the twelfth article of amendment.

SECTION 2

The Congress shall have power to enforce this article by appropriate legislation.

AMENDMENT XXIV

Passed by Congress August 27, 1962. Ratified January 23, 1964.

SECTION 1

The right of citizens of the United States to vote in any primary or other election for President or Vice President, for electors for President or Vice President, or for Senator or Representative in Congress, shall not be denied or abridged by the United States or any State by reason of failure to pay poll tax or other tax.

SECTION 2

The Congress shall have power to enforce this article by appropriate legislation.

AMENDMENT XXV

Passed by Congress July 6, 1965. Ratified February 10, 1967.

Note: Article II, section 1, of the Constitution was affected by the Twenty Fifth Amendment.

SECTION 1

In case of the removal of the President from office or of his death or resignation, the Vice President shall become President.

SECTION 2

Whenever there is a vacancy in the office of the Vice President, the President shall nominate a Vice President who shall take office upon confirmation by a majority vote of both Houses of Congress.

SECTION 3

Whenever the President transmits to the President pro tempore of the Senate and the Speaker of the House of Representatives his written declaration that he is unable to discharge the powers and duties of his office, and until he transmits to them a written declaration to the contrary, such powers and duties shall be discharged by the Vice President as Acting President.

SECTION 4

Whenever the Vice President and a majority of either the principal officers of the executive departments or of such other body as Congress may by law provide, transmit to the President pro tempore of the Senate and the Speaker of the House of Representatives their written declaration that the President is unable to discharge the powers and duties of his office, the Vice President shall immediately assume the powers and duties of the office as Acting President.

Thereafter, when the President transmits to the President pro tempore of the Senate and the Speaker of the House of Representatives his written declaration that no inability exists, he shall resume the powers and duties of his office unless the Vice President and a majority of either the principal officers of the executive department or of such other body as Congress may by law provide, transmit within four days to the President pro tempore of the Senate and the Speaker of the House of Representatives their written declaration that the President is unable to discharge the powers and duties of his office. Thereupon Congress shall decide the issue, assembling within forty-eight hours for that purpose if not in session. If the Congress, within twenty-one days after receipt of the latter written declaration, or, if Congress is not in session, within twenty-one days after Congress is required to assemble, determines by two-thirds vote of both Houses that the President is unable to discharge the powers and duties of his office, the Vice President shall continue to discharge the same as Acting President; otherwise, the President shall resume the powers and duties of his office.

AMENDMENT XXVI

Passed by Congress March 23, 1971. Ratified July 1, 1971.

Note: Amendment 14, section 2, of the Constitution was modified by section 1 of the 26th Amendment.

SECTION 1

The right of citizens of the United States, who are eighteen years of age or older, to vote shall not be denied or abridged by the United States or by any State on account of age.

SECTION 2.

The Congress shall have power to enforce this article by appropriate legislation.

AMENDMENT XXVII

Originally proposed Sept. 25, 1789. Ratified May 7, 1992.

No law, varying the compensation for the services of the Senators and Representatives, shall take effect, until an election of representatives shall have intervened.

UNIVERSAL DECLARATION OF HUMAN RIGHTS, ADOPTED AND PROCLAIMED BY GENERAL ASSEMBLY RESOLUTION 217 A (III) OF DECEMBER 10, 1948

PREAMBLE

∽ Whereas recognition of the inherent dignity and of the equal and inalienable rights of all members of the human family is the foundation of freedom, justice and peace in the world,

∽ Whereas disregard and contempt for human rights have resulted in barbarous acts which have outraged the conscience of mankind, and the advent of a world in which human beings shall enjoy freedom of speech and belief and freedom from fear and want has been proclaimed as the highest aspiration of the common people,

∽ Whereas it is essential, if man is not to be compelled to have recourse, as a last resort, to rebellion against tyranny and oppression, that human rights should be protected by the rule of law,

∽ Whereas it is essential to promote the development of friendly relations between nations,

∽ Whereas the peoples of the United Nations have in the Charter reaffirmed their faith in fundamental human rights, in the dignity and worth of the human person and in the equal rights of men and women and have determined to promote social progress and better standards of life in larger freedom,

∽ Whereas Member States have pledged themselves to achieve, in co-operation with the United Nations, the promotion of universal respect for and observance of human rights and fundamental freedoms,

∽ Whereas a common understanding of these rights and freedoms is of the greatest importance for the full realization of this pledge,

Now, Therefore THE GENERAL ASSEMBLY proclaims THIS UNIVER-SAL DECLARATION OF HUMAN RIGHTS as a common standard of achievement for all peoples and all nations, to the end that every individual and every organ of society, keeping this Declaration constantly in mind, shall strive by teaching and education to promote respect for these rights and freedoms and by progressive measures, national and international, to secure their universal and effective recognition and observance, both among the peoples of Member States themselves and among the peoples of territories under their jurisdiction.

ARTICLE 1

All human beings are born free and equal in dignity and rights. They are endowed with reason and conscience and should act towards one another in a spirit of brotherhood.

ARTICLE 2

Everyone is entitled to all the rights and freedoms set forth in this Declaration, without distinction of any kind, such as race, colour, sex, language, religion, political or other opinion, national or social origin, property, birth or other status. Furthermore, no distinction shall be made on the basis of the political, jurisdictional or international status of the country or territory to which a person belongs, whether it be independent, trust, non-self-governing or under any other limitation of sovereignty.

ARTICLE 3

Everyone has the right to life, liberty and security of person.

ARTICLE 4

No one shall be held in slavery or servitude; slavery and the slave trade shall be prohibited in all their forms.

ARTICLE 5

No one shall be subjected to torture or to cruel, inhuman or degrading treatment or punishment.

ARTICLE 6

Everyone has the right to recognition everywhere as a person before the law.

ARTICLE 7

All are equal before the law and are entitled without any discrimination to equal protection of the law. All are entitled to equal protection against any discrimination in violation of this Declaration and against any incitement to such discrimination.

ARTICLE 8

Everyone has the right to an effective remedy by the competent national tribunals for acts violating the fundamental rights granted him by the constitution or by law.

ARTICLE 9

No one shall be subjected to arbitrary arrest, detention or exile.

ARTICLE 10

Everyone is entitled in full equality to a fair and public hearing by an independent and impartial tribunal, in the determination of his rights and obligations and of any criminal charge against him.

ARTICLE 11

(1) Everyone charged with a penal offence has the right to be presumed innocent until proved guilty according to law in a public trial at which he has had all the guarantees necessary for his defence.

(2) No one shall be held guilty of any penal offence on account of any act or omission which did not constitute a penal offence, under national or international law, at the time when it was committed. Nor shall a heavier penalty be imposed than the one that was applicable at the time the penal offence was committed.

ARTICLE 12

No one shall be subjected to arbitrary interference with his privacy, family, home or correspondence, nor to attacks upon his honour and reputation.

Everyone has the right to the protection of the law against such interference or attacks.

ARTICLE 13

(1) Everyone has the right to freedom of movement and residence within the borders of each state.

(2) Everyone has the right to leave any country, including his own, and to return to his country.

ARTICLE 14

(1) Everyone has the right to seek and to enjoy in other countries asylum from persecution.

(2) This right may not be invoked in the case of prosecutions genuinely arising from non-political crimes or from acts contrary to the purposes and principles of the United Nations.

ARTICLE 15

(1) Everyone has the right to a nationality.

(2) No one shall be arbitrarily deprived of his nationality nor denied the right to change his nationality.

ARTICLE 16

(1) Men and women of full age, without any limitation due to race, nationality or religion, have the right to marry and to found a family. They are entitled to equal rights as to marriage, during marriage and at its dissolution.

(2) Marriage shall be entered into only with the free and full consent of the intending spouses.

(3) The family is the natural and fundamental group unit of society and is entitled to protection by society and the State.

ARTICLE 17

(1) Everyone has the right to own property alone as well as in association with others.

(2) No one shall be arbitrarily deprived of his property.

ARTICLE 18

Everyone has the right to freedom of thought, conscience and religion; this right includes freedom to change his religion or belief, and freedom, either alone or in community with others and in public or private, to manifest his religion or belief in teaching, practice, worship and observance.

ARTICLE 19

Everyone has the right to freedom of opinion and expression; this right includes freedom to hold opinions without interference and to seek, receive and impart information and ideas through any media and regardless of frontiers.

ARTICLE 20

(1) Everyone has the right to freedom of peaceful assembly and association.

(2) No one may be compelled to belong to an association.

ARTICLE 21

(1) Everyone has the right to take part in the government of his country, directly or through freely chosen representatives.

(2) Everyone has the right of equal access to public service in his country.

(3) The will of the people shall be the basis of the authority of government; this will shall be expressed in periodic and genuine elections which shall be by universal and equal suffrage and shall be held by secret vote or by equivalent free voting procedures.

ARTICLE 22

Everyone, as a member of society, has the right to social security and is entitled to realization, through national effort and international co-operation and in accordance with the organization and resources of each State, of the economic, social and cultural rights indispensable for his dignity and the free development of his personality.

ARTICLE 23

(1) Everyone has the right to work, to free choice of employment, to just and favourable conditions of work and to protection against unemployment.

(2) Everyone, without any discrimination, has the right to equal pay for equal work.

(3) Everyone who works has the right to just and favourable remuneration ensuring for himself and his family an existence worthy of human dignity, and supplemented, if necessary, by other means of social protection.

(4) Everyone has the right to form and to join trade unions for the protection of his interests.

ARTICLE 24

Everyone has the right to rest and leisure, including reasonable limitation of working hours and periodic holidays with pay.

ARTICLE 25

(1) Everyone has the right to a standard of living adequate for the health and well-being of himself and of his family, including food, clothing, housing and medical care and necessary social services, and the right to security in the event of unemployment, sickness, disability, widowhood, old age or other lack of livelihood in circumstances beyond his control.

(2) Motherhood and childhood are entitled to special care and assistance. All children, whether born in or out of wedlock, shall enjoy the same social protection.

ARTICLE 26

(1) Everyone has the right to education. Education shall be free, at least in the elementary and fundamental stages. Elementary education shall be compulsory. Technical and professional education shall be made generally available and higher education shall be equally accessible to all on the basis of merit.

(2) Education shall be directed to the full development of the human personality and to the strengthening of respect for human rights and fundamental freedoms. It shall promote understanding, tolerance and friendship

among all nations, racial or religious groups, and shall further the activities of the United Nations for the maintenance of peace.

(3) Parents have a prior right to choose the kind of education that shall be given to their children.

ARTICLE 27

(1) Everyone has the right freely to participate in the cultural life of the community, to enjoy the arts and to share in scientific advancement and its benefits.

(2) Everyone has the right to the protection of the moral and material interests resulting from any scientific, literary or artistic production of which he is the author.

ARTICLE 28

Everyone is entitled to a social and international order in which the rights and freedoms set forth in this Declaration can be fully realized.

ARTICLE 29

(1) Everyone has duties to the community in which alone the free and full development of his personality is possible.

(2) In the exercise of his rights and freedoms, everyone shall be subject only to such limitations as are determined by law solely for the purpose of securing due recognition and respect for the rights and freedoms of others and of meeting the just requirements of morality, public order and the general welfare in a democratic society.

(3) These rights and freedoms may in no case be exercised contrary to the purposes and principles of the United Nations.

ARTICLE 30

Nothing in this Declaration may be interpreted as implying for any State, group or person any right to engage in any activity or to perform any act aimed at the destruction of any of the rights and freedoms set forth herein.

SOURCES AND PERMISSIONS

We have made every effort to secure the permission to reprint all of the pieces in this book. If any copyright holders have been inadvertently overlooked, we offer our sincere apologies and welcome you to contact us. Any additional copyright information will be published in future printings of this book.

The editor wishes to thank each of the copyright holders for granting us permission to include their piece in this book.

ADAMS, ABIGAIL AND JOHN. An Exchange of Letters, March 31, 1776 and April 14, 1776. In *Letters of John Adams and His Wife Abigail Adams, during the Revolution. With a Memoir of Mrs. Adams,* edited by Charles Francis Adams. Freeport, New York: Books for Libraries Press, 1875.

AFKHAMI, MAHNAZ. "A Prologue." From *Women in Exile.* University of Virginia Press, 1994. Copyright © 1994 by the University of Virginia Press. Reprinted by permission of the University of Virginia Press.

ANGELOU, MAYA. "Still I Rise." In *And Still I Rise.* New York: Random House, 1978. Copyright © 1978 by Maya Angelou. Reprinted by permission of Maya Angelou.

ANTHONY, SUSAN B. An Account of the Proceedings on the Trial of Susan B. Anthony, on the Charge of Illegal Voting, at the Presidential Election in Nov. 1872, and on the Trial of Beverly W. Jones, Edwin T. Marsh and William B. Hall, the Inspectors of Election by Whom Her Vote Was Received. 1874.

BALDWIN, JAMES. "My Dungeon Shook: Letter to My Nephew on the One Hundredth Anniversary of the Emancipation." In *The Fire Next Time.* New York: Vintage Books, 1962. Copyright © 1962, 1963 by James Baldwin. Copyright renewed 1990, 1991 by Gloria Baldwin Karefa-Smart. Reprinted by permission of the James Baldwin Estate.

BALZAR, JOHN. "Let That Old-Time Freedom Ring Out." In *The Los Angeles Times*. July 4, 2001. Copyright © 2001 by *The Los Angeles Times*. Reprinted by permission of *The Los Angeles Times*.

BERLIN, IRVING. "God Bless America." Copyright © 1938, 1939 by Irving Berlin. Copyright renewed 1965, 1966 by Irving Berlin. Copyright assigned the Trustees of the God Bless America Fund. Reprinted by permission of Williamson Music, a division of The Rodgers & Hammerstein Organization on behalf of the Irving Berlin Music Company.

BRADLEY, BILL. "America's Challenge: Revitalizing Our National Community." Speech at the National Press Club, Washington, D.C., February 9, 1995.

BROKAW, TOM. Commencement Address delivered at the College of Santa Fe, New Mexico, May 15, 1999. Copyright © 1999 by Tom Brokaw. Reprinted by permission of Tom Brokaw.

Brown v. Board of Education. Supreme Court of the United States, 347 U.S. 483. Decided May 17, 1954.

BUCHMAN, SIDNEY. *Mr. Smith Goes to Washington,* 1939. Copyright © 1939, renewed 1967 by Columbia Pictures Industries, Inc. Reprinted by permission of Columbia Pictures.

BUCK, PEARL S. "What America Means to Me." In *What America Means to Me.* New York: The John Day Company, 1942. Copyright © 1942 by Pearl S. Buck. Reprinted by permission of Harold Ober Associates for Pearl S. Buck.

CAMUS, ALBERT. "The Myth of Sisyphus." In *The Myth of Sisyphus*. Translated by Justin O'Brien. New York: Vintage Books, a division of Random House, 1955. Copyright © 1955 by Alfred A. Knopf, a division of Random House, Inc. Reprinted by permission of Alfred A. Knopf, a division of Random House, Inc.

CARTER, JIMMY. "Farewell Address to the Nation," delivered January 14, 1981, in Washington, D.C. In *Public Papers of the Presidents of the United States, Jimmy Carter: Containing the Public Messages, Speeches, and Statements of the President, 1980-81, Book III—September 29, 1980 to January 20, 1981.* Washington, D.C. United States Government Printing Office, 1981.

CATT, CARRIE CHAPMAN. "An Address to the Congress of the United States." In *Pamphlets in American History.* New York: National Woman Suffrage Publishing Co., 1917.

CHAPMAN, TRACY. "Talkin' Bout a Revolution," from the album *Tracy Chapman,* 1988. Copyright © 1988 by EMI April Music, Inc./Purple Rabbit Music. All rights controlled and administered by EMI April Music, Inc. All rights reserved. International copyright secured. Reprinted by permission.

CHAVEZ, CESAR E. "UFWU Appeal to the California Grape and Tree Fruit League, Good Friday, 1969." Copyright © 2003 by the Cesar E. Chavez Foundation. Reprinted by permission of the Cesar E. Chavez Foundation. *www.chavezfoundation.org*

CLINTON, WILLIAM J. Remarks delivered at the 86th Annual Holy Convocation, the Church of God in Christ, Memphis, Tennessee, on November 13, 1993.

CONNELL, STEVE. "I Am an American." Copyright © 2003 by Steve Connell. Reprinted by permission of Steve Connell.

DARROW, CLARENCE. Clarence Darrow's closing argument in the Henry Sweet Case, May 19, 1926. Copyright © 1926 by the NAACP. Reprinted by permission of the National Association for the Advancement of Colored People.

DECLARATION OF SENTIMENTS AND RESOLUTIONS BY THE WOMEN'S RIGHTS CONVENTION, Seneca Falls, New York, 1848. In *History of Women's Suffrage,* edited by Elizabeth Cady Stanton, Susan B. Anthony, and Matilda Joslyn Gage, New York, 1881.

DE TOCQUEVILLE, ALEXIS. *Democracy in America. Part the Second, The Social Influence of Democracy*. Translated by Henry Reeve, Esq. New York: J. & H. G. Langley, 1840.

DONNE, JOHN. "Meditation XVII: No Man is an Island." In *Devotions upon Emergent Occasions*. London: Printed by A.M., 1624.

DOUGLASS, FREDERICK. "Frederick Douglass to His Former Master, Capt. Thomas Auld." In the *North Star,* September 8, 1848.

DU BOIS, WILLIAM EDWARD BURGHARDT. Address to the Second Annual Meeting of the Niagara Conference, Harper's Ferry, West Virginia, on August 16, 1906. Reported in *The New York Times,* August 20, 1906.

DUMAS, HENRY. "America." In *Knees of a Natural Man: The Selected Poetry of Henry Dumas,* edited by Eugene B. Redmond. New York: Thunder's Mouth Press, 1989. Copyright © 1968–2003 by Loretta Dumas and Eugene B. Redmond. Reprinted by permission of the Henry Dumas Estate.

DYLAN, BOB. "Chimes of Freedom," from the album *Another Side of Bob Dylan,* 1964. Copyright © 1964 by Warner Bros. Inc. Copyright © 1992 renewed by Special Rider Music. Reprinted by permission of Bob Dylan.

EMERSON, RALPH WALDO. "Self-Reliance." In *The Works of Ralph Waldo Emerson, Volume 1, Essays, First and Second Series*. New York: The Caxton Society, 1841.

FAULKNER, WILLIAM. Acceptance speech at the Nobel Banquet in Stockholm, Sweden, on December 10, 1950. Copyright © 1950 Nobel Foundation. Reprinted by permission of The Nobel Foundation.

FLOOD, CURT. Letter to Bowie Kuhn, December 24, 1969. In Marvin Miller's *A Whole Different Ball Game: The Sport and Business of Baseball*. Secaucus, NJ: Carol Publishing Group, 1991. Copyright © 1991 by Marvin Miller. Reprinted by permission of Marvin Miller.

FORD, GERALD R. Speech delivered in Philadelphia, Pennsylvania on July 4, 1976. In *Public Papers of the Presidents of the United States, Gerald R. Ford: Containing the Public Messages, Speeches, and Statements of the President, 1976–77, Book II—April 9 to July 9, 1976.* Washington, D.C.: United States Government Printing Office, 1979.

FRANK, ANNE. Diary entry on July 15, 1944. In *The Diary of a Young Girl: The Definitive Edition,* edited by Otto H. Frank and Mirjam Pressler, translated by Susan Massotty. Copyright © 1995 by Doubleday, a division of Random House, Inc. Reprinted by permission of Doubleday, a division of Random House.

FROST, ROBERT. "The Gift Outright." In *The Poetry of Robert Frost,* edited by Edward Connery Lathem. Copyright © 1942 by Robert Frost, © 1975 by Lesley Frost Ballantine, © 1969 by Henry Holt and Company. Reprinted by permission of Henry Holt and Company, LLC.

FROST, ROBERT. "The Road Not Taken." In *The Poetry of Robert Frost,* edited by Edward Connery Lathem. Copyright © 1942 by Robert Frost, © 1975 by Lesley Frost Ballantine, © 1969 by Henry Holt and Company. Reprinted by permission of Henry Holt and Company, LLC.

GUTHRIE, WOODY. "This Land is Your Land." Words and music by Woody Guthrie. Copyright © 1956, 1958, 1970, 1972 by TRO (copyrights renewed) Ludlow Music, Inc., New York, NY. Reprinted by permission of TRO—The Richmond Organization.

HAVEL, VÁCLAV. "Letter to Olga, August 29, 1981." In *Letters to Olga: June 1979–September 1982.* New York: Henry Holt and Company, 1989. Copyright © 1983 by Václav Havel. Reprinted by permission of Václav Havel.

HUGHES, LANGSTON. "Let America Be America Again." In *The Collected Poems of Langston Hughes.* Copyright © 1994 by the Estate of Langston Hughes. Reprinted by permission of Alfred A. Knopf, a division of Random House, Inc.

JOHNSON, HARRIET McBRYDE. "Courage." On NPR's *The Infinite Mind,* August 21, 2000. Copyright © 2001 by Harriet McBryde Johnson. Reprinted by permission of Harriet McBryde Johnson.

JOHNSON, LYNDON B. Special Message to the Congress: "The American Promise," delivered on March 15, 1965. In *Public Papers of the Presidents, Lyndon B. Johnson, Containing the Public Messages, Speeches, and Statements of the President, 1965, Book I—January 1 to May 31, 1965.* Washington, D. C.: Government Printing Office, 1966.

JOHNSON, LYNDON B. "The Great Society" delivered at the University of Michigan on May 22, 1964. In *Public Papers of the Presidents, Lyndon B. Johnson, Containing the Public Messages, Speeches, and Statements of the President, 1963–1964. Book I—November 22, 1963 to June 30 1964.* Washington, D. C.: Government Printing Office, 1965.

JONES, MARY HARRIS "MOTHER." Letter to President Theodore Roosevelt. Printed in the Philadelphia *North American,* July 31, 1903.

JORDAN, BARBARA. Democratic National Convention Keynote Address: "Who Then Will Speak for the Common Good?" Delivered in New York, New York, on July 12, 1976.

KEMPNER, MARION LEE "SANDY". Letter from Marion Lee "Sandy" Kempner to His Great-Aunt Mrs. Louis "Fannie" Adoue, October 20, 1966. In *Dear America: Letters Home from Vietnam,* edited by Bernard Edelman. Published originally by W.W. Norton & Company in 1985. Reissued by Norton in 2002. Copyright © the New York Vietnam Veterans Memorial Commission. Reprinted by permission of Bernard Edelman.

KING JR., MARTIN LUTHER. "The American Dream." Speech delivered at Ebenezer Baptist Church, Atlanta, Georgia, on July 4, 1965. Copyright © 1963 by Martin Luther King, Jr. Copyright renewed 1991 by Coretta Scott King. Reprinted by permission of Intellectual Properties Management, Atlanta, Georgia, as Manager of the King Estate.

MANKILLER, WILMA. Commencement Address delivered at Northern Arizona University, Flagstaff, Arizona, on December 18, 1992. Copyright © 1992 by Wilma Mankiller. Reprinted by permission of Wilma Mankiller.

MARSHALL, THURGOOD. "Reflections on the Bicentennial of the United States Constitution." In the *Harvard Law Review,* 101. November 1987. pp. 1–5. Copyright © 1987 by the Harvard Law Review Association. Reprinted by permission of the Harvard Law Review Association.

McCULLOUGH, DAVID. "The Argonauts of 1776." In *The New York Times,* Op-Ed, July 4, 2002. Copyright © 2002 by David McCullough. Reprinted by permission of David McCullough, author and historian.

NASH, GRAHAM. "Teach Your Children," from the album *Four Way Street,* 1971. Copyright © 1971 (Renewed) by Nash Notes. Reprinted with permission of Sony/ATV Music Publishing, 8 Music Square West, Nashville, TN, 37203.

NERUDA, PABLO. "October Fullness." In *Isla Negra,* translated by Alastair Reid. New York: Farrar, Straus and Giroux, 1981. Translation copyright © 1970, 1979, 1981 by Alastair Reid. Translated from the Spanish, *Memorial de la Isla Negra,* copyright © 1964 by Editorial Losada, S.A., Buenos Aires. Reprinted by permission of Farrar, Straus and Giroux, Inc.

OSUNDARE, NIYI. "I Sing of Change." In *Pages from the Book of the Sun: New & Selected Poems.* Trenton, N.J.: African World Press, 2002. Copyright © 2002 by Niyi Osundare. Reprinted by permission of Niyi Osundare.

PEART, NEIL AND GEDDY LEE. "Something for Nothing." Copyright © 1976 by Core Music Publishing Co. All Rights Reserved. Reprinted by permission of Warner Bros. Publications U.S. Inc., Miami, Florida.

RATUSHINSKAYA, IRINA. "I Will Live and Survive." In *Beyond the Limit,* translated by Frances Padorr Brent and Carol J. Avins. Evanston:

Northwestern University Press, 1987. English translation and notes, foreword, and translator's introduction copyright © 1987 by Frances Padorr Brent and Carol J. Avins. Reprinted by permission of Northwestern University Press.

"Reasoning the Fourth." In *The New York Times,* Editorial, July 4, 1999. Copyright © 1999 The New York Times Co. Reprinted by permission of The New York Times Agency.

RICH, ADRIENNE. "Why I Refused the National Medal for the Arts." In *Arts of the Possible: Essays and Conversations.* Copyright © 2001 by Adrienne Rich. Reprinted by permission of Adrienne Rich and W.W. Norton & Company, Inc.

ROCKEFELLER, JOHN D. JR. Speech to New York City Parents and Neighbors, July 8, 1941, Folder 188, Box 4, Subseries 8: Speeches, Series Z: JDR Jr. Personal Papers, Record Group 2: Office of the Messrs. Rockefeller, Rockefeller Family Archives, Rockefeller Archive Center, Sleepy Hollow, New York.

ROOSEVELT, ELEANOR. "Keepers of Democracy." In *Virginia Quarterly Review,* pp. 1–5, January 15, 1939. Copyright © 1939 by Eleanor Roosevelt. Reprinted by permission of Nancy Roosevelt Ireland.

ROOSEVELT, FRANKLIN D. State of the Union Message: "Four Freedoms." Delivered January 6, 1941. In the *Congressional Record,* 77th Congress, first session, LXXXVII, part I, pp. 45-47.

SAFIRE, WILLIAM. Commencement Address delivered at James Madison University, Harrisonburg, Virginia, on May 5, 2001. Copyright © 2001 by William Safire. Reprinted by permission of William Safire.

SAMUELSON, ROBERT J. "Pay Attention, Kids." In *The Washington Post,* August 23, 2000. Copyright © 2000 by The Washington Post Writers Group. Reprinted by permission of The Washington Post Writers Group.

SANDBURG, CARL. "Open Letter to the Poet Archibald MacLeish Who has Forsaken His Massachusetts Farm to Make Propaganda for Freedom." In *The Complete Poems Of Carl Sandburg*. San Diego: Harcourt Brace Jovanovich, Publishers, 1970. Copyright © 1970, 1969 by Lilian Steichen Sandburg, Trustee. Reprinted by permission of Harcourt, Inc.

SCHMICH, MARY. "Advice, Like Youth, Probably Just Wasted on the Young." In the *Chicago Tribune,* June 1, 1997. Copyright © 1997 Chicago Tribune Company. Reprinted by permission of the Chicago Tribune Company.

SCOTT-HERON, GIL. "The Revolution Will Not Be Televised," from the album *Flying Dutchman,* 1974. Copyright © 1971, 1988 by Bienstock Publishing Company (ASCAP). Copyright © Renewed. Reprinted by permission of Carlin America, Inc., on behalf of Bienstock Publishing Company.

SEATTLE, CHIEF. Public Speech,1854. Originally published in the *Seattle Sunday Star,* October 29, 1887.

SHAARA, MICHAEL. *The Killer Angels.* New York: Ballantine Books, 1974. Copyright © 1974 by Michael Shaara. Reprinted by permission of David McKay Company, a division of Random House, Inc.

SIA, BEAU. "Generations of Lost Angels Found." Copyright © 2003 by Beau Sia. Reprinted by permission of Beau Sia.

SMITH, MARGARET CHASE. "Declaration of Conscience." Statement delivered by Senator Smith to the Untied States Senate, June 1, 1950.

SORKIN, AARON. *The American President,* 1995. Copyright © 1995 by Aaron Sorkin. Reprinted by permission of Aaron Sorkin.

SULLIVAN, KATHRYN. "A Glimpse of Home." In *Time,* August 26, 2002, pp. A4 and A5. Copyright © 2002 TIME. Reprinted by permission of TIME.

WAYNES, ARIANA. "To the Patriots and the Activist Poets." Copyright © 1999 Ariana Waynes. Reprinted by permission of Ariana Waynes.

WIESEL, ELIE. "The Perils of Indifference: Lessons Learned from a Violent Century." Speech delivered on April 12, 1999. Copyright © 1999 by Elie Wiesel. Reprinted by permission of Elie Wiesel.

WILLIAMS, WILLIAM CARLOS. "To William Eric Williams: March 13, 1935." In *Selected Letters of William Carlos Williams,* edited by John C. Thirwall. New York: New Directions, 1984. Copyright © 1957 by William Carlos Williams. Reprinted by permission of New Directions Publishing Corp.

WILSON, E.O. "Prologue: A Letter to Thoreau." In *The Future of Life.* New York: Alfred A. Knopf, 2002. Copyright © 2002 by E.O. Wilson. Reprinted by permission of Edward O. Wilson.

INDEX

F

G

Y

ABOUT THE EDITOR

Daniel R. Katz has worked in the nonprofit sector for over twenty years. In 1986, at the age of 24, he co-founded the Rainforest Alliance, and built it into one of the premier international conservation organizations. He provides consulting services to several other organizations and manages The Overbrook Foundation's environment program. Mr. Katz lectures widely on leadership, and co-edited the 1995 anthology *Tales from the Jungle: A Rainforest Reader*. He lives in New York City with his wife and son.